THE LOST MANDATE OF HEAVEN

GEOFFREY D. T. SHAW

The Lost Mandate of Heaven

The American Betrayal of
Ngo Dinh Diem,
President of Vietnam

With a Foreword by James V. Schall, S.J.

IGNATIUS PRESS   SAN FRANCISCO

Cover photo © Bettmann/CORBIS

Cover design by Riz Boncan Marsella

© 2015 by Ignatius Press, San Francisco
All rights reserved
ISBN 978-1-58617-935-9
Library of Congress Control Number 2014959911
Printed in the United States of America ∞

The superior man understands virtue;
the mean man understands gain.

—Confucius

CONTENTS

FOREWORD

Political society, in one basic sense, was originally conceived as a method to escape the feud whereby one violation of justice was followed by another, and then another and another. Cicero considered the killing of a tyrant to be a noble act. The killing of Caesar by his friend Brutus was justified in terms of killing a tyrant, an enemy of the republic. Christian theologians have considered tyrannicide to be sometimes justified. The attempts to kill Hitler by a group that included General Erwin Rommel were applauded. However, Lincoln was shot by a man who thought that the president was a tyrant. Many assassinations of good political leaders dot recent centuries. One school of thought maintains that only violence accomplishes change. Another sees such violence as the cause of civil disorder. A third thinks a reasonable possession and use of force is always necessary given the present human condition.

In one sense, we can look on the periodic elections of presidents or other political leaders as a way to avoid the problems caused when no peaceful way is found to change political rule. One of the advantages of hereditary monarchies is that they usually provide a clear and orderly succession of rule. Their problem is that one can never be sure of the ability or the character of a new hereditary monarch. The search for a wise ruler who is able to lead and protect citizens is an ancient one. We usually can detect a difference between a constitutional method whereby designated rulers are regularly changed and the actual workings of these various methods. It turns out that democracies can produce both corrupt and mediocre rulers as well as, at times, good ones. Many rulers chosen by the Confucian Mandate of Heaven or by aristocratic or tribal means turn out to be decent public guides. Moreover, a difference can usually be found between good military leaders needed to protect a people and good political ones. Ruling in time of warfare and in time of peace require different talents.

All of these related issues come into play when considering the central theme of this book of Geoffrey D. T. Shaw. More than half a

9

century has passed since the Vietnam War was fought. It is a courageous
academic task to return to its bitterly controversial events to determine,
as best we can, its justification and its results. It is of considerable importance that we do not deceive ourselves about wars. We sometimes hear
that wars are unnecessary or that they are only evil and only causes of
destruction. But one must always wonder about who is one's enemy.
Both winning wars and losing them have consequences that cannot be
denied and must be dealt with. If one is constrained to protect himself
from an aggressive enemy, it is good to know the nature of that enemy's
arms and manpower. But it is even more necessary to know his intentions and the philosophy on which they are based. Wars can be won or
lost on battlefields, but more often the battlefields reflect the ideas that
are chosen by the combatants. This book, to be sure, is a book about
battles, but it is first a book about reasons and justifications. As such, it
is an exercise of what Christopher Dawson once called "the judgment
of the nations".

In 1954 I was in studies at Mount Saint Michael's in Spokane, Washington. At the time, I recall reading about the defeat of the French colonial
forces in Vietnam at the Battle of Dien Bien Phu. The victorious Vietnamese Communist commander at the time, General Vo Nguyen Giap,
went on to lead North Vietnamese forces in their successful undermining
of Laos and Cambodia and the conquest of South Vietnam. From this
French defeat, the Geneva peace settlement divided Vietnam at the seventeenth parallel. Thereafter, it established North Vietnam as a Communist
state, under Ho Chi Minh, while South Vietnam was formed as an independent country under the emperor Bao Dai, who was soon replaced by
Ngo Ninh Diem as president.

At the time, French pleas for U.S. military assistance were made,
but President Dwight D. Eisenhower, after Korea, did not want to be
involved in another foreign war. On reading of these dire events, I dis-
tinctly recall considering this French defeat to be much more ominous
than most people were willing to recognise. It set the stage for further
Communist expansion throughout the area. Military losses define an
era. The fortune and the geography of nations are the results of military
losses as much as they are of military victories. Who wins and who loses
are not insignificant questions. But wars, especially in democracies, are as
much the results of domestic politics as of foreign affairs. What responsibility does one nation have for another that is being unjustly attacked?

In 1972 I was in Saigon for about a week. The French Canadian Jesuits had a mission there. I walked about the city as best I could. A large Catholic church stood with what seemed like a large traffic circle in front of it. I entered the church. Someone had told me that this was the church in which Ngo Dinh Diem had been killed on All Souls' Day 1963. He and his brother Ngo Dinh Nhu, though captured on church grounds, were actually killed in a military vehicle by a Vietnamese officer under the command of the Vietnamese general known as "Big" Minh (Duong Van Minh). He later took Diem's place, but only briefly. Diem had been to Mass that morning. President John F. Kennedy, significant members of the State Department, Senator Mike Mansfield, and much of the press, especially the *New York Times*, had, in principle, as this book recounts, either set up or approved that assassination. This killing always seemed to me to be closer to a martyrdom than a political murder. But there is no reason it could not have been both.

In this book, Canadian scholar Geoffrey D. T. Shaw has given us a careful, candid account of the killing of Ngo Dinh Diem; the reasons for it; who was responsible; why it happened; and the disastrous results. It is not a happy story except in the sense that here we finally have a clear picture of the events and the personages surrounding this assassination. The hero of the book is the Virginia-born American ambassador to South Vietnam Frederick Nolting. In retrospect, he best understood Diem, American interests, the Vietnamese situation, the Communists, and what to do about it all. Shaw's massively documented book sets out to do nothing less than present a frank account of the steps that led to the killing of the great South Vietnamese leader, a man whose unjust vilification in the American media is one of almost unbelievable ignorance and willful blindness to the truth.

A central issue in political philosophy has always been, following Socrates, why is the just and good man killed "legally" in existing cities, especially democracies? Diem was not killed by the North Vietnamese, who respected him. They did want him out of the way, of course, as they understood his importance to the Vietnamese. They were rather astonished to see that, at the behest and the connivance of the Americans, a treacherous South Vietnamese general did it for them. They did not have to lift a finger. The one man who could prevent their victory by establishing a viable South Vietnam, Diem himself, was eradicated by the instigation of his presumed friends. The irony is almost too sad.

The nuance, in the case of Diem, was that the democracy most responsible for his killing—the killing of a good and competent man—was not his own country but that of his not-so-steadfast allies, the Americans.

The death of Christ under Roman jurisdictions also has many parallels to the death of Diem, without making Diem a god. As Shaw testifies, it was an unprincipled willingness to "kill one man" for the good of the country that drove and justified, in their own eyes, the perpetrators of this bloody deed. Get rid of him, and all will be fine. But as Nolting— along with British, French, Australian, and Filipino advisors—warned, this killing would make things considerably worse. And it did. It unnecessarily caused a war to continue for another decade, amidst huge casualties and destruction on all sides. We still live with its results. In the end, it led to an American defeat not on the battlefield but through opinion in the home democracy that did not stick to principles long enough to accomplish its announced purpose. Once the great Socratic civilizational principle that *it is never right to do wrong* was violated by abandoning Diem, the moral integrity of the Americans was undermined.

What is particularly agonising for Americans who read this clearly stated and tightly argued book is the fact, to repeat, that the final Vietnam defeat was not really on battlegrounds but on political and moral grounds—or even worse, on personal grounds of prideful diplomats and reporters. The Vietnam War need not have been lost. This fact is another basic theme of Shaw. Overwhelming evidence supports it. The original plan was sound. We were to support President Diem. He was a legitimate leader, encouraged to lead his own country. Vietnam was not to be taken over by our forces. Diem at one point was concerned that, having defeated the French, his country was being taken over by the Americans. Americans insisted on imposing an American-style democracy in an alien Confucian culture, in the midst of a war against shrewd and ruthless opponents. This effort was basically folly. Diem understood this fact, as did Ambassador Nolting, CIA Saigon Chief William Colby, Vice President Lyndon Johnson, most of the American military, and especially the British Malaysian war expert Sir Robert Thompson, who was called in as an advisor.

The character of President Kennedy—who was, in turn, shot in Dallas exactly three weeks after the killing of Diem—is particularly upsetting, especially for Catholics. Diem was a faithful Catholic and an honourable politician and patriot. That fact should have been a bond. Everyone knew that. Kennedy was accused at home by Diem's enemies of religious bias if he did not disassociate himself from him. Diem was accused of being anti-Buddhist, a charge that can in no way be sustained. Diem's record on religious fairness is simply unassailable. After the war, the North Vietnamese acknowledged that the bonzes who burned themselves in supposed defiance of Diem's "anti-Buddhist" policies were their agents within minority Buddhist monasteries in Vietnam. This information never appeared in the American press at the time.

The character of President Kennedy on this issue comes across as weak and vacillating. The character of Diem is consistent, noble, and aware of the slander waged against him. The members of the State Department—Averell Harriman, Roger Hilsman, Henry Cabot Lodge, and others—are seen as vain and vindictive, ideological, and poorly informed. Laos' neutrality was dealt with in such a way that the North Vietnamese could use the country as a conduit to bypass the northern border of South Vietnam. This Laotian "neutrality" was the work of Harriman and made defending South Vietnam almost impossible. North Vietnamese units came from Laos into South Vietnam. This result was particularly the case when the enemy was seen by many Americans to be Diem and not the Viet Cong and North Vietnam.

One of the most upsetting elements of this book is the theme of the unreliability of the Americans. Many in Eastern Europe at the time had seen their own subjection to the Soviet forces to be the result of this occasional unreliability. The major concern of Diem became, more and more, can the Americans be trusted? He knew that Nolting and some of his advisors could be. But he could not trust the president or members of the State Department. The press seemed to be the major force in his undoing. There were some reporters, like Marguerite Higgins, who did understand the overall issue. But the main press that most people read was unrelenting in its insistence that the problem was Diem, and the solution his removal.

Though this book is a work of careful scholarship, it is also a work of dramatic proportions. Tragedy revolves around a tragic flaw that leads to the downfall of a man who is in many ways good. This book is not an account of the perfidy of the Communists. It recognises that they are ruthless, powerful, and out to win. But they are not the focus of the text. They are, rather, the recipients of the tragedy, the ones left to follow in its wake. Had the North Vietnamese with Chinese support simply overrun South Vietnam with superior tactics and force, there would have been nothing to write about. The most powerful rule by right of conquest. But that is not a criterion of justice, only of war's de facto results. The unjust often win.

Nor is this book about a North Vietnamese victory caused by Communism's overwhelming power and moral attraction. The Communists did finally win and still control the land. But their victory was the consequence of moral and intellectual faults on the part of American advisors. The South Vietnamese could have established their homeland had the original plan that Americans agreed to support been carried out. Thus, this book watches the North Vietnamese conquest of South Vietnam, together with similar results in Laos and even more terrible ones in Cambodia. The book recounts the profound venality and ignorance of well-educated and aristocratic American diplomats and journalists who insisted that they better understood the situation than did the local leader and the Americans who grasped what he was doing in the light of the enemies he had to deal with.

President Kennedy comes across as a man intimidated by events that he really did not understand. He agreed to the original policy that probably would have succeeded had he remained loyal to President Diem. He backed this policy until press reports and pressure from the State Department weakened his resolution. He was concerned about the 1964 election. But in the president's case, the old Truman principle, "The buck stops here", was in force. He was the ultimate voice who approved the overall plan to get rid of Diem. He might have stopped it. State Department officials spoke of "eliminating" Diem. No one quite said outright that he would be executed. But it was clear that eliminating Diem was the intention. The doing of the actual dirty work was the initiative not of the Vietnamese generals but of the State Department officials led by Harriman, who put them up to it.

Once the bloody deed was accomplished, the Americans and the Vietnamese had to scurry to replace Diem and his brother. They never really succeeded. Good men like Ambassador Nolting withdrew in what was no doubt a private sadness and horror that such things could happen. The war went on and was lost. The book is not an account of the next decade of warfare. Its purpose is to reexamine the killing of a good and honourable politician by his friends. In that sense, the book has tragic qualities. We come away from it sobered not over the Communist rule and its own bloody prosecution but over the way good men are killed in their own city when other men cross the Socratic line that holds that it is never right to do wrong. Once that line is crossed, a new regime is implicitly established, one that does not feel itself bound by basic principle.

A reason can be given for most political actions. This position is likewise true in the death of Diem. The line of responsibility is clear enough with regard to its final authorisation. The efforts to justify the action are varied. No one can permit such an action without trying to justify it. This book provides not so much an account of the efforts to justify the killing but a documentation of the steps that led to it, showing who was ultimately responsible and what were the immediate results. This book is not a happy read. But it is a careful record to set the issue straight. The redemption of memory is a necessary step in restoring the order of truth to its prime position in our thinking and in our polity. Shaw has provided the evidence for this redemption. Presenting this evidence is what a historian can do for the public good. The killing of Ngo Dinh Diem was not another death of a corrupt politician. It was a step in the death of the basic principle on which civilization rests.

James V. Schall, S.J.
Professor Emeritus
Georgetown University

PREFACE

The overarching thesis of this book is that the first president of South Vietnam, Ngo Dinh Diem, possessed the Confucian Mandate of Heaven, a moral and political authority that was widely recognised by the South Vietnamese, Buddhist and Catholic alike. This devout Roman Catholic leader never lost his mandate to rule in the eyes of his people; rather, it was removed by his erstwhile allies in the U.S. government. U.S. Ambassador to South Vietnam Frederick "Fritz" Nolting also shares some prominent space in this book, because he was the best and highest-placed U.S. witness to the decency of Ngo Dinh Diem and the injustice of his assassination, which some Vietnamese consider a martyrdom.

The foundations of this work began some twenty-four years ago, when I came across the popularly held negative portrayal of Diem, which abounds in books about the Vietnam War. A military historian, I was looking for standard sets of military clues that would indicate why the Vietnam War was lost. But these clues seemed to be almost completely absent in the foundational years of American entanglement with Vietnam. Indeed, all the standard markers seemed to be pointing toward a counterinsurgency campaign that was gaining substantial ground by 1963. Even the Communists acknowledged that they were having a very hard go of it then. Consequently, I shifted my focus off the military aspects and toward the political ones.

As I did so, I found that the standard claims made about Diem in popular American histories were at odds with his political, economic, cultural, and military accomplishments. The histories referring to Diem's "corrupt government" simply did not add up with the reality of the man I found recorded elsewhere—the Diem who was up for Mass at 6:30 every morning and who was venerated by the Vietnamese as a great leader at all levels of government and as a kind man who did not like even the thought of Viet Cong guerrillas being killed. This discrepancy drew me further and further into the study of Diem's presidency, the Americans who had supported him, and those who later decided to destroy him. Did I find a veritable Conradian "heart of darkness"? Yes, I did, but not in the quarter to which all popular American sources were pointing their accusatory fingers—in other words, not in Saigon but in Washington, D.C., within the circle of President John F. Kennedy's closest advisors.

The actions of these men led to Diem's murder. And with his death, nine and a half years of careful work and partnership between the United States and South Vietnam was undone. Within a few weeks, any hope of a successful outcome in Vietnam—that is, of a free and democratic country friendly toward the United States—was extinguished. Truly, in order to solve a problem that did not exist, the Kennedy administration created a problem that could not be solved. And that remains the essence of the mystery of this particular iniquity.

Geoffrey D. T. Shaw, Ph.D.
November 7, 2013

ACKNOWLEDGEMENTS

The author is indebted to many people whose help made this work possible and thanks the following individuals for their kind assistance and encouragement:

Francis F. M. Carroll—professor, Department of History, University of Manitoba

Lawrie Cherniack—lawyer and senior partner, Cherniack and Smith

William E. Colby—former director of the CIA

Father Dennis Dickson—priest-in-charge, Saint Thomas Becket Anglican Catholic Church

Vivian Dudro—senior editor at Ignatius Press

Oleh Gerus—professor, Department of History, University of Manitoba

General Nguyen Khanh—former premier of South Vietnam and commander in chief of the Army of the Republic of Vietnam

Rev. M. McLean—warden of Saint John's College at the University of Manitoba

Major Ralph Millsap—revolutionary warfare course director at the United States Air Force Special Operations School, Hurlburt Field, Florida

Mark Moyar—Senior fellow at the Joint Special Operations University and the Foreign Policy Research Institute

Rena Niznick—Lawrie Cherniack's very competent legal assistant

Grace Lindsay Nolting—daughter of Frederick and Lindsay Nolting, and family historian

Lindsay Nolting—wife of and confidant to Ambassador Frederick Nolting

Douglas Pike—professor and assistant director of the Vietnam Center and Archive, Texas Tech University

James Reckner—professor and director of the Vietnam Center and Archive, Texas Tech University

Steven Sherman—U.S. Army First Lieutenant, Fifth Special Forces Group, Vietnam, 1967–1968

Kenneth Thompson—professor and director of the Miller Center, University of Virginia

In addition to the support that I have received from the individuals in the preceding list I would also like to thank my family for all of their very tangible support—in both material and morale.

ABBREVIATIONS

ARVN	Army of the Republic of Vietnam
CIA	Central Intelligence Agency
CINCPAC	commander in chief, U.S. Pacific Command
CIP	Counterinsurgency Plan
Deptel	Department of State telegram
DOD	U.S. Department of Defense
DOS	U.S. Department of State
DRV	Democratic Republic of Vietnam
FRUS	*Foreign Relations of the United States*
GVN	government of South Vietnam
ICC	International Control Commission
MAAG	Military Assistance Advisory Group
NATO	North Atlantic Treaty Organisation
NLF	National Liberation Front
NVA	North Vietnamese Army
PAVN	People's Army of Vietnam (another name for NVA)
SHP	Strategic Hamlet Program
SVN	South Vietnam
VC	Viet Cong

INTRODUCTION

Ngo Dinh Diem

On November 2, 1971, the eighth anniversary of Ngo Dinh Diem's assassination, several thousand people gathered in Saigon to commemorate the death of the former president of Vietnam. "A yellow-robed Buddhist monk offered a Buddhist remembrance, and Catholic prayers were said in Latin. Banners proclaimed Diem a saviour of the South. The previous day, All Saints Day, Catholics had come to the cemetery from the refugee villages outside Saigon, carrying portraits of the slain president."[1]

Indeed, ever since 1970 the loss of Ngo Dinh Diem has been publically mourned throughout many communities in Vietnam, albeit somewhat secretly at times. His memory has been kept alive more openly by the Vietnamese diaspora around the world.[2] The question becomes, then, who was this slain South Vietnamese leader who has remained at the centre of the history of post-1945 Vietnam? It is hoped that this introduction will give the reader at least a reasonable grounding in the man's background, which in turn makes the true story of his tragic death less opaque.

Probably the single most important theme of this work is the role of Ngo Dinh Diem in American diplomatic, military, and domestic political planning from the beginning of his presidency until his murder—or martyrdom, according to the long-suffering Vietnamese

---

[1] Ellen J. Hammer, *A Death in November: America in Vietnam, 1963* (New York: E.P. Dutton, 1987), 317.

[2] Hoang Ngoc Thanh and Than Thi Nhan Duc, *Why the Vietnam War? President Ngo Dinh Diem and the US: His Overthrow and Assassination* ([San Jose, Calif.:] Tuan-Yen and Quan-Viet Mai-Nam, 2001), 485.

23

Roman Catholic community.[3] Unquestionably, his Catholic faith, often described as monk-like with a touch of severity, was at the heart of this man's spirit. Without his presence there would have been no South Vietnam of any consequence and certainly not one that, in the face of the most militant, atheistic Communism, could have flourished and succeeded as a fledging nation-state caught in the very midst of the Cold War.

There is simply no gainsaying the fact that the impact of Ngo Dinh Diem upon the history of post-1945 Vietnam is of such significance that even the academic historical schools concerning the Vietnam War are essentially demarked by where a scholar stands on the man: those who condemn him depend on this harsh judgement as if it were the very glue that binds all so-called orthodox adherents together; those who recognise his great charitableness, as made manifest in his love of God, the Catholic Church, and his fellow Vietnamese, constitute the disciples of the inadequately named "revisionist school". Those whose worldview is more horizontal see Diem as an obstacle to progress, and bluntly, some of them hate him; those with a transcendent view of man, who embrace his capacity for nobility through humility, duty, and self-sacrifice, lionise Diem. Either way, Ngo Dinh Diem stands at the epicentre of all historical studies of America's Vietnam War. If it is acceptable for Vietnamese Roman Catholics to gather every November 2 at the site of Diem's murder and there to offer up prayers for his revered soul, then perhaps it is fitting for this non-Catholic Canadian "revisionist" historian of America's involvement in the Vietnam War to offer up his own form of veneration.

Most of the popular sources on the Vietnam War, American and Vietnamese, cite the city of Hue as the birthplace of Ngo Dinh Diem, yet careful study of older Vietnamese records convinced French journalist and historian Bernard Fall that the more likely location was Dai-Phuong, in Quang Binh Province, north of what was to become the demilitarised zone between North and South Vietnam. Determining the birthplace of Ngo Dinh Diem is important for understanding why,

---

[3] The Roman Catholic Church has been established in Vietnam since the sixteenth century, but she has also suffered periods of persecution. Jacob Ramsay's *Mandarins and Martyrs: The Church and the Nguyen Dynasty in Early Nineteenth-Century Vietnam* (Stanford, Calif.: Stanford University Press, 2008) attempts to explain how persecutions could arise even when it appeared that the Church was well accepted in Vietnamese society.

many years later, he directed his foreign minister at the 1954 Geneva Conference to protest forcefully against a partitioned Vietnam. In Vietnamese culture, the tie between individuals and their place of birth, their ancestral and family home, is at the core of how they view themselves in the world. The Americans (aid advisors, diplomats, and politicians) seem never to have fully grasped Diem's long-term goal and deep desire to reunite Vietnam under an anti-Communist central government.

Although born in the north, Diem had ties to the mandarin centre of all Vietnam, Hue. In fact, his elevated social position was derived from links to the imperial court there, connections that had been established several centuries earlier. Diem was a member of one of the great families of Vietnam, and "by tradition, by capacity, and through Confucian sense of duty", it was proper for members of that family to take their places amongst the mandarins of the imperial court.[4] Diem's father, Ngo Dinh Kha, was the court minister of rites and the grand chamberlain to the emperor. He was a devout Roman Catholic who also embraced the teachings of Confucius. One of the few Vietnamese of his generation to be educated both in Vietnam and in a foreign country (Malaya), he directed his sons, particularly Diem and Nhu, to gain both a Western and a Vietnamese education.

At an early age Diem had already absorbed his father's dedication to education. He would get up before dawn and study by the light of an oil lamp until it was time for him to go to his French Catholic school. His steadfastness went well beyond his early-morning study sessions after he won his first school prize at the age of six. As one of his brothers later recalled for *Time* magazine, once Diem snuck off to school along the dike tops when he and his brothers had been told by their father to stay home because of flooding. When his father punished him for his disobedience, Diem had no sense of any injustice being done and accepted his father's discipline with equanimity.[5] Diem's exceptional determination, which did not falter in the face of adversity, became the mark of the man's later political life.

There was a political dimension to Diem's education, upon which his father had substantial influence. His father hosted all manner of Vietnamese leaders in the family home, including Emperor Thanh Tai and

[4] Charles Keith, *Catholic Vietnam: A Church from Empire to Nation* (Berkeley: University of California Press, 2012), 98.

[5] "South Viet-Nam: The Beleaguered Man", *Time*, April 4, 1955, 23–24.

Emperor Duy Tan, as well as many other powerful men who came to garner Ngo Dinh Kha's support or to seek his advice.[6] It was Diem's good fortune to have discussed current events with these leaders during his formative years. When many Vietnamese nationalists were debating whether to overthrow French colonial rule, and when this subject was broached at home, Diem's father was unshakable in his opposition to violence or bloodshed. He stressed that revolution must come only through education. When the Vietnamese people were ready to look after their affairs, he argued, Vietnam would gain its independence from France naturally, with no need for killing. The impact of this schooling in politics at his father's knee was profound; for when Diem was president of South Vietnam and hard-pressed by his American allies to ramp up the physical destruction of the Viet Cong (VC), Diem would express a visceral reaction against the very idea of killing his fellow Vietnamese. A good friend of the Ngo Dinh family, Andre Nguyen Van Chau, recalled the gentleness of Diem's character when he noted that the man never liked being harsh with anyone.[7] Douglas Pike, a leading American authority on the Viet Cong, concurred with Van Chau's assessment that Diem, despite the portrait drawn by his critics, was not a violent man, nor even the authoritarian type.[8]

Diem proved just as capable at higher education as at his childhood studies. He attended the National College, an institution established by his father so that Vietnamese mandarins could be introduced to Western thought. He earned such high marks in the final examinations that

[6] Ngo Dinh Kha was well respected by Catholics and Buddhists alike and had a reputation for wisdom and good judgement. He nevertheless suffered occasional persecution, and his patience through these ordeals won him even more admiration. See Keith, *Catholic Vietnam*, 169–70.

[7] Andre Nguyen Van Chau, "The Late President Ngo Dinh Diem of Vietnam as Seen by Members of the Family and Some of His Friends", paper presented at the conference "The Rise and Fall of Ngo Dinh Diem: Its Implications for the United States and for Vietnam", Vietnam Center and Archive, Texas Tech University, Lubbock, Texas, October 24, 2003.

[8] Douglas Pike became acquainted with President Diem while a Foreign Service officer in Saigon. He said, "Diem fit neither the classical nor the contemporary American stereotype of a tyrant. He was not brutal, mean, or arrogant. He was educated, cosmopolitan, and far more liberally minded than the emperor Bao Dai who preceded him.... However politically misguided Saigon's undemocratic practices may have been, they were chiefly a military response to [an] external challenge. By that measure they were neither excessive nor unreasonable." Douglas Pike, "South Vietnam: Autopsy of a Compound Crisis", in *Friendly Tyrants: An American Dilemma*, ed. Daniel Pipes and Adam Garfinkle (New York: St. Martin's Press, 1991), 38, 47, 52–53.

the French offered him a scholarship to attend university in Paris. But Diem's great desire was to serve the Vietnamese people, and he turned down the French offer, choosing instead to stay in Vietnam, where he continued to excel academically. In 1921 he graduated at the top of his class at the French-run School for Law and Administration in Hanoi.

During his studies, Diem became increasingly aware that Catholicism and Confucianism had many similarities, including a shared understanding of ethics. As a result, Diem would think and move in a way that was almost incomprehensible to the secular-minded and politically expedient Americans with whom he would later collaborate. A modern Western or American policy perspective asserts that individual rights and the freedom to pursue personal happiness are paramount, almost to the exclusion of every other consideration. Diem, however, believed that the individual needed to submit his will and talents to the greater good of the family, the community, and the nation. In his political philosophy, the individual did not have a right to political activity that threatened the downfall of a legitimate government. Diem's Catholic faith and Confucian principles were so robustly integrated as to make his political philosophy all but impermeable to contrary argument.

Catholicism and Confucianism both stress that the well-being of the family is the most important social responsibility of a people and their rulers. Diem never lost sight of this responsibility, even as the modern world threatened to destroy traditional Vietnamese culture. Indeed, this seems to be an area where Diem's soul burned with a righteous fire: he lamented that the faith and the family life of his countrymen had diminished under French rule. When he became president, Buddhism, for example, was in such decline that it seemed like a discard from a bygone era. This loss grieved Diem, and during his presidency he appropriated government funds for the restoration of Buddhist places of worship. In effect, Diem was a true conservative: he wanted to conserve the traditional Vietnamese way of life. First and foremost, he wanted to restore the family to its Confucian status as the legal personality and the responsible entity within the village community. Toward this end, and in accordance with his Christian faith, he wanted to outlaw polygamy and concubinage.[9] As it would turn out, Diem's sturdy emphasis on

---

[9] Dennis J. Duncanson, *Government and Revolution in Vietnam* (London: Oxford University Press / Royal Institute of International Affairs, 1968), 214.

religious, familial, and social duties placed a spiritual, moral, and intellectual gulf between him and many of his American advisors, the latter finding this an extremely difficult chasm to cross. Such matters are weightier than other sorts of policy concerns because they stem from the heart of what a man essentially is.

One of the more revealing historical footnotes about Diem is that his earliest ambition was to be a priest; indeed, he attended a seminary when he was fifteen, before deciding to become a civic leader. Catholicism was always closer to Diem's heart than purely political ideas. His lengthy monologues irritated many of the American officials who attended meetings with him because they were a bit too much like sermons. A member of Diem's family drew journalist Denis Warner's attention to Diem's otherworldliness when he stated, "You think you can have a meeting of minds with Diem ..., [but] I tell you it is impossible. To a Westerner, Diem does not just come from another culture and another hemisphere. He comes from another planet."[10]

Diem's committed Catholicism was inculcated by his father, and it had a practical utility inasmuch as it was intended to strengthen his sons for the inevitable anti-Christian hostility that would come their way. From the time that Diem's great-grandfather embraced Christianity, the Ngo Dinh family endured considerable anguish whenever the Church was identified with the French, and the French with oppressive colonialism. Like many other Vietnamese Catholics, the Ngo Dinhs then had to pay a high price for their faith. It should be added, however, that the persecution of Christians in Vietnam was by no means unrelenting; often there were periods of peaceful acceptance.[11]

Diem's firm Catholic faith was buttressed by another significant character trait that had profound appeal to the Confucianist soul of Vietnamese society: asceticism. He led a disciplined life, and this was something the Vietnamese people revered because they believed that the quality of a man was determined by his ability to withstand hardship. Diem's scholarly, monk-like personality made him far more attractive to the

---

[10] Denis Warner, *The Last Confucian: Vietnam, Southeast Asia, and the West*, rev. ed. (Sydney, Australia: Angus and Robertson, 1964), 92.

[11] There had been periods of benign acceptance and periods such as the "great persecution" under Emperor Ming Mang during the mid-nineteenth century, wherein over 130 priests, missionaries, and other lay Church leaders were executed. See Ramsay, *Mandarins and Martyrs*, 68.

Vietnamese people as a leader than, for example, a Western-styled, big-toothed, glad-handing, baby-kissing politician. Indeed, such a politician offended Vietnamese sensibilities, and yet it was this very model that many American advisors tried to push on Diem.

There is another reason Diem found favour with the Vietnamese people. As Vietnamese writer Tran Van Dinh explained, according to Confucian ethics and Taoist concepts of harmony and universal order, those who seek wealth to the near exclusion of all else and attain it are held in low regard. Their motives are suspect, and consequently, so is their morality. Even the name for them is derogatory: *troc phu*, which translates as "filthy rich". As was expected of a mandarin, Diem and his family had nothing to do with chasing money, and this also may have had some bearing on why, later in his career, Diem did not take a liking to W. Averell Harriman, the celebrated scion of American high society who became one of President Kennedy's most influential foreign policy advisors. Opposite the *troc phu* is the *thanh ban*, or the learned "immaculate poor"; thus, the impecunious scholar had social appeal in Confucian Vietnamese society. Ho Chi Minh did his level best to appear as *thanh ban* to the average Vietnamese, because he knew he would be judged by them according to the Vietnamese-Confucian ideas of a good leader. Ho, however, was a bit disingenuous about his image, whereas Diem was the genuine article by birth and training.

In nearly every meaningful way, traditional Vietnamese society had values that were diametrically opposed to those of modern, secular Western societies, particularly the United States. Vietnamese social order, from top to bottom, looked something like this: at the top were the *si*, or scholars, men of letters like Ngo Dinh Diem and his brother Ngo Dinh Nhu; second down the scale could be found the *nong*, or peasant farmers; the next lower echelon was occupied by the *cong*, or workers; considerably further down in esteem were the *thuong*, or the businessmen and merchants; and finally, last in the Confucian Vietnamese order were the *binh*, or soldiers, who like our modern-day sanitation workers were seen as doing a necessary but dirty job.[12] The low standing of soldiers in Vietnamese society explains why the Washington-backed coup against Diem was doomed to failure, because it replaced a *si* with

---

[12] Tran Van Dinh, "Why Every American Should Read Kim Van Kieu", in *We the Vietnamese: Voices from Vietnam*, ed. François Sully (New York: Praeger, 1971), 236–37.

a group of *binh*. Moreover, the "revolving door" coups of military men that followed left the average Vietnamese wondering who had turned the world upside down. Political legitimacy, in the form of the Confucian Mandate of Heaven, could never rest upon a military regime.

The Vietnamese held that only a man who had trained himself in hardship and had disciplined himself through the denial of his physical passions could truly lead the people, and Diem was known to be such a man. In an interview with the author, General Nguyen Khanh said that Diem's purity and simplicity of life made him exemplary to the Vietnamese, Catholic and Buddhist alike. The general, who had participated in the coup that resulted in Diem's murder, recalled how Diem, while living in the presidential palace, would have nothing to do with ostentation. He slept on an old army cot in his office, for example. Amongst the Vietnamese there is still, to this day, a deep reverence, bordering on awe, when they talk of the former president. Vietnam expert Paul Mus, a French scholar who grew up in Vietnam, told historian Ellen Hammer that only one man in Vietnam vied successfully with Ho Chi Minh for power: Ngo Dinh Diem. Mus knew both Ho and Diem, and he emphasised that it was Diem's reputation for virtue that made him such a challenge to Ho. He told American officials back in 1949 that Diem was the only viable alternative to the Communists, but he also warned them that Diem could not be bought and would never be "their man" in Saigon.[13]

Many of the finer accolades of Diem came from his enemies. For example, General Tran Van Don, a leader of the military conspiracy that overthrew Diem in 1963, admitted that he was an ardent patriot who had been a resolute defender of national independence and whose rectitude was unassailable.[14] Another military leader and coconspirator, Nguyen Cao Ky, praised Diem for his honesty and integrity.[15] The most famous testament to the unimpeachable character of Diem came from none other than Ho Chi Minh, the leader of the Communist take-over of Vietnam and Diem's implacable enemy. In September 1945 Diem's

---

[13] Hammer, *Death in November*, 47.

[14] Tran Van Don, *Our Endless War: Inside Vietnam* (San Rafael, Calif.: Presidio Press, 1978), 48.

[15] Nguyen Cao Ky, *Twenty Years and Twenty Days* (New York: Stein and Day, 1976), 19, 31–33.

brother Khoi was murdered by Viet Minh guerrillas, and Diem, having also been captured, was brought before their leader, Ho Chi Minh. Ho tried to convince Diem to join the Viet Minh in their war against French rule. Diem refused, stating that he could never work with the Communist murderers of his brother, who were destroying his country. Ho remonstrated with him, saying that the orders to kill Khoi had not come from him and that any violence against his family was carried out in error. Flattering Diem about his well-known nationalist credentials, he tried to cajole him. Diem would have none of it, and deeply impressed with Diem's courage, Ho—amazingly—let him go, perhaps thinking that once Diem had had enough of what the French were doing and had gotten a whiff of the Americans, he would be back.[16]

After Diem's college graduation in 1921, he entered the provincial administration of French-controlled Vietnam as a district chief in charge of some 225 villages. This was no small task for such a young man, but regardless of his youth and inexperience, he displayed genuine leadership qualities as he developed a counterstrategy to Ho Chi Minh's insurgents working in Vietnamese villages. Diem set up his own intelligence within the Communist political infrastructure. He would then, at the opportune moment, arrest Ho's operatives, reeducate them, and then turn them against the Communists. He was extraordinarily successful at this because he eschewed bloodshed.[17] In order to implement such an effective operation, Diem thoroughly studied Marxism and Communism as they were applied in Vietnam, thereby becoming one of the first Vietnamese officials fully to discern the extent to which the Communists had gained support in the country.[18]

Although the French ignored his perceptive reports on the nature and the extent of the Communist threat in the villages, they nevertheless rewarded Diem for his work in 1929 by appointing him, at age twenty-eight, governor of Phan Thiet Province. During the next four years, Diem became well known as an honest and competent administrator and a formidable opponent to violent revolutionaries. Significantly, he

---

[16] Some of this story is related by Stanley Karnow. He discussed this incident in early 1981 with the propaganda chief of the Vietnamese Communist Party, Hoang Tung, who told him that Ho had made a serious mistake concerning Diem and should have had him killed. See Stanley Karnow, *Vietnam: A History* (New York: Viking, 1983), 216–17.

[17] "South Viet-Nam", 24.

[18] Robert Shaplen, "A Reporter in Vietnam: Diem", *New Yorker*, September 22, 1962, 103.

depended on the rule of law, and not his own personal authority, to maintain order, and thus he was able to please both the French and the Vietnamese, at least briefly. The French found him to be an outstanding civil servant, and the Vietnamese respected him for his ability to work hard on their behalf while not resorting to corruption or repression to get the job done—a very rare administrative talent in the recent memory of most Vietnamese.[19]

All was not perfect, however, in the relations between Diem and the French colonial administration, for Diem had been unrelenting in his plea to the French for greater freedom for the Vietnamese people. Specifically, he requested that more autonomy be granted to the Vietnamese peasants at the village level, especially in the context of increasing Communist activity in the countryside. The French, however, consistently ignored him, because they believed that the gravest threat came from neither the Communists nor the peasants but rather from the Vietnamese nationalists—in other words, from Vietnamese just like Ngo Dinh Diem. Nevertheless, Diem continued to argue that not only were the Communists a major threat but so too was the growing apathy or, conversely, hostility toward government of any kind amongst the hard-pressed peasants. Diem tried to demonstrate that the Communist inroads, which largely depended on propaganda and intimidation, could be headed off by simple government assistance at the village level, but the French were not listening.[20]

Regardless of their disdain for Diem's harangues and warnings on the state of the peasants in the countryside, the French recognised his extraordinary administrative talents and advised their man, Emperor Bao Dai, to install Diem as the minister of the interior, which in effect was the prime minister. Trouble began almost immediately, though, when the French discovered that, unlike Bao Dai, Diem could not be bought so as to be more amenable to their will. To the contrary, and true to his forthright nature, Diem complained bitterly to the French that the government had little authority and even less political legitimacy in the eyes of the people. Moreover, he said that he would not stand by while Emperor Bao Dai's powers were reduced to nothing. As a result, animosity formed between Diem and the French colonial administration.

---

[19] Warner, *Last Confucian*, 89.
[20] Shaplen, "Reporter in Vietnam", 103.

It seemed as if the French never forgave Diem for exposing and complaining about the true nature of the Bao Dai regime, that it was a government firmly under French control. When it became obvious to Diem that the French would not permit any meaningful reform, he resigned and became subject immediately to French retaliations. They stripped him of his awards for his excellent work and threatened him with deportation. The French, however, were loath to carry their retribution too far, because they did not want to make a martyr out of a leader so deeply respected by his own people;[21] it would take the less experienced Americans to make that grievous error many years later.

Having been judged a troublemaker who had the most disconcerting inability to be purchased, Diem found himself subject to constant harassment by French colonial officialdom over the next ten years. During his hiatus from any sort of public office, Diem spent much of his time living with his younger brother Ngo Dinh Can in the city of Hue. Prayer and daily Mass were regular parts of each day, along with much reading and study. Occasionally he would go riding, dabble in photography, or tend the family garden. Many Vietnamese nationalists beat a path to the Ngo Dinh residence in Hue, and Diem visited the same people in Saigon. While many talked of revolution, nothing came of such discourse. The one truly outstanding political relationship that Diem forged at this time was with Vo Nguyen Giap, who later became the successful commander of the Viet Minh. Resisting Diem's arguments for a nonsocialist approach, Giap, for his part, attempted to win Diem to the socialist cause. Neither one was successful in converting the other, although they created a sort of mutual admiration society.[22]

A significant event occurred during Diem's years of political exile that lent further legitimacy to his nationalist credentials. When the Japanese moved into Indochina during the Second World War, Diem, believing an opportunity to help his country was at hand, asked them to grant independence to the Vietnamese people. The French took a dim view of Diem's overture, and the Vichy government placed him under even closer surveillance. In 1944, Vichy openly denounced Diem as a subversive and placed his name on their "most wanted" list. But the French need not have bothered, because the Japanese were

---

[21] Ibid., 106.
[22] Ibid., 108.

not interested in Vietnamese political aspirations; they were far more concerned with maintaining efficient control over their Greater East Asia Co-prosperity Sphere. In 1945, however, the Japanese attempted to bring Diem into their Indochina administration by offering him the prime ministership of a government they had hastily cobbled together in Hanoi. Diem, true to his character, would have nothing to do with what he believed was a thinly disguised Japanese puppet regime created more out of desperation than anything else, given that these were the dying days of their empire.[23]

During the post-war period, Diem was confronted with two substantial problems: first, he was still on the French wanted list and was being pursued by them relentlessly; and second, Ho Chi Minh had already set up a temporary government in Hanoi. These developments compelled Diem to leave the relative safety of his friends in Saigon and head north in order to warn the ordinary people there about Ho's true intentions. It was during this trip that he was captured by the Viet Minh, as previously mentioned. Although he was eventually set free by Ho himself, his hostility toward the Viet Minh remained;[24] this was not surprising given that the Viet Minh not only had murdered his brother, by burying him alive, but had raided the Ngo Dinh family home, destroying its library of more than ten thousand books in the process.[25]

Almost immediately after he was released by the Viet Minh, Diem began organising anti-Communist bases in North Vietnam. But he lacked the necessary funds and supply of arms for such an undertaking, and nothing but threats against his life were the result. In desperation, he took refuge with some Canadian monks living in Vietnam until a temporary accord with the Viet Minh and the French was signed on March 8, 1946.

Diem was not discouraged from making other attempts to organise Vietnamese nationalists, and in the spring of 1947 he founded a political party, the National Union Front, with the set purpose of achieving

---

[23] Frances Fitzgerald, *Fire in the Lake: The Vietnamese and the Americans in Vietnam* (New York: Vintage Books, 1989), 103. Another account of Diem's relationship with the Japanese is given by Ellen Hammer, who had personally queried Diem on this point. He denied that they had tried to make him a prime minister. See Shaplen, "Reporter in Vietnam", 51.

[24] Bernard B. Fall, *The Two Viet-Nams: A Political and Military Analysis* (New York: Praeger, 1963), 240.

[25] "South Viet-Nam", 24.

dominion status for Vietnam within the French Union.[26] The National Union Front published a newsletter in Saigon until the French closed down the party and the paper after jailing one of its editors. Another editor was murdered by hired gangsters. As a result, Diem experienced political disappointment once again.

From 1947 to 1948 the French made a concerted effort to reinstall their favourite emperor, Bao Dai. Diem also made an overture to Bao Dai: he travelled to the latter's place of exile in Hong Kong, where he beseeched him not to accept the French offer without an unequivocal French commitment to grant Vietnamese independence within the near future. Regardless of Diem's entreaties, Bao Dai unconditionally returned to his role as the emperor of French-controlled Indochina. In May 1949 he requested Diem to become his prime minister, and in disgust Diem refused.[27] The French, like the Japanese and later the Americans, had failed to take Diem's obstinate adherence to his principles and his commitment to Vietnamese independence into their political calculations.[28]

By 1950 Diem's aspirations for his country were firmly established, yet he was still searching for the necessary means by which he could gain the power of national leadership necessary to realise them and thus save his country from many more years of colonial rule or something even worse. Along with his brothers Ngo Dinh Nhu and Bishop Ngo Dinh Thuc, the apostolic vicar of Vinh Long, Diem had been hard at work in creating new political movements such as the Christian Socialist Party, but the Viet Minh and the French authorities, each for their own reasons, thwarted most of these efforts. Politically frustrated and wishing to escape a death sentence imposed by the Viet Minh, Diem and

[26] Both Ngo Dinh Diem and his brother Ngo Dinh Nhu admired the French thinker Emmanuel Mounier and his ideas concerning the need for Catholics to take an active role in the world while maintaining the vision of their true destiny in the heavenly Jerusalem. Mounier called his philosophy "personalism" as set forth in his book *Be Not Afraid*, and the Ngo Dinhs attempted to incorporate it into their political thought. See Keith, *Catholic Vietnam*, 239.

[27] Shaplen, "Reporter in Vietnam", 116.

[28] Ellen Hammer explained this well: "His standing among his own people as a political leader was grounded on a stubborn refusal to compromise his principles and on an unswerving attachment to the cause of Vietnamese independence. The Americans who admired him had no idea that these same qualities one day would lead him into conflict with the Washington government." Hammer, *Death in November*, 52–53.

Bishop Thuc left Vietnam in August 1950 to look for support overseas. Much to Diem's surprise, those warmhearted neophytes from the Occident, the Americans, would soon be backing his patriotic ambitions.

Diem's first stop was Japan, where apart from visiting an old friend, he attempted to solicit General Douglas MacArthur's help in obtaining American support for a nationalist Vietnamese government. Preoccupied with Korea, MacArthur was not interested, so Diem sought other Americans in Japan for advice and assistance. Not surprisingly, some of these were impressed and inspired by Diem and his anticolonial patriotism, including a young professor of political science from Michigan State University, Wesley Fishel, who advised Diem to take his plea for an independent Vietnam directly to the United States, advice Diem followed.[29] On his way from Japan to the United States, Diem stopped in Rome, where he was granted a private audience with the Pope, a visit some have suggested was intended to impress America's Catholic elite.[30] But there is another explanation: 1950 was a Holy Year, when many devout Roman Catholics made pilgrimages to Rome. At this time, Diem and his bishop brother would have been naturally drawn to Rome, where the latter had studied at the Gregorian University. For pious reasons alone they would have sought a papal audience.

During his two-year stay in America, Diem lived in Maryknoll Mission Society seminaries in upstate New York and New Jersey.[31] Diem embraced the Maryknoll way of life, doing the same menial chores as the seminarians. Visitors of high import in American politics were stunned to see Diem taking out the garbage, washing the floors, and doing other lowly labours without complaint. Plainly, the man was seeking political power not for his own aggrandisement but out of dedication to God and his fellowmen, whom he wished to serve. Diem greatly impressed Francis Cardinal Spellman, archbishop of New York, who introduced him to everyone he knew in Washington who might help him. As a result, Diem made friends with Supreme Court Justice William O. Douglas, Senator Mike Mansfield, and the rising political star Congressman John F. Kennedy.[32]

---

[29] Fall, *Two Viet-Nams*, 242.

[30] Shaplen, "Reporter in Vietnam", 116.

[31] Philip E. Catton, *Diem's Final Failure: Prelude to America's War in Vietnam* (Lawrence, Kans.: University Press of Kansas, 2002), 6.

[32] William O. Douglas, *North from Malaya* (New York: Doubleday, 1953), 180–81.

What seems to have appealed to these Washington power brokers, apart from Diem's Catholicism, was his resolute stand against both Communism and French colonialism. Justice Douglas, one of the original creators of the Diem "miracle man" myth, concluded after visiting Southeast Asia in 1954 that Ngo Dinh Diem was "revered by the Vietnamese because he is honest and independent and stood firm against French influence—a hero in Central and North Vietnam, with a considerable following in the South too".[33] Diem seemed to be exactly what the Americans were looking for—a popular, incorruptible, non-Communist nationalist. What Douglas and other Americans seemed not to realise was that the very qualities they admired in Diem would later lead their government into conflict with him.

Although the Washington contacts would become more significant for him as time passed, in the short term Diem had no concrete plans for engaging this robust American support. To the contrary, he stepped back for a while to assess things, and he left the United States in May 1953, heading for a Benedictine monastery in Belgium. There he took refuge from the world in order to draw closer to God. By this time in his life, Diem had formed a pattern of going in and out of worldly affairs, a pattern he would continue until his death. When troubled, under threat, or just in need of quiet and reflection, he would retreat into a monastery or a similar religious institution. After his soul had been calmed and his thoughts organised through Christian contemplation, he would return to the hurly-burly of politics once more. After his Belgium retreat in 1953, he travelled to Paris to visit his brother Luyen, who had been seeking and organising support for Diem within the large Vietnamese community there.

Diem appeared torn between his attraction to the religious life and his sense of civic duty. In an apparent attempt to fulfil both, on January 12, 1954, he joined the third order of the Benedictines, making a commitment to live according to the rule of Saint Benedict as befitted a layman.[34] Many years later, in a moment of exasperation with Diem's political naïveté during the Buddhist crisis of 1963, his brother Ngo Dinh Nhu shouted that he should have been a monk and not a president.[35] Everyone who knew the man realised that if not for his sense of

---

[33] Ibid., 181.

[34] Van Chau, "Late President".

[35] This story, attended by a smile and a chuckle, was related to this writer by the late General Nguyen Khanh, who had been present at Nhu's frustrated outburst.

filial duty to both his family and his country, he would have entered a monastery.

The support that Diem had garnered during his visit to America began to expand at a prodigious rate a year later when it became apparent to the U.S. government that the Communists were intent on bringing all of Southeast Asia under their sway. They already controlled China, North Korea, and, after the 1954 Geneva Accords, North Vietnam. Championing Diem in this important period were formidable Americans such as Senators John F. Kennedy and Mike Mansfield; Kenneth Young of the Department of State; Allen Dulles and John Foster Dulles, both with the U.S. Central Intelligence Agency (CIA); and Edward Geary Lansdale, a military intelligence officer who became a true friend to Diem.[36] Outside of the Eisenhower administration, Diem's advocates included the editors of *Life* and *Time*; and the powerful lobby group led by Cardinal Spellman, Justice Douglas, Professor Fishel, Leo Cherne of the Research Institute of America, and Cherne's associate Joseph Buttinger, a well-known socialist activist and author from Austria.[37] Later in 1955, when Diem was president, both Fishel and Buttinger acted as advisors to him in Saigon. Eventually Buttinger became disillusioned with Diem.

Another important figure in Diem's founding relationship with the United States was Wolf Ladejinsky, a colourful New Deal Democrat. More importantly for Diem's credentials as a reorganiser, Ladejinsky was an Asian land reform expert, having served the U.S. government in that capacity in both post-war Japan and Chiang Kai-shek's Taiwan. A Jewish refugee of the Russian Revolution, Ladejinsky was fired from the Department of Agriculture in 1954, when he was accused of being involved in "un-American activities". Nevertheless, when Diem hired Ladejinsky as his land reform tsar, the move created substantial goodwill

---

[36] As a military intelligence officer, Edward Geary Lansdale successfully countered insurgents in the Philippines with President Ramon Magsaysay. He then advised French troops fighting against the Viet Minh in Indochina before the foundation of South Vietnam and its government, which he helped to establish. Lansdale took a near-instant liking to President Diem, and this friendliness was reciprocated by the Vietnamese leader. After he retired from the military with the rank of major general, Lansdale returned to Vietnam, where he worked in the American embassy in Saigon. Even when the U.S. government turned against Diem in 1963, Lansdale remained his staunch defender.

[37] Robert Scheer, "The Genesis of United States Support for Ngo Dinh Diem", in *Vietnam: History, Documents, and Opinions of a Major World Crisis*, ed. Marvin E. Gettleman (Greenwich, Conn.: Fawcett Publications, 1965), 248–52.

on the part of America's liberal elite, because they took this as proof of Diem's sincerity with regard to that important issue.[38]

Finally, a brief note needs to be included here regarding Diem's attitude toward Buddhism. Diem deeply respected Buddhism. Indeed, in a moment of candour he admitted to a close family friend that he preferred Buddhist practice to Confucian philosophy because the former involved looking inward and mending one's own life.[39] As a devout Roman Catholic, Diem knew that the best way to win anyone to Christ was via the example of his own conduct; the very notion of forcing his religious beliefs on anyone was anathema to the Vietnamese leader. Additionally, Diem saw in Buddhism a means of reinvigorating Vietnamese identity. French colonialism had, for the most part, robbed the people of their traditional culture, a vacuum that was at risk of being filled by Communism. Diem hoped that a revitalised Buddhism at the village level would provide the people with a spiritual centre of gravity that would prevent the Communists from taking over the countryside. Even without such a strategy in mind, Diem could never have attacked Buddhism as his critics have claimed; his Confucian ethic of honouring his parents and ancestors would not have permitted him to dishonour the Buddhism of his great-grandfather and other forebears.

[38] Ibid., 250.

[39] In his own words, Diem stated: "The Buddhists are calm and more contemplative; they look inside themselves and they try to improve themselves; they are not going out into society and trying to create trouble." Van Chau, "Late President".

I

Diplomacy in South Vietnam
from the Late 1950s to 1960

This work is concerned with the history of a specific era in American-Vietnamese relations wherein President Ngo Dinh Diem was betrayed and murdered, owing to the collusion of his erstwhile allies with local Vietnamese plotters. Thus, this first chapter provides the backdrop to this American betrayal of an ally in a time of war.

After the Americans helped Diem become president of South Vietnam in 1955, he immediately set out to improve his country. Diem's Communist adversaries were realists, and they understood that with Diem's competent administration and his ambitious development projects in the rural areas they had a problem on their hands. South Vietnam was not disintegrating into the kind of chaos that would have made a reintegration with the Communist North a foregone conclusion.

The Communists understood the many grievances that they could exploit to organise an indigenous revolutionary movement in the South, which came to be called the National Liberation Front (NLF). No emerging nation, at least in Southeast Asia, was immune from such problems.[1] But political action with a duly subordinated military campaign was needed to break the bonds being formed between the Diem government and the people. This took the form of terrorism, which was iniquitous in design and execution and ironically labelled the Destruction of the Oppression. By March 1958, Destruction of the Oppression had assassinated more than four hundred village officials. In 1959 they began murdering schoolteachers, mostly in the key Mekong

---

[1] Sir Robert Thompson gave a competent overview of these problems in his *Defeating Communist Insurgency: Experiences from Malaya and Vietnam* (London: Chatto and Windus, 1966); see esp. 21–23.

Delta provinces of Long An, Kien Hoa, and Dinh Tuong. This campaign contributed to the subsequent lack of schooling for nearly thirty thousand children—children who, to the advantage of the Communists, no longer had any positive relationship with the government of South Vietnam.[2]

Destruction of the Oppression was not only tactically selective in terms of those targeted for torture and murder but also strategically overarching, designed to frighten the general populace away from helping and supporting the government. Indeed, as the Communists testified themselves: "Our purpose was not only to eliminate those who could be harmful to the movement but also with a view toward making the people afraid and to prevent them from co-operating with the government."[3] Thus, the Communists were intent on undermining the legitimacy of the government to the point where it would no longer be viable.[4] Specifically, they were targeting Diem's leadership, which they knew had a unique standing in the eyes of the Vietnamese.

French scholar Paul Mus was well acquainted with both Ho Chi Minh, the Communist leader of North Vietnam, and Ngo Dinh Diem, and he understood that only "a man who is known to be virtuous and who leads an austere life" constituted a legitimate leader for the Vietnamese. As a result, he said to historian Ellen Hammer, "Only one man could ever hope to challenge Ho Chi Minh for leadership—Ngo Dinh Diem. Because he alone has the same reputation for virtue and austerity as Ho."[5] Mus had grown up in Vietnam, and his expert knowledge of the country was highly regarded by the French government, which made him its official emissary to Ho Chi Minh during the First

[2] William R. Andrews, *The Village War: Vietnamese Communist Revolutionary Activities in Dinh Tuong Province, 1960–1964* (Columbia, Mo.: University of Missouri Press, 1973), 51, 54–55. Andrews' work is supported by RAND Corporation and Military Assistance Command, Vietnam J-2, "Studies of the National Liberation Front of South Vietnam" (Saigon, n.d.), DT-86, 2; DT-99, 2; DT-84, 2; DT-88, 1.

[3] Quotation in RAND Corporation and Military Assistance Command, Vietnam J-2, "Studies of the National Liberation Front", DT-99, 2. Found in the notes of Andrews, *Village War*, 51, 54–55.

[4] See Alexander Dallin and George W. Breslauer, *Political Terror in Communist Systems* (Stanford, Calif.: Stanford University Press, 1970), 7, for an explanation of why Communist insurgents are so dependent on the use of terror.

[5] Ellen J. Hammer, *A Death in November: America in Vietnam, 1963* (New York: E. P. Dutton, 1987), 47.

Indochina War. Mus related his observations to the Americans in 1948 as both a commendation of Diem and a warning that he could not be used as "their man".[6] In an interview with the author, Vietnamese General Nguyen Khanh, who participated in the overthrow of Diem, concurred with Mus' assessment of him. Diem's legitimacy with the people was based on his virtue, he said. "The number one thing was the example of the way of his life; how he lived his life. He sacrificed himself!"[7]

The ongoing Destruction of the Oppression spanned the gamut from few or no killings to outright slaughter that even the Americans at their undisciplined worst[8] would not come close to matching.[9] In their pitiless analysis, the Communists understood that terror worked best when it paralysed the greatest amount of people; thus, it was most effective when it seemed to be only partially selective, like lightning, that way, no one could predict who would get hit next.[10]

Analyst William R. Andrews, in his studies, tours, and interviews within South Vietnam, determined that the killings of village officials, schoolteachers, public health workers, and other civil servants reached

[6] Ibid.

[7] General Nguyen Khanh, interview by author, June 16, 1994, United States Air Force Special Operations School, Hurlburt Field, Fla., transcript, 61, Vietnam Center and Archive at Texas Tech University, Lubbock, Tex., and the United States Air Force Special Operations School, Hurlburt Field, Fla.

[8] Even the massacre that took place at My Lai, many years later, paled in comparison to what the Communists did.

[9] At other times, in different circumstances, the terror of the Destruction of the Oppression, which apologists for the party have often excused on the grounds that it was "selective", could take on the appearance of a charnel house. In a Cai Lay village that had changed hands between the Communist National Liberation Front and the South Vietnamese government four times in as many years, twenty persons, including women, were accused of being government spies: "They all had their heads cut off and their bodies were thrown in the street. On them were pinned the charges written on a piece of paper." In another execution, "The hamlet chief in this instance had been tied to a stake in the middle of the market place in full view of the assembled villagers. The man was slowly disembowelled, his children decapitated, and his pregnant wife then tied to the same stake and similarly disembowelled." Malcolm Browne, *The New Face of War* (New York: Bobbs-Merrill, 1965), 103.

[10] "The Party at times accused and then executed or humiliated certain persons for their pro-Government activities when even a cursory examination would have revealed the charges to be baseless. Had the Party been consistently discriminatory, eliminating only those persons widely known to be class enemies, then the terror would have become highly predictable and incapable of creating the desired level of anxiety response among the villagers." Andrews, *Village War*, 57–58.

its peak in 1963, with a definite decline in 1964.[11] Andrews has argued that the sharp drop in killings of civil servants in 1964 was owing to a combination of factors. In the first place, by 1964 the Destruction of the Oppression had been effective in eliminating government workers from areas that had been penetrated by the party earlier on; second, the South Vietnamese officials in the rural areas were no longer exposing themselves; they were avoiding death by withdrawing their involvement with the people living in rural villages.[12]

There is, however, a third explanation, which has primary strategic implications and is linked directly to the central thesis of this book, which is the singular importance of Ngo Dinh Diem. By 1964 it was no longer necessary to kill civil servants and to discredit the government of South Vietnam (GVN) to the same extent because Diem, the government's most powerful and substantial pillar of political legitimacy, had been removed. Even with military power attempting to fill the political vacuum created by the demise of Diem, it was just a matter of time before the whole structure collapsed. Communist though they were, the insurrectionists were also Vietnamese, and they knew that soldiers could never take the place of a leader like Diem in the hearts and the minds of their people. Thus, the strategic political victory granted to the Communists by the murder of Ngo Dinh Diem cannot be overstated.

All of this has a great deal of bearing upon just who was responsible for the insurrection in the South: Was it the allegedly corrupt and incompetent administration of President Diem, as some of his detractors have argued, or the carefully planned and executed Communist insurgency? Evidence suggests that a superb Communist organisational structure was already in place even before Diem had taken up the reins

---

[11] Here are Andrews' figures:

Year	Assassinations
1957–1960	1,700
1961	1,300
1962	1,700
1963	2,000
1964	500

Source: Ibid., 60.

[12] These figures of Andrews are supported by the studies of Viet Cong expert Douglas Pike. See his *Viet Cong: The Organization and Techniques of the National Liberation Front of South Vietnam* (Cambridge, Mass.: MIT Press, 1966), 102.

of power.[13] Certainly the Communists in the North made no attempt to hide their control of the insurrection in the South. This was made manifest when in 1963 they offered Ngo Dinh Nhu, Diem's younger brother and chief political advisor, a cease-fire in exchange for the beginning of an American withdrawal from Vietnam. Indeed, Seymour M. Hersh argued that the Kennedy administration engineered and supported the coup that removed Diem from power because Kennedy and his officials worried that the Ngo Dinhs were, in fact, going to come to such terms with the North.[14]

Dennis Duncanson, in his studies of 1950s Vietnam, observed that the Communists had been conducting their campaign of terror from the earliest days of Diem's administration. They had not been idle during or after President Diem's initial triumphs over the militarised sects Binh Xuyen, Cao Dai, and Hoa Hao.[15] According to Duncanson, they had a "sleeper", or a hidden party base, in most villages,[16] and threats, coercion, and selective assassinations kept peasants in a perpetual state of terror. When Diem refused to hold nationwide elections with the Communist-controlled North in 1956, as called for by the Geneva Accords that ended the First Indochina War between the French and the Viet Minh, the Communists found a new justification, and a new propaganda tool, for their terror campaign and escalated their violent activities.[17] A British counterinsurgency expert and an advisor to Diem's

[13] See Douglas Pike, *History of Vietnamese Communism, 1925–1976* (Stanford, Calif.: Hoover Institution Press, 1978), 115–18.

[14] Seymour M. Hersh, *The Dark Side of Camelot* (Boston: Little, Brown, 1997), 423.

[15] The sects—the Cao Dai, the Hoa Hao, and the criminal Binh Xuyen—had been a challenge to Diem's political legitimacy from the beginning of his government (see Bernard B. Fall, *The Two Viet-Nams: A Political and Military Analysis* [New York: Praeger, 1963], 239). These groups, which had fought against the French during the First Indochina War, controlled key areas of South Vietnam and had access not only to a bounty of arms and soldiers for hire but also, at least in the case of the Binh Xuyen, to government officials and police in Saigon (see Dennis J. Duncanson, *Government and Revolution in Vietnam* [London: Oxford University Press / Royal Institute of International Affairs, 1968], 220–21). To govern a united South Vietnam and to resist attempts by the North to take over the country, Diem needed to counter these groups. In the case of Binh Xuyen, he knew that "as a matter of both government integrity and his own survival, the police must be under his control." David L. Anderson, "J. Lawton Collins, John Foster Dulles, and the Eisenhower Administration's 'Point of No Return' in Vietnam", *Diplomatic History*, no. 12 (Spring 1988): 132.

[16] Duncanson, *Government and Revolution*, 252.

[17] After Ngo Dinh Diem repudiated demands for all-Vietnam elections, the rate at which murders were committed seems to have increased. Although the government's limited

government, Sir Robert Thompson, noted that the published figures for murders and abductions by insurgents exceeded twelve thousand civilians and government workers between 1960 and 1961.[18]

The Communists were seeking to estrange the people from their government, not only by killing its workers but also by destroying the relative peace and stability it had achieved in rural South Vietnam between 1955 and 1958. Another British counterinsurgency expert, P.J. Honey, who was attached to Thompson's advisory mission to President Diem, duly noted the calm during this era:

> The country has enjoyed three years of relative peace and calm in which it has been able to carry on the very necessary work of national reconstruction. The most destructive feature in the national life of Vietnam throughout recent years has been the lack of security in the countryside, which obliged farmers and peasants to abandon the rice fields and to flee to the large cities for safety. Today it is possible to travel all over South Vietnam without any risk. The army and security forces have mopped up most of the armed bands of political opponents of the Government, of Communists and of common bandits.[19]

Contrary to their arguments, the Communists were not terrorizing the countryside in retribution for Diem's refusal to participate in reunification elections. The fact is, the Communists in the North were in no position to hold such elections, and they were lying about their adherence to the Geneva Accords.[20] In short, through violence they created

---

administrative control obscured much of what was going on, it is now generally thought that during the nine years that Diem was in power, close to twenty thousand people lost their lives to Communist insurgents. See Duncanson, *Government and Revolution*, 252.

[18] Thompson, *Defeating Communist Insurgency*, 27.

[19] Congress, House, Committee on Armed Services, "Rebellion against My-Diem", tab 2 of *Evolution of the War: Origins of the Insurgency, 1954–1960*, section IV.A.5 of bk. 2 of *United States–Vietnam Relations, 1945–1967: Study Prepared by the Department of Defense* (Washington, D.C.: United States Government Printing Office, 1971), 46.

[20] Edward Geary Lansdale, who had led undercover operations in North Vietnam, had predicted that just prior to the planned 1956 elections, the North itself would probably have found a convenient way around the process and blame the South for violating the Geneva Accords, which the South had not signed, because they had serious political problems of their own making (see Edward Geary Lansdale, *In the Midst of Wars: An American's Mission to Southeast Asia* [New York: Harper and Row, 1972], 346). One of these problems was the bungling of their land reform, which had led to open revolt (see Pike, *History of Vietnamese Communism*, 108–13). Furthermore, although the Ho Chi Minh regime did sign the Geneva Accords, it was committing violations of its own, not least of which was the build-up of their army: from 7 to

a situation in which nationwide elections were unthinkable to Diem and his supporters, including the Americans, and then used their non-participation as a stick to beat them with. All of their actions were calculated to erode the people's trust in Diem.[21] Their lack of trust would, in turn, bring about strategic paralysis in the governing of South Vietnam, because the people would be deterred from supporting Saigon. In essence, the Communists were involved in an all-out effort to destroy the legitimacy of Ngo Dinh Diem and his government.[22]

While this attack on the legitimacy of the Diem government was already under way at the tactical, village level in South Vietnam,[23] in May 1959, at the fifteenth plenum of the Communist Central Committee, the leaders of North Vietnam made the formal decision to direct strategically the entire insurgency in the South. The North Vietnamese Communist leadership considered a number of questions; chief amongst these was whether to send their own North Vietnamese Army (NVA) troops or simply to increase support for the Viet Minh organisation already in the South. In their estimation, it was better to expand support for the Viet Minh (later called Viet Cong) while leaving the option open for using regular troops of the NVA, also known as the People's Army of Vietnam (PAVN), should the Southern resistance prove too strong. One of the benefits of this course of action was that it would not attract worldwide condemnation for a Korean-style invasion of the South. Should it become necessary, such an invasion could be launched later under the guise of supporting "the freedom-loving peoples of the South in their fight against oppression". Expanding their Southern insurgency,

---

20 divisions, from 200,000 to 550,000 troops, and from 600 to 700 Chinese instructors. A total of several thousand Chinese and Russian advisors were in all echelons of the army. Congress, House, Committee on Armed Services, "Failure of the Geneva Settlement", tab 1 of *Evolution of the War: Origins of the Insurgency, 1954–1960*, 29–30.

[21] Andrews, *Village War*, 20.

[22] "Disorientation is the objective par excellence of the terrorist removing the underpinnings of the order in which his targets live out their daily lives. The primary responsibility of any incumbent group is to guarantee order to its population, and the terrorist will attempt to disorient the population by demonstrating that the incumbent's structure cannot give adequate support." Thomas Perry Thornton, "Terror as a Weapon of Political Agitation", in *Internal War: Problems and Approaches*, ed. Harry Eckstein (New York: Free Press, 1968), 83.

[23] This observation is supported by RAND Corporation studies. See Stephen T. Hosmer, *Viet Cong Repression and Its Implications for the Future*, Report Prepared for the Advanced Research Projects Agency; R-475/1-ARPA (Santa Monica, Calif.: RAND Corporation, 1970), 7–8.

then, became the order of the day, which placed the Viet Minh under the same general command as the NVA.[24]

William Colby, who was CIA station chief in Saigon between 1959 and 1962, observed that given Diem's progress in stabilising and rebuilding South Vietnam, the Communists had little choice but to increase their violent attacks; otherwise, they would lose not only the South but potentially the North as well.[25] Colby described the GVN's programs to rebuild the basic infrastructure of the rural areas of the South, between 1956 and 1959, as "the total social and economic regeneration of South Vietnam". Villages that had been abandoned during the Viet Minh war were repopulated. Land reform had made the peasant farmers more productive; for example, rice production was increasing. New schools were being built in rapid order. Colby noted that in one particular province he visited, there had been only two or three schools at the end of the Viet Minh war, all in the province capital. By the spring of 1959, there were approximately forty new schools spread throughout the province.[26] These were practical and therefore powerful indicators to the ordinary Vietnamese that Diem took their welfare into account as he developed the country. In short, the Communists recognised that their campaign to take the South was finished unless they escalated the violence and thereby separated the people from the GVN.[27] The

[24] "A conventional attack by Ho Chi Minh's People's Army of Viet-Nam patterned after the invasion of South Korea probably would have succeeded because the Army of the Republic of Viet-Nam was weak and fragmented, but two factors mitigated against such a move: world opinion and the alternative means possessed by the Lao Dong to destroy the South Vietnamese Government.... [which] bypassed the difficulties of conventional military action; that means was revolutionary guerrilla warfare. Conditions in South Viet-Nam, no matter how improved, were advantageous for such an undertaking." Andrews, *Village War*, 20–21.

[25] "And of course the communists' conclusion out of this was, no chance. No chance of playing a role, and we're being crushed by the momentum of the government, by this positive momentum of the economic and social development that was in the process. And I think that is what led them to the decision, we've got to go back to the war. Otherwise we've lost it, and we've not only lost it in South Vietnam, we may lose it in North Vietnam as well." William Colby, interview by Ted Gittinger, June 2, 1981, Washington, D.C., interview 1, transcript 1, Lyndon Baines Johnson Presidential Library Oral History Collection, University of Texas at Austin, pp. 1, 7–9.

[26] Ibid.

[27] Edward Geary Lansdale's observations corresponded to Colby's: "Paradoxically, the Communist campaign of terrorism started just as life in the countryside was beginning to show great promise for the people on the land. It wasn't only that the armies had departed from the former battlegrounds in the rice paddies, letting farmlands be tilled in peace; there were, as well, a multitude of new efforts being made to improve the whole agrarian economy

time, then, for substantial Northern assistance for the stay-behind cadres in the South was at hand, and it became clear to most observers that by 1960 the Viet Minh were embarking upon another major war, the political target being Ngo Dinh Diem, who turned out to be more assailable through the Americans than through the Vietnamese.[28]

From the time Diem became president in 1955, he was opposed by some of the more liberally minded, educated, and articulate South Vietnamese, particularly those with political aspirations of their own. In the face of violent threats from first the militarised sects and then the Communist insurgents, Diem took a tough approach to any political opposition, including outlawing certain groups, shutting down their newspapers, and arresting some of their leaders. These actions Diem thought necessary to prevent the fledgling republic from collapsing. Some South Vietnamese, however, saw Diem and his family as antiquated and authoritarian mandarins, and they feared, as opposition leader Phan Quang Dan told *Life* reporter John Osborne, that Diem was building a "Ngo dynasty".[29]

Some members of Diem's opposition put forward a manifesto of grievances, which they first enunciated at the Caravelle Hotel in Saigon and thus became known as the Caravellists.[30] In their "Manifesto of the Eighteen",[31] which they gave to the international press, they claimed that Diem and his brother Nhu were playing into the hands of the Communists with their "state-of-emergency" methods of government.[32] Furthermore, they argued that Diem was being insulated from the truth by members of the government's executive branch and that he needed to act upon Caravellist advice if the country was to be spared from complete destruction at the hands of a rebellious populace.[33] But more circumspect American military intelligence reports indicated that many of this Caravellist Eighteen were suspect in terms of their impartiality.

---

of Vietnam. Each time that I visited President Diem in his office, I would find him deep in the study of some new program, often of vast dimensions." *In the Midst of Wars*, 354.

[28] Denis Warner, *The Last Confucian: Vietnam, Southeast Asia, and the West*, rev. ed. (Sydney, Australia: Angus and Robertson, 1964), 146.

[29] John Osborne, "The Tough Miracle Man of Vietnam: Diem, America's Newly Arrived Visitor, Has Roused His Country and Routed the Reds", *Life*, May 13, 1957, 168.

[30] Duncanson, *Government and Revolution*, 267.

[31] Congress, House, Committee on Armed Services, "Rebellion against My-Diem", 34.

[32] Duncanson, *Government and Revolution*, 267.

[33] Congress, House, Committee on Armed Services, "Rebellion against My-Diem", 39.

All of them were involved in Saigon politics with their sights set upon leadership roles.[34]

President Diem and his advisor brother, Ngo Dinh Nhu, were not moved by the arguments of the Caravellists. According to Colby, "Diem and Nhu contemptuously rejected the petition, remarking on the plush surroundings of the Caravelle Hotel in which this group of Saigon politicians had gathered, and on their lack of contact with the rural areas where the real battle against both the Communists and underdevelopment were underway."[35] The Caravellists' cry for "freedom" and "democracy" made great play in the liberal U.S. press, however, which in turn put U.S. Ambassador to South Vietnam Elbridge Durbrow in conflict with Diem. Essentially, under pressure from Washington, Durbrow argued that democratic reforms had to flow rapidly or the supposed proverbial dam of South Vietnamese political outrage would burst. Diem countered that in any fledgling government representing an emerging nation, authority had to be maintained while democratic institutions were being constructed; this was especially the case in South Vietnam, where not just Communist insurgents were hard at work undermining lawful authority but several sects with private armies had been attempting to do the same thing. Diem further argued that the Caravellists had no following beyond the cafés of Saigon, where the U.S. news media swarmed to garner the latest anti-Diem gossip.[36]

Diem responded to the criticism by intensifying the very measures that had initially caused it: press censorship, detention without trial, implementation of the Agroville Program,[37] and Can Lao Party[38] control of the army.[39] Meanwhile, although the Caravellists were unable to come up with any practical method for dealing with the Communists, American advisors continued to urge Diem to implement democratic

[34] Edward Geary Lansdale, "Memorandum for Secretary of Defense [and] Deputy Secretary of Defense; Subject: Vietnam" [between January 14 and 17, 1961], in "U.S. Perceptions of the Insurgency, 1954–1960", tab 4 of Evolution of the War: Origins of the Insurgency, 1954–1960, 67, 69, 73.

[35] William Colby and Peter Forbath, Honorable Men: My Life in the CIA (New York: Simon and Schuster, 1978), 159.

[36] Colby, interview by Gittinger, interview 1, p. 11.

[37] Launched in 1959, the Agroville Program moved peasants from areas being destabilised by Communist insurgents to areas secured by the Army of the Republic of Vietnam.

[38] The Can Lao Party, led by Diem's brother Ngo Dinh Diem, was created to support the Diem government.

[39] See Duncanson, Government and Revolution, 267.

reforms in order to gain the confidence and support of the people.[40] But the net "effect of the [Caravellists'] petition was to start a political war within Saigon to go along with and complicate the guerrilla war in the countryside".[41]

American criticism at this time also took aim at Diem's land reform. Historian George C. Herring offered a leftist critique of Diem's program, saying not enough peasants were benefiting from the redistribution of land. He accused Diem of "a singular lack of concern and near-callous irresponsibility".[42] Herring's analysis, however, did not take into account the social conditions Diem was trying to overcome and the undermining effects of Communist propaganda.

William Colby, on the other hand, appreciated the practicality of Diem's approach in the face of tremendous challenges. When U.S. advisors complained that the parcels of land being taken from the French and sold to the Vietnamese were too large and left powerful landlords in place, Colby explained, Diem said he could not make them smaller without harming the middle class. Diem thus urged his allies to be patient, because he was "going to use the apparatus of social order that exists in order to conduct this longer-term transition". Meanwhile, noted Colby, the Communists were subverting the program by trying to convince the peasants that the land reforms were set up to make them pay more taxes.[43]

Along with the redistribution of existing farmland, the Diem government made more land available for cultivation, introduced new crops, and built model rural communities in which Vietnamese farmers could flourish free of Communist insurgent activities. "One of the actualities

[40] Robert Shaplen, "A Reporter in Vietnam: Diem", *New Yorker*, September 22, 1962, 125.

[41] Colby, *Honorable Men*, 159.

[42] George C. Herring, *America's Longest War: The United States and Vietnam, 1950–1975*, 2nd ed. (New York: Alfred A. Knopf, 1986), 65.

[43] "[T]he land reform worked according to the way most of the successful land reform programs had worked in the past [e.g., Japan and Taiwan] in which the government took the land from the larger landowners, and particularly the French, and then loaned the peasant the money, which he then repaid over the next few years. Now the communists very intelligently focused on that as just a way of insisting on further payment of taxes. Because during the intervening years, the years of the war, there were no taxes collected because the backcountry was in a turmoil and in an uproar, and so the peasants weren't paying any taxes. So that the interpretation successfully put forward by the communists, which was in a sense accurate, was that this legal mumbo jumbo meant that the peasants would be required to pay taxes today that they hadn't been required to pay before." Colby, interview by Gittinger, interview 1, pp. 13–14.

was the development of the trans-Bassac region, the land between the Bassac branch of the Mekong River and the Gulf of Thailand. The first phase called for settling over a hundred thousand people in new model farm communities in the Cai Sab area and draining the low-lying land by constructing 125 miles of navigable canals."[44] As mentioned earlier, Diem hired American land reform expert Wolf Ladejinsky to help him to plan these communities.

> The two men became close friends in 1956, and Ladejinsky was given a house next to the presidential palace and joined Diem at breakfast nearly every morning. Thus Diem's daily routine began with these breakfast sessions, discussing the implementation of the land reform measures drafted by Ladejinsky and issued as decrees by Diem, as well as the myriad problems of the whole range of agricultural projects afoot. Both men shared the dream of making an Eden of Vietnam, with bounty for all its inhabitants and with ample foods for other nations in the Pacific basin.[45]

Diem's critics found plenty wrong with these ambitious projects. They accused Diem of being too authoritarian, of exercising too much control in order to aggrandise himself.

In an attempt to prove that Diem was a power-hungry dictator, or at least a bungler, Diem's critics derided his 1956 suspension of local democratic elections. Calling the action Diem's "most fateful decision", Bernard Fall wrote, "In defiance of one of the most hallowed Vietnamese traditions, according to which the power of the central authorities stops at the bamboo hedge of the village, the Saigon administration abolished by a stroke of the pen elected village chiefs and village councils and replaced them by appointive members."[46] Historian Larry Cable agreed that Diem made "a massive and egregious error in 1956, when he prohibited the traditional and deeply cherished village elections and instead appointed as village chiefs fellow Catholic refugees from the North. This was a blunder which even the French and the Japanese had not committed during their terms as occupiers of Vietnam. It was a cause of massive discontent among the rural population of South Vietnam."[47] The

---

[44] Lansdale, *In the Midst of Wars*, 354–56.

[45] Ibid.

[46] Bernard B. Fall, *Last Reflections on a War: Bernard B. Fall's Last Comments on Vietnam* (Garden City, N.Y.: Doubleday, 1967), 198–99.

[47] Larry E. Cable, *Conflict of Myths: The Development of American Counterinsurgency Doctrine and the Vietnam War* (New York: New York University Press, 1986), 185.

criticism is misleading, because it ignores that many villages had already been infiltrated by violent Communist subversives, necessitating GVN intervention. As we have seen, in such places the choices were stark for villagers: submit to the will of the Communists or die a horrible death along with all of your family members.

What was lacking in so much Western criticism of Diem was any fair comparison between his leadership and that of his rival in the North, Ho Chi Minh. Fall claimed that the Communists in the North had not been so stupid as to interfere with village leadership, but this assertion is disproved by the unfortunate historical facts. Under Communist rule, North Vietnamese peasants accomplished little by political protest other than their own deaths. In 1956 there was a massive rebellion against Ho Chi Minh's land reform (which was, in effect, Stalinist collectivisation). Ho sent in the army, with the result that approximately ten thousand Vietnamese peasants lost their lives.[48] Some estimate that at least 50,000 were murdered.[49] Lansdale stated that the Communist officials, who were adept at running guerrilla warfare, proved to be terrible at running the Hanoi government. He claimed that the Northern Communists were so unpopular at this time that they would have been soundly defeated by Diem had the 1956 plebiscite reunification elections been held.[50]

Although Fall admitted that there had been a substantial stay-behind Communist organisation in the South, he failed to ascribe to it any thoroughgoing revolutionary capability.[51] He did not take seriously the threat the Communists posed to Diem's GVN, never mind how the president was supposed to deal with it. Nor did he credit Diem for the fact that his interference at the village level was temporary. Once his Strategic Hamlet Program (SHP) was in place, village elections were reinstated by the GVN, because the protected peasant communities were no longer subject to Communist intimidation.[52]

---

[48] Lansdale, *In the Midst of Wars*, 346.

[49] Jean-Louis Margolin, "Vietnam and Laos: The Impasse of War Communism", in *The Black Book of Communism: Crimes, Terror, Repression*, trans. Mark Kramer and Jonathan Murphy (Cambridge, Mass.: Harvard University Press, 1999), 569.

[50] Lansdale, *In the Midst of Wars*, 345.

[51] See Fall, *Last Reflections*, 198.

[52] Robert Thompson, however, did not ignore what Diem said or did in this context, and he supported the Vietnamese president in his attempts to purge Communist control from the villages. See Thompson, *Defeating Communist Insurgency*, 78–79.

The Caravellists' criticism of Diem's land reform programs marked the beginning of a schism that began to develop in American policy toward the government in South Vietnam and the burgeoning guerrilla threat. The CIA was caught in the middle of what would turn out to be a long and bitter fight between the Department of Defense (DOD) and the Department of State (DOS). According to eyewitness Colby, DOD took a predictable stand by viewing the rising Viet Cong insurgency as the outbreak of war. As a result, officers in the U.S. military, such as General Sam Williams, argued that South Vietnamese troops needed to be shaped up and reorganised in order to meet the possibility of an invasion from North Vietnam. Consequently, the American military advisory in Vietnam reorganised the command structure of the Army of the Republic of Vietnam (ARVN) in 1959 and called for an increase in men from 150,000 to 170,000 soldiers.[53] It should be noted that regardless of the varying views on the design of the Vietnamese force necessary to defeat the Communists—more soldiers versus more policemen—Diem and his officials had quite good relations with the American military for the most part.

The conflict that arose between Saigon and Washington, Colby recalled, was between Diem and DOS. The disagreement was over the direction he and the U.S. military were taking. For DOS, the solution was for Diem to make his regime more democratic and less authoritarian. Thus, DOS viewed U.S. military aid as leverage to pressure Diem to reform his government. Quite naturally, the American military advisors were infuriated with DOS, who presumed to know the best way to counter the advances of North Vietnam.[54]

While observing the fight between DOD and DOS, Colby formed his own conclusions on counterinsurgency, which diverged from those of both departments and were heavily influenced by British successes and French failures. The North Vietnamese strategy in 1960, Colby saw, did not include conventional warfare. Rather, it was designed to create a "people's war". He recognised the telltale indicators of the first stage: the mobilisation and organisation of insurgent Communist forces.[55] Since the immediate challenge was political subversion, it could not be easily

[53] Colby, *Honorable Men*, 159–60.
[54] Ibid.
[55] Ibid., 161–70.

addressed by the standard military doctrines being advocated by American military advisors. Colby was quick to add, however, that the calls for a more democratic government in Saigon were also, for the most part, irrelevant to the task at hand. As he quipped in an interview with the author, "It's difficult to talk about draining the swamp when you are up to your—in alligators."

The real battle, Colby noted, was what Sir Robert Thompson had famously described as the struggle for "the hearts and the minds of the people". According to Thompson, "An insurgent movement is a war for the people."[56] And Colby could see that the side that won over the Vietnamese villagers would win.

> The real contest, it seemed to me, was in the villages, where the issues were more fundamental. Did association with the Saigon government offer a better future, both economic and political, for the villager? Or did the national and revolutionary appeal of the Communist organiser, reinforced by the authority of guerrilla squads, convince the villager or leave him no alternative but to join the revolt? My travels in the countryside had shown how wide was the gap between the French-influenced urban class and the traditional Vietnamese villager. But it had also shown the latter's enthusiastic acceptance of economic and social development and his willingness to work hard toward it. In the long term, villagers would certainly insist on more of a voice in their national affairs, even along the lines advocated by the oppositionists in Saigon, but in the near term, they were far more interested in the practical improvements that could be made in their lives and in the life-and-death issue of protection from the armed bands circulating in their regions. Thus, the real way to contest the Communists, it seemed to me, would be to mobilize, organize and involve the villagers in the economic and social improvements that the government was providing and to strengthen them so that they could help defend themselves against Communist pressures.[57]

Colby agreed with Thompson that a government could win over its people without being a Western-style democracy. An authoritarian government that applied the rule of law equally to all while engaging in constructive and progressive national policies, as Diem's was doing, could garner popular support. Diem's government needed only to prove

[56] Thompson, *Defeating Communist Insurgency*, 51.
[57] Colby, *Honorable Men*, 161–70.

its program equalled results while the Communist insurgency guaranteed the opposite.[58]

Unfortunately, the very fact that a Communist insurgency had begun to spread through rural South Vietnam in the late 1950s caused many Americans to take a critical view of Diem. By 1960 American experience with him and the GVN had created much controversy in Washington. To many American liberals, Diem was an enigma—and one they suspected was unsympathetic to their worldview. Between the lines of what they said and wrote about Diem and his brother Ngo Dinh Nhu, one can detect a subtle but definite distaste. Over time this distaste blossomed into hatred.

[58] Thompson, *Defeating Communist Insurgency*, 68.

2

U.S. Ambassador Elbridge Durbrow

Elbridge Durbrow was posted as American ambassador to South Vietnam in 1957. Durbrow, who had been educated as a lawyer, joined the U.S. Foreign Service in 1930 and served in Warsaw and Bucharest before being assigned to Moscow for three years, a posting that began in 1934. During the 1930s and 1940s, Durbrow had been on what became known as the "East European shuttle", a DOS exercise that exposed a diplomat to all of the capitals, and therefore all of the governments, of the region. As a result of his experience with the Soviets under Joseph Stalin, Durbrow developed a shrewd and realistic understanding of the ruthless political machine America was dealing with in Moscow, placing him at odds with the accomodationists in President Franklin D. Roosevelt's administration.[1] In fact, a real knock-down fight developed between the New Dealer political appointments in the administration and the professional diplomats within the DOS, between those who wished to believe the best about Stalinist Russia and those who were experienced with Stalin's regime. Indeed, Roosevelt had prepared the ground for this ongoing quarrel by trying to sidestep what he perceived to be an unruly department of "stuffed shirts" that would not go along with his foreign policy objectives.[2] This antagonism carried over into Harry Truman's administration.

Elbridge Durbrow was a formidable opponent of potential American policies that did not confront the reality of Soviet expansionism. Furthermore, he outlived Roosevelt and outlasted the policies of the New Dealers.[3] Durbrow's expertise was recognised when he received

---

[1] Martin Weil, *A Pretty Good Club: The Founding Fathers of the U.S. Foreign Service* (New York: W. W. Norton, 1978), 53, 235, 268.

[2] Smith Simpson, *Anatomy of the State Department* (Boston: Beacon Press, 1968), 75, 138, 142.

[3] Weil, *Pretty Good Club*, 267.

his posting to Saigon, and nearly all cable traffic directed to him was addressed to "Durby", his well-known Eastern European nickname. His credentials as a Soviet expert were second to none within the State Department, and since Soviet expansion was perceived as being behind the Viet Minh effort in Southeast Asia, his appointment as ambassador to South Vietnam in 1957 was logical. The problem, though, was that Indochina was not Eastern Europe.

The Vietnamese approach to politics, in both the North and the South, was different from that of the Soviets, and this difference proved to be a substantial stumbling block for Durbrow and another powerful and well-versed Soviet expert who would play a leading role in the downfall of President Diem, Averell Harriman. To keep power in Vietnam, even the head of the Communists, Ho Chi Minh, had to pay homage to the Confucian understanding of what a true leader of the people should be; and in his personal life and physical appearance he attempted to emulate Confucian ideals. Ngo Dinh Diem, however, was the consummate Confucian. As we have seen of the two men, Diem was by far the more worthy to rule. But Durbrow in 1960 and Harriman a year later paid little heed to the important differences between the two. Perhaps, with their long experience with Russian Communist perfidy, they were too cynically focused on Soviet machinations in the region.

There also were other reasons for their lack of appreciation for Diem. By early 1960, the reports of expanding Viet Cong strength, ongoing weaknesses in the South Vietnamese Army, and increasing dissatisfaction with Diem's government were not at all encouraging to Ambassador Durbrow.[4] As he noted in a despatch to Washington, "Diem cannot be completely absolved of blame for this unsatisfactory situation in the rural

[4] In a despatch (desp. no. 278) sent to Washington via diplomatic pouch, Durbrow noted the following: (1) VC tactics had changed from attacking individuals to carrying out more frequent and daring attacks upon government security forces. (2) VC planned more guerrilla warfare for 1960 and intended to stage a coup that same year. (3) ARVN weaknesses were becoming more apparent, and more training was needed; and (4) people in rural areas were unhappy with Diem. The primary cause was the sustained VC terror campaign. The GVN was seen as not protecting them, and local officials, who in their frustration at attempting to overcome the inroads made by VC terror, were opting for coercion in implementing programs decided upon in Saigon. See Elbridge Durbrow, "Special Report on Current Internal Security Situation", in *1956 French Withdrawal–1960*, section V.B.3.d of bk. 10 of *United States–Vietnam Relations, 1945–1967: Study Prepared by the Department of Defense*, by Congress, House, Committee on Armed Services (Washington, D.C.: United States Government Printing Office), 1255–56.

areas. Considerable evidence has existed that he has not in the past kept himself properly informed of what is going on. Officials have tended to tell him what he wants to hear, largely because of fear of removal if they indicate that mistakes have been made or reply that projects he is pushing should not be carried out as rapidly as he desires."[5] Indeed, the growing lack of patience being displayed by the Americans toward Diem and his government, on the surface at least, would appear to be justified.

Yet, beneath the surface of the negative reports was a more complex reality, in which much of what the Americans were complaining about was their own fault, for they had burdened Diem with an army that did not understand how to conduct a counterinsurgency campaign. The ARVN had been designed by the Americans as a conventional army that could dovetail into their command structure and forces should a large-scale invasion be embarked upon by the North Vietnamese and their foreign supporters, as had happened in Korea. The Americans were loath to let Diem develop the kind of forces needed to break an insurgency, meaning well-equipped special constabulary and police. Yet it was precisely these sorts of forces, drawn from local Vietnamese, who could live in the rural communities and thus secure an intimate understanding of the people they were seeking to protect. In time, an effective intelligence of the local population would evolve. In turn, the police would be able to secure the locals' trust through effectively protecting them from terrorist activity. The British had demonstrated that the strategic use of local policing was crucial in effective counterinsurgency warfare; they had made this type of police program the foundation of their success against the Communist guerrillas in Malaya from about 1948 to 1960.[6]

To the Americans, these measures, quite apart from placing the main thrust of counterinsurgency in Diem's hands, seemed to be militarily unacceptable because they appeared to be passive and not offensive enough. It was this attitude of the American military that ensured that

---

[5] Ibid.

[6] Early Pentagon analyst reports indicate that police forces were effective in curbing Communist insurgent activity, even though they had not been developed in anywhere near the numbers and capabilities of those in Malaya: "The police services, which include the 7,500-man Vietnamese Bureau of Investigation, and 10,500-man police force stationed in the main cities, have had considerable success in tracking down subversives and terrorists and are developing into efficient organizations." Congress, House, Committee on Armed Services, "Major Trends in South Vietnam", in *1956 French Withdrawal–1960*, 1193.

the ARVN would be engaged in a war for which it was not designed. For those versed in the American military doctrine that the offensive had to be taken aggressively against the guerrilla through overwhelming firepower, the U.S. military reluctance to endorse what seemed to be a passive approach had a consistent logic. Also, the Americans appeared to be embracing their own cultural, and historically inaccurate, myth that the British were not offensively minded enough when it came to taking the fight to the enemy. British ideas for countering insurgents by a circumspect approach therefore became an area of disagreement between the British advisory team and the American Military Assistance Advisory Group (MAAG). MAAG, after all, was under instructions from Washington not to let Diem have total control of the Counterinsurgency Plan, or CIP.

Meanwhile, Diem had fewer and fewer quality civil servants in the places they were most needed. The first reason for this was that the best were being killed off by the Viet Cong. The second reason was that the Americans demanded he not choose more government workers from the Roman Catholic community. To the Americans, Diem seemed to be showing partiality in this regard, but they failed to appreciate that the best-educated Vietnamese—and there were precious few—were the products of Catholic schools. Buddhism had no similar educational infrastructure that offered the kind of formation and training desperately needed to govern an emerging modern nation.[7] Also lost on the Americans was the fact that Roman Catholic Vietnamese were the ones most loyal to the anti-Communist cause, as nearly one million of them had fled the brutal persecution of religion underway in North Vietnam.[8] They needed no ideological coaxing or propaganda to convince them of their need to fight the Communists. The Vietnamese Catholics were therefore an ideal recruiting pool for Diem's government and counterinsurgency efforts.[9]

---

[7] According to author Marguerite Higgins: "With education left in a lamentable state by the French, it is true that the Catholics, being better organised than other faiths, tended to be better educated." *Our Vietnam Nightmare* (New York: Harper and Row, 1965), 43.

[8] For the persecution of Vietnamese Catholics by Ho Chi Minh's Communists in the Democratic Republic of Vietnam in the 1950s, see Charles Keith, *Catholic Vietnam: A Church from Empire to Nation* (Berkeley: University of California Press, 2012), 238.

[9] William Colby stated: "Diem of course had no hesitation in arming a Catholic community because he had confidence that they would fight, and they did." Interview by Ted Gittinger, June 2, 1981, Washington, D.C., interview 1, transcript, 34, Lyndon Baines Johnson Presidential Library Oral History Collection, University of Texas at Austin.

Yet American fears of political dominance by a Catholic minority were keeping Diem from fully engaging the potential of this population. American policy ensured that most of Diem's own cabinet and general staff were made up of Buddhists.[10] At the time, one of the greatest ironies for Vietnamese Catholics, who had endured centuries of persecution and humiliation for staying true to their faith in Christ, was that when one of their very best was president, and he with their assistance offered the best chance of building anything remotely like a Western-style democracy, they were being overlooked for government jobs because of pressure from an outside power.[11] As a result, Diem was in the terrible position of both needing and resisting U.S. interference. He looked upon the Americans as "great big children—well intentioned, powerful, with a lot of technical know-how, but not very sophisticated in dealing with him or his race, or his country's problems".[12]

Diem's differences with the Americans led Ambassador Durbrow to suggest his removal as early as 1960.[13] The problem of political legitimacy was coming to the fore, as the American press had begun to talk about religious bias, corruption, and abuses of authority in the Diem

[10] Higgins explained: "But in Diem's immediate entourage—his cabinet—there were only six Catholics out of seventeen men. The Vice-President of Vietnam, Nguyen Ngoc Tho, was a Buddhist and was in charge of the efforts to achieve a truce with the Buddhist extremists. In the military sphere most generals were Confucianists, Buddhists, and Cao Dai. Out of seventeen generals on active duty, three were Catholic and the rest non-Catholic." *Our Vietnam Nightmare*, 43–44.

[11] Fr. Piero Gheddo, *The Cross and the Bo-Tree: Catholics and Buddhists in Vietnam*, trans. Charles Underhill Quinn (New York: Sheed and Ward, 1970), 136–37.

[12] Interview with Everett Bumgardner on "America's Mandarin (1954–1963)", program 2 of *Vietnam: A Television History*, PBS, 1983, http://www.pbs.org/wgbh/amex/vietnam/series /pt_02.html. A hard-copy transcript is available in the Frederick (Fritz) Ernest Nolting Jr. Papers, accession 12804, Special Collections, Alderman Library, University of Virginia, Charlottesville, box 28, Professional Papers—Historical Backgound Records, 8 of 10 (hereafter cited as Nolting Papers; quote is located on p. 8).

[13] "We believe US should at this time support Diem as best available Vietnamese leader, but should recognize that overriding US objective is strongly anti-Communist Vietnamese government which can command loyal and enthusiastic support of widest possible segments of Vietnamese people, and is able to carry on effective fight against guerrillas. If Diem's position in country continues deteriorate as result failure to adopt proper political, psychological, economic and security measures, it may become necessary for US Government to begin consideration alternative courses of action and leaders in order achieve our objective." "Telegram from the Ambassador in Vietnam (Durbrow) to the Department of State", September 16, 1960, Saigon, in United States Department of State, *Foreign Relations of the United States, 1958–1960*, ed. John P. Glennon, vol. 1, *Vietnam* (Washington, D.C.: United States Government Printing Office, 1986), document 197, p. 579 (hereafter cited as *FRUS, 1958–1960*).

government. Washington believed that unless Diem's government quickly improved its public image, both at home and abroad, its capacity to stem the tide of Communist encroachment in Southeast Asia would be greatly diminished. On December 23, 1960, Durbrow delivered a memorandum to the South Vietnamese president that with a seemingly cordial and advisory tone made the following demands:

1. Make the workings of Diem's cabinet and his ministers' budgets, which were debated in the Vietnamese Assembly, more accessible to the press.
2. Permit the elected assembly to conduct investigations of any branch of the government.
3. Develop a more liberal press code, thereby allowing more freedom of information to the press.
4. Take seriously the importance of developing more favourable relations with the foreign press.
5. Develop a broader credit program for the rural peasants and conduct "fireside chats" with them.[14]

Such American advice could be seen as condescending and demeaning to the leader of a sovereign government. This was especially the case when one considers that Diem, on many occasions, had already proven his ability to govern equitably and consistently at the local, provincial, and ministerial levels. Indeed, those who knew the South Vietnamese president understood that such a communication could have only a negative effect and would increase his suspicion about the Americans and what they wanted.

Predictably, Diem's reaction to Durbrow's memo was blunt, as duly noted by the ambassador in a telegram to DOS. According to Durbrow's telegram, Diem told him that reform was a wonderful thing so long as it was doable and did not make South Vietnam more vulnerable to the Communists. American proposals for the rural areas however, were impossible to implement if holding political debates and elections in villages merely made better targets for guerrilla terrorist action. Adding to Diem's concern was the situation across the border in Laos, which was

---

[14] See Elbridge Durbrow, "Memorandum Handed to President Diem by Ambassador Durbrow on December 23, 1960", in Congress, House, Committee on Armed Services, *1956 French Withdrawal–1960*, 1353–55.

under attack from the NVA and likely to fall into Communist hands. He therefore stressed the need for at least twenty thousand more trained soldiers. As far as press relations were concerned, Diem said the foreign press should try to be more objective; they sought out only those stories that were sensational and critical of the GVN and ignored many favourable success stories. Diem dismissed the attempts to make his executive branch more answerable to the elected assembly, which could be used against him by the Communists.[15]

Apart from the fact that Diem did not like being told what to do by the Americans, he had a counterinsurgency strategy substantially different from theirs even at this relatively early date. This divergence was displayed in Durbrow's messages to DOS. In effect, Diem subscribed to the British understanding of counterinsurgency, which began with a premise: stronger not weaker government is needed in a time of war. As Robert Thompson explained, emergency government must, out of rational necessity, be a far cry from American-style liberal democracy. Tough laws are needed to crush an insurgency, and they do not alienate the population if they are administered effectively and equitably.[16]

In this context, the role that the American liberal news media played in destroying the relations between Ngo Dinh Diem and the U.S. government should not be underestimated. According to William Colby, Diem's fatal error was that he did not realise the impact the news media had on political leaders in the United States and consequently allowed negative coverage to spread unchallenged. "Therefore he let the issue grow as to whether Vietnam was democratic enough, rather than the issue grow as to whether Vietnam was progressing. Because if the latter had become the main issue, then I think he would have had support."[17]

[15] Elbridge Durbrow to the Department of State, telegram, December 24, 1960, Saigon, no. 1216, in Congress, House, Committee on Armed Services, *1956 French Withdrawal–1960*, 1348–51.

[16] "Some very tough laws were enacted in Malaya. One enabled the government to seize and deport all Chinese found in a declared bad area. Another allowed the government to impose a collective fine on all the inhabitants of an area where the people were uncooperative.... Laws imposing strict curfews, a mandatory death penalty for carrying arms, life imprisonment for providing supplies or other support to terrorists, restricted residence or detention for suspected terrorist supporters and so on were introduced and used effectively. The main point about them was that they were seen by the population to be effective and were applied equally to all." Robert Grainger Thompson, *Defeating Communist Insurgency: Experiences from Malaya and Vietnam* (London: Chatto and Windus, 1966), 53.

[17] Colby, interview by Gittinger, interview 1, p. 11.

The more the American news media portrayed Diem as a corrupt dictator, the more the political pressure mounted at home. Thus, Durbrow began communicating to Diem that either he liberalise his government or the United States would find others to run his country. At the same time, Washington fully expected Diem to win the war. South Vietnam's former vice president, Nguyen Hgoc Tho, recalled several years later that Diem had been caught in a terrible dilemma owing to the "crushing and contradictory demands of the Americans that he win the war and at the same turn South Vietnam into an American-style democracy".[18]

Regardless of what America wanted for Vietnam, it was plain to Diem that he had to provide his people with security if the stability of and the confidence in his government were to grow. Indeed, its very political legitimacy was at stake. But on top of America's stress on liberalisation was the fact that guerrilla warfare had begun to expand exponentially in 1959, making national security an increasingly difficult task.[19] Moreover, it was a task that would be made practically impossible if Western democratic principles, like freedom of movement or the requirement of search warrants for the invasion of private dwellings, were implemented. The Communists were well aware of Diem's dilemma, and they realised that the tensions growing between Diem and the Americans could be exploited to their own advantage if they increased their terror campaign in the villages and thus invited even further undemocratic responses from Diem. The simple truth was that these two contradictory demands— democracy and counterinsurgency—could not be reconciled within the political reality that existed in South Vietnam at that time. Nonetheless, this truth evaded the educated men in power in Washington and the American press in Vietnam.[20]

Prior to the December memorandum to Diem, Durbrow had been working on some other ideas to reform Diem's government in the wake of increased guerrilla activity. In a telegram Ambassador Durbrow sent to Washington in September 1960, he explained that he wanted to administer a "shock" to the Communists and non-Communists alike.

---

[18] Ellen J. Hammer, *A Death in November: America in Vietnam, 1963* (New York: E.P. Dutton, 1987), 37–38.

[19] Congress, House, Committee on Armed Services, "Rebellion against My-Diem", tab 2 of *Evolution of the War: Origins of the Insurgency, 1954–1960*, section IV.A.5 of bk. 2 of *United States–Vietnam Relations, 1945–1967: Study Prepared by the Department of Defense* (Washington, D.C.: United States Government Printing Office, 1971), 46.

[20] Hammer, *Death in November*, 38.

His measures to achieve this included directly interfering with Diem's cabinet appointments and disbanding Diem and Nhu's Can Lao Party, which in turn would shuffle Diem's own brother, Ngo Dinh Nhu, out of the way.[21]

Colby, who was privy to the motivation and the details of these recommendations before they were sent to Washington or moderated for presentation to Diem, believed that Durbrow was making a big mistake. Durbrow's suggestions would change the locus of power in Vietnam while not giving any clear or definitive picture of what the results would be on the war in the rural areas. Colby understood that America wanted South Vietnam to be democratic, but Durbrow's methods and timetable were not relevant to the nature of the Vietnamese situation and were, specifically, hostile toward Diem. In fact, Colby believed that the "psychological shock" that Durbrow wished to administer would lead to nothing but confrontation with no requisite gain for the United States, especially since it included "the suggestion that we might have to look for 'other leaders' if Diem did not take our advice as to what was 'proper' for him to do. The confrontation with Diem had begun."[22]

The confrontation became manifest in October 1960, when Durbrow handed Diem a memorandum spelling out several of the ambassador's far-ranging suggestions, which were essentially the same as those Durbrow had sent to Washington in September, sans the "or else" clause.[23] As we have seen, Durbrow's December memo to Diem included similar reforms. In both memos the suggestions were made to circumvent the corruption of lower-level officials, because Ambassador Durbrow believed that some of the government's problems could be traced to administrative deficiencies in the villages. But he was also insistent about the need to remove certain cabinet officials and to send Diem's brother

---

[21] Other changes included making Vice President Nguyen Hgoc Tho, a Southerner totally subservient to Diem, minister of the interior; Diem giving up the ministry of defence and appointing a new full-time minister; sending Diem's brother Nhu to a foreign embassy; naming one or two members of the opposition party to the cabinet; lifting controls on the press; stimulating National Assembly investigations, on the American model, into corruption and mismanagement; and implementing a series of economic measures such as subsidies to rice farmers. See William E. Colby, *Lost Victory: A Firsthand Account of America's Sixteen-Year Involvement in Vietnam*, with James McCargar (Chicago: Contemporary Books, 1989), 74–75.

[22] Ibid.

[23] Elbridge Durbrow, "English Text of Memorandum Handed to President Diem", in *FRUS, 1958–1960*, vol. I, pp. 598–602.

Nhu on an extended holiday out of the country.[24] Diem's reaction was to defend his brother, and he implored Ambassador Durbrow to consider that many of the rumours being spread about Nhu were coming from the Communists. He also stated that the ongoing guerrilla campaign made it difficult to implement reform in the countryside.[25] Essentially, Diem asked the Americans for more patience and time. He could not react to the various problems merely as an American puppet: the solutions had to be his, and they had to be Vietnamese.

The Americans were not the only ones running out of patience. As Communist attacks increased in 1960, Colonel Nguyen Chanh Thi, commander of the ARVN airborne brigade, attempted a coup on November 11. He and his followers blamed Diem for the security failings in the South and said that his ouster would allow the military and the country's other non-Communist politicians to crush the insurrection.[26] But they also acted on their assessment of the American political situation. According to George Carver, a CIA operative in Saigon at the time, "The military coup planners were a bit hazy on the finer points of U.S. constitutional procedure and more familiar with European parliamentary practice in which one government's 'fall' was promptly followed by the opposition's acquisition of power. They wanted to give President Kennedy's incoming administration a fresh Vietnamese hand to play. They also wanted to pre-empt any risk that a new Catholic American president might throw the full weight of American support irrevocably behind the Catholic Ngo Dinh Diem."[27] Diem was able to weather the coup attempt and remain in office, but he never forgave the army's senior officers, such as Major General Duong Van Minh "Big Minh", for sitting calmly on the sidelines and waiting to join whichever party prevailed.[28] Furthermore, the Vietnamese president believed that he now had additional reasons to doubt the reliability of his American sponsors.

Lansdale, who personally knew Diem, understood how the Vietnamese president would interpret the American response to the coup attempt.

---

[24] Elbridge Durbrow, "Telegram from the Ambassador in Vietnam (Durbrow) to the Department of State", in *FRUS, 1958–1960*, 1:596.

[25] Ibid., 595.

[26] Congress, House, Committee on Armed Services, "Rebellion against My-Diem", 44.

[27] George A. Carver Jr., "An Unheeded Firebell: The November 1960 Coup Attempt", in *Kennedy in Vietnam*, by William J. Rust and the editors of U.S. News Books (New York: Scribner, 1985), 2.

[28] Rust, *Kennedy in Vietnam*, 7.

On November 15, 1960, General Lansdale, then the deputy assistant secretary of special operations, sent a memorandum on the subject to James H. Douglas, deputy secretary of defense, with several detailed critical observations about the American treatment of Diem. The president would be making comparisons between the 1954 coup attempt and the most recent one, he wrote, specifically, between how the Americans reacted in each situation. For example, the Americans had persuaded Diem not to jail the coup leaders in 1954, who afterwards began—within a few weeks of their attempt—to instigate a revolt against Diem by stirring up the religious sects. This led to much violence and bloodshed. During both coup attempts, the coup leaders, who were military men, had links to and support from the deposed emperor Bao Dai. Similarly, the coup leaders appealed to vague democratic ideals, which coincided with what the Americans wanted to hear. Thus, Lansdale was concerned that Diem would see a link between the coups and Durbrow's attempts to pressure him for democratic reforms, especially since Durbrow had urged Diem to acquiesce to the rebels' demands while the coup attempt was still underway, and he had tried to get other diplomats to urge Diem to compromise with the leaders. Lansdale was therefore worried that the most charitable view Diem could hold of Durbrow was that he was badly misinformed. He would certainly regard the ambassador's mission with ever-deepening suspicion. In short, Lansdale reported, the U.S. position in Southeast Asia had been weakened by America's handling of the coup.[29]

CIA Saigon Station Chief Colby concurred with Lansdale. Colby noted to Secretary of State Dean Rusk after the second coup attempt: "I think President [Diem] interpreted U.S. even-handedness as disloyalty to him.... I think he felt we should have been much more supportive, much more positive."[30] Colby was being circumspect, because he later observed in the spring of 1993 that the American treatment of Diem during these crucial times was a mistake of strategic proportions.[31]

There is little doubt that 1960 heralded the beginning of a severe breach between Diem and Washington. Diem could not forget the

[29] Edward Geary Lansdale, "Memorandum for Deputy Secretary Douglas", in Congress, House, Committee on Armed Services, *1956 French Withdrawal–1960*, 1330–31.

[30] Colby, quoted in Rust, *Kennedy in Vietnam*, 19.

[31] Colby made this remark privately to me and during his talk at the first conference on Vietnam, "Paris and 20 April 1993", given by the Vietnam Center and Archive at Texas Tech University, Lubbock, Texas.

attempted coup and the less than supportive American response, and he resented Washington's desire to get rid of his brother Nhu. The Americans failed to take into account Diem's past and how it indicated the way he would react to attacks on family members. Diem had been prepared to sacrifice both his political career and even himself over the death of his brother Khoi.[32]

One reason Nhu was disliked was his Movement for National Revolution and his secretive Can Lao Party (Can Lao Nhan Vi), which was accused by its detractors of being the Vietnamese equivalent of Hitler's SS. A more objective analysis of the Can Lao was rendered by Pentagon analyst Michael Field, who acknowledged its secretive design and intelligence-gathering capabilities but refused to give any credence to the more lurid SS-like descriptions that had popped up in the American press. "It was no ordinary party and can best be described as a sort of ginger group within the regime," wrote Field, "organized and acting like a secret society which reported on the attitudes and actions of politicians, officials and the population. Closely associated with the Can Lao was a secret political intelligence service which reported direct to Nhu himself."[33] According to Field, Nhu's purpose was similar to the Communists' in that he wanted to create a party that could bring political discipline to the people. It was organised very much like a Communist party with its system of cadres and cells. This structure permitted the Can Lao to be active at every level of Vietnamese life. To advance in professional circles, one had to have Can Lao connections or credentials. The Can Lao could boast that at least one-third of the cabinet were members, and up to one-half of the elected assembly. Similarly, it controlled the government's official political party, the Movement for National Revolution.[34]

In fairness to Nhu, it should be noted that the U.S. Foreign Service had endorsed the Can Lao. Indeed, Lansdale had warned his fellow Americans—particularly Ambassador Durbrow—that the creation of the

---

[32] Robert Shaplen, "A Reporter in Vietnam: Diem", *New Yorker*, September 22, 1962, 110.

[33] Michael Field, *The Prevailing Wind: Witness in Indo-China* (London: Methuen, 1965), 314.

[34] There was one notable area where the Can Lao had no jurisdiction, and that was the administrative region around Hue controlled by Diem's brother Ngo Dinh Can. Can's control of this area was almost medieval in its absoluteness and near-Stalinist in its ability to gather intelligence on any and all dissidents operating in the area. See Congress, House, Committee on Armed Services, *1956 French Withdrawal–1960*, 1192.

party, largely the brainchild of a senior U.S. Foreign Service officer, could cause significant problems if it became the favoured party and forced older parties underground.[35] In essence, the Can Lao had been an American conception through which, it was hoped, political activity and support would coalesce around the Ngo Dinh brothers.

In addition to fears about Nhu's political machinery, his intellectual and rhetorical capabilities played a significant role in building apprehension and resentment amongst the government's opponents. He was a brilliant man who had been educated at the formidable École Nationale des Chartes in Paris, where he had studied a great deal of philosophy. Furthermore, he had a true believer's attitude with regard to the correctness of the government's path.[36] Field noted that "to listen to Nhu discussing the political errors and deviations of his countrymen was like listening to a Jesuit discoursing on heresy.... Nhu's persuasiveness was considerable. In the space of an hour's conversation he almost broke down the most sceptical resistance to his beliefs, which he held with quietly fanatical conviction."[37]

Ngo Dinh Nhu in many ways was indispensable to Diem's government. He was not merely a nepotistic appointment but "undoubtedly one of the most astute Vietnamese politicians of his generation" and, really, the designer of Diem's rise to the premiership of South Vietnam.[38] Indeed, Ngo Dinh Nhu had already assumed the role of advisor to Diem during the 1954 Geneva Conference, and this had been duly noted by DOS.[39] Nhu was with Diem every step of the way in planning

[35] See Edward Geary Lansdale, "Memorandum for Secretary of Defense [and] Deputy Secretary of Defense; Subject: Vietnam" [between January 14 and 17, 1961], in "U.S. Perceptions of the Insurgency, 1954–1960", tab 4 of Congress, House, Committee on Armed Services, *Evolution of the War: Origins of the Insurgency, 1954–1960*, 74.

[36] John Osborne, "The Tough Miracle Man of Vietnam: Diem, America's Newly Arrived Visitor, Has Roused His Country and Routed the Reds", *Life*, May 13, 1957, 166.

[37] Field, *Prevailing Wind*, 314.

[38] "It was probably Ngo Dinh Nhu who created the situation in 1954 in which his elder brother was the most obvious candidate for the premiership, and it was probably he who worked out the tactics by which the Caodaists and the Hoa-Hao were out-manoeuvred in Cochinchina during the following year." Ralph Smith, *Viet-Nam and the West* (Ithaca, N.Y.: Cornell University Press, 1971), 152.

[39] Robert McClintock, "The Chargé at Saigon (McClintock) to the Department of State" in *Foreign Relations of the United States, 1952–1954*, by United States Department of State, ed. John P. Glennon, vol. 13, pt. 2, *Indochina* (Washington, D.C.: United States Government Printing Office, 1982), pp. 1762–63 (hereafter cited as *FRUS, 1952–1954*).

the necessary moves to offset the myriad political intrigues and plots hatched by the discontented politicians and generals in Saigon. Thus, Ngo Dinh Nhu was an exceptionally dangerous man for the opponents of Diem's government to cross, and thus he was feared and hated.

Before Frederick Nolting officially replaced Ambassador Durbrow, he became well acquainted with Nhu in a variety of social and informal settings.[40] Perceptive and thoughtful, Nolting was not given to either hurried analysis or extreme views. His testimony about Nhu is worth examining in the context of counterinsurgency warfare. First, he described the man's position this way: "With me, he never put himself forward as a spokesman for the government. Unlike Attorney General Robert Kennedy, he held no official position. But like Bobby Kennedy, he was considered to be (rightly, I think) his President's closest advisor."[41] Nolting found Nhu to be a genuine scholar, a strong anti-Communist patriot, and a man with a mission to come up with a philosophical and practical bulwark to Communism—all of which seemed to point Nhu in the direction of the British counterinsurgent tool par excellence, strategic hamlets. Nolting described Nhu's philosophy as a form of personalism. It was not directed toward oligarchy or family rule, as was frequently reported in the press. On the contrary, it was a doctrine of individual development—self-realisation combined with self-sacrifice, as understood by both Christianity and Confucianism.[42] As Nolting took over the reins of the American embassy in Saigon, and as he came into increasing contact with Diem and Nhu, he came to understand that much of what the American advisors had been blaming on Nhu—such as intransigent resistance to new policies—actually was the result of stubborn opposition from Diem, who simply refused to be cajoled by the Americans in what he declared were internal Vietnamese affairs.[43]

In his reports to Washington, Lansdale stated that the complexities of Vietnam had exhausted Durbrow, who had been in the "forest of tigers" too long and whose actions were mistrusted by the Diem government.

---

[40] Frederick Nolting, *From Trust to Tragedy: The Political Memoirs of Frederick Nolting, Kennedy's Ambassador to Diem's Vietnam* (New York: Praeger, 1988), 101.

[41] Ibid.

[42] Nolting continued, "Quoting Aristotle, I said to Nhu, 'You mean that the essence of man is to strive to be human.' With some elaboration he agreed." Ibid.

[43] Ibid., 103–4.

Lansdale thus had advised that Durbrow be transferred.[44] Lansdale had been right. Ambassador Durbrow's extended term had led to a deterioration in relations between Saigon and Washington. Durbrow was no longer seen as a friend by the Diem government. As such, Nolting's appointment was timely. Having lost the confidence of Diem, American policy in South Vietnam was in disarray when Frederick Nolting took over the post of U.S. ambassador in 1961.

[44] Edward Geary Lansdale, "Memorandum for Secretary of Defense [and] Deputy Secretary of Defense", in U.S. *Involvement in the War, Internal Documents: The Kennedy Administration, January 1961–November 1963, Book I*, section V.B.4 of bk. 11 of *United States–Vietnam Relations, 1945–1967: Study Prepared by the Department of Defense*, by Congress, House, Committee on Armed Services (Washington, D.C.: United States Government Printing Office, 1971), 3–4.

3

Enter Ambassador Frederick Nolting

Edward Geary Lansdale had a shrewd and accurate assessment of what was required of the U.S. government to undo the disarray in which Ambassador Durbrow's mission had left American-Vietnamese relations. He told his superiors that the new Kennedy administration must restore Ngo Dinh Diem's faith in American foreign policy in Southeast Asia. The new ambassador, Frederick Nolting, would therefore need "to get on the same wave-length with Diem".[1]

Who was Ambassador Nolting, and what was his background? Frederick "Fritz" Ernest Nolting Jr. was born on August 24, 1911, in Richmond, Virginia, where his ancestry was deeply rooted and his family well respected.[2] He spent his childhood in Richmond, attending Saint Christopher's School; later, as an undergraduate, he attended the University of Virginia in Charlottesville. In 1933, after only three years of study, he earned his bachelor of arts in history. At that time the Depression had devastated the family business, and his skills and education were required to help out. Thus, Nolting worked for five years in his father's bank in Richmond.[3]

---

[1] Edward Geary Lansdale, "Annexes to a Program of Action for South Vietnam", in *U.S. Involvement in the War, Internal Documents: The Kennedy Administration, January 1961–November 1963, Book I*, section V.B.4 of bk. 11 of *United States–Vietnam Relations, 1945–1967: Study Prepared by the Department of Defense*, by Congress, House, Committee on Armed Services (Washington, D.C.: United States Government Printing Office, 1971), 102.

[2] Nolting's paternal grandfather had emigrated from Germany in 1839 and immersed himself in the tobacco business in Virginia. Nolting's father, before the Depression, had been involved in the business of investment banking in Richmond. Nolting's mother could trace her American heritage back to the Revolutionary War in Virginia. Lindsay Nolting, interview by Geoffrey D.T. Shaw, February 3, 1999. Also see Jeanne C. Pardee, "Biographical Sketch", p. 1, in rg-21/102.921, The Nolting Papers.

[3] Ibid.

In 1939 Frederick Nolting returned to his studies at the University of Virginia, where he earned a master of arts in philosophy in 1940. That same year he married Olivia Lindsay Crumpler, who remained his lifelong spouse and friend.[4] Owing to his extraordinary capabilities, he won a fellowship to attend graduate studies at Harvard. There he added religion to his study of philosophy, a background that would later help him to understand Diem and his brother.[5] One of Nolting's professors was Lord Bertrand Russell; and regardless of his disagreements with the celebrated atheist, Nolting was able to earn top marks.[6] In 1941 Harvard awarded Nolting a master's in philosophy, and in 1942 a doctorate. Having just completed his graduate education, he found his life interrupted by the Second World War.[7]

Nolting rose through the ranks of the U.S. Navy and was a lieutenant commander when the war ended. His naval service was not without peril: he served on a munitions ship in the Mediterranean theatre, where he was involved with military operations in North Africa and Italy.[8] In 1946 Nolting entered the service of the U.S. Department of State, and during the next eighteen years served in a variety of postings in Washington and overseas.[9] To this service he brought a mind developed by his academic accomplishments and a will disciplined by his military training. Because he eventually was a special assistant to the secretary of state for mutual security affairs, he was also heavily involved with the North Atlantic Treaty Organisation (NATO). He would later become the deputy chief of the U.S. delegation to NATO, and as such the alternate U.S. representative to the North Atlantic Council. While

[4] Ibid., 2.

[5] Frederick Nolting, *From Trust to Tragedy: The Political Memoirs of Frederick Nolting, Kennedy's Ambassador to Diem's Vietnam* (New York: Praeger, 1988), 23.

[6] Lindsay Nolting still has one of her husband's papers, upon which Bertrand Russell wrote: "If you had agreed with my book—I would have given you an A plus." As it stood, Russell had given him an A minus. Lindsay Nolting, interview, February 4, 1999.

[7] Lindsay Nolting recalled that Frederick had been extremely fortunate in completing his university education before signing up with the U.S. Navy after Pearl Harbor had been bombed in December 1941. Lindsay Nolting, interview, February 3, 1999.

[8] Ibid.

[9] Nolting, *From Trust to Tragedy*, 11. Lindsay Nolting told this writer that her husband had no special contacts within DOS that would have guaranteed him a diplomatic career. Nevertheless, with his war service record, his considerable academic achievements, and his interest in foreign policy, he was able to enter the Foreign Service. Lindsay Nolting, interview, February 3, 1999.

serving in this capacity, he was asked to be the U.S. ambassador to South Vietnam.[10]

In his memoirs, Nolting admits candidly that most of his experience in Washington and elsewhere had been concerned with European countries. Yet as a student he had spent several months in Japan and North China, and as an assistant to Secretary of State John Foster Dulles, he had heard Premier Pierre Mendès-France's last desperate plea for U.S. naval and air support in France's war with the Viet Minh. From that point on, Nolting began to develop a special interest in Indochina. Still, when Secretary of State Christian Herter asked him to serve as ambassador to Laos, Nolting's chief, Ambassador Warren Randolph Burgess, urged that he remain at NATO.[11]

Concurrent with Nolting's growing interest in Southeast Asia, there was a growing realisation in Washington that a crisis was developing in South Vietnam.[12] The new U.S. president, John F. Kennedy, and his administration were concerned by the pronounced deterioration in relations between Washington and Saigon that had occurred during the mission of Ambassador Elbridge Durbrow, and U.S. policy was under review at the time of Nolting's appointment as U.S. ambassador to South Vietnam in April 1961. A task force headed by Roswell L. Gilpatric had been reshaping this policy during the late winter and the early spring of that year.[13]

Initially, there was continuity in policy between the previous administration (of Dwight D. Eisenhower) and the Kennedy administration. Fundamentally, policy remained the same in that it was designed to assist

[10] Frederick E. Nolting, interview by Joseph E. O'Connor, May 14, 1966, Paris, interview 1, transcript, 1, John F. Kennedy Oral History Collection, John F. Kennedy Presidential Library, Boston.

[11] Nolting, *From Trust to Tragedy*, 11.

[12] "When Kennedy took office, the prospect of an eventual crisis in Vietnam had been widely recognized in the government, although nothing had yet been done about it. Our Ambassador in Saigon [Durbrow] had been sending worried cables for a year, and twice in recent months (in September 1960 and again in December) had ended an appraisal of the situation by cautiously raising the question of whether the U.S. would not sooner or later have to move to replace Diem." Congress, House, Committee on Armed Services, *The Kennedy Program and Commitments, 1961*, bk. 1 of *The Evolution of the War: Counterinsurgency; The Kennedy Commitments, 1961–1963*, section IV.B of bk. 2 of *United States–Vietnam Relations, 1945–1967: Study Prepared by the Department of Defense* (Washington, D.C.: United States Government Printing Office, 1971), i.

[13] Nolting, interview by O'Connor, 2.

the GVN in strengthening itself and defending the country.[14] In 1961, however, the new Kennedy program for South Vietnam diverged from Eisenhower's by substantially increasing matériel aid for the ARVN, which was delivered to the various departments and military personnel through the GVN. "The Americans had decided to increase their aid to the Vietnamese, to pay the expenses of another 20,000 men in the army who would be trained in guerrilla warfare, and to add 100 American advisers to the 685 men in the U.S. Military Assistance Advisory Group (MAAG)."[15] According to Nolting, the Kennedy administration believed that this increase in aid was necessary in order to offset the increasing pressure by the Viet Cong, who were receiving substantial support from Hanoi.[16] "By this time Ho Chi Minh was supplying the Viet Cong with training, equipment, strategic advice and even men— perhaps 2000 a year by 1960."[17]

Also to restore Washington-Saigon relations, Vice President Lyndon B. Johnson, his wife, and members of the Kennedy family went to South Vietnam only two days after Nolting had arrived. The vice president was very "forthright" about America's support of Diem, Nolting said. "He was extremely cordial to President Diem and the members of his family and his government, both publicly and privately. There was a strong joint communiqué issued at the end of that visit which, in effect, underlined the determination of both governments to maintain the independence of South Vietnam."[18]

As previously mentioned, Deputy Secretary of Defense Gilpatric had been asked by the president to appraise the situation in South Vietnam and to recommend a series of actions.[19] Nevertheless, the deputy secretary had other problems to contend with in proposing a new initiative for South Vietnam. Not least of these problems to be considered was

[14] Ibid., 3.

[15] Ellen J. Hammer, *A Death in November: America in Vietnam, 1963* (New York: E. P. Dutton, 1987), 34.

[16] Nolting, interview by O'Connor, 3.

[17] Arthur M. Schlesinger Jr., *A Thousand Days: John F. Kennedy in the White House* (Boston: Houghton Mifflin, 1965), 538–39.

[18] Nolting, interview by O'Connor, 3.

[19] Congress, House, Committee on Armed Services, "The Spring Decisions—I", in *The Kennedy Program and Commitments, 1961*, bk. 1 of *The Evolution of the War: Counterinsurgency; The Kennedy Commitments, 1961–1963*, section IV.B of bk. 2 of *United States–Vietnam Relations, 1945–1967: Study Prepared by the Department of Defense* (Washington, D.C.: United States Government Printing Office, 1971), 19.

the crisis in Laos, which was a strategic nightmare for the U.S. policy planners. As early as 1957, in meetings with American officials, Diem had pointed out that Laos was going to prove critical to the security of South Vietnam and that the Communist insurgency there had to be countered with firmness and resolve.[20] As the soldierly instincts of Eisenhower had discerned, however, Laos was a linchpin: on the one hand, it would secure the Southeast Asian theatre; on the other, it would open it up to assault. The Laotian border not only ran the entire length of North Vietnam and much of the length of South Vietnam but also abutted China, Burma, Thailand, and Cambodia. Kennedy, though not the soldier Eisenhower was, was a formidable politician and recognised that attempting to defend Laos had the makings of political disaster—quite apart from the military concerns that would only be compounded after his Bay of Pigs fiasco.[21]

As a result of his reluctance to be further involved in a land war in Asia, Kennedy's political estimation was that Laos would have to be declared neutral. But this presented substantial problems. Neutrality would be extremely embarrassing and perhaps costly for the United States in Southeast Asia, because it would involve abandoning a non-Communist leader, Phoumi Nosavan, who had come to power with the full support and assistance of the United States.[22] To abandon Phoumi for a neutralist government would place the Kennedy administration in an excruciatingly awkward position. After neutrality was temporarily imposed upon Laos in 1962, American fickleness toward Phoumi was never fully compensated for by Washington's attempts to assuage the

[20] R. A. Robbins Jr., "Meeting between President Diem and Deputy Secretary Quarles", May 10, 1957, in *1956 French Withdrawal–1960*, section V.B.3.d of bk. 10 of *United States–Vietnam Relations, 1945–1967: Study Prepared by the Department of Defense*, by Congress, House, Committee on Armed Services (Washington, D.C.: United States Government Printing Office, 1971), 1103–7.

[21] "Kennedy would have had Eisenhower's personal support if he decided to fight in Laos. But the young president was chastened by one disaster—the rout of the invasion he had authorized against Fidel Castro at the Bay of Pigs [April 1961]—and did not want to risk another. When Kennedy put hard questions to the chiefs of staff, he found them ready to go to war in Laos but unable to promise an easy victory, or any victory at all, without the right to use nuclear weapons." Congress, House, Committee on Armed Services, "The Spring Decisions—I", 28–29.

[22] Arthur Schlesinger maintained that there was some disagreement between DOS and DOD over where U.S. support should go in Laos. In the end, DOD won out in their support of Phoumi, who took power through a CIA-backed coup. See Schlesinger, *Thousand Days*, 325–26.

fears of other Southeast Asian governments, including Diem's, of being similarly abandoned.[23]

Kennedy's government was well aware of its growing lack of credibility amongst its Southeast Asian allies and gave Deputy Secretary Gilpatric a near carte blanche in designing a policy that would restore trust, especially with President Diem.[24] Nevertheless, Frederick Nolting did not go to South Vietnam with any preconceived notions that Diem must be supported by the United States. He had heard a number of negative reports about Diem, and these influenced him somewhat; however, he decided to withhold his judgement until he met the man himself.[25] Just before taking up his assignment in Saigon, Nolting discussed Diem with various European officials and Vietnamese exiles in Paris, most of whom were stridently against him. The negative opinions abroad seemed to match those at home. Yet Nolting remained concerned that they were having a greater impact on the American policies taking shape than they merited. He was also concerned about the membership of President Kennedy's special task force on South Vietnam, which was being headed up by a military man who, by his own admission, knew nothing about the country.[26] Years later Nolting said, "It was a puzzle to me from the beginning why, in this situation which was more political and economic and social than it was military at that time—it was a puzzle to me why the Task Force was chaired by the Deputy Secretary of Defense rather than by, let's say, the Undersecretary of State."[27] Puzzled and uncertain, the new ambassador

---

[23] Congress, House, Committee on Armed Services, *Kennedy Program and Commitments, 1961*, 50–51. Also see "Spring Decisions—I", 53.

[24] Ibid., 20.

[25] Nolting, *From Trust to Tragedy*, 12.

[26] Membership of the presidential task force on South Vietnam, led by Roswell Gilpatric, included General Edward Geary Lansdale (Operations); Colonel Edwin F. Black, military assistant to the deputy secretary of defense (executive secretary and DOD representative); Walt Rostow (White House representative); Major General Charles H. Bonesteel III, secretary of the general staff, U.S. Army (Joint Chiefs of Staff representative); Thomas C. Sorenson, deputy director, U.S. Information Agency; U. Alexis Johnson, deputy undersecretary of state; and for the CIA, Desmond Fitzgerald. "Editorial Note", in "Creation of the Presidential Task Force on Vietnam and the Drafting of a Program of Action on Vietnam, April–May", pt. 3 of United States Department of State, *Foreign Relations of the United States, 1961–1963*, ed. John P. Glennon, vol. 1, *Vietnam, 1961* (Washington, D.C.: United States Government Printing Office, 1988), document 31, p. 74 (hereafter cited as *FRUS, 1961–1963*).

[27] Frederick Nolting, interview by Dennis O'Brien, May 6, 1970, New York, interview 2, transcript, 36–37, John F. Kennedy Oral History Collection, John F. Kennedy Presidential Library, Boston.

developed a sense of foreboding about his mission before even having arrived in Saigon.[28]

During Nolting's second meeting with the task force, as they were drafting recommendations for the ambassador's mission, Lansdale made them reconsider what they were doing. Essentially, he wanted them to avoid the kind of condescension that had plagued Durbrow's relations with Diem. He did not want Nolting to meet Diem with introductory letters that insisted the president "be a good boy".[29] Lansdale was the most knowledgeable member of the task force and had even been considered by President Kennedy as the possible ambassador to South Vietnam.[30] He expressed a solid faith in Diem and his capabilities, and he had been persuasive in his arguments in favour of increased U.S. support for his government. According to Nolting, Lansdale "did acknowledge that 'there are a lot of criticisms that can be leveled against this government in South Vietnam, but compared to others in Southeast Asia, it's a beaut.' "[31]

Yet, despite Lansdale's expertise,[32] there were problems with the approach being taken by the task force, and these were duly noted by the new ambassador. Nolting was particularly concerned with the near-total focus on Vietnam to the exclusion of Laos and Cambodia. He knew that not taking into account the whole theatre was a mistake. Time would tell just how erroneous it was for the American planners to deal with Indochina on a piecemeal basis rather than as a strategic whole.[33]

William Colby, with his substantial firsthand experience in Vietnam, understood one of the reasons for the lack of broader vision: the ever-increasing DOS and DOD personnel in Saigon who were making decisions more in keeping with their own career advancement than with

[28] Nolting, *From Trust to Tragedy*, 12.

[29] Seymour Weiss, "Draft Memorandum of the Conversation of the Second Meeting of the Presidential Task Force on Vietnam", May 4, 1961, the Pentagon, in *FRUS, 1961–1963*, vol. 1, document 43, p. 121.

[30] Nolting, *From Trust to Tragedy*, 13.

[31] Ibid.

[32] In interviews with General Nguyen Khanh, when the subject of American expertise in Southeast Asia was broached, the former prime minister of South Vietnam always seemed to accord Lansdale a mantle of greatness. This was a respect that was clearly lacking in the general's estimations of nearly every other American advisor (with the exceptions of William Colby and Frederick Nolting).

[33] Nolting, *From Trust to Tragedy*, 14.

a clear understanding of Vietnam.[34] Colby saw that during the early years of the Diem government, while the Communists were growing in power, another "battlefront" had been forged—between Washington and Saigon. Colby believed that Diem was fully aware of this conflict and deplored it, yet was unable to do anything about it because American attitudes were shaped by so many factors over which he had no control.[35] For example, amongst the many Americans in Saigon, there were few who had any experience with the earlier French regime. Neither had they witnessed Diem's struggle to build an orderly, legitimate government amidst the chaos and gang warfare that ensued as the French withdrew. The solid years that followed French rule were the direct result of Diem's efforts to create the Republic of South Vietnam from 1954 to 1956, yet most Americans working in Saigon in their air-conditioned offices, listening to the political gossip and intrigue in the cafés, failed to see what Diem had accomplished.[36] Their blindness was compounded by the fact that they spent so much time in meetings amongst themselves, which "encouraged the Americans to think of the Diem Government in confrontational terms, the shadowy Viet Cong hardly counting in the balance sheet".[37]

In setting up the task force and choosing Nolting as ambassador, the Kennedy administration had hoped to ameliorate the conflict with Diem that had been caused by American ignorance and heavy-handedness. The final draft of Gilpatric's proposals, which was delivered to President Kennedy, made it clear that Nolting's role as ameliorator had strategic implications for U.S. policy in South Vietnam. Gilpatric warned that there were no alternatives to Diem, and he repeated Lansdale's warning,

---

[34] "The representatives, even the chiefs, of the various American agencies in Saigon were career officers whose hopes and futures lay in their agencies. An officer's success or failure—that is, his subsequent assignments and professional progress—would be determined by his fulfilment of the agenda of his own agency." William E. Colby, *Lost Victory: A Firsthand Account of America's Sixteen-Year Involvement in Vietnam*, with James McCargar (Chicago: Contemporary Books, 1989), 104–5.

[35] Ibid., 104.

[36] Ibid.

[37] "Like the blind men around the elephant, the Foreign Service Officers of the State Department, the Agency for International Development, the United States Information Service, the CIA, and the comparatively large contingent of the American military—Army, Navy, Air Force, and Marines—gathered about the Diem Government, each dealing with different pieces and sections of its problems and defining the animal accordingly." Ibid., 105.

almost verbatim, that American success or failure depended heavily on Nolting's ability to "get on the same wave-length" with him.[38]

Nolting was given the official mission brief, which was focused on the special understanding that good relations had to be restored with Ngo Dinh Diem. As Nolting explained,

> The new element in my instructions was to get this thing on a firm footing, to get a rapport between the two partners, to create confidence in each other's motives, and to use that confidence to build real advances in social, political and economic matters, as well as in the more military part of the anti-subversion campaign, because it was completely recognized that this whole effort was of a piece, that you couldn't put down the Viet Cong or pacify the country without a very broad and deep program of winning the people.[39]

To underscore that the new government in Washington wanted to secure and maintain good relations with President Ngo Dinh Diem, President Kennedy wrote the following words in a personal letter to President Diem: "I wish on the occasion of your second inauguration to offer to you and to the Vietnamese people my personal congratulations and those of the American people. We have watched with sympathy your courageous leadership during your country's struggle to perfect its independence and its efforts to create a better life for its people. The United States stands firmly with you in this struggle and in these efforts."[40]

According to Colby, the U.S. president could not have picked a better man than Nolting to forge a new beginning in America's relations with South Vietnam. Though Nolting had no real experience with Asia, he readily grasped the complex nature of Washington's relationship with Saigon. His quiet but steadfast approach had proved invaluable with allies in Europe just after the trauma of World War II, Colby said. Nolting knew the diplomat's art of influencing a leader as a friend,

---

[38] "We must continue to work through the present Vietnamese government despite its acknowledged weakness. No other remotely feasible alternative exists at this point in time which does not involve an unacceptable degree of risk.... Given Diem's personality and character and the abrasive nature of our recent relationships, success or failure in this regard will depend very heavily on Ambassador Nolting's ability to get on the same wave-length with Diem." Congress, House, Committee on Armed Services, "Spring Decisions—I", 47–48.

[39] Nolting, interview by O'Connor, interview 1, p. 4.

[40] John F. Kennedy, "Letter from President Kennedy to President Diem", April 26, 1961, Washington, in FRUS, 1961–1963, vol. 1, document 34, 81.

he added, and he refrained from pressuring heads of allied nations as if they were foes.[41] Thus, soon after his arrival in South Vietnam on May 9, 1961, Ambassador Nolting told President Diem that the United States would be a reliable ally. He said that Washington understood the special problems that both he, as president, and his country faced. He assured him that their two governments, working together, would be able to devise a way to defeat the Communist offensive.[42]

One of Nolting's first tasks as ambassador was to prepare for the visit of Vice President Johnson and his wife on May 11. The purpose behind Johnson's visit was many-layered. While on one level it was an excellent photo opportunity for the U.S. government to show its support for Diem's struggle against Communism, it held a deeper purpose— and according to Nolting, this was not lost on Diem.[43] President Kennedy had sent members of his own family, Jean Kennedy and Stephen Smith, to accompany Johnson. This presence was to assure Diem that "the Kennedy administration appreciated strong family ties, and, unlike its predecessor, did not want to divorce Diem from his family [i.e., Ngo Dinh Nhu]."[44] By all accounts, Johnson's visit was a significant diplomatic success that ended with a joint communiqué in which Diem was highly praised by the vice president and was promised an increase in American moral and matériel support. As Nolting recalled, the formal dinner and speeches, coupled with the strength of the communiqué the following day, could not be construed as anything less than the strongest American support for Diem.[45]

There were rumours, maintained primarily by American journalists who did not like Diem or what he represented, that Johnson waxed eloquent about Diem merely because he was the "only boy" America had in South Vietnam. But Johnson expressed admiration for Diem and consistently advised against any moves to remove him from office.[46] In his written report of his visit to Southeast Asia, the vice president wrote

[41] Colby, *Lost Victory*, 109–10.
[42] Ibid., 110.
[43] Nolting, *From Trust to Tragedy*, 20.
[44] Ibid.
[45] Ibid., 21.
[46] Johnson explained his unfaltering support of Diem in his memoirs: Lyndon Baines Johnson, *The Vantage Point: Perspectives of the Presidency, 1963–1969* (New York: Popular Library, 1971), 54–62.

that South Vietnam was a lot more stable than the American media were suggesting. He noted that there was an obsession with security amongst many of the American mission personnel in Vietnam, which was creating the impression that the country was about to disintegrate. American officials were relying too much on the opinions of disgruntled Vietnamese intellectuals, Johnson said, and panic on Washington's part would only make matters worse. He said the destabilisation of the country would occur only if Diem were assassinated by the Communists or thrown out of power by a coup. Johnson concluded his report by stating that there was no other realistic alternative to Diem and that there was no question of Diem's will and capability to resist the insurgents.

For his part, Diem was impressed by the vice president's warm and friendly manner. After Johnson's visit, however, the South Vietnamese leader warned Ambassador Nolting that "there are profound differences between the Vietnamese and American people, in customs, outlook, political training, and philosophy. I hope we can find a bridge between Eastern and Western cultures."[47]

Throughout the early days of his mission, Nolting diligently investigated what had been going on between the Americans and the Vietnamese. He conducted interviews and meetings with diplomatic colleagues and representatives of the numerous U.S. government agencies in Saigon. As a consequence, Nolting determined that many Americans there, particularly DOS officials, were dissatisfied with Diem's government.[48] Joseph Mendenhall, the embassy's counsellor for political affairs, expressed serious doubts about the abilities of Diem and his government to bring peace to South Vietnam or to help its people.[49] Immediately upon returning to the United States, Mendenhall wrote a critique of Diem and the GVN. In a thesis at the National War College, he stated that a military regime would serve South Vietnam best. While Mendenhall did not recommend a coup, Nolting said, "the government he envisioned was like the one that succeeded the Diem government after the 1963 overthrow." John Anspacher, counsellor for public affairs, and Arthur Gardiner, counsellor for economic affairs, also were critical of the

---

[47] Nolting, *From Trust to Tragedy*, 22.
[48] Nolting, interview by O'Brien, interview 2, pp. 32–33.
[49] Nolting, *From Trust to Tragedy*, 24–25.

GVN. Gardiner, Nolting noted, was more discouraged by than antago-nistic toward Diem.[50]

In spite of the fellow diplomats who were negative about Diem, the ambassador noticed that those who were actively gathering intelligence in the field were positive about U.S. efforts in Vietnam. Not least to be considered amongst these individuals was the calm and competent CIA station chief William Colby. Cautious optimism also came from MAAG, headed by Lieutenant General Lionel McGarr. The advi-sory effort was independent from the embassy yet was required to work closely with it. Nolting recalled that McGarr had a difficult and demanding soldier-diplomat role, and as such, he was obviously under instructions from Washington to keep Diem from interfering in military operations while at the same time not annoying the Vietnamese presi-dent.[51] Regardless of the occasional clashes between McGarr and Diem, there was a mutual respect between them.

In addition to studying the American side of the equation, Ambas-sador Nolting also studied Diem and his government. He recognised, almost from the very beginning of his posting, that the way to improve relations with Diem was to allow him to be independent of Ameri-can direction. Perhaps, more importantly—at least in the context of the contest between Diem's nationalist credentials and those of Ho Chi Minh—it was crucial that Diem *appear* to be independent. Diem and his brother Nhu were highly sensitive to the accusation made by the Communists that they were the lackeys of the neocolonialist Amer-icans. For example, early Communist propaganda linked Diem with Eisenhower's secretary of state, John Foster Dulles. Indeed, Australian sympathiser with the Communist cause Wilfred G. Burchett endorsed this linkage in much of his written work on the subject.[52] The Viet Cong assertion that the South Vietnamese government was "My-Diem" (American-Diemist) was particularly galling to the patriotic Ngo Dinh

---

[50] "He had been in the country since February 1958. Arthur was an old friend, and I sus-pect that, rather than being anti-Diem, he was disillusioned and disheartened. He had worked very hard and ably and felt that the Vietnamese economy should have responded better to the infusions of money it was receiving, as well as to his ... efforts in training and advice." Ibid., 24–25.

[51] Ibid.

[52] See, e.g., Wilfred G. Burchett, *Vietnam: Inside Story of the Guerrilla War* (New York: International Publishers, 1965), 177.

brothers. The unflattering characterization was more than a personal affront; it was at the very heart of the Communist misinformation campaign against the government of South Vietnam.[53] Nolting was aware of the persuasive power of Communist propaganda, of its capacity to make Diem's government appear far more inept or corrupt than it actually was while making Ho Chi Minh's look righteous. Meanwhile, the Communists had a much easier task than Diem, for as author Weldon A. Brown noted: "We built; the Vietcong destroyed."[54]

Seeing the important reasons to cut Diem more slack, Nolting overcame his previous foreboding and came to embrace the Kennedy directives for his mission, which had been endorsed by the presidential task force. He did so not for the sake of being "with the program". Instead, his full-fledged support for Diem had come about through his own observations of the Vietnamese leader's qualities and abilities, not least of which were integrity and dedication. Diem was inept when it came to public relations, especially with the American press, said Nolting, but his attempts to work with the Americans to the degree he was able were as genuine as his efforts to defeat the Communists.[55] Nolting also believed that the U.S. effort in South Vietnam would add substantial credibility to other American assistance programs for beleaguered countries elsewhere. This credibility, however, would hinge on American restraint, wisdom, and consideration regarding Ngo Dinh Diem and his government.

[53] "Every insurgency, particularly a communist revolutionary one, requires a cause.... The basic cause was ready at hand: anti-colonialism. It was on this that the Emergency was based and also the war against the French in Indo-China. It did not quite fit the situation prevailing in South Vietnam after 1954, but by twisting the cause to anti-imperialism it could be made to apply to the United States' presence in South Vietnam at the invitation of and in support of the Ngo Dinh Diem government." Robert Grainger Thompson, *Defeating Communist Insurgency: Experiences from Malaya and Vietnam* (London: Chatto and Windus, 1966), 21–22.

[54] Brown elaborated: "By very costly and careful efforts we sought to influence the villages to support Saigon through appeals to their hopes; while by terror and murder the Vietcong tried to win power through popular fears. Only as long as American or Saigon troops stayed in the village to protect it was security possible. With their departure the enemy returned and resumed his destruction. Rural turbulence made life a nightmare for millions." Weldon A. Brown, *Prelude to Disaster: The American Role in Vietnam, 1940–1963* (Port Washington, N.Y.: Kennikat Press, 1975), 160.

[55] "[A]s is the case with anybody new, one wants to find out by getting to know a person and getting to know his philosophy and his way of doing things, his character, and that of his principal assistants. And, so I spent a lot of time when I first got out there on this. And I came out with what I felt was a fresh conclusion: that this was an extremely able and dedicated man, working in a very difficult situation, subject to a great deal of unjust criticism, having weaknesses, of course, as all of us do. But a person of real integrity, whose philosophy I could agree with." Nolting, interview by O'Brien, interview 2, pp. 34–35.

After being in Saigon for approximately three months, Nolting sent a telegram to DOS expressing his understating of the situation in Vietnam. Diem was not a dictator who relished power for its own sake, Nolting said. In fact, Diem was almost monk-like in his dedication to high principles and as such not a typical politician who enjoyed the exercise of power and its privileges. His philosophy was sound and compatible with American interests, although a little over the heads of most Vietnamese, and his objectives were reasonable. Therefore, there was nothing to prevent the Kennedy administration from "backing Diem to the hilt".[56]

Nolting's telegram continued that Diem was confident that he could govern South Vietnam better and more equitably than any other possible candidate. Nolting concurred with Diem's self-assessment but feared that because the leader was so exemplary and quite irreplaceable, he would prove to be a weakness for South Vietnam and U.S. involvement there. In short, he was vulnerable to both Communist and non-Communist enemies.[57]

The ambassador's telegram also stated that in places where Washington thought Diem was wrong, the Americans could gradually bring about changes and improvements so long as they maintained Diem's trust. In the classified section of his report, Nolting said that Diem's confidence in the United States had improved in recent months despite the negative developments in Laos. Actions of substance were backing up American assurances, and these were starting to win over political fence-sitters to the GVN side. There was, however, a tricky and negative aspect to this improved relationship: it seemed to validate the "My-Diem" image. Diem worried that if the Communists convinced his people that his government stood or fell because of the Americans, his political legitimacy would be increasingly challenged. Thus, Nolting warned Washington that there had to be a subtlety of execution in its support of Diem.[58]

Diem's popularity amongst the Vietnamese had not increased much in spite of what he had accomplished, Nolting wrote. There was a widespread misconception that the leader had little interest in the welfare of the common people and was indifferent to their problems. This view

---

[56] Nolting, *From Trust to Tragedy*, 146; Frederick E. Nolting, "Telegram from the Embassy in Vietnam to the Department of State", July 14, 1961, Saigon, in *FRUS, 1961–1963*, vol. 1, document 92, pp. 217-19.

[57] Ibid.

[58] Ibid.

was completely at odds with the man, his interests, and his actions, added Nolting, who had accompanied Diem on his many trips into rural Vietnam, where the Vietnamese leader seemed to be most at ease. His interest and expertise in farming, fishing, and all manner of practical things proved that the picture of him as an aloof mandarin was utterly false. Yet this false picture, manufactured by his enemies, was spreading in the news media, and it was hurting Diem and his administration. Nolting warned that Diem could not afford to allow the slander to drag on indefinitely, or he would suffer from another coup attempt or worse. He said Diem had to make a public relations "breakthrough".[59]

The ever-watchful William Colby kept a steady eye on how Nolting conducted his diplomatic mission. The CIA station chief noted that the new U.S. ambassador, unlike his predecessor, grew close to both the Vietnamese leadership and its opposition. Just as importantly, Nolting spent a considerable amount of time and effort attempting to understand the ordinary Vietnamese in both the city of Saigon and the countryside. He was not naïve about the cruel realities of Vietnam and certainly did not view Diem's government as a model of democracy. Yet he recognised the political necessity of Diem's mandarin-style leadership in the face of a violent Communist insurgency.[60]

According to Colby, Nolting was one of the few Americans who understood that the war for Vietnam was not like that fought in Korea—a conventional soldier's war. The ambassador discerned from his earliest days in Saigon that the main battles were political and needed to be won in the villages. The key to winning over the Vietnamese villagers was not Western-style democracy, which was an alien concept in Southeast Asia. Thus, Nolting understood, the leaders of South Vietnam could not be expected to "do our will, as Americans are wont to expect foreigners to do in every possible circumstance; they had to assert their nationalism if they were to contest the nationalist appeal that the enemy was offering to the population."[61]

[59] Ibid.

[60] William Colby, speech to the Miller Center at the University of Virginia, in *Diplomacy, Administration and Policy: The Ideas and Careers of Frederick E. Nolting, Jr.*, Frederick C. Mosher, and Paul T. David, ed. Kenneth W. Thompson (Lanham, Md.: University Press of America, 1995), 8.

[61] Ibid., 8–9.

4

The Continuing Laotian Question

Southeast Asia was a strategic whole. "As events tend to show more and more," wrote Bernard Fall in 1967, "it is impossible to conceive a coherent policy for, say, Cambodia or South Viet-Nam that does not affect Laos or North Viet-Nam as well."[1] President Eisenhower had understood this and, as stated previously, had recognised Laos as the strategic linchpin to the theatre. He had also promised to commit U.S. forces to protect the territorial integrity and political independence of countries threatened by aggression from any nation controlled by international Communism, the so-called Eisenhower Doctrine. Yet even with Eisenhower's understanding of the importance of Laos, his foreign policy, according to Ngo Dinh Diem, did not adequately address the burgeoning Communist infiltration of this neighboring country. John F. Kennedy's administration inherited the Laotian question, and to the peril of the United States and its allies in the region, also failed to find an answer to it.

In May 1959, a major offensive was initiated by Communist Pathet Lao guerrillas against the royal Laotian government. This offensive was carried out mainly by North Vietnamese units against the government's frontier posts.[2] The Pathet Lao, meaning "Lao Nation", had been established many years before by Vo Nguyen Giap, the most important military and political leader in North Vietnam after Ho Chi Minh.

During elections in the spring of 1960, Pathet Lao representatives were eliminated from the Laotian National Assembly. Unwilling to abide by the elections, neutralist Captain Kong Le of the Royal Lao

[1] Bernard B. Fall, *Last Reflections on a War: Bernard B. Fall's Last Comments on Viet-Nam* (Garden City, N.Y.: Doubleday, 1967), 118.
[2] See Paul F. Langer and Joseph J. Zasloff, *North Vietnam and the Pathet Lao: Partners in the Struggle for Laos* (Cambridge, Mass.: Harvard University Press, 1970), 202–5.

Army unleashed a successful coup that was endorsed by the Pathet Lao. Neutralist Prince Souvanna Phouma was returned to power as prime minister through the efforts of Kong Le, who as a paratrooper recognised his own political limitations. The Communists benefited from the confusion that had followed the Kong Le coup and continued to make territorial gains.[3] Highly suspicious of the supposed neutrality of Kong Le and Prince Phouma, the U.S. government was not encouraged by the official opening of diplomatic relations with the Soviet Union and cut off its aid to the royal Laotian government.[4] Meanwhile, the Thais, alarmed at the Laotian slide toward the Communists, began an economic blockade of Laos.

The leaders of the conservative forces in Laos, Prince Boun Oum and General Phoumi Nosavan, retook the Laotian capital city of Vientiane in September 1960, forcing Prince Phouma and Kong Le to flee. Nevertheless, a month later the Laotian government created closer ties with the Pathet Lao and the Soviet Union, which responded by sending its first ambassador to Laos. In addition to this diplomatic support, the Soviet Union began an airlift of arms from Hanoi to Kong Le's forces.[5]

By the end of 1960, intelligence reports indicating sizeable movements of North Vietnamese troops into Laos, in support of the Communist Pathet Lao guerrillas, were causing real concern in Washington and especially in the Eisenhower White House.[6] Previously, CIA Director Allen Dulles had given his own report, which confirmed that China, North Vietnam, and Russia were supporting the Pathet Lao. Although

---

[3] Ibid.

[4] Since 1956 the Americans had been keeping a watchful and concerned eye on Prince Souvanna Phouma because he had come to an agreement with Pathet Lao about the need for a cease-fire in the disputed areas, a foreign policy of neutrality, and the political rights of the Pathet Lao. When the prince made a two-week trip to Peking and Hanoi, "this trip was the turning point for many people in Washington—proof that Souvanna would knuckle under to the Asian Communist leaders. American officials tried hard to prevent the trip by repeated warnings of the dangers of getting too close to the Communists. Coming so soon after the agreement . . . the journey was symbolic confirmation that Souvanna meant to work with the devil." Charles A. Stevenson, *The End of Nowhere: American Policy toward Laos since 1954* (Boston: Beacon Press, 1972), 40–41.

[5] Langer and Zasloff, *North Vietnam and the Pathet Lao*, 202.

[6] United States Department of State, "Memorandum of a Conference with the President, White House, Washington, December 31, 1960, 11:30 A.M.", in *FRUS, 1958–1960*, vol. 16, *East Asia–Pacific Region; Cambodia; Laos* (Washington, D.C.: United States Government Printing Office, 1992), 1025.

the extent of their help was difficult to determine, Dulles believed that they had already sent considerable supplies to Laos. For example, the Soviets had expanded the Communist airlift capacity in the area by delivering AN-12 transport planes. On December 26, Soviet leader Nikita Khrushchev told a British ambassador, "Moscow regards current activity in Laos as a long-term operation which might last for seven years without a major war resulting."[7] From the flood of intelligence streaming into the White House, it appeared that the Pathet Lao, supported and supplied via the Dien Bien Phu valley in North Vietnam, had secured the entire province of Phong Saly in Laos.[8] Biographer John Colvin noted that cautious Americans, such as President Eisenhower, were beginning to discover that Giap's "reach was as long as his grasp"[9] and that Laos was subject to both.

Although Eisenhower said he needed more information before he could counter a North Vietnamese invasion of Laos with U.S. troops, he argued to his National Security Council that the situation demanded co-ordinated and decisive action. On December 31, 1960, the president stated that the time was drawing near to deploy the U.S. Navy's Seventh Fleet with its contingent force of Marines.[10] But first the non-Communist Laotian leader (at that time Boun Oum) needed to be legitimised and America's allies needed to be consulted. If the United States and her allies could not agree on a course of action, however, America would take unilateral action to defend Laos, he said, because it "cannot sit by and see Laos go down without a fight."[11]

President Eisenhower then enumerated the following action steps: (1) The United States would persuade the contested Laotian prime minister, Prince Souvanna Phouma, to resign and to leave the country for retirement in France; (2) the United States would motivate Prince Boun Oum to permit his government to be legitimised by the Laotian assembly;[12] (3) the U.S. government would consolidate its positions

[7] Editorial note in FRUS, 1958–1960, vol. 16, document 496, p. 1021.

[8] United States Department of State, "Memorandum of Conference with President, December 31, 1960", 1025.

[9] John Colvin, Giap: Volcano under the Snow (New York: Soho Press, 1996), 116–17.

[10] United States Department of State, "Memorandum of Conference with President, December 31, 1960", 1025.

[11] Ibid., 1028–29.

[12] Prince Oum's regime was officially recognised by the U.S. government in mid-December 1960.

with both the British and the French; (4) the Eisenhower administration would alert the Southeast Asia Treaty Organisation (SEATO) Council about the serious situation in Laos, without calling for immediate military action; and (5) the United States would make the necessary changes to its own military assets so as to bring maximum force to bear on the North Vietnamese should an attack become essential. Concerned as to how Diem would view the Communist assault on Laos and the American reaction to it, Eisenhower also told the council to inform the press that America would not allow Laos to fall to the Communists even if such prevention meant that the United States had to act alone.[13]

President Eisenhower then authorised Llewellyn Thompson, the U.S. ambassador to the Soviet Union, to convey a warning directly to Nikita Khrushchev.[14] He told Thompson to inform the Soviet leader that the United States viewed the deteriorating Laotian situation "with grave concern" and was moving the positions of its forces to assure, if necessary, that the legitimate government will not be destroyed, and that in the event of major war America "will not be caught napping".[15]

In January 1961, when President Eisenhower handed over the reins of power to President-elect Kennedy, they discussed Laos. The outgoing president made it absolutely clear that for strategic reasons Laos must not be forsaken. "It was his opinion that if Laos should fall to the Communists, then it would be just a question of time until South Vietnam, Cambodia, Thailand and Burma would collapse.... President Eisenhower said with considerable emotion that Laos was the key to the entire area of Southeast Asia."[16] Proving that Russia, China, and North Vietnam were determined to seize Laos, Eisenhower gave a brief overview of the country's recent political history. The Communists must not be allowed

[13] United States Department of State, "Memorandum of Conference with President, December 31, 1960", 1028–29.

[14] See Patrick Anderson, *The President's Men: White House Assistants of Franklin D. Roosevelt, Harry S. Truman, Dwight D. Eisenhower, John F. Kennedy and Lyndon B. Johnson* (Garden City, N.Y.: Doubleday, 1969), 285.

[15] "Memorandum of Conference with President, December 31, 1960", 1028–29.

[16] "Memorandum of Conference on January 19, 1961 between President Eisenhower and President-elect Kennedy on the Subject of Laos", copy of original 1961 memorandum sent from Clark Clifford to President Johnson, September 29, 1967, in *1956 French Withdrawal–1960*, section V.B.3.d of bk. 10 of *United States–Vietnam Relations, 1945–1967: Study Prepared by the Department of Defense*, by Congress, House, Committee on Armed Services, 1360–63.

to insert themselves in the Laotian government, he added, otherwise they would take power by that means as they had done in China.[17]

Kennedy seems to have been persuaded by Eisenhower to make Laos his number one foreign policy concern. Within the first two weeks after his inauguration, when Theodore Sorensen, special counsel to President Kennedy, was asked to identify the administration's foreign policy priorities, Sorensen answered, "Laos." He gave the same answer to the question, "What about Vietnam?"[18] Kennedy also seems to have agreed with Eisenhower's assessment that military force should be used in Laos if necessary. But, as shall be seen, the Eisenhower take on Laos did not guide Kennedy's foreign policy for long.

First of all, Kennedy was not a general like Eisenhower, and the Laos question turned into a problem for him when he learned the actual details of military intervention. Secondly, his priorities shifted as he began to digest how serious the Vietnamese situation had become. Indeed, in the early period of his administration the president blurted out in frustration, "Eisenhower briefed me about everything—but Vietnam."[19] Kennedy did not stop with blaming Eisenhower. He also began to doubt the efficiency and the professionalism of DOS. He believed that they stumbled through one muddle after another, and he was even quoted as saying to his national security advisor: "I get more done in one day in the White House than they do in six months in the State Department." He also said, "They never have any ideas over there.... The State Department is a bowl of jelly."[20] Strong words, no doubt, but also words coming from a man who was afraid of the chaos he saw in Southeast Asia.

Initially, and on the surface, Kennedy's Laos Task Force appeared to be pro-interventionist with a tilt toward using ground forces if needed. Even if Kennedy at first leaned in the same direction, "he was soon disenchanted with the prospects [of military force]. His military aide has written that he showed 'stunned amazement' on learning that if only 10,000 men were sent to Southeast Asia, there would be practically no strategic reserve left for any other contingencies. Nor could those troops

[17] Ibid.

[18] John P. Leacacos, *Fires in the In-Basket: The ABC's of the State Department* (Cleveland: World Publishing, 1968), 89.

[19] Ibid.

[20] Smith Simpson, *Anatomy of the State Department* (Boston: Beacon Press, 1968), 228.

be deployed with the speed necessary to counter any large-scale intervention by the Chinese."[21]

The membership of Kennedy's Laos Task Force included Assistant Secretary of State J. Graham Parsons; his deputy, John Steeves; Assistant
Secretary of Defense Paul Nitze; men from the CIA; the Joint Chiefs
of Staff; Walt Rostow, representing the White House; and some lower-
echelon DOS officials. According to historian Charles A. Stevenson,
these individuals were the type most likely to take a hard-line approach
to the Communist intervention in Laos. Parsons and Steeves had detailed
knowledge of what was going on in Laos, and they also brought a distrust
of Souvanna to the task force. They were indeed willing to support military intervention if it proved to be necessary, and they did not perceive
that as a problem for a president who spoke so often of "taking action".[22]

Before the task force could submit its recommendations, however,
Kennedy was assailed with questions about Laos by the news media,
and before the cameras and microphones his political instincts were
revealed: he indicated a preference for diplomatic not military action. In
his first news conference, on January 25, 1961, he said the United States
sought to establish an "independent, peaceful, uncommitted country" in
Laos.[23] Kennedy reiterated this hoped-for solution at a news conference
on March 23, 1961:

> First, we strongly and unreservedly support the goal of a neutral and inde-
> pendent Laos, tied to no outside power or group of powers, threatening
> no one, and free from any domination.... We are earnestly in favor of
> constructive negotiation among the nations concerned and among the
> leaders of Laos which can help Laos back to the pathway of independence
> and genuine neutrality.... We are always conscious of the obligation,
> which rests upon all members of the United Nations to seek peaceful
> solutions to problems of this sort.... I want to make it clear to the Amer-
> ican people and to all the world that all we want in Laos is peace, not war;
> a truly neutral government, not a cold war pawn; a settlement concluded
> at the conference table and not on the battlefield.... We will not be pro-
> voked, trapped, or drawn into this or any other situation.[24]

---

[21] Stevenson, *End of Nowhere*, 135.

[22] Ibid.

[23] Ibid.

[24] John F. Kennedy, "The President's News Conference of March 23, 1961", in *Public
Papers of the Presidents of the United States: John F. Kennedy*, vol. 1, *1961* (Washington, D.C.:
United States Government Printing Office, 1962), document 92, p. 214.

As Kennedy spoke to the press of diplomacy and peace, his task force on Laos discussed the option of military intervention. A key observer of these discussions was Roger Hilsman, whom Kennedy's Secretary of Defense Robert McNamara described as a "smart, abrasive, talkative West Point graduate who had been involved in guerrilla combat in World War II and had subsequently become an academic".[25] Hilsman had been a professor of international politics at Princeton before entering public service. During World War II he had served with a U.S. Army commando unit in Japanese-occupied Burma known as Merrill's Marauders.[26] In the early days of the Kennedy presidency, Hilsman was DOS' director of research and intelligence and the administration's leading proponent of a "political approach" to Laos, one that emphasised "political, economic and social action into which very carefully calibrated military measures were interwoven".[27] His ideas on fighting Communist guerrillas approximated those of Sir Robert Thompson, a thinking soldier whom Hilsman respected and admired.[28] Hilsman advised, "Protect the people, don't chase the Viet Cong, just use the troops to protect the people. Then behind the screen you have social and political reform."[29]

Most of the task force's discussion of military intervention, Hilsman observed, took place against the backdrop of the Korean War. He noted that many of the military planners considered the stalemate that ended the Korean War a humiliation. They believed that restrictions placed on bombing north of the Yalu River and other constraints on the use of force prevented the possibility of military victory.[30] As a result, the Joint Chiefs of Staff came to a position that was more like a tenet: the United States should never again fight a restricted or limited ground war in Asia. Its corollary was this: if the United States were to engage again in land warfare in Asia, its use of force should be unlimited, meaning it should have the option of using nuclear weapons.[31]

[25] Robert S. McNamara, *In Retrospect: The Tragedy and Lessons of Vietnam*, with Brian VanDeMark (New York: Random House, 1995), 52.

[26] Larry E. Cable, *Conflict of Myths: The Development of American Counterinsurgency Doctrine and the Vietnam War* (New York: New York University Press, 1986), 197.

[27] Ellen J. Hammer, *A Death in November: America in Vietnam, 1963* (New York: E.P. Dutton, 1987), 39.

[28] Cable, *Conflict of Myths*, 197.

[29] Hammer, *Death in November*, 39.

[30] Martin E. Goldstein, *American Policy toward Laos* (Cranbury, N.J.: Associated University Presses, 1973), 234.

[31] Ibid.

The task force predicted that if the Communists took Laos, they would have access to a north–south invasion route, later called the Ho Chi Minh Trail, which sliced through the very heart of Southeast Asia, allowing the Communists to mount pressure on South Vietnam, Cambodia, and Thailand through the Mekong lowlands (which is what happened in the following years). It also determined that if in an effort to prevent such an outcome, American armed force was introduced into Southeast Asia in a limited way, a Korean-style war would probably ensue. Conversely, an unrestricted deployment of American armed force could possibly escalate into World War III.

Neither of these potential scenarios appealed to President Kennedy, nor did the political cost of being the president to lose Southeast Asia. Thus, he opted for diplomatic action aimed at Laotian neutrality instead of military intervention. If diplomatic negotiations proved fruitless, he reasoned, the United States could then threaten the use of force. Such a threat would be a bluff, however, and all that was required to undo Kennedy's plan for Laotian neutrality was for the Communists to perceive it as such—and as events unfolded, that is precisely what happened.[32]

It needs to be noted that the notion of a negotiated settlement that would lead to Laotian neutrality had not spontaneously blossomed forth out of the president's fears. Instead, all indications, which can be corroborated with documents, suggest that the policy was whispered into his ear by Undersecretary of State Chester Bowles. During his election campaign, President Kennedy had proclaimed Bowles his chief advisor on foreign policy. But Bowles' advice on Laos, as gathered from his own testimony, seems to have been based more on his own idealism than on his knowledge of Southeast Asia:

> The only realistic approach, I believed, was to buy whatever time we could by maintaining a military power balance, but with no illusions about its fragile nature. We could only hope that within this period the necessary peacekeeping apparatus could somehow be created within a strengthened United Nations, which ultimately would become the basis for a system of world order.... As the leader of the kind of world-wide liberal movement which I envisioned, a new American President would be faced with the opposition of many powerful vested interests committed to the status quo. But on his side would be all the human forces for

[32] Ibid.

freedom, proclaimed in our own Revolution, which had been gradually evolving and were now inspiring young leaders in every corner of the world.[33]

Bowles thought very little of Eisenhower's approach to Laos, calling it "one of the most appalling, naive, misguided and badly administered efforts that has come to my attention in the last few years".[34]

Regardless of what Bowles and Kennedy thought or hoped would stabilise Laos, Vo Nguyen Giap knew exactly what had to be done there to assault the salients of South Vietnam. Giap was born on August 28, 1911, in the village of An Xa, situated in the province of Quang Binh. Thus, like Ngo Dinh Diem and Ho Chi Minh, Giap was from central Vietnam, or more traditionally, Annam. There can be no denying that he was an extraordinary individual: from his youth on, he had demonstrated remarkable intelligence and unique powers of leadership and organisation. Politically involved since his teens, he joined the Communists in the early 1930s. He acquired a degree in law and political economics from the University of Hanoi in July 1937.[35] He worked as a journalist for revolutionary newspapers for a couple of years and by 1940 was teaching history at a private school near Hanoi.[36] On December 22, 1944, Giap oversaw the inception of the first military-propaganda unit of what would become the People's Liberation Army of Vietnam.[37] Starting out with thirty-four soldiers, he ended up commanding more than one million during his war with the Americans. Although he made several disastrous mistakes during his campaigns against the French and the Americans, he was victorious in the end.[38]

To the creation of his army Giap brought a firm grasp of Vietnamese and military history. He was a great admirer of Napoleon Bonaparte and could recite the French commander's campaigns and battles in detail in

[33] Chester Bowles, *Promises to Keep: My Years in Public Life, 1941–1969* (New York: Harper and Row, 1971), 286–87.

[34] Ibid., 334.

[35] Peter Macdonald, *Giap: The Victor in Vietnam* (New York: W. W. Norton, 1993), 16–17, 22.

[36] William J. Duiker, *The Communist Road to Power in Vietnam*, 2nd ed. (Boulder, Colo.: Westview Press, 1996), 69.

[37] Ibid., 83.

[38] Macdonald, *Giap*, 17.

rapid-fire lectures accompanied by precise maps drawn on a blackboard. Though he religiously studied Lenin, Marx, Engels, and Mao to understand the nature of revolutionary warfare, he nevertheless admitted to the French general Raoul Salan that he had discovered the secrets of successful guerrilla warfare from a British soldier: T.E. Lawrence, better known as Lawrence of Arabia. His seminal work, *The Seven Pillars of Wisdom* (1935), gave Giap "practical examples of how to apply minimum military force to maximum tactical and strategic effect".[39]

Giap's understanding of the practical realities of unconventional warfare in Indochina led him early on to consider Laos as his strategic linchpin. Communist though he was, Giap manifested qualities of a Confucian philosopher-leader: respect for Sun Tsu's martial thought, incredible patience, and a long-term view.[40] Thus, Giap saw Laos as part of an integrated strategy for winning the war in Vietnam. Indeed, Giap's biographer John Colvin explained how Giap used Laos in his war against the French.[41]

Kennedy's decision to engage in negotiations for a neutral Laos seemed to many observers to overlook the country's strategic importance to the North Vietnamese. In April 1961 White House counsel Theodore C. Sorenson called for "a more realistic approach" to Vietnam. In a memo to the president he wrote, "To the extent that [the administration's] plan depends on the communists being tied down in Laos or lacking further forces, on our blocking land corridors through which communist support flows, or on our obtaining effective anti-infiltration action against Laos ... the outcome is highly doubtful."[42] The president's task force on South Vietnam also had doubts about the outcome of the Laotian talks. The task force members had observed a relationship between the Pathet Lao Communists, the Laotian

---

[39] Ibid., 23.

[40] Ibid., 41–42.

[41] "After the Black River campaign of 1952, Giap withdrew to regroup, replace losses of men and equipment, and to plan the assault on Laos.... The opportunities for dividing the forces of the French Union once again and concentrating the Viet Minh against a weakened and dispersed enemy in the Red River Delta, Laos, Tonkin or the Central Highlands, were strategically evident to Giap. In April 1953 his troops advanced in multi-divisional strength into Laos." Colvin, *Giap*, 113.

[42] Theodore C. Sorenson, "Memorandum from the President's Special Counsel (Sorenson) to the President", April 28, 1961, Washington, in *FRUS, 1961–1963*, vol. 1, document 37, pp. 84–85.

neutralists, and the Communist offensive in South Vietnam.[43] In other words, the connection between declared Communist intentions and actual violent events in Laos and Vietnam was far too close to suggest anything other than a very well-organised campaign master-minded in Hanoi. Furthermore, the task force members warned President Kennedy that if the Laos talks resulted in unenforceable neutrality, and therefore a porous border between Laos and Vietnam, such an outcome would play right into the Communists' hands.[44]

There was something else to understand about the geopolitical landscape of Southeast Asia: Vietnam's traditional attempts to assert hegemony over at least parts of what the French in the last century designated as Laos.[45] In other words, Laos was not simply a conduit for North Vietnamese troops and supplies in order for the Communists to conquer

[43] "At the North Vietnamese Communist Party Congress in September 1960, the earlier declaration of underground war by the Party's Control Committee was re-affirmed. This action by the party Congress took place only a month after Kong Le's coup in Laos. Scarcely two months later there was a military uprising in Saigon. The turmoil created throughout the area by this rapid succession of events provides an ideal environment for the Communist 'master plan' to take over all of Southeast Asia." Roswell Gilpatric, "A Program of Action to Prevent Communist Domination of South Vietnam", attachment to "Memorandum from the Deputy Secretary of Defense (Gilpatric) to the President", May 3, 1961, Washington, in *FRUS, 1961–1963*, vol. 1, document 42, p. 93.

[44] "The effect of these negotiations on the situation in Vietnam will be threefold: First, the very fact that the Fourteen Powers are meeting under essentially the same ground rules as the 1954 Geneva Accords, including the concept of an ICC [International Control Commission] mechanism in Laos, Vietnam and Cambodia, could have a politically inhibiting effect on any significant measures which the U.S. might undertake to prevent a Communist take-over in South Viet-Nam.

"Second, as has been their practice in the past, the Communists can be expected to use the cover of an international negotiation to expand their subversive activities. In this case, close coordination of their efforts in Southern Laos, Cambodia and Viet-Nam can be expected. The 250-mile border between South Viet-Nam and Laos, while never effectively sealed in the past, will now be deprived of even the semblance of protection which the friendly, pro-western Laos offers.

"Third, the three principal passes through the Annamite Mountains—the Nape Pass, Mugia Gap, and the pass that controls the road from Quang Tri to Savannakhet—lie in Southern Laos. These passes control three key military avenues of advance from North Viet-Nam through Laos into the open Mekong valley leading to Thailand and South Viet-Nam. A Lao political settlement that would afford the Communists an opportunity to maintain any sort of control, covertly or otherwise, of these mountain passes would make them gate keepers to the primary inland invasion route leading to Saigon and flanking the most important defensive terrain in the northern area of South Viet-Nam." Ibid., 94–95.

[45] Langer and Zasloff, *North Vietnam and Pathet Lao*, 1.

South Vietnam but part of the conquest itself. This intention of the Vietnamese Communists could be seen through their spring 1961 offensive, by which they began seizing, along with Pathet Lao fighters, nearly all of upland Laos.

In spite of this Communist offensive and the warnings from both of his task forces, President Kennedy went forward with the negotiations on Laos. In April 1961, shortly after the failed U.S. Bay of Pigs invasion of Cuba, the United States and the USSR agreed on a cease-fire in Laos. Then from May 16, 1961, to July 23, 1962, the International Conference on the Settlement of the Laotian Question met in Geneva to hammer out the details of an agreement, which culminated in the Declaration of Laotian Neutrality. The fourteen signatories of the declaration agreed to refrain from interference in Laos and to disengage from military activity in the country.

Southeast Asian scholars Paul F. Langer and Joseph J. Zasloff noted that in compliance with the declaration, American and Filipino troops who had been fighting on the side of the Royal Lao government were withdrawn from the country. Meanwhile, the North Vietnamese left in place their estimated ten thousand men, the backbone of the Pathet Lao military. The North Vietnamese denied the remaining presence of their fighting units, and their duplicity was made possible by the built-in ineffectiveness of the International Control Commission (ICC): the ICC's Communist member, representing Poland was able to veto or to obstruct any investigative action that would have uncovered the truth.[46]

It should have been obvious to the Kennedy administration that the North Vietnamese had no intention of honouring Laotian neutrality, because they had openly displayed a negative attitude about international inspection and enforcement from the beginning of the meetings in Geneva. The North Vietnamese delegation had insisted that the neutrality of Laos should be mainly safeguarded by the Laotians themselves. Their Pathet Lao allies threatened that they would not tolerate inspections by an international body.[47]

By the time the declaration was signed, the North Vietnamese along with the Pathet Lao controlled approximately the same amount

[46] Ibid., 79.
[47] Ibid., 80.

of territory as the Viet Minh had at the end of the 1954 war with France. In reality this meant that approximately half of Laos was under Communist control.[48] After the declaration, North Vietnamese troops continued to occupy this territory and pass between Laos and North Vietnam at will. The Communists had achieved a net gain out of the Laotian affair, and the negotiated settlement served only to cement this gain in writing.[49] The student of military history and strategy can only assume that Kennedy's leading advocates for a new policy toward Laos had strayed into serious error. They had believed that neutrality would succeed where arms and the best efforts of the more experienced French had been unsuccessful. But as Sir Robert Thompson said, "The French experience in Indochina was almost totally written off and disregarded [by the Americans]."[50]

Further proof that Kennedy's men failed at what they set out to do in Laos manifested itself years later when the Americans were heavily engaged with their own forces in South Vietnam. By then, according to Douglas Pike, the NVA totally controlled the Pathet Lao. In 1968, there were more than forty thousand NVA troops within the Pathet Lao area of Laos, and all Pathet Lao decisions were made by North Vietnamese advisors.[51] In other words, North Vietnam was exercising complete suzerainty over much of Laos.

Looking on in dismay at the Kennedy administration's policy toward Laos, President Diem became more doubtful about the Americans. The growing tension between him and DOS, notwithstanding Ambassador Nolting's best efforts, caused President Kennedy's ambassador-at-large, W. Averell Harriman, and his faction within DOS to insist that the Vietnamese president be removed from power. Yet, as the Americans were

[48] "From their own point of view, the North Vietnamese had made substantial gains: Not only was the area of the Ho Chi Minh Trail now securely in Communist hands, but the northern provinces bordering on Vietnam were also clearly within Communist control, thereby providing a buffer between Vietnam and a potential enemy. In the future, this buffer zone could serve as a staging area for further advances into other parts of the country. Laos was now divided, and it seemed unlikely that peaceful reunification could be achieved without North Vietnamese consent." Ibid., 79–80.

[49] Ibid.

[50] Thomas C. Thayer, "Patterns of the French and American Experience in Vietnam", in *The Lessons of Vietnam*, ed. W. Scott Thompson and Donaldson D. Frizzell (New York: Crane, Russak, 1977), 35–36.

[51] Douglas Pike, *War, Peace, and the Viet Cong* (Cambridge, Mass.: MIT Press, 1969), 44.

to find out, whatever they decided about Diem would not change the reality of Laos— that it had been given over to the North Vietnamese.

At this juncture it becomes necessary to take a closer look at W. Averell Harriman, the man above the task forces who steered American policy in Laos and Ambassador Nolting's mission to South Vietnam. Son of a railroad baron, Harriman was well established and well known in elite American society. Having held one important political position after another, including U.S. secretary of commerce and ambassador to the Soviet Union, he wielded considerable political power. When in late 1961 President Kennedy made Harriman his assistant secretary of state for Far Eastern affairs, he described him as a man who had held "probably as many important jobs as any American in our history, with the possible exception of John Quincy Adams".[52]

The combination of Harriman's long, prestigious political career and his financial backing of Kennedy's presidential campaign made him a key figure in the Kennedy administration. Harriman had contributed more than thirty thousand dollars to Kennedy's campaign, and though the president had run on a theme of young American idealism, he could not overlook the venerable Harriman when time came to make political appointments. Soon after the election, special advisors Arthur Schlesinger and John Kenneth Galbraith drove this point home to the new president, who had paid all his political debts except to Harriman. When they told Kennedy that a Democratic administration without him was unthinkable, he asked Harriman to design his own job within DOS. On December 30, 1960, Harriman was sworn in as ambassador-at-large, a role with historic precedent as it once was held by Benjamin Franklin.[53]

As Harriman was reinserting himself into Washington politics, after serving as the governor of New York from 1955 to 1958, he saw settling the Laos question as his ticket to influence in the corridors of American power.[54] He had a long association with the Soviets that went back to the days of World War II, when he had acted as President Roosevelt's

[52] John F. Kennedy, "The President's News Conference of November 29, 1961", in Kennedy, *Public Papers*, vol. 1, document 488, p. 760.

[53] Ruby Abramson, *Spanning the Century: The Life of W. Averell Harriman, 1891–1986* (New York: William Morrow, 1992), 578–82.

[54] Walter Isaacson and Evan Thomas, *The Wise Men: Six Friends and the World They Made; Acheson, Bohlen, Harriman, Kennan, Lovett, McCloy* (New York: Simon and Schuster, 1986), 214.

chief expediter of the lend-lease program of war matériel to America's Russian ally.[55] In his early dealings with the Soviets, Harriman developed a good sense of how they negotiated and generally was able to interpret their intentions with a reasonable degree of accuracy.[56] Based on this experience, Harriman was convinced during the Laos negotiations that the Soviets would keep their promise to bring the necessary pressure to bear on the Pathet Lao and their direct sponsors, the North Vietnamese, to abide by an agreement. According to Ambassador Nolting, Harriman told him he based his confidence in the Soviets on his expert "fingertips feeling". Nolting replied that his "fingertips" told him "just the reverse".[57]

Throughout the Laos negotiations, Harriman built himself a formidable reputation. In meetings he would lull those who opposed him with the appearance of docility and then, at the appropriate moment, suddenly snap back. Thus, Harriman became known as the "old Crocodile" around Washington. Harriman liked the moniker, and the reputation that went with it, and used it as his code name for some DOS correspondence.[58]

Through the force of his remarkable will and skills, Harriman forged an agreement on Laotian neutrality that had the official support from all parties concerned, including the North Vietnamese. About President Kennedy's support, Harriman wrote: "Throughout the period President Kennedy's position was unchanging. He fully supported the negotiations for a political settlement. In fact after one meeting with his advisers in late August, which I attended, he telephoned me personally to make sure I understood clearly his position. He said, 'The alternative to an understanding with Souvanna is not one that I would like to contemplate.'"[59] The

[55] Ibid.

[56] W. Averell Harriman, *America and Russia in a Changing World: A Half Century of Personal Observation* (Garden City, N.Y.: Doubleday, 1971), 28–29, 31, 33–34.

[57] Frederick Nolting, interview by Dennis O'Brien, May 7, 1970, Washington, D.C., interview 3, transcript, 89–90, John F. Kennedy Oral History Collection, John F. Kennedy Presidential Library, Boston.

[58] "His episodes of impatient snapping in the genteel atmosphere of the White House caused McGeorge Bundy to liken him to an old crocodile arousing from a feigned doze with flashing jaws.... Harriman loved the image because it enhanced a reputation for toughness which he had valued and long cultivated by sprinkling cables and memoranda with references to how 'blunt' or 'brutal' or 'tough' he had been with one foreign official or another." Abramson, *Spanning the Century*, 603.

[59] Harriman, *America and Russia*, 112–13.

Soviets were more than willing to go along with Harriman's deal, because it gave them substantial prestige in the region at a relatively cheap cost. They agreed to ensure that all the Communist states would comply with the neutrality declaration. Furthermore, they accepted the agreement's language stipulating that Laotian territory could not be used in the affairs of a neighbouring state. Specifically, the North Vietnamese could not use Laos as a supply route in support of the insurgency in South Vietnam.[60]

Regardless of his triumph in getting the Soviets to sign the declaration of neutrality, in his haste to prove himself to Kennedy, Harriman had overlooked the fact that signatures on a piece of paper were one thing while the reality on the ground was quite another. While the Laos negotiations had seen the emergence of the "old Crocodile" and had enhanced his reputation as a diplomat who got things done, the affair was, in fact, much worse than "a good bad deal", as Harriman called it.[61] Laotian neutrality was a catastrophe for Southeast Asia; and when this became obvious to Harriman, he attributed the failure of the Laos agreement not to its inherent flaws, of which he was the architect, but to unexpected "intransigence" on the part of the Pathet Lao and the North Vietnamese.[62]

Foreseeing the looming disaster, some U.S. officials were tougher customers than the Russians, so much so that Harriman found it easier to agree with the Soviet negotiator than with his colleagues in Washington. In fact, Harriman collided with leading DOS officials who insisted that the ICC have the authority to travel in Laos at will in order to report any violations of the neutrality accords. Secretary of State Dean Rusk championed this fight and told President Kennedy that the ICC's freedom of movement in Laos was absolutely critical, "especially on the routes for present [North Vietnamese] infiltration into South Vietnam".[63] According to Harriman's wife Pamela, her husband had calculated an artful

---

[60] Abramson, *Spanning the Century*, 586–87.

[61] Isaacson and Thomas, *Wise Men*, 618.

[62] "However, due to Pathet Lao intransigence and the North Vietnamese violations of the agreement, a de facto partition of the country has resulted.... In violation of the specific terms of the agreement, the North Vietnamese have continued to use the Ho Chi Minh Trail and have supported the Pathet Lao in order to achieve this objective." Harriman, *America and Russia*, 112–13.

[63] Abramson, *Spanning the Century*, 586–87.

"end run" around his DOS opponents by befriending Robert Kennedy.[64] Ambassador Nolting agreed:

> Unlike Rusk, who personally and professionally resented the attorney general, Harriman courted the President's brother, serving as a contact, adviser, and sounding board. Though the collaboration was at the start calculated and self-serving on the part of both, they were natural allies, impatient, intolerant, sometimes ruthless, and consummately loyal to the President.... The home base of the Harriman–Bob Kennedy team was eventually established in a high-powered National Security Council committee created to coordinate the United States' response to Communist-backed "wars of liberation."[65]

Through his friendship with Robert Kennedy, Harriman was able to convince the president that ICC oversight, which was opposed by Laos and North Vietnam, was an area where the United States would have to compromise. Incredibly the president agreed with him over the objections of not only Rusk but neutrality advocate Chester Bowles, Deputy Undersecretary of State U. Alexis Johnson, and Walter McConaughy, the assistant secretary for Far Eastern affairs. Thus, Harriman proved his clout both inside and outside the Kennedy administration. "He had a political and social constituency that spanned decades and stretched around the world. When it suited him, he could ignore bureaucratic protocol and use his personal channels into far-flung governments, not to mention the White House and the inner circles of Kennedy's advisers."[66] In the future, rather than quarrel with Harriman, leading DOS officials would tend either to get on board with his policy initiatives or to look the other way while he proceeded with his course of action, although some of these later dubbed the Ho Chi Minh Trail the Averell Harriman Memorial Highway.[67]

Ambassador Nolting confronted Harriman during the Laos negotiations, because he knew that without oversight a neutrality agreement

[64] Sally Bedell Smith, *Reflected Glory: The Life of Pamela Churchill Harriman* (New York: Simon and Schuster, 1997), 257.

[65] Frederick Nolting, "Kennedy, NATO, and Southeast Asia", in *Diplomacy, Administration, and Policy: The Ideas and Careers of Frederick E. Nolting, Jr., Frederick C. Mosher, and Paul T. David*, ed. Kenneth W. Thompson (Lanham, Md.: University Press of America; Charlottesville, Va.: Miller Center, University of Virginia, 1995), 34–35.

[66] Abramson, *Spanning the Century*, 601.

[67] Ibid., 587.

would cause serious national security problems for South Vietnam and further weaken the relationship between Saigon and Washington. He and Harriman had "rather hot and heavy" arguments on several occasions, he said.

> And when it finally shaped up so that practically all of the safeguards were removed, President Diem and his government had grave misgivings as to whether they should sign the agreement. By and large, I agreed with that point of view because I felt that without the safeguards, the treaty would be violated. The Ho Chi Minh Trail would be, in effect, opened up completely to the North Vietnamese for infiltrating South Vietnam. And this would make it very difficult to maintain, to carry out, the policy of the Kennedy Administration, vis-à-vis South Vietnam—which was to support their independence. So, at that point, difficulties did begin to develop between our mission and Averell Harriman.[68]

Before the declaration of neutrality was signed, the Harriman-Nolting dispute spilled into the American press. In a newspaper interview, Nolting said that he told Harriman he could not support the agreement in good conscience because it was immoral for the U.S. government to break promises it had made to President Diem. According to Nolting, Harriman had retorted that they were not working for God but for the Kennedy administration.[69]

As previously mentioned, Harriman became assistant secretary of state for Far Eastern affairs after he negotiated the Laotian deal. It would seem he had such a promotion in mind by the way he maintained such a singular determination to please President Kennedy, by giving him an alternative to military intervention in Laos almost regardless of the cost. He reversed course from the one spelled out in his earlier public statements about the need for enforcement of Laotian neutrality, for example: "In the view of my Government,... we cannot have an effective cease-fire agreement without the widespread investigation by the ICC and cooperation from the parties in Laos."[70] And he bullied the president of South Vietnam to override his better

---

[68] Nolting, interview by O'Brien, interview 3, pp. 84–86.

[69] Editorial, Week's End, *Richmond News Leader*, June 9, 1962, 10, Nolting Papers, box 23, Professional Papers—Newsclippings, 1 of 2.

[70] Statements made at Geneva, May 31, 1961, in United States Department of State, *American Foreign Policy* (Washington, D.C.: United States Government Printing Office, 1961), 1013, quoted in Goldstein, *American Policy toward Laos*, 249.

judgement also. After Harriman won the Russian's acceptance of the agreement, he met with President Diem in Saigon to demand that he sign it. As Nolting recalled, Harriman "had a long talk with President Diem and rather forcefully told him that he'd better sign it despite President Diem's well-founded misgivings. And this was a rather rugged interview between the two of them."[71]

Harriman and Diem had met before, when Harriman had travelled to Saigon in 1961 to compel Diem to support the direction the Laos talks were taking. From that first fateful meeting, Harriman and Diem "took a violent dislike to each other", said Nguyen Dinh Thuan, South Vietnam's secretary of state for security co-ordination. "It was very unfortunate. Diem did not understand Harriman's role in the Democratic Party and Harriman did not understand Diem."[72] One could argue that the two men understood each other very well, that each took the measure of the other and did not like what he saw. While in that first meeting with Diem, Harriman turned off his hearing aid and dozed while the South Vietnamese president explained that the Communists could not be trusted, listing all of the nefarious ways they had already behaved. An American embassy official took Harriman's behaviour as calculated rudeness to demonstrate his disdain for Diem.[73]

To please the Americans, Diem reluctantly agreed to send a delegation to Geneva to sign the neutrality agreement, even though he knew it would put South Vietnam in a terrible position: it would give North Vietnam free reign with its troops in Laos while preventing the South Vietnamese and their allies from incursions into Laos to defend themselves against them. The solution hammered out by Harriman was perceived by the GVN as worse than no solution at all.[74] Some Kennedy observers hailed the Laotian settlement of 1962 as a diplomatic triumph. "Well, if that was a triumph of diplomacy," said Ambassador Nolting years later in a speech at the University of Virginia, "I don't

---

[71] Nolting, interview by O'Brien, interview 3, 88–89.

[72] Quoted in Hammer, *Death in November*, 31.

[73] Abramson, *Spanning the Century*, 606.

[74] Hammer stated: "In 1961, Diem might have accepted a partitioned Laos if that were the only way to cut the Ho Chi Minh Trail, even (he said) a hostile Laos where he would have been free to harass Communist bases and communication lines. But not this 'neutrality' preached by Harriman that would stigmatize South Vietnamese forces as aggressors if they entered Laos, while leaving the North Vietnamese free to use Laotian territory as they chose because the treaty lacked any enforceable safeguards." Hammer, *Death in November*, 30.

the meaning of the word." He then gave the following summary of the evolution of the agreement:

> Averell Harriman was the negotiator. He told me that he was under instructions from President Kennedy to get a settlement of the Laotian question at any cost. In the early days of the Kennedy Administration, President Kennedy went on television and said we were going to take a stand in Laos. Those of you who know the inaccessibility of Laos can understand how horrified the Joint Chiefs of Staff were to hear that the President had decided to make a stand in Laos. There wasn't any way to get in there except by air and that didn't make much sense. So the President backed-off of that idea and decided Vietnam was the place to make the stand. But then, as if in order to open up the flank of Vietnam, he ordered the Laotian settlement. This treaty definitely weakened, both physically and from the point of view of morale, the chances of the successful defense of South Vietnam.[75]

What proved to be one of the most damaging, and ultimately fatal, outcomes of the Laotian settlement, at least for Ngo Dinh Diem, was the ill will it produced between the governments of the United States and South Vietnam. As the failure of the policy became more and more apparent, an ever-widening gulf grew between Harriman and his DOS faction on one side and Diem, Nolting, and their DOS and DOD supporters on the other side. As Laos was overrun by the North Vietnamese and the attacks on South Vietnam increased, Kennedy's original promise of a noninterference in the GVN was compromised more and more. Further, the DOD and DOS became divided over how to defeat the Communists in South Vietnam. The foundation for the tragic ending of American involvement in Vietnam, therefore, was the Laotian agreement.

[75] Nolting, "Kennedy, NATO, and Southeast Asia", 20.

5

The Counterinsurgency Plan

Kennedy's government had stumbled badly over the Laotian deal, and now American plans to counter the insurgency in South Vietnam would have to be conducted in the face of this blunt reality. As Sir Robert Thompson explained, the 1962 Laos agreement gave the North Vietnamese "free run down through Laos and Cambodia, and it kept the United States out of Laos." For North Vietnam and its Communist allies, "that was the whole purpose of the Agreement."[1] With their unfettered access to South Vietnam, the Communist insurgents would become an even greater threat.

Even before the agreement was signed, the situation in South Vietnam was deteriorating. In November 1961 a report stating as much was submitted to President Kennedy by Walt Rostow, deputy national security advisor, and General Maxwell Taylor, Kennedy's chief military advisor.[2] To stop the insurgency, the Taylor-Rostow report recommended improved training of ARVN troops, greater use of helicopters, increased bombing of the North, and deployment of more U.S. combat troops. Such a response was needed, according to a memo from Rostow to President Kennedy, because the number of infiltrators who had crossed the Laotian border had grown from two thousand to sixteen thousand within two years.[3] Rostow warned Kennedy not to focus

---

[1] Robert Thompson, "Rear Bases and Sanctuaries", in *The Lessons of Vietnam*, ed. W. Scott Thompson and Donaldson D. Frizzell (New York: Crane, Russak, 1977), 101.

[2] After the failed Bay of Pigs invasion of Cuba in April 1961, President Kennedy lost faith in his Joint Chiefs of Staff and appointed Korean War commander Taylor as his chief military advisor. On October 1, 1962, Kennedy made Taylor chairman of the Joint Chiefs of Staff.

[3] Walt W. Rostow, "Memorandum from the President's Deputy Special Assistant for National Security Affairs (Rostow) to the President", November 14, 1961, Washington, in *FRUS, 1961–1963*, vol. 1, document 251, p. 601. These figures are a little in excess of Hanoi's own records, which show North Vietnam sent approximately 14,573 infiltrators to the South

on whether Diem was the right leader for South Vietnam, as if the country's problem was its head of state. Rather, the "gut issue", he wrote, was whether the United States was going to take immediate and decisive action against the Communists. Rostow expressed his worry that American indecision would allow the enemy to gain too much ground, possibly leading to an American overreaction and then war. At this stage, Rostow defended Diem. Later, under pressure from the Harriman group, he would turn against Diem.

In October 1961, Ngo Dinh Nhu invited the U.S. deputy assistant for special operations, General Edward Lansdale, to a meeting about the Laos negotiations. As Lansdale reported back to Washington, Nhu informed him that Southeast Asian governments from Thailand to the Philippines were shocked by the direction of the talks. Meanwhile, they were giving the Communist insurgents in South Vietnam a propaganda tool. In southern rural areas, the insurgents were telling the people that the agreement would be a victory for their side and a portent of their future success; therefore they had better join the winning team. Thus, the Communists were making meaningful political gains at the village level, Lansdale warned, while the West, particularly the United States, still failed either to appreciate their losing score or to do something about it.[4]

Owing to the increase in insurgent activity in South Vietnam in 1961, the Americans began to search for ways to combat it successfully, hence the Taylor-Rostow report. The post–World War II years had not been kind to the American armed forces. Their budgets had been slashed and their manpower demobilised. More important, there had been no real new thinking about internal war based on either recent experience or analysis in the U.S. service academies. As late as 1964, warfare expert David Galula noted:

> Although analyses of revolutionary wars from the revolutionary's point of view are numerous today, there is a vacuum of studies from the other side, particularly when it comes to suggesting concrete courses of action

---

in this period. Steven Young, "A Very Accurate Threat Assessment: The State Department Vietnam White Papers of 1961 and 1964 in Retrospect", paper presented at "After the Cold War: Reassessing Vietnam", Second Triennial Symposium, Vietnam Center and Archive, Texas Tech University, Lubbock, Tex., April 18–20, 1996.

[4] Edward Lansdale, "Memorandum from the Secretary of Defense's Deputy Assistant for Special Forces (Lansdale) to the President's Military Representative (Taylor)", October 21, 1961, Saigon, in FRUS, 1961–1963, vol. 1, document 182, pp. 411–12.

for the counterrevolutionary. Very little is offered beyond formulas—which are sound enough as far as they go—such as, 'Intelligence is the key to the problem,' or 'The support of the population must be won.' How to turn the key, how to win the support, this is where frustrations usually begin, as anyone can testify who, in a humble or in an exalted position, has been involved in a revolutionary war on the wrong—i.e., the arduous—side.[5]

Because Kennedy's advisors were bereft of new ideas, they reached for the strategy that had been drafted by the previous Eisenhower administration, in spite of having campaigned against it, and developed the Counterinsurgency Plan (CIP).[6] Official U.S. Army historian and analyst General S. L. A. Marshall argued that all the Kennedy administration did was warm over the old Korean War model of limited warfare. "Promoted ostensibly as a safeguard against the possibility of a small war getting beyond containment and mushrooming into an atomic eclipse, it postulated that a great power could conduct fighting operations with a stringent economy of force and could, in effect, buy success at the lowest possible price. I could not believe one word of it."[7] General Marshall, who had served as an operations analyst of U.S. forces during the Korean War, wrote that the CIP reflected Defense Secretary Robert McNamara's predilection for a "bean-counter's" war "on the cheap", but beefing up the ARVN and sending in some helicopters was not

[5] Galula then listed those on the arduous side: "The junior officer in the field who, after weeks and months of endless tracking, has at last destroyed the dozen guerrillas opposing him, only to see them replaced by a fresh dozen; the civil servant who pleaded in vain for a five-cent reform and is now ordered to implement at once a hundred-dollar program when he no longer controls the situation in his district; the general who has 'cleared' Sector A but screams because 'they' want to take away two battalions for Sector B; the official in charge of the press who cannot satisfactorily explain why, after so many decisive victories, the rebels are still vigorous and expanding; the congressman who cannot understand why the government should get more money when it has so little to show for the huge appropriations previously granted; the chief of state, harassed from all sides, who wonders how long he will last—these are typical illustrations of the plight of the counterrevolutionary." David Galula, *Counter-Insurgency Warfare: Theory and Practice* (New York: Frederick A. Praeger, 1964), xii.

[6] L. L. Lemnitzer [chairman, Joint Chiefs of Staff], "Memorandum for the Secretary of Defense; Subject: Recommendations on South Vietnam", April 11, 1961, in *U.S. Involvement in the War, Internal Documents: The Kennedy Administration, January 1961–November 1963, Book I*, section V.B.4 of bk. 11 of *United States–Vietnam Relations, 1945–1967: Study Prepared by the Department of Defense*, by Congress, House, Committee on Armed Services (Washington, D.C.: United States Government Printing Office, 1971), 19–21.

[7] S. L. A. Marshall, "Thoughts on Vietnam", in Thompson and Frizzell, *Lessons of Vietnam*, 47.

going to defeat the insurgents in Vietnam.[8] Critics such as Marshall, however, had nothing else to offer Kennedy other than to suggest that America either withdraw from Vietnam or move in with massive force. To the politically astute Kennedy, both of Marshall's options were unsavoury, and he authorised the implementation of the CIP.

Dean Rusk cabled the heart of the CIP to the American embassy in Saigon. First, U.S. funding for the Vietnamese armed forces was increased to $28.4 million for fiscal year 1961/1962 so that another twenty thousand men could be added to the ranks. Second, $12.7 million was allocated to increase the Civil Guard to thirty-two thousand men, who would protect villages from terror attacks. Third, $660,000 was to be spent on psychological operations and the purchase of communications equipment.[9] This was a substantial financial commitment on the part of the Kennedy administration, and the president himself had personally approved this pledge.[10]

In Rusk's correspondence to Ambassador Nolting, he stressed that the aid to South Vietnam was contingent on President Diem liberalising his government and gaining cooperation from his opposition in Saigon.[11] The Kennedy administration demanded changes in the roles and the relationships within the GVN as they pertained to the CIP. For example, Diem was to abandon his bilinear chain of command "in favor of a single command line with integrated effort at all levels within the government, and to create the governmental machinery for coordinated national planning". Implicit in this requirement was the judgement that President Diem was an ineffectual leader who needed to give control, especially of the armed forces, over to the Americans.[12] A month later,

---

[8] Ibid., 48.

[9] Dean Rusk to American embassy in Saigon, "Joint State-Defense-ISA [Office of International Security Affairs] Message; [subject: counterinsurgency plan]", telegram, February 3, 1961, no. 2761, in Congress, House, Committee on Armed Services, *U.S. Involvement in the War: Book I*, 14.

[10] John F. Kennedy, "Memorandum For: The Secretary of State [and] the Secretary of Defense", January 30, 1961, White House, Washington, in Congress, House, Committee on Armed Services, *U.S. Involvement in the War: Book I*, 13.

[11] Rusk, "Joint State-Defense-ISA Message", 14–16.

[12] Congress, House, Committee on Armed Services, *Evolution of the War: The Strategic Hamlet Program, 1961–1963*, section IV.B.2 of bk. 3 of *United States–Vietnam Relations, 1945–1967: Study Prepared by the Department of Defense* (Washington, D.C.: United States Government Printing Office, 1971), 7–8.

in another telegram to Ambassador Nolting, mention was made of the successful British counterinsurgency in Malaya. Nolting was told to approach them to see if they would help in the training of the ARVN and the Civil Guard even before Diem approved the CIP.[13]

Before examining the conceptual flaws in the CIP, it is important to recognise its usurpation of Diem's authority. General Lansdale commented on the arrogance of this approach in his communications with government officials,[14] and his admonishments were partially responsible for the assignment of Ambassador Nolting in the spring of 1961. Nevertheless, even after Nolting had taken over the U.S. mission to Saigon, the influential individuals within DOS, such as Averell Harriman, continued to insist that the way to deal with Diem was to lay down the law. Nolting's assignment proved to be simply a pause in their plan to remove Diem. Indeed, during Durbrow's tenure as ambassador, DOS official John Steeves had drawn up a top secret plan for replacing the Vietnamese president, which was sent to Nolting as a "contingency plan" in the event Diem did not follow American orders.[15]

Returning to the problems associated with the CIP, a brief look at how the Americans viewed the ARVN in the 1960s is useful. DOD analysts indicated in September 1960 that the ARVN had the capability and the flexibility to fight either external aggressors (i.e., the NVA) or internal guerrillas (i.e., the Viet Cong). There was, however, an acknowledgement that "militia type home guards and civil guards should be trained and equipped. Accelerated efforts should be undertaken to develop the paramilitary and police forces."[16] In addition, as the British had done

[13] Dean Rusk, "Telegram from the Department of State to the Embassy in Vietnam", March 1, 1961, Washington, in *FRUS, 1961–1963*, vol. 1, document 16, pp. 40–41.

[14] For example, see Edward Geary Lansdale, "Memorandum for Secretary of Defense [and] Deputy Secretary of Defense; Subject: Vietnam", [between January 14 and 17, 1961], in "U.S. Perceptions of the Insurgency, 1954–1960", tab 4 of Congress, House, Committee on Armed Services, *Evolution of the War: Origins of the Insurgency, 1954–1960*, 69, 73.

[15] United States Department of State, "Memorandum Prepared in the Department of State: Suggested Contingency Plan", October 20, 1961, Washington, enclosure to "Letter from the Assistant Secretary of State for Far Eastern Affairs (McConaughy) to the Ambassador in Vietnam (Nolting)", by Walter McConaughy, in *FRUS, 1961–1963*, vol. 1, document 181, pp. 408–11.

[16] "Contrasting DOD [Department of Defense] and State Appreciations", Defense 982994 to CINCPAC, 162156Z Sep 60, in "U.S. Perceptions of the Insurgency", tab 4 of Congress, House, Committee on Armed Services, *Evolution of the War: Origins of the Insurgency, 1954–1960*, 62.

in Malaya, "for the duration of the emergency campaign, operational control of all security activities should be under centralized direction."[17] In spite of these nods to the British expertise in counterinsurgency warfare, DOD focus continued to be on conventional warfare controlled by MAAG through the ARVN in the field. When it became apparent that the ARVN was unable to contain and destroy the source of the insurgency, the solution appeared to be the CIP, which, as previously indicated, called for substantial increases in South Vietnamese armed forces. It also called for major changes in Diem's government, because supposedly his resistance to outside control of his government was partly responsible for the failure to stop the insurgency.[18]

General Lansdale, however, did not assign blame to the GVN but put the onus on the Americans. He acknowledged in one of his many memos to General Taylor that "the Vietnamese governmental machinery seems to be bogged down, and somehow things simply don't get done effectively enough."[19] But sending more aid and changing organisational structures will not correct the inefficiency, he added, because the root of the problem is America's condescending treatment of the South Vietnamese. He therefore advised a more respectful and collaborative approach:

> The Vietnamese are an able and energetic people. They don't seem to be themselves today. They are going to lose their country if some spark doesn't make them catch fire to go to work to win this war. The spark could well be to place the right Americans into the right areas of the Vietnamese government to provide operational guidance. These Americans should be collaborators, who quietly advise some key Vietnamese leaders on how to get things moving effectively, and are physically close enough to them to permit the guidance to be constant. Such work will require Americans of talent and compassion, who will engage in the task with considerable empathy. Perhaps the wisest method of selecting them would be to let each

[17] Ibid.

[18] "The unsuccessful U.S. attempts to secure organizational reforms within the Diem government had assumed psychological primacy by the time of General Taylor's October 1961 mission to Saigon. The American position was essentially that no operational plan could succeed unless GVN was reorganized to permit effective implementation." Congress, House, Committee on Armed Services, *Evolution of the War: Strategic Hamlet Program*, 9–10.

[19] Edward Geary Lansdale, "Memorandum from the Secretary of Defense's Deputy Assistant for Special Operations (Lansdale) to the President's Military Representative (Taylor)", October 23, 1961, Saigon, in *FRUS, 1961–1963*, vol. 1, document 185, pp. 418–19.

Vietnamese name the American he would like as an advisor; then the U.S. should go to work to make those people available.[20]

Lansdale's emphasis was clear: it was the Americans who were causing the Vietnamese to react in the lethargic manner being reported. Many of the advisors treated the Vietnamese with frustration or contempt, which in turn only engendered more distrust and slowness of action. In stressing the damage this was doing to the fight against the Viet Cong, Lansdale warned that the future of South Vietnam hung in the balance. He believed that the Vietnamese would lose their existential fight against the Communists unless the Americans helped them in a more positive manner.

Lansdale sent several other memoranda to Taylor. The theme remained consistent: the Americans needed to correct their relations with the Vietnamese; they especially needed to stop their harangue of Diem. Lansdale wrote a fairly tough letter to General Samuel T. Williams, the former commander of MAAG, seeking his help against the growing anti-Diem group in Washington. It lays bare the depth of the problem with regard to the powerful Americans who thought they could fix South Vietnam by removing its president:

> One of the conclusions drawn in town, and both Taylor and Rostow say it isn't one of theirs (although I'm suspicious) is that we cannot help the VN [Vietnamese] win against the VC as long as a dictator (Diem) holds power. So, one of the thoughts being ginned up is that I go over as his personal advisor and, presumably, clobber him from up close. I pointed out that this was a duty without honor and I'd be damned if I'd do that.... We probably will be boosting our help by a lot more men, money and material. However, what's really lacking is something of the spirit, something of leadership qualities on our part, which would give meaning to our aid. It's pure hell to be on the sidelines and seeing so conventional and unimaginative an approach being tried.... Rather than end this on a gloomy downbeat, let's noodle out how to lick the crowd. One of the main problems is here at home, with Washington being only one phase. Do you feel up to entering the fray again—against folks of Durbrow's ilk—but much subtler?[21]

[20] Ibid.

[21] Edward Geary Lansdale, "Letter from the Secretary of Defense's Assistant for Special Operations (Lansdale) to General Samuel T. Williams", November 28, 1961, Washington, in *FRUS, 1961–1963*, vol. 1, document 293, pp. 687–89.

The phrase "folks of Durbrow's ilk—but much subtler" refers to Averell Harriman and other anti-Diem officials.[22] General Williams was known to have influence at the Pentagon, and Lansdale knew he needed some powerful men on his side when he went up against them. Even with Williams' support, Lansdale's numerous memos and letters had little effect on the implementation of the CIP.

Although the CIP referred to the British counterinsurgency in Malaya, it left out some of its key principles of success, and one of these was that the military cannot replace proper civilian authority. The British had understood, perhaps out of their own raw impecunious necessity in the aftermath of World War II, that bombs and bullets cannot replace a functioning government. As Robert Thompson explained, the insurgent challenge in Malaya was the same as it was in Vietnam: the insurgents in both places were contesting the incumbent regime's legitimacy and offering themselves as the authentic voice of the people. The fundamental difference between the British campaign in Malaya and the American-sponsored endeavour in Vietnam was that the British never lost sight of the paramount necessity of maintaining the legitimacy of the current government, while the Americans, taking their cues from Communist propaganda, did. Heeding the complaints of Diem's critics, Washington tried to compel Diem's government to become more democratic, in violation of another key principle of British success: in a Communist insurrection, it is vastly more important for the people to feel protected by their national government than for them to feel that they have a say in their government. Indeed, in order to provide national security, the British emergency measures and laws in Malaya were far tougher and more undemocratic than anything the Americans were prepared to countenance in Vietnam.[23]

---

[22] Harriman's attitude toward Diem can be seen in these words in a letter he wrote during the Laos negotiations and the development of the CIP: "The best any international settlement can do is to buy time. If the Government of South Viet-Nam continues a repressive, dictatorial and unpopular regime, the country will not long retain its independence. Nor can the United States afford to stake its prestige there. We must make it clear to Diem that we mean business about internal reform. This will require a strong ambassador who can control all U.S. activities (political, military, economic, etc.) and who is known by Diem to have the personal intimacy and confidence of the President and the Secretary." W. Averell Harriman, "Letter from the Ambassador at Large (Harriman) to the President", November 12, 1961, Washington, in *FRUS, 1961–1963*, vol. 1, document 239, pp. 580–82.

[23] Robert Grainger Thompson, *Defeating Communist Insurgency: Experiences from Malaya and Vietnam* (London: Chatto and Windus, 1966), 20.

Thompson kept a steady and critical eye on Washington's tendency to be swayed by the criticisms of Diem's government. While the GVN was not without fault, he argued, the exaggerated accusations being made by the Communists were without basis in reality and should therefore not have been the basis of American policy:

> If the Vietcong had had a good cause within South Vietnam, the whole country would have collapsed long ago. This does not mean that there may not have been a good cause at some time in the past before the present conflict, because that was essential to establish the basic organisation for People's Revolutionary War in the first place.... The Vietcong's basic organisation was already in existence and was inherited from the Vietminh. The shortcomings of the Diem regime and the contradictions within Vietnamese society were the excuse rather than the reason for the insurgency.[24]

The Americans were vulnerable to Communist propaganda because they lacked patience, Thompson wrote, which is one of the three indispensable qualities in counterinsurgency, along with determination and an offensive spirit.[25] American politicians expected rapid results to flow from their wealth and power and they needed them in order to please the press and, through them, their constituencies. Hanoi took advantage of this weakness by denying the Americans a quick victory. The North Vietnamese, according to Thompson, had seen four main avenues to victory: (1) failure of American resolution; (2) failure of South Vietnamese resolution; (3) failure of the Americans and the Vietnamese to adopt the correct counterstrategy; and (4) failure of the South Vietnamese to build, even with American aid, a stable and viable government.[26] Even if only one of these avenues was open, Hanoi stood a good chance of winning and achieving its minimum war aim, reunification of Vietnam under Communist rule. The maximum war aim was to visit

---

[24] Thompson added, "The original organisation [of the Viet Cong] was built up during the Japanese War and then forged during the Vietminh War against the French colonial power. This organisation could not have been created from scratch in South Vietnam, on the basis of the cause which the Vietcong were promoting at the beginning of the present war in the short time available between 1954 and 1959. If that had been the case President Diem would have had little difficulty in dealing with it as he dealt with the Binh Xuyen bandits in Saigon immediately after he came to power." Robert Thompson, *No Exit from Vietnam*, updated ed. (New York: David McKay, 1970), 30–31.

[25] Thompson, *Defeating Communist Insurgency*, 171.

[26] Thompson, *No Exit from Vietnam*, 63–64.

a humiliating defeat on the United States. The key to Hanoi's strategic planning, then, was American impatience, because all four avenues to Communist victory incorporated varying degrees of this crucial American shortcoming.

As previously noted, Vo Nguyen Giap was a student of history, and military history in particular, and he therefore likely knew how America fought its wars. Given Giap's background, Thompson wrote, he knew that the longer the insurgency dragged on, the more anti-war pressure would mount within American society. The requirements of counterinsurgency warfare, including its political necessities, and the failure of the American public to understand them would lead to an eventual American withdrawal. Thus, Thompson concluded, Hanoi would make the war a test of wills, not a test of strength, and would expect the Americans, regardless of their power, to prove as faltering as the French had.[27]

Robert Thompson arrived in Saigon in the fall of 1961 at the request of President Diem. As head of the British Advisory Mission to South Vietnam, his primary task was to advise Diem and his American allies on a strategy for pacifying the rural areas that were being infiltrated, and those that were already being controlled, by the Viet Cong.[28] He began developing a plan at the same time that the U.S. government was formulating the CIP, and some American officials worried that a rivalry between the two plans would ensue.[29]

For his part, Ambassador Nolting "welcomed the British initiative". As he wrote in his memoirs, "The Malaya experience was something of a counterpart to Vietnam, and we could learn from it." Nolting was impressed with Thompson, who had been highly recommended to Diem by Malaysian Prime Minister Tunku Abdul Rahman.

---

[27] Ibid.

[28] Robert B. Asprey, *War in the Shadows: The Guerrilla in History* (New York: William Morrow, 1994), 739–40.

[29] "Thompson provided Diem with his initial 'appreciation' (or, in U.S. terminology, 'estimate of the situation') in October 1961. His assessment was well received by the President, who asked him to follow it up with a specific plan. Thompson's response, an outline plan for the pacification of the Delta area, was given to the President on 13 November. In effect, Thompson was in the process of articulating one potentially comprehensive strategic approach at the same time that the U.S. was deeply involved in fashioning a major new phase in U.S.-GVN relations in which major new U.S. aid would be tied to Diem's acceptance of specified reforms and, inferentially, to his willingness to pursue some agreed, coordinated strategy. Thompson's plan was, in short, a potential rival to the American-advanced plans represented by the CIP and the geographically phased MAAG plan of September 1961." Congress, House, Committee on Armed Services, *Evolution of the War: Strategic Hamlet Program*, 10.

Thompson had only about half a dozen people working for him, all of whom … had served under Sir Gerald Templar in Malaya. They did not have much more than their individual experience to work with, but they were effective. They worked closely with the South Vietnamese and with us, advising on pacification and anti-infiltration methods. Thompson himself was very persuasive and had considerable influence with President Diem.[30]

Thompson advised the Vietnamese government to select an area in the Mekong Delta that could be adequately cleared of Viet Cong by the army and then be protected from further Communist activity through a system of fortified hamlets protected by their own civil defence units. This plan came to be called the Strategic Hamlet Program (SHP), and in it Ngo Dinh Diem found a way to avoid the impending American control of his government and thus becoming, or at least appearing as, an American puppet. Some Americans called Thompson's ideas "advice without responsibility".[31] There was much more, however, to Thompson's SHP than the possibility of saving Diem from further U.S. control. Simply put, it was based on recent Southeast Asian experience, and it had common sense logic that would balance the advice and pressure coming from Washington.

According to the Pentagon analysts, Thompson shared a common understanding with General Taylor: both men saw that the Viet Cong were attempting to force a political outcome in their favour by using military actions combined with political ones as opposed to a straight-out attempt to take over the country by force. But General Taylor, along with General Lionel McGarr, commander of MAAG, thought the Viet Cong would focus their efforts on seizing control of the unpopulated areas in order to use them as bases from which they could launch attacks on Saigon (such an area existed northeast of Saigon and was known as War Zone D). These bases would also be used by the Viet Cong to project an image of political control and legitimacy to the people of South Vietnam.[32]

Thompson, on the other hand, believed the real thrust of the Viet Cong would be to assault the political stability of the populated rural

---

[30] Frederick Nolting, *From Trust to Tragedy: The Political Memoirs of Frederick Nolting, Kennedy's Ambassador to Diem's Vietnam* (New York: Praeger, 1988), 37.

[31] Congress, House, Committee on Armed Services, *Evolution of the War: Strategic Hamlet Program*, 10.

[32] Ibid.

areas. In other words, while recognising that the Communist threat to assail Saigon was valid, Thompson thought the real war, the contest for political legitimacy, would be fought in the small agrarian villages. American planners, like McGarr and Taylor, were still thinking in terms of classic military assault, albeit via guerrilla action, on the capital. Thus, their plans were based on the belief that the Communists' political and military objectives could be smashed if the Viet Cong forces were destroyed. Thompson argued that the main GVN and American goal should be not merely to destroy the Viet Cong's field forces but to offer the people of South Vietnam an attractive, constructive, and positive option in place of the Communists' appeals. The focus for the GVN and the Americans, therefore, should be national reconstruction with infra-structure development in the populated rural areas—a tough, lengthy, and expensive gambit.[33]

The program envisioned by Thompson would require thoroughgoing and tight security measures, but these procedures could be successfully undertaken by police as opposed to soldiers. His experience dictated that policemen could establish a close rapport with the people as they lived and worked in the very communities they protected. Army units could not do this because they were constantly needed in those areas where the fiercest fighting required their resources. Not only that, but if an army unit spent too long in a given area, daily life for the average Viet-namese would take on the regimen of military occupancy. Therefore, in the Thompson understanding, the army's purpose was to keep main Viet Cong units off-balance in order to prevent them from carrying out insurgent attacks in the areas the GVN was trying to stabilise with recon-struction and police programs. Additionally, the army could be used to reinforce the police in extreme situations. In short, the focus of SHP was to win the loyalty of the people, their hearts and minds, rather than to kill Viet Cong. Thompson's plan of toned-down violence naturally appealed to Diem, who detested violence; even the killing of the most radical Communists was abhorrent to him.

Given the priority of winning support for the government, Thomp-son chose an area in the Mekong Delta that had seen little Viet Cong main force activity. He argued that the GVN needed to "clear and hold" this area and that such a direction had to replace the counterproductive ARVN "search and destroy" sweeps that, to date, had been advised

[33] Ibid.

and directed by American military advisors. He acknowledged that the ARVN could be used to protect the villages temporarily while the inhabitants organised their own civil defence and that the ARVN could come to the aid of a village that needed reinforcement, but performing big sweeps through an area and then subsequently leaving it had to be abandoned. All these sweeps had done was to destabilise the villagers and their way of life when what they really needed from their government was the assurance of physical security so that the economic and social improvements being attempted could proceed without violent and destabilising interruptions.

Once the area was cleared of Viet Cong, the strategic hamlets would be constructed. The typical strategic hamlet would be a lightly guarded village in a relatively low-risk area. Defended hamlets would be more heavily fortified villages in areas where there had been more Viet Cong activity. These would also receive people who had been removed from areas already subverted by the Viet Cong. Defended hamlets would be particularly useful in areas closer to the Cambodian border, through which the Viet Cong were constantly moving.

SHP caused real and immediate problems for the Americans, since Diem seemed prepared to implement it immediately and to circumvent American control of the counterinsurgency effort. Ambassador Nolting sent a telegram to Washington saying that Thompson's plan was first-rate but that it should be submitted to the Kennedy administration for review; after all, the Americans would be paying the costs and should therefore have a real say in the program's implementation.[34] This telegram disproves the assertion that Nolting was so sympathetic toward Diem that he ignored U.S. policy directives. In fact, the telegram reported that Nolting had held a meeting with British Ambassador Henry Arthur Frederick Hohler, Robert Thompson, and General McGarr to register Washington's disapproval of what the British had done.[35] At that meeting, Nolting supported General McGarr's proposal to go after the Viet Cong–infested area of War Zone D north of Saigon. He also explained that the U.S. government disagreed with the command structures that Thompson had proposed to Diem, which would have allowed the president to go around the field command of the ARVN and thus MAAG

---

[34] Frederick Nolting, "Telegram from the Embassy in Vietnam to the Department of State", November 30, 1961, Saigon, in *FRUS, 1961–1963*, vol. 1, document 299, pp. 698–700.
[35] Ibid.

by directing military operations straight from the palace—something the Americans had been trying to eliminate. Ambassador Nolting was caught in a dilemma. On one hand he genuinely liked both Diem and Thompson and could see the value of the very practical, nonmilitary approach that Thompson was advocating. On the other hand, it was his duty, as U.S. mission chief in South Vietnam, to adhere to his instructions from Washington and to implement American policy.

Despite the disagreement between the Americans and the British, one aspect of Thompson's advice—that the real contest was for the hearts and minds of the peasants in rural South Vietnam—clearly won everyone over. Even the Communists saw the potential of this program to create a wedge between them and the peasants in South Vietnam. Communist General Nguyen Chi Thanh called the idea of establishing strategic hamlets "a relatively clearheaded conclusion".[36]

There was a Vietnamese predecessor to the SHP, the 1959 Agroville Program. The main purpose of this earlier plan was to strengthen the government's ties with the rural population. Like the later SHP, the Agroville Program involved moving peasants who lived far distances from each other along the Mekong River canals into settlements where they could be protected from guerrilla coercion, propaganda, and terror. The population density of the agrovilles would make defending the people easier. It would also allow the GVN to provide electricity, schools, and medical centres, as well as training in new agricultural techniques. It was Diem's hope that these settlements would "stabilize the government's authority in the face of increasing incidents of assassination and kidnapping of rural officials".[37] Although the U.S. government supplied nearly 60 per cent of the funding for the agrovilles, it had hardly any control of the program, which ultimately failed. This fact would weigh substantially in future American involvement with this sort of counter-insurgency effort in South Vietnam.

The Agroville Program failed but for reasons more complex than those allowed by the standard versions of history, which cite poor planning and mismanagement.[38] According to historian Dennis Duncanson,

[36] Quoted in Ellen J. Hammer, *A Death in November: America in Vietnam, 1963* (New York: E. P. Dutton, 1987), 41.

[37] Richard A. Hunt, *Pacification: The American Struggle for Vietnam's Hearts and Minds* (Boulder, Colo.: Westview Press, 1995), 20.

[38] See Stanley Karnow, *Vietnam: A History* (New York: Viking Press, 1983), 231.

an acknowledged authority on the political history of South Vietnam, the agrovilles were not initially intended for bringing all rural South Vietnamese closer together. Instead, they were to bring "unreliable families" together in order to divorce them from the sway of the Viet Cong. These families, however, were never free of Communist pressure.[39] Recognising the threat of the agrovilles, the Viet Cong mounted raids on the settlements "but most often employed terrorism and threats against government officials to intimidate people and impede work".[40]

William Colby noted that the agrovilles had potential but proved to be indefencible. It was a fine idea, he said, to "move the people together and then give them these amenities, these steps toward modernization and organizing and so forth".[41] But as the families were drawn closer together in the agrovilles, Colby explained, they became distanced from their rice fields. Although there were complaints about the distance, the greater challenge was to defend the space in which the families actually lived. The GVN gave each family dwelling a plot of land for growing vegetables and maintaining livestock. These plots of land extended the distance between dwellings to the point that there was an average of ten family dwellings per square kilometre. This was closer than the inhabitants had been when they were stretched out along the canals, and it certainly permitted them to access new schools and hospitals. Had there been no insurgency, the agrovilles probably would have worked, Colby maintained, but they could not be defended owing to the large areas through which the guerrillas could freely move. Setting up a defended perimeter around several families spread out over a few square kilometres was beyond the resources of the GVN. Colby saw the moving of ancestral graves, which was criticised by Diem's detractors,[42]

[39] Dennis Duncanson, *Government and Revolution in Vietnam* (London: Oxford University Press / Royal Institute of International Affairs, 1968), 261–62.

[40] Hunt, *Pacification*, 20.

[41] William Colby, interview by Ted Gittinger, June 2, 1981, Washington, D.C., interview 1, transcript, 15–16, Lyndon Baines Johnson Presidential Library Oral History Collection, University of Texas at Austin.

[42] Stanley Karnow made the classic complaint with regard to the Agroville Program: "For one thing, peasants assigned to the agroville had been uprooted from their native villages and ancestral graves, and their traditional social pattern disrupted, for reasons they could not fathom." Karnow, *Vietnam*, 231. Gabriel Kolko wrote that the project was detested by the South Vietnamese and that they did not cooperate with the program. Gabriel Kolko, *Anatomy of a War: Vietnam, the United States, and the Modern Historical Experience* (New York: Pantheon Books, 1985), 96, 103, 131.

as a minor problem compared with the difficulty of Viet Cong penetration.[43] In other words, the Agroville Program failed because the Communists successfully destabilised the settlements.

Although the agrovilles failed, Diem and his brother Ngo Dinh Nhu recognised the potential of the SHP, which offered not only the same agroville amenities but also the means for the villages to defend themselves. Other Vietnamese leaders also saw the potential. South Vietnamese Generals Cao Van Vien and Dong Van Khuyen praised the program as

> a judicious national policy, a true antidote to Communist subversive and total warfare. Its chief merit lay in the fact that it had been comprehensively designed to improve the people's living standards through socioeconomic developments at the rice-roots level. It was a sound strategic concept whose objective was to neutralize and counter balance the effects of a war without front lines by transforming the countryside into a system of mutually-supporting fortifications. It sought to build and consolidate the spirit of self-assurance, self-reliance, and voluntary participation which would sustain the nation's efforts in a protracted war of attrition.[44]

Roger Hilsman, who was no fan of Diem, also agreed with the Vietnamese president on the SHP. He too wished to see a reduction of the emphasis on traditional military answers in favour of more political solutions. SHP, he said, was more than a means to fight the Viet Cong but "a strategic concept based upon a true understanding of the nature of internal war".[45]

William Colby, who was in Vietnam when the SHP was implemented, explained how Ngo Dinh Nhu perceived something more in the strategic hamlets than even effective protection of the Vietnamese. More than wrap barbed wire around people, the settlements would engender community. By banding together to develop and to defend themselves, the people would experience a sense of accomplishment and take pride in what they were doing—a necessary step if they were to withstand the Communists.[46]

[43] Colby, interview by Gittinger, interview 1, pp. 15–16.

[44] Cao Van Vien and Dong Van Khuyen, *Reflections on the Vietnam War*, Indochina Monographs (Washington, D.C.: United States Army Center of Military History, 1980), 9.

[45] Quoted in Larry E. Cable, *Conflict of Myths: The Development of American Counterinsurgency Doctrine and the Vietnam War* (New York: New York University Press, 1986), 197.

[46] Colby, interview by Gittinger, interview 1, pp. 17–18.

The strategic hamlets were not as disruptive to the traditional Viet-namese way of life as some of its critics have suggested. Indeed, a historian who wrote at the time of the Vietnam War observed that as Vietnamese migrated into the southern areas of the country, in the seventeenth and eighteenth centuries, "they made use of settlement techniques which sound an echo of fortified hamlets of more recent years."[47] Over time, the farmers spread out along the canals of the Mekong Delta to be close to their land, and as a result they became isolated from each other and estranged from any national leadership, which made them vulnerable to the Viet Cong. To Diem and Nhu, the strategic hamlets held out the promise of overcoming this isolation and estrangement and stopping the insurgency. The only way they would be able to accomplish this, however, would be if the GVN could prove it had the Confucian Mandate of Heaven by being able to protect the people in the strategic hamlets and to enourage their well-being there.[48]

In 1960 a strategic hamlet had been established in Ninh Thuan Province by ARVN Colonel Nguyen Khanh.[49] Having assisted the French in fortifying villages in North Vietnam's Red River Delta, Khanh was able to transfer this knowledge to the South, where he set up several villages with fences and volunteer militia. Another early defended village was in Darlac Province under the direction of a Catholic priest. Ngo Dinh Nhu welded all these experiences together with the British advice and "created the conceptual framework for the plan and set its pace for completion".[50]

The best overview of how Ngo Dinh Nhu set the SHP into motion is found in William Colby's recollections on the subject. As Colby pointed out, the initial American response to the escalating insurgent effort was entirely predictable and formed the backbone of the Taylor-Rostow report and recommendations. The American military planners did not agree with the proposals made by Thompson and the British Advisory Mission, Colby explained, because they believed that the focus for

[47] Milton E. Osborne, *Strategic Hamlets in South Viet-Nam: A Survey and Comparison*, Data Paper 55, Cornell University, Southeast Asia Program (Ithaca, N.Y.: Southeast Asia Program, Department of Asian Studies, Cornell University, 1965), 20.

[48] Ibid.

[49] William A. Nighswonger, *Rural Pacification in Vietnam*, Praeger Special Studies in International Politics and Public Affairs (New York: Frederick A. Praeger, 1966), 54.

[50] Ibid., 55.

fighting the insurgents needed to be on the military and not on the local civil defence units called for by the SHP. General Lyman Lemnitzer, chairman of the Joint Chiefs of Staff, was particularly against the idea of the police replacing the military even for local force work.[51] The main reason for his objection was that the Joint Chiefs of Staff believed "the situation in Vietnam had degenerated to a level which police mechanisms could not deal with effectively."[52]

Ngo Dinh Nhu, however, was not convinced that the Americans were right about the SHP. On the contrary, in meetings each week with William Colby, he came to see it as the key to saving South Vietnam. In these meetings, when the two men discussed the gains that had been made by the insurgents, Nhu observed the Communists' impressive ability to recruit and to organise the peasants, training them first for small guerrilla units and then graduating them to main-force battalions. Nhu admitted to Colby that the ARVN could not stop the organisational juggernaut that the Communists had put into action. He also realised that the detailed planning in Saigon translated into little in the countryside and that the political depth of his own Can Lao Party was insubstantial compared with that of the Communist Party.[53] Thus, Colby and Nhu began to explore the ways they could use the SHP to stimulate the rural communities to defend themselves from the nocturnal raids that the Viet Cong were so masterfully carrying out. Even a few motivated armed villagers would be able to prevent them from assembling villagers for night-time political harangues and intimidating recruitment tactics. These armed villagers would also be able to prevent the extortion of "taxes" by the Viet Cong.[54]

Because of the civil defence component of the strategic hamlets, Nhu recognised that they had more potential for success than the ill-fated agrovilles. Moreover, he believed they could constitute the foundation for a new social and political order. This new polity would find its roots in rural South Vietnam and would replace the elite in Saigon that was a holdover from French colonial days. Nhu was concerned that if the Americans had too large a hand in the strategic hamlets, they would

[51] William E. Colby, *Lost Victory: A Firsthand Account of America's Sixteen-Year Involvement in Vietnam*, with James McCargar (Chicago: Contemporary Books, 1989), 98–99.

[52] Cable, *Conflict of Myths*, 191.

[53] Colby, *Lost Victory*, 98–100.

[54] Ibid.

undo the necessary desire within the South Vietnamese for self-reliance. Douglas Pike recalled that Nhu was very adamant about this point.[55] Colby, for his part, was not as concerned about the spoiling effects of American aid and control as he was excited over the fact that Nhu's vision held the necessary political elements for defeating the Communists.[56] Because President Diem's past experience as a village and district chief predisposed him to favour SHP, Nhu was able to persuade his brother to make the program a major national undertaking.[57]

[55] Douglas Pike, *Viet Cong: The Organization and Techniques of the National Liberation Front of South Vietnam* (Cambridge, Mass.: MIT Press, 1967), 66–67.

[56] Colby, *Lost Victory*, 98–100.

[57] Anne Miller, "And One for the People: The Life Story of President Ngo Dinh Diem" (unpublished manuscript, July 30, 1965), microfilm, 2:337–46. Copies of the manuscript are available through the Vietnam Center and Archive, Texas Tech University, Lubbock, Tex.

6

Policemen versus Soldiers

At the core of the SHP was the assumption that the real fight for South Vietnam was between the Communists and the South Vietnamese people, not between the Viet Cong and the South Vietnamese government. When President Diem wholeheartedly adopted the SHP, the message communicated to the Americans, both directly and indirectly, was that he rejected their counterinsurgency plan, which was based on immediate democratic reforms of his government and conventional warfare by Vietnamese and American forces controlled by the U.S. military.[1]

Their understanding of where the true fight was taking place led Robert Thompson and Ngo Dinh Nhu to slightly different conclusions about strategic hamlet security. Based on Thompson's previous Malaya experience, he thought armed forces should surround the fledgling community to protect it from attacks by the enemy and to sever any links between the inhabitants and the Viet Cong.[2] Nhu, with the help of William Colby, argued that the protection of the hamlet should begin with the inhabitants. Taking responsibility for their own defence,

---

[1] See Howard L. Burris, "Memorandum from the Vice President's Military Aide (Burris) to Vice President Johnson", March 30, 1962, Washington, in United States Department of State, *FRUS, 1961–1963*, ed. John P. Glennon, vol. 2, *Vietnam, 1962* (Washington, D.C.: United States Government Printing Office, 1990), document 136, pp. 284–85.

[2] "While all this is being created during the hold phase of operations, the close defence of the hamlet must be provided by the paramilitary forces, with the army holding the ring to prevent attacks by major insurgent units. Both the paramilitary forces and the army should be so deployed at this stage that they can rescue hamlets if attacked by more than local village guerrilla squads, which the hamlet militia should be capable of keeping at bay." Robert Grainger Thompson, *Defeating Communist Insurgency: Experiences from Malaya and Vietnam* (London: Chatto and Windus, 1966), 124.

he reasoned, would both flow from and help to strengthen the political core of the community.[3]

Ngo Dinh Nhu led the implementation of SHP.[4] To inaugurate the program, he formed committees, which held lectures and discussions, to organise the leadership of the strategic hamlets.[5] Nhu also established three initial goals for the program. First, the GVN would link the peasants in the strategic hamlets into a communications network while also providing them with local defence units that could fight off insurgent raids. These local defence units would establish an emergency reserve that could rapidly deploy to meet immediate security needs. Second, the program would motivate the inhabitants to unite and to involve themselves in the political affairs of the community. Third and most important, the program was to improve the living standards of the rural Vietnamese.[6] With these goals Nhu was attempting to create a comprehensive political and economic alternative to the Viet Cong and thereby prevent them from establishing themselves as the legitimate authority in the countryside.

Contrary to the reports in the *New York Times*, Nhu was not a disembodied intellect brooding in his study in Saigon.[7] Rufus Phillips, a CIA operative subordinate to William Colby, said Nhu had been uncertain about his ideas until he was able to visit the hamlets and to see for himself whether the SHP was working. These trips convinced Nhu that the

---

[3] According to Colby, he shared "Nhu's view, of course, having argued its advantages with him, so this difference between Thompson and myself persisted for years. We so closely agreed on the necessity of a village-based approach, however, over the military one that we remained the closest of friends and collaborators." William E. Colby, *Lost Victory: A Firsthand Account of America's Sixteen-Year Involvement in Vietnam*, with James McCargar (Chicago: Contemporary Books, 1989), 100.

[4] Sterling J. Cottrell, "Memorandum from the Director of the Vietnam Task Force (Cottrell) to the Assistant Secretary of State for Far Eastern Affairs (Harriman)", April 6, 1962, Washington, in *FRUS, 1961–1963*, vol. 2, document 149, p. 311.

[5] Milton E. Osborne, *Strategic Hamlets in South Viet-Nam: A Survey and Comparison*, Data Paper 55, Cornell University, Southeast Asia Program (Ithaca, N.Y.: Southeast Asia Program, Department of Asian Studies, Cornell University, 1965), 26.

[6] Richard A. Hunt, *Pacification: The American Struggle for Vietnam's Hearts and Minds* (Boulder, Colo.: Westview Press, 1995), 21.

[7] According to *New York Times* reporter David Halberstam, "Nhu made no attempt to conceal his lack of interest in the needs of the Vietnamese people; he was an intellectual and an aristocrat, and they were not." *The Making of a Quagmire: America and Vietnam during the Kennedy Era*, rev. ed. (New York, Alfred A. Knopf, 1988), 51.

program was sound.[8] He explained to Phillips that the strategic hamlets could defeat the Communists while assisting the rural Vietnamese people in the improvement of their way of life.

Nhu told Phillips that he envisioned a gradual blossoming of democratic institutions in the countryside through the SHP, which based local governance on free elections of hamlet chiefs and hamlet councils. As the people in the hamlets practiced self-government and experienced its positive results, Nhu explained, democracy would develop organically throughout the rural areas. Democratic reforms imposed by Saigon, under pressure from the Americans, Nhu had observed, had brought only political chaos, which the Communists had exploited, causing the need for more dictatorial powers to be exercised by the central authority. Thus, Nhu concluded that the SHP was a better way to introduce democracy.[9]

Nhu realised that the Vietnamese adoption of democracy would be a gradual process. When he visited the settlements, he investigated how their local elections were held. He explained to the villagers that election by a show of hands was not good enough because it made voters vulnerable to intimidation. Hamlet governments elected by this means could be considered only provisional, he told them, and would need to be replaced or endorsed by elections with secret ballot voting. Nhu instructed GVN workers in the strategic hamlets not to tell the people whom they should vote for.[10]

---

[8] According to Phillips: "Mr. Nhu said that although he had originated the strategic hamlet program, it was only an idea, a 'pipe-dream', to him until the last four months. Since that time he has been making constant trips to the provinces, particularly to the south. During his more recent trips, all ceremonies were eliminated and he insisted on only single course meals. Most of his time was consumed by visits to hamlets and meetings with strategic hamlet teams, hamlet chiefs, province chiefs, district chiefs and committees. These discussions often lasted as long as five hours. He found the trips very tiring but at the same time exhilarating because he had been able to test out his theories about strategic hamlets through actual experience." Rufus Phillips, "Memorandum from the Special Consultant for Counterinsurgency, United States Operation Mission (Phillips) to the Acting Director of the Mission (Fippin)", June 25, 1962, Saigon, in FRUS, 1961–1963, vol. 2, document 227, pp. 470–71. This writer met Phillips at a conference given by the Lyndon Baines Johnson Presidential Library in 1993. Phillips touched upon the strategic hamlets, amongst other topics. His recollections were consistent with the memoranda he wrote in 1962.

[9] From Phillips' memo: "He said the imposition of democracy at the top in an underdeveloped country brought anarchy, which resulted in dictatorship. Democracy must be instituted at a level where the people can understand it and where it can be a revolution to eliminate the existing system of privileges and the defeatism and separatism which exists in the minds of the people." Ibid.

[10] Ibid.

Nhu also told Phillips that Viet Cong should be allowed to surrender and to rejoin their communities. This tactic was in keeping with the British experience in Malaya, where Communist guerrillas had been successfully encouraged to switch sides. Nhu and Deim hoped to minimise the killing of insurgents by winning over as many as possible, and this concept was later developed into the Open Arms Program, or *Chieu Hoi*.[11] This avoidance of bloodshed whenever possible sprang from the Ngo Dinh brothers' Catholic faith.

William Colby, who had more influence over the direction of the SHP than any other American,[12] discerned that Nhu had embarked on a program that had real potential for stopping and reversing Communist political advances in the countryside. Thus, he directed that all CIA special projects be incorporated into, and in some cases subordinated to, Nhu's revolutionary program.[13] According to Colby's account, he was not the only influential American to get behind Nhu's SHP: also supportive was Ambassador Nolting, who directed that the entire U.S. mission in South Vietnam assist the GVN in this effort.[14]

Ambassador Nolting defended the SHP on a number of occasions and in his telegrams to DOS. He argued that the American Task Force on Counterinsurgency had the means to fund the strategic hamlets while at the same time fulfilling U.S. priorities. In January 1962, the task force

---

[11] Ibid.

[12] Roger Hilsman claimed credit for the Strategic Hamlet Program when, in fact, his ideas were essentially borrowed from Thompson. Nevertheless, Hilsman went on record as one of the major critics of the way Nhu implemented the program. See Kent M. Streeb, paper based on interview with Roger Hilsman, November 26, 1994, Reston, Va. (available through the Vietnam Center and Archive, Texas Tech University, Lubbock, Tex.). See also Hilsman, *To Move a Nation: The Politics of Foreign Policy in the Administration of John F. Kennedy* (Garden City, N.Y.: Doubleday, 1967), 464.

[13] "Those local officials who had a CIA-sponsored project in their area (and by 1962 there were some 30,000 armed members of such projects throughout the country) had an advantage of course, as they could—and did—simply fold their projects into the strategic hamlets program, giving them an instant accomplishment to report. And despite some grumbling, from the Station about the loss of our direct influence over the experimental communities we had armed, I saw their incorporation into the strategic hamlets program as a means by which the approach they represented could become the much-needed fundamental strategy of the Diem Government to fight the people's war it faced. I thus welcomed this as a step taking us beyond the limited capabilities of the CIA to a national effort." Colby, *Lost Victory*, 101.

[14] Colby stated: "The Americans were somewhat bewildered by the sudden appearance of a major activity that had not been processed through their complex co-ordinating staffs. Under the leadership of Ambassador Nolting, however, they subordinated their injured pride and swung into support of what appeared to be a genuinely Vietnamese initiative." Ibid., 101–2.

drew up a geographically phased approach to counterinsurgency efforts, which placed emphasis on defending the environs of Saigon–War Zone D, as requested by MAAG, before defending the Mekong River Delta Zone outlined by Thompson.[15] Nolting informed Washington that the GVN was committed to implementing the SHP on a nation-wide basis. He emphasised that, while there might be some local failures in such a massive program, the experts in Vietnam held that there was no substantial risk that the program would prove fatal to the GVN.

There were indeed some local failures, as noted by Colby. Some of these were caused by corrupt GVN officials, who claimed that hamlets were being fortified when the reality was otherwise, cheated on the figures, or even abused some of the peasants. The reason Colby knew of such instances was that Diem sent out inspectors to report any corruption so that it could be rectified. Diem's attitude was that missteps were bound to happen during the implementation of a huge program and that they could be fixed along the way. As Colby said, in answer to Diem's critics, "The fact that you get these reports doesn't mean that the program is no good." Only if nothing is done about such reports is the program bad.

Not every U.S. official was as sanguine about the program as Nolt-ing and Colby. Averell Harriman, assistant secretary of state for Far Eastern affairs, "was dubious about what he heard from the American embassy because he considered Ambassador Frederick Nolting too close to Diem".[16] Secretary Harriman had heard that the SHP was a mess, that "the enclaves had not been located in a manner to create an expanding secure zone. Instead, they had been set up at breakneck speed across the country, many of them no more secure than the old villages whose inhabitants had been uprooted and driven into hamlets as virtual

---

[15] In a telegram, Nolting stated: "Although Task Force Saigon fully appreciates importance establishment geographical priorities for Strategic Hamlet program, we favor somewhat different approach from that suggested.... Task Force some time ago agreed on geographically phased counter-insurgency program including priorities.... This program has served as basis US advice to GVN on Strategic Hamlet Program and in deciding allocation of US resources to specific clear and hold operations. Believe we now have more effective means of applying these priorities de facto to ongoing Strategic Hamlet Program." Frederick Nolting, "Telegram from the Embassy in Vietnam to the Department of State", July 20, 1962, Saigon, in *FRUS, 1961–1963*, vol. 2, document 245, pp. 539–40.

[16] Rudy Abramson, *Spanning the Century: The Life of W. Averell Harriman, 1891–1986* (New York: William Morrow, 1992), 608.

prisoners."[17] Harriman seemed to have purchased the criticism of the
SHP found in the American press, which reported that the program was
spreading itself too thin and leading to the mistreatment of the Vietnamese peasants. In particular, *New York Times* reporter David Halberstam
and Associated Press reporter Neil Sheehan wrote negative articles about
Diem's SHP and Nolting's support of it.[18] Regardless of his sources, Secretary Harriman pressed Ambassador Nolting for quicker and better results.[19]

Thompson, who was involved in implementing the program, gave a
different report from that given by the media and DOS. He noted that
contrary to reports of massive and abusive relocations of peasants, "It was
not the intention that any householder should be relocated more than a
reasonable distance from his land, i.e., up to a maximum of three miles.
Only in the remaining 5 per cent was it likely to be necessary to move all
houses entirely to a new site, a measure that would entail loss of existing
land."[20] Moreover, he added,

> It may come as a surprise to learn that, both in Vietnam and in Malaya,
> there were many occasions when large numbers of the population asked
> to be moved and did so voluntarily without any pressure being brought to
> bear on them. In fact it can be said that, throughout, the Vietnamese
> peasant understood perfectly well the whole purpose in the programme,
> and was prepared to play his part in carrying it out even to the extent of
> devoting full-time labour for the construction work involved.[21]

One of the sources of disagreement between Thompson and the Kennedy administration was the way they perceived the kind of war they

[17] Ibid., 610.

[18] For Halberstam's critique of the SHP, see his *Making of a Quagmire*, 184–87.

[19] Harriman wrote to Nolting: "I would like your views on whether we are doing everything possible to put in administrative support in villages which have been recently liber-
ated.... While I realize that progress is being made in improving the GVN's image, for
example President Diem's speech at the opening of the National Assembly, I am still concerned that the Viet Cong propaganda machine is more effective. In general I think that the
question will be solved through concrete steps taken to help the villagers, while unfounded
public claims by the GVN will only hurt their cause.... In general I feel that we are doing
better militarily but that more must be done to help the villagers themselves, not only by
arming them more rapidly but also socially and economically." W. Averell Harriman, "Letter
from the Assistant Secretary of State for Far Eastern Affairs (Harriman) to the Ambassador
in Vietnam (Nolting)", October 12, 1962, Washington, in *FRUS, 1961–1963*, vol. 2, document 300, pp. 693–96.

[20] Thompson, *Defeating Communist Insurgency*, 122.

[21] Ibid., 127.

were fighting and the role of the SHP in the overall strategy. Thompson and the British Advisory Mission viewed the strategic hamlets as a means to deprive the Communists of political legitimacy. The British recognised that armies, by their very nature, tend to lend a certain amount of political legitimacy to their opponents. Proper police forces, on the other hand, maintain an air of law and order and cast a mantle of criminality upon their opponents. After all, policemen arrest and jail criminals—they do not necessarily want to slay them as enemies on a battlefield or put them in prisoner-of-war camps, where they no longer enjoy the rights of citizens. This observation seemed to be missed by the Americans in their search for greater efficacy in the war effort (which almost always translated into more haste).

In Thompson's November 1961 report to President Diem about the plan for pacifying the Mekong Delta, of which SHP was a part, he called for the development of a National Police force.[22] Because the purpose of the overall pacification plan was to create an attractive and constructive alternative to Communist rule in the countryside, the government's focus needed to be on development of the rural areas. "To do so would require extensive and stringent security measures, to be sure, but these measures required primarily police rather than regular military forces. The police could establish a close rapport with the populace; the army could not. The army should have the mission to keep the VC off balance by mobile action in order to prevent insurgent attacks on the limited areas in which GVN would concentrate its initial pacification efforts."[23]

In his overall aims for the police, Thompson said their goal was to win over the people, not to kill Communists. He noted: "If the main emphasis is placed merely on killing terrorists there is a grave risk that more Communists will be created than are killed. Winning the people must, therefore, be kept in the forefront of the minds of every single person, whether military or civilian, who is engaged in anti-terrorist

[22] Robert Thompson to Ngo Dinh Diem, enclosure 1, despatch 205, November 11, 1961, Saigon, in *U.S. Involvement in the War, Internal Documents: The Kennedy Administration, January 1961–November 1963, Book I*, section V.B.4 of bk. 11 of *United States–Vietnam Relations, 1945–1967: Study Prepared by the Department of Defense*, by Congress, House, Committee on Armed Services (Washington, D.C.: United States Government Printing Office, 1971), 345–46.

[23] United States Department of Defense, "The Strategic Hamlet Program, 1961–1963", in *The Pentagon Papers: The Defense Department History of United States Decisionmaking on Vietnam*, ed. Mike Gravel (Boston: Beacon Press, 1971), 2:139–40.

operations."[24] Thompson stated that staying focused on winning the people would produce the following results:

1. Extended protection of the rural population
2. Increased mobility of security forces, particularly the ARVN
3. Greater flexibility in the use of forces within the whole area where insurgents were operating
4. Improvement in the economy of force as a result of increased mobility and flexibility and better communications
5. Increased confidence of the people toward their government, and improved morale of the security forces
6. Better intelligence about Communist insurgents and their organisation due to the people's increased confidence in their government
7. More kills of the hard-line Communist cadres as a result of better intelligence

According to Thompson's argument, if these results were achieved, then "protection, confidence, intelligence and kills should become a constantly expanding circuit" that would end with the effective destruction of the Communist insurgent infrastructure and its ability to wage any kind of war.[25] While the military certainly had a role to play in Thompson's plan, it was not the dominant force in his counterinsurgency proposal. Needless to say, Thompson's vision clashed with that of the U.S. military.

In addition to the SHP, there were many other types of development programs being carried out in South Vietnam by various U.S. government agencies, simultaneous with the CIP and in conjunction with it. In spite of the good work being done, these efforts were constantly under attack by the Viet Cong. Thus, the GVN and the Americans were concerned about how to protect the civilian populace and the civilian agencies at work throughout the country. In this regard, even the most democratically minded Americans realised that one could not set up a polling station if one could not protect it from insurgent violence.

With these considerations in mind, the U.S. military advisors and the ARVN agreed with Thompson that the Viet Cong had to be separated

[24]Robert Thompson to Ngo Dinh Diem, enclosure 2, memorandum [subject: counterinsurgency plan], despatch 205, November 13, 1961, Saigon, in Congress, House, Committee on Armed Services, *U.S. Involvement in the War: Book I*, 347.

[25]Ibid., 357–58.

from the people via the SHP. But to their way of thinking, the purpose of this separation was to force the Communists to give battle on terrain where they would be destroyed by the superior firepower of the professionally trained Vietnamese and American armed forces. There was nothing intrinsically wrong with this classic military strategy. Undoubtedly, if one can subject an enemy to superior firepower, one will win the battle. The problem for the American and Vietnamese armies became what to do when the enemy does not accept defeat after losing the conventional battles. Recognising that the battlefield in Vietnam was not necessarily only a military one but also a political one would prove difficult for any soldier. The American commanders and advisors, capable though they were, found this reality almost inconceivable.

The American military advisors in South Vietnam, or MAAG, had ingrained the ARVN with the doctrine that their primary purpose was to repel a formal attack from the NVA, very much as the United States and its allies had done in Korea. There was little doubt amongst the likes of General Lionel McGarr that programs such as the SHP were secondary in importance to making the ARVN more aggressive and efficient. In short, military strategy and tactics were to predominate over other considerations. This approach translated in the field into a single command: Kill more Viet Cong, more efficiently.[26] The protection of civilians within strategic hamlets or defended villages was all well and good to MAAG, but it was second, at best, to the necessity of utilising military means to destroy the insurgents. This attitude contradicted the British experience in Malaya, in which they saw that the more insurgents one indiscriminately kills, with all the horrible attendant collateral damage, the more guerrillas are created from the friends and the relatives of the fallen. In other words, simply killing insurgents would reach, quite rapidly, the point of diminishing returns for the government.

Opposite MAAG were Thompson and the British Advisory Mission, who advocated denying the Communists the battle they wanted to fight: the battle for political legitimacy. As previously noted, this is the battle

---

[26] Lionel McGarr, "Letter from Chief of MAAG Lt. General Lionel C. McGarr to Admiral Heinz", Progress of CIP Plan, Jan.–Feb.–Mar.–Apr. 1961, Spector Files, RG 319, Box 11, SEA-RS-798, pp. 1–6; and Kent M. Streeb, "A Fragmented Effort: Ngo Dinh Diem, the United States Military and State Department and the Strategic Hamlet Program of 1961–1963" (paper, George Mason University, December 10, 1994), 15, Vietnam Center and Archive, Texas Tech University, Lubbock, Tex.

South Vietnam would lose if they overused their army. It is worth reiterating that police forces tend to deny their opponents legitimacy because they impute them with criminality. It is the job of good policemen to arrest wrongdoers. Then through due process, the government can jail or otherwise punish convicted criminals. However, when an army captures enemy soldiers on a battlefield, they become prisoners of war and subject to different treatment.[27]

It was central to the British counterinsurgency concept that the public saw policemen doing their justifiable duty conferred upon them by the lawful authority of the state; justice not only had to be done but had to be seen by the people as being done. This foundation of civil legal authority superseding armed might was never entirely accepted in American military thinking on the subject. Nevertheless, Thompson made it very clear that it was essential to subordinate the military to the civil authority. Indeed, Thompson maintained that winning the people over and retaining their support could be achieved only if strong civil authority had full reign over the means of protecting the populace.[28] Of course, this did not mean that the military was eliminated from the process; instead, the military's role was one of working in concert with the police in isolating and eliminating the Viet Cong.[29] Thus, Thompson spelled out the specific roles of the Civil Guard and the ARVN: the main work of defence in the villages and hamlets was to be conducted by

[27] Indeed, prisoner-of-war status invokes international conventions and laws that legitimise guerrillas and insurgents and separate them from civil and criminal law. This has been a very complex issue since 1945, when the United Nations began to grapple with the problem of legal combatant status for insurgents.

[28] From Thompson's plan: "This is a battle for the control of the villages and the protection of the population. If security and Government control are restored, then, with the assistance of the people themselves, the elimination of the Vietcong will automatically follow. The Vietcong cannot exist unless they can intimidate and gain the support of elements in the population. They depend on these elements for supplies, food, intelligence and recruits. This is a continual traffic and represents the weakest link in the Vietcong organisation."

Robert Thompson, "Draft Paper by the Head of the British Advisory Mission in Vietnam (Thompson)", National Security Council, Policy Directive No. ... [ellipsis in original], Delta Plan [February 7, 1962?], Saigon, in *FRUS, 1961–1963*, vol. 2, document 51, pp. 101–2.

[29] The British had used some very formidable military units in Malaya to engage the Communist guerrillas. For example, the Special Air Service (SAS) and the Gurkhas were used to take over from the police at the jungle's edge in what Americans might call a "tag team" effort. Noel Barber, *The War of the Running Dogs: Malaya, 1948–1960* (London: Arrow Books, 1989), 184. See also Anthony Kemp, *The SAS: Savage Wars of Peace, 1947 to the Present* (London: Penguin / Signet Books, 1995), 22.

the Civil Guard (what the British called special constables in both Kenya and Malaya) and the military was to assist them.[30]

It would not be farfetched to suggest that Thompson, having been made aware of General McGarr's objection to the primary role of policemen over soldiers, had replaced the term "police" with paramilitary descriptions such as "Self-Defence Corps" and "Civil Guard". Nevertheless, not more than four years later, in his seminal work on counterinsurgency warfare, *Defeating Communist Insurgency: Experiences from Malaya and Vietnam*, Thompson underscored exactly what he was getting at with these terms, and why the police or special constabulary forces were so important.

In Malaya, Thompson explained, there were basically two government forces: the police and the army. The strength of the police force was deliberately maintained at more than twice that of the army, and this remained the case even when Commonwealth battalions were factored into the equation. The Home Guard, arguably a third force, operated under the direction of the police force even though its members were recruited and administered separately. When the Malayan Emergency broke out in 1948, the police had 11,285 men in all ranks. During the course of the Communist insurgency, this force was rapidly built up to incorporate 30,000 regular policemen and another 30,000 special constables. The special constables were assigned the tasks of defending villages, estates, and mines. The Malaya police also put into place a field force made up of platoons and companies that were equivalent to light infantry. All of these forces were carefully controlled and co-ordinated in such a manner as to allow the police to carry on their normal functions while providing protection against insurgent attacks and undertaking counterinsurgency operations. The armed forces acted as a buttress to this civil power. This dominance of the policemen, Thompson pointed out, enhanced political stability while making certain that there was a

---

[30] "The framework will depend for close defence mainly on the Self-Defence Corps supported by the Republican youth as part-time members of the Self-Defense Corps. Immediate close support in a mobile role will be provided by the Civil Guard. Where defended hamlets are established in areas which have been heavily penetrated by the Vietcong it may be necessary to employ Civil Guard in their close defence until such time as reliable Self-Defence Corps units can be called. During the establishment of the framework it will be the task of the Army to keep regular units of the Vietcong harassed and off balance so that the security framework can be consolidated." Thompson, "Draft Paper", 102.

continuance of legitimate governance by rule of law throughout the duration of the insurgency.[31]

Thompson's description of the balance of forces in Malaya compared with that of Vietnam in the early 1960s warranted more serious consideration than it was given by MAAG chief General McGarr. Another item deserving scrutiny was the high number (at least eighty) of security organisations that existed in South Vietnam during this period. Thompson noted that they overlapped each other, which led to confusion of roles and duties in the implementation of security measures—simply co-ordinating them all was problematic for the GVN. In Thompson's opinion, many of these forces should have been amalgamated, and their roles clearly defined. The very size of the army, in addition to all of South Vietnam's paramilitary organisations, tended to increase political instability and to endorse the rule of force over the rule of law.[32]

Unfortunately for all concerned, the Americans perceived Thompson's recommendations to be in direct conflict with their new plan, which tied the release of substantial sums of new aid to President Diem's acceptance of U.S.-specified governmental reforms and his willingness to co-ordinate his counterinsurgency strategy with that formulated by U.S. military experts. As stated previously, since Thompson's plan gave President Diem a way to circumvent both conditions, the Americans saw it as a rival to their own.[33] A specific point of contention between Thompson and the Americans was the offensive planned by MAAG. Unlike the U.S. military advisors, Thompson viewed the primary threat to be to the political stability of the populated rural areas. Consequently, and as noted previously, he regarded Lionel McGarr's proposed initial operation in War Zone D to be a step in the wrong direction.[34] Understandably General McGarr did not appreciate Thompson's opinion. He was not moved by professional jealousy or pettiness but by a profoundly different approach to fighting an insurgency.

[31] Thompson, *Defeating Communist Insurgency*, 103.

[32] Ibid., 103–4.

[33] Congress, House, Committee on Armed Services, *Evolution of the War: The Strategic Hamlet Program, 1961–1963*, section IV.B.2 of bk. 3 of *United States–Vietnam Relations, 1945–1967: Study Prepared by the Department of Defense* (Washington, D.C.: United States Government Printing Office, 1971), 10.

[34] Ibid., 11.

Also, it must be remembered, if Diem adopted Thompson's plans he would not adopt the chain of command changes desired by the Americans.[35] According to Vietnam War scholar Kent M. Streeb, McGarr had been hoping that the utterly confusing web of the ARVN's command structure would be streamlined by strict adherence to Washington's CIP.[36] The Americans recognised that Diem had kept this intricate interweaving and overlapping command structure in place to reduce the possibility of coup attempts. MAAG, however, came to view Diem's command structure as a hindrance to the proper functioning of the ARVN. Thus, they ignored the fact that for Diem "to accede to the American military's chain-of-command request would afford his forces the opportunity to co-ordinate and coalesce into numbers sufficient to overthrow him".[37] In effect, American advisors such as McGarr wanted to curb the Vietnamese president's control over the CIP, because it was Diem's alleged inabilities that were partially responsible for the need for greater American intervention.

Another area of dispute between Thompson and the Americans was control of intelligence. Thompson wanted the new National Police to direct and to co-ordinate all intelligence activities, which would be, ultimately, under President Diem's control.[38]

> The best organisation to be responsible for all internal security intelligence is the special branch of the police force rather than a completely separate organisation. It is a great advantage if intelligence officers have police powers and are able to call when necessary on the other branches of the police force for support and assistance in developing their intelligence network. The police force is a static organisation reaching out into every corner of the country and will have had long experience of close contact with the population. If it can possibly be avoided, the army should not be responsible for internal security intelligence. The army will have had little concern

[35] "Thompson's recommended command arrangements, if adopted, would demolish the prospect of a unitary chain of command within ARVN, an objective toward which he [McGarr] had been working for over a year. Additionally, the Thompson proposals would leave Diem as the ultimate manager of an operation dealing with only a portion (the Delta) of RVN [the Republic of Vietnam]. The elimination of practices such as this had been an explicit objective of the entire U.S. advisory effort for a long time." Ibid.

[36] Streeb, "Fragmented Effort", 8.

[37] Ibid.

[38] Congress, House, Committee on Armed Services, *Evolution of the War: Strategic Hamlet Program*, 11–12.

with subversion before the open insurgency breaks out; it will have had very limited experience of contacting the people, particularly rural communities, which are inherently suspicious of troops; and its units are always liable to be re-deployed throughout the country in accordance with the situation. Any intelligence lines which these units may have established are then immediately uprooted.[39]

Internal intelligence directed by one organisation avoids all kinds of problems, Thompson added, such as unreliable information being assumed reliable because it came from more than one source or competition between organisations leading agents to undercut each other in the field. "Mutual suspicion and jealousies will arise, quite likely with the result that the separate organisations merely end up spying on each other."[40]

General McGarr balked at the very idea of conducting a war from a static security framework,[41] that is, strategic hamlets defended largely by policemen.[42] To American military thinkers, civic action in static positions smacked of too much reliance on the defensive; in fact, it constituted a switching over to the strategic defensive. Thompson addressed this criticism directly:

> Certainly the first object of the programme is the protection of the population, and each hamlet must therefore be capable of defending itself. But the concept as a whole is designed to secure a firm base and then to expand from that into disputed, and finally enemy-controlled, territory. If the programme is strategically directed, and supported by the armed forces, it becomes an offensive advance which will wrest the military initiative from the insurgent. This is far more aggressive, because it is effective, than launching thousands of operations with hundreds of troops in each, all wading through the paddy fields with their rifles cocked to no purpose.[43]

Thompson's insistence that the size and the role of the conventional military should be downgraded and that police forces should be brought to

---

[39] Thompson, *Defeating Communist Insurgency*, 84–86.

[40] Ibid.

[41] United States Department of Defense, "Strategic Hamlet Program", in *Pentagon Papers*, 2:141.

[42] McGarr, "Letter from Chief of MAAG", 1–6; Streeb, "Fragmented Effort", 9.

[43] *Defeating Communist Insurgency*, 126.

the fore was directly at odds with General McGarr, who thought the size and the role of the military must be upgraded in order to win the war.[44] He was not alone in his opinion. Joint Chiefs Chairman Lemnitzer also saw the need for the military to have priority over the police. He wrote in October 1961, "It seems clear that in recent months the insurgency in South Vietnam has developed far beyond the capacity of police control." In the same memo he explained that the police turned Civil Guard were being specially targeted by the Viet Cong:

> It is most important to note that the heaviest casualties in the Vietnam insurgency have been suffered by the Civil Guard previously trained as police. Almost without exception, the Viet Cong have attacked the untrained Civil Guard rather than the better trained Army units. This has resulted in a heavy loss of weapons and equipment to the Viet Cong. Untrained Civil Guard units have, in fact, been an important source of weapons and supplies for the Viet Cong, and their known vulnerability has been an invitation for the Viet Cong to attack. General McGarr believes that reversion of the Civil Guard to police control would set back the counter-insurgency operation in Vietnam by at least a year.[45]

The general mentioned the time consideration elsewhere in the memo. He wrote that making better use of police was generally a good idea but that it takes a long time to build up a competent police force: "It took the British nearly 12 years to defeat an insurgency which was less strong than the one in South Vietnam."[46] General McGarr also thought Thompson's ideas would take too long to implement, because time was needed for hamlet administration and defences to grow organically from the effort. "Not only would the Viet Cong not wait," McGarr thought, "it was simply unsound policy not to use the tools at hand. It would not do to reduce the ARVN and increase police forces while the VC

---

[44] "Thompson's stated desire to emphasize police forces in lieu of regular military forces was regarded by the U.S. military advisory chief as unrealistic—a transferral of Malayan experience to a locale in which the existing tools of policy were very different." Congress, House, Committee on Armed Services, *Evolution of the War: Strategic Hamlet Program*, 13.

[45] L. L. Lemnitzer, "Memorandum for General Taylor; Subject: Counterinsurgency Operations in South Vietnam", October 18, 1961, Washington, in *U.S. Involvement in the War, Internal Documents: The Kennedy Administration, January 1961–November 1963, Book I*, section V.B.4 of bk. 11 of *United States–Vietnam Relations, 1945–1967: Study Prepared by the Department of Defense*, by Congress, House, Committee on Armed Services (Washington, D.C.: United States Government Printing Office, 1971), 324–26.

[46] Ibid.

continued their successes. It was necessary, in sum, to act in a limited area but to act quickly."[47]

In short, the leading U.S. generals considered that "Thompson's recommendations did not look to quick action, emphasized the wrong area, were designed to emphasize the wrong operational agency, and proposed unacceptable command lines."[48] Ambassador Nolting, in spite of his desire to fulfil U.S. policy directives, saw the merit in Thompson's ideas, and he warmed to the man on a personal level.[49] He sensed, however, that the Kennedy administration would not heed Thompson's advice as it was looking for a quick military fix to the insurgency in South Vietnam, and that meant it would turn to conventional warfare, no matter how counterproductive it was in a political fight with the Communists.

Nolting saw the turn toward conventional warfare in the Taylor-Rostow report, and he was disturbed by it. The report called for the deployment of five thousand U.S. combat engineers to the Mekong Delta, ostensibly for the purpose of helping the GVN with flood control. But the American unit had full military capability, which meant it could defend itself if engaged in combat and cut off from the ARVN. Seeing the writing on the wall, Nolting sent his concerns to Washington: "When I cabled my comments to Washington, I noted that I was in thorough accord with the ideas that had been discussed in Vietnam, but not with this new addition. My opposition stemmed from the conviction that the introduction of American combat forces would set a precedent and eventually lead to a shuffling of responsibility from the Vietnamese Army onto the stronger, better equipped Americans."[50]

[47] Congress, House, Committee on Armed Services, *Evolution of the War: Strategic Hamlet Program*, 13.

[48] Ibid.

[49] "Bob Thompson was very good. He had a very small mission—six men. I think all of them had served at one point or another in Malaya under Sir Gerald Templar. Bob Thompson was the head of the British mission. He got there, I believe, shortly after I did. I liked him, worked closely with him, learned a lot from him. He was quite persuasive, vis-à-vis President Diem, who could see that he knew what he was talking about because of his experience in Malaya. We quite often went together to put up a proposal. Yes, they did a lot of good work. They did not have much to work with other than their experiences as individuals. They didn't have any supplies.... I had a high respect for Bob Thompson." Frederick Nolting, interview by Dennis O'Brien, May 6, 1970, New York, interview 2, transcript, 55–56, John F. Kennedy Oral History Collection, John F. Kennedy Presidential Library, Boston.

[50] Frederick Nolting, *From Trust to Tragedy: The Political Memoirs of Frederick Nolting, Kennedy's Ambassador to Diem's Vietnam* (New York: Praeger, 1988), 36.

Nolting knew that such a noticeable foreign military presence within the country would undermine Diem's authority in the perceptions of the Vietnamese and therefore give the Communists a political weapon against the GVN. Although President Kennedy did not initiate such a deployment straightaway, Nolting knew that the military intervention advocates held a strong hand in the administration, and that Thompson's advice was not likely to win against it.

Although the leading American military men had their criticisms of the plan, as we have seen, none wanted to reject wholesale the British advice given to President Diem. By early 1962 some of the British ideas had garnered considerable interest in Washington at the highest levels. General Maxwell Taylor and Roger Hilsman liked much of what Thompson had to say.[51] Hilsman actually incorporated much of Thompson's advice into his own plan, which he presented to President Kennedy, who expressed that he was in favour of such a scheme.[52]

In many ways the American concerns about British counterinsurgency methods were not at all obvious to the outside observer; after all, it appeared as though the Americans wholeheartedly agreed with the implementation of the SHP, because thousands of these communities were being quickly built with American financial help. Yet, in order to preserve good relations amongst MAAG, Diem's government, and the British Advisory Mission, subtle but profound changes in the Thompson plan occurred on the ground in Vietnam. For example, Thompson agreed to revise his program so as to remove American objections to his proposed command arrangements. He also decided to drop, at least

---

[51] Consider, for example, Hilsman's praise for Thompson: "The more I reflected on my own experience as a guerrilla in Burma and imagined what it would have been like if we had been facing strategic hamlets during World War II, the more I was persuaded.... It seemed more and more possible that an effective strategic concept could be developed by combining Thompson's strategic hamlet plan with the work in Washington and Fort Bragg on both the military tactics to be pursued and the measures to combat the strains of modernization with which Rostow was concerned.... What was clear above all else was that the single most important principle of all—as the British had discovered in Malaya—was that civic, police, social, and military measures had to be combined and carefully co-ordinated in an over-all counter-guerrilla program and that there had to be a unified civilian, police, and military system of command and control." Roger Hilsman, *To Move a Nation: The Politics of Foreign Policy in the Administration of John F. Kennedy* (Garden City, N.Y.: Doubleday, 1967), 434–35.

[52] Congress, House, Committee on Armed Services, *Evolution of the War: Strategic Hamlet Program*, 14.

temporarily, his push for police primacy over the army in the pacification plan.[53]

Objectively, these changes may or may not have been a detriment to fighting the Communists. It cannot be denied, however, that the ascendancy of conventional warfare controlled by a foreign power undermined the Vietnamese president's legitimacy in the eyes of his people, and this was no small matter. Unfortunately for both the Americans and the Vietnamese, this was to prove very costly—for all the reasons that Robert Thompson had explained.

[53] Ibid.

7

The Abrogation of Nolting's Rapprochement

On February 27, 1962, a seemingly innocuous letter was sent from the U.S. assistant secretary of state, Averell Harriman, to the ambassador in Vietnam, Frederick Nolting. The letter read as follows:

> Dear Fritz: In the light of today's attack on the palace I have reviewed Walter McConaughy's letter to you of October 20, 1961 and the "Suggested Contingency Plan" of the same date which was enclosed with that letter.
>
> It seems to me that the "Suggested Contingency Plan" is still valid. I regret that we did not have time to discuss it during your hurried visit to Washington.
>
> If you have any comments to make on it in view of the present situation I would be glad to read them. Knowing that you are very busy I will assume that if I do not hear from you this plan remains satisfactory to you. We are very pleased with your handling of the reporting on today's attack on the palace.
>
> With best personal regards,
> Yours very sincerely,
> Averell[1]

Despite appearances to the contrary, the true thrust of this inquiry was anything but harmless: Harriman was sounding out just where Nolting stood with regard to the removal of Ngo Dinh Diem from power, because that was the precise nature and content of McConaughy's Suggested Contingency Plan.

---

[1] W. Averell Harriman, "Letter from the Assistant Secretary of State for Far Eastern Affairs (Harriman) to the Ambassador in Vietnam (Nolting)", February 27, 1962, Washington, in *FRUS, 1961–1963*, vol. 2, document 89, pp. 182–83.

In earlier telegrams to Nolting, Harriman hinted that he and other leaders had grave doubts about President Diem. For example, in his telegram from Geneva on October 13, 1961, during the Laotian neutrality negotiations, Harriman said that throughout his travels over the last six months he had heard nothing but concern about Diem's "dictatorial regime, Palace Guard, family and corruption".[2] Diem's presidency started out well enough, he added, but his later leadership style, particularly after the 1960 coup attempt, was encouraging speculation about his competency: "Various accounts indicate lack of confidence among military, provincial government officials, intellectuals, business, professional and university groups. There is general prophesy [sic] that another coup is apt to happen, in which case insurgents will not be as considerate of Diem as last year." Harriman assured Nolting that the sources for these observations were friendly to the United States. Even the British, he said, were hoping the Americans could pressure Diem to undertake major reforms, including the "elimination of undesirable family influence". Harriman ended this cable by telling Nolting that he had no recommendations but believed "we may well be sitting on powder keg that could blow up, conceivably not disastrous if it was touched off by constructive forces." The implication was clear enough: Harriman was suggesting that the United States might want to get behind a coup. He concluded: "I only want to add my voice to those who believe more recognition must be given to political situation which no amount of military assistance or participation can cure."[3]

Masterfully, Harriman was marshalling forces while sounding out Nolting's opinion about betraying Diem. Nolting's measured response was sent three days later. In his telegram, he said there were some steps that needed to be taken to strengthen Diem and to preserve a free Vietnam. "A very careful balance has to be struck between the ideal and the possible," he wrote, "assuming Diem's continuance at the helm and given his extraordinary blend of quality, fortitude, deep conviction, determination, lack of political instinct, lack of organizing

---

[2] W. Averell Harriman, "Telegram from the Consulate General in Switzerland to the Department of State", October 13, 1961, Geneva (forwarded by Harriman to President Kennedy at Hyannis Port, Mass., on October 13, 1961), in *FRUS, 1961–1963*, vol. 1, document 164, pp. 363–64.

[3] Ibid.

and administrative ability and many others."[4] Diem was not perfect, Nolting realised, but he was a good man worthy of American support. In dealing with him and his government, Washington needed to realise that diplomacy, like politics, should be concerned with the art of the possible.

There is little doubt that Averell Harriman had taken a strong dislike to Ngo Dinh Diem. Harriman was not alone in this. Another extremely influential individual, John Kenneth Galbraith, also disapproved of Diem—and Galbraith had direct access to President Kennedy.

John Kenneth Galbraith was born in 1908 in Canada, where his father was a farmer and a school teacher involved in the United Farmers of Ontario, a political party that promoted cooperative business ownership, nationalised railways, and progressive taxation.[5] After finishing his undergraduate studies in agricultural economics at the Ontario Agricultural College, which was then a part of the University of Toronto (the college later became the University of Guelph), Galbraith moved on to the University of California at Berkeley, where he completed a doctorate in the same field in 1934. He then began his long and ofteninterrupted tenure at Harvard as a professor of economics. While there he penned his influential work *The Affluent Society* and began to involve himself in American liberal politics and causes.[6] He helped to found the Americans for Democratic Action in 1947, when his politics and academic career began to merge into one.[7]

Galbraith's endorsement of Kennedy as the Democratic nominee for president had its roots in 1957, when Kennedy eagerly sought the support of the widely published and highly esteemed Harvard professor.[8] By 1960 Galbraith was part of an elite group of influential liberals organised

---

[4] Frederick Nolting, "Telegram from the Embassy in Vietnam to the Department of State", October 16, 1961, Saigon, in *FRUS, 1961–1963*, vol. 1, document 171, pp. 383–86.

[5] James Ronald Stanfield, *John Kenneth Galbraith* (New York: St. Martin's Press, 1996), 1.

[6] Ibid., 2–3.

[7] According to James Ronald Stanfield, Galbraith's biographer: "Galbraith's ardent partisanship is quite unusual. To be sure, political activity is not uncommon among economists. There are highly visible advisers to candidates and administrations and frequent testimony to congressional committees. There are popular essays that convey the author's political slant. Economists at least tend to know each other as inclined to one political persuasion or another. But Galbraith's uninhibited partisanship coupled with his refusal to neatly separate his politics from his economics sets him well apart from his more conventional colleagues." Ibid., 4.

[8] Arthur M. Schlesinger Jr., *A Thousand Days: John F. Kennedy in the White House* (Boston: Houghton Mifflin, 1965), 11–15.

by John L. Saltonstall Jr. to back Kennedy's presidential bid.[9] Galbraith's loyalty throughout the presidential campaign earned him the appointment as American ambassador to India.[10]

Ambassador Galbraith visited Vietnam in 1961 and concluded that President Diem was to blame for the ongoing insurgency. In support of this contention, Galbraith stated that even a moderately effective government coupled with a relatively powerful military would be able to stop the Communist insurgents.[11] Thus, Galbraith wrote, "There is no solution that does not involve a change of government. To say there is no alternative is nonsense for there never has seemed to be where one man has dominated the scene. So while we must play out the ineffective and hopeless course on which we are launched for a little while, we must look ahead very soon to a new government."[12]

The use of the word "nonsense" was a swipe at Ambassador Nolting, who considered Diem the best possible leader of Vietnam given the alternatives. In an earlier report Galbraith recommended the "replacement of Ambassador Nolting by an ambassador of the character and prominence of Governor Harriman. We need someone who can hold his own with both Diem and the United States military, who will insist once and for all on government reform, and who will understand the United States political implications of developments there."[13]

In spite of the contempt for Nolting shown by Galbraith and Harriman, Kennedy showed respect for his personally selected ambassador to South Vietnam even after he succumbed to the pressure to remove him. According to Averell's biographer, in a critical and heated meeting at the White House, during the days leading up to Diem's assassination, Harriman "sailed into Nolting for being too cozy with Diem. And when the former ambassador tried to defend himself, Harriman snapped that

[9] Ibid., 28.

[10] Ibid., 152.

[11] John Kenneth Galbraith, "To Director, CIA, from Bangkok, 20 November 1961: For the President from Ambassador Galbraith", in *U.S. Involvement in the War, Internal Documents: The Kennedy Administration, January 1961–November 1963, Book I*, section V.B.4 of bk. 11 of *United States–Vietnam Relations, 1945–1967: Study Prepared by the Department of Defense*, by Congress, House, Committee on Armed Services (Washington, D.C.: United States Government Printing Office, 1971), 406–8.

[12] Ibid.

[13] John Kenneth Galbraith, "Paper Prepared by the Ambassador to India (Galbraith): A Plan for South Vietnam", November 3, 1961, Washington, in *FRUS, 1961–1963*, vol. 1, document 209, p. 475.

he should keep his mouth shut because no one cared what he thought. With that, Kennedy curtly interrupted. He was fond of Nolting, and he told Harriman that the President, for one, was interested in hearing what Nolting had to say."[14]

Six days after his telegram stating the need for the removal of President Diem, Galbraith sent a telegram to DOS stating that "unless there is penetrating and non-routine reason to contrary," he would like to meet with a Hanoi representative about matters in South Vietnam when he arrived in New Delhi. He said he would tell the Democratic Republic of Vietnam (DRV) diplomat that although neither the U.S. nor the South Vietnamese governments intended any "menace" to North Vietnam, both were seriously determined to preserve the independence of South Vietnam.[15]

Secretary of State Dean Rusk promptly replied to Galbraith that such a meeting was a bad idea. Given the direction of the Laos talks, Diem and his government might think such a meeting meant the United States was going to settle with the North Vietnamese and abandon South Vietnam to the Communists. Said Rusk, "Since it is our policy give full support to GVN we must avoid any move that might appear, or which DRV propaganda could cause to appear, as prelude to US reduction its commitments to Viet-Nam."[16] Rusk made sure that his reply also went to Harriman in Geneva and Nolting in Saigon. Rusk and Galbraith did not care for each other. In Galbraith's memoirs of the Kennedy years, he recalled being told that Rusk and some of the other "more pompous people in Washington" had come to suspect he did not have a very high regard for them. Then the former ambassador to India quipped, "This does credit to their perceptions."[17]

Despite Galbraith's obvious disdain for some of his colleagues, he won converts to the idea of removing Diem. One of these was Walt Rostow, Kennedy's assistant national security advisor, who wrote the president in November 1961 that he had no objection to Galbraith's plan

[14] Rudy Abramson, *Spanning the Century: The Life of W. Averell Harriman, 1891–1986* (New York: William Morrow, 1992), 622.

[15] John Galbraith, "Telegram from the Embassy in India to the Department of State", November 26, 1961, New Delhi, in *FRUS, 1961–1963*, vol. 1, document 282, p. 671.

[16] Dean Rusk, "Telegram from the Department of State to the Embassy in India", November 28, 1961, Washington, in *FRUS, 1961–1963*, vol. 1, document 290, p. 681.

[17] John Kenneth Galbraith, *Ambassador's Journal: A Personal Account of the Kennedy Years* (Boston: Houghton Mifflin, 1969), 294.

to replace the government in Saigon. His only concern about a coup was that "the management of that crisis will take great skill to avoid exploitation by the Communists; but I think it not impossible."[18] Rostow also indicated that "contingency planning might quietly begin." Meanwhile, Galbraith continued to press his case with President Kennedy, as can be seen in his spring 1962 correspondence: "It must be recognized that our long-run position cannot involve an unconditional commitment to Diem. Our support is to non-communist and progressively democratic government not to individuals. We cannot ourselves replace Diem. But we should be clear in our mind that almost any non-communist change would probably be beneficial and this should be the guiding rule for our diplomatic representation in the area."[19]

As leading diplomats Galbraith and Harriman tried to steer the course on America's Vietnam policy, what was Secretary of State Dean Rusk thinking and doing? Answering that question requires tracing Rusk's path to Washington. Born into a farming family in Cherokee County, Georgia, on February 9, 1909, Rusk's beginnings could not have been more different from those of Harriman. Unable to keep their farm economically viable, the Rusks were forced to sell their property. They moved to Atlanta, where they lived in relative poverty and young Dean was subjected to all the humiliations of being poor.[20] Nevertheless, with a combination of intelligence, guts, and determination, he did well in school. In 1931, he won a Rhodes Scholarship to Oxford, where despite the rampant scepticism, he was able to maintain a quiet, steady, and devout Christian faith.[21] During World War II, Rusk was assigned as deputy chief of staff to General Stilwell and Colonel Frank Merrill (commander of Merrill's Marauders) in the China-Burma-India theatre.[22] In 1945, after the war, DOS offered Rusk a job, and two

---

[18] Walter Rostow, "Memorandum from the President's Deputy Special Assistant for National Security Affairs (Rostow) to the President", November 24, 1961, Washington, in *FRUS, 1961–1963*, vol. 1, document 274, p. 661. Under cover of a brief letter of November 25, 1961, Rostow sent Galbraith a copy of this memorandum.

[19] John Kenneth Galbraith, "Memorandum from the Ambassador to India (Galbraith) to the President", April 4, 1962, Washington, in *FRUS, 1961–1963*, vol. 2, document 141, p. 298.

[20] Thomas J. Schoenbaum, *Waging Peace and War: Dean Rusk in the Truman, Kennedy, and Johnson Years* (New York: Simon and Schuster, 1988), 29–32.

[21] Ibid., 53.

[22] Ibid., 84–92.

years later he was effectively serving as an assistant secretary of state in his official role as director of special political affairs.[23] According to his biographer, Thomas J. Schoenbaum, Rusk brought a unique perspective to DOS that might partially explain his ultimate lack of enthusiasm for trying to save South Vietnam from the Communists:

> His faith in the Anglo-Saxon tradition of law and liberty as a beacon for the entire human race led Rusk to be, paradoxically, a convinced anti-colonialist. He accurately predicted the swift and inevitable dissolution of colonial empires after the war [World War II], and thought that the United States and Britain should assist this process. Nevertheless, he was enough of a realist to leaven these views with a dose of pragmatism. He did not believe in universal American intervention to set the world right, but in the limited use of American power based on what was possible in any given situation.[24]

Given where he had started from, Rusk had arrived when President Kennedy appointed him secretary of state in 1961, but in some ways he never would arrive. DOS was a stronghold of East Coast Ivy Leaguers, and a humble Southerner like Rusk would never be fully accepted in such a milieu.[25] Thus, Rusk was not given the opportunity to design the department to his liking and was put in the position of deferring to people whose credentials carried more weight than his, such as Averell Harriman.

Rusk was not as involved in shaping foreign policy toward Vietnam as Ambassador Nolting would have liked. As he wrote in his memoirs, "Dean Rusk, as Secretary of State, failed, in my view, to supply the oversight required in American policy toward Southeast Asia in the early 1960's, when the problems there were more political than military. True, he was preoccupied with larger issues, in particular the tense confrontation with the Soviet Union over Berlin and Cuba."[26] Especially after the Laos agreement of 1962, Rusk deferred the situation in South Vietnam

---

[23] Ibid., 142–43.

[24] Ibid., 135.

[25] In the words of Rusk's biographer: "It was a very exclusive group in which everyone was on a first name basis, and not without a certain haughtiness, a feeling of being anointed to decide questions of war and peace for the rest of the nation. Presidents might come from obscure origins in places like Independence, Missouri, but not the foreign policy establishment." Ibid., 143.

[26] Frederick Nolting, *From Trust to Tragedy: The Political Memoirs of Frederick Nolting, Kennedy's Ambassador to Diem's Vietnam* (New York: Praeger, 1988), xiii–xiv.

first to the Pentagon and then more and more to Averell Harriman: "During my tenure as Ambassador, he never set foot in Vietnam, nor did he attend any of the Honolulu conferences. I could never get him to focus on our problems while I was in Vietnam. Policy fell by default first to Bob McNamara in Defense and then to Averell Harriman. As late as August 1963, when I went to ask Rusk to talk about Vietnam, he told me, 'Averell's handling this.' "[27]

As we have seen with the Laos accords, Harriman put great faith in the power of negotiations between world powers to pacify Southeast Asia, or at least to please the constituencies of President Kennedy. Even if Harriman were not a true believer, Chester Bowles certainly was, as can be seen in his proposal to create not only a neutral Laos but a neutral Thailand, Burma, Cambodia, Malaysia, South Vietnam, and Singapore: "In February, 1961, I first urged Dean Rusk to consider the expansion of the neutrality concept ... to embrace the rest of Southeast Asia, excluding North Vietnam and East Pakistan.... Neutral status, I said, might be guaranteed by the United States, Britain, France, the Soviet Union, India and Japan. It was even conceivable that such a plan might appeal to the Soviet Union's interest in keeping Communist China from moving to absorb Southeast Asia into its sphere of influence." Bowles thought that such an effort would "transfer the debate from the military to the political arena" and that it should be attempted while Laotian neutrality was being hammered out in Geneva. Bowles claimed that Averell Harriman reacted favourably to his proposal: "As head of our negotiating team he had developed working relationships with representatives of the other side and, while recognising the difficulties, felt that some such plan might be feasible. The Soviet Union, he thought, might be persuaded to share responsibility for insuring the provisions of the agreement."[28]

Less than ten days before the Laotian accords were signed, Bowles once again floated his proposal for spreading neutrality throughout Southeast Asia in a memo to Secretary Rusk.[29] At the same time, he wrote emergency memos to President Kennedy urging him to reconsider

[27] Ibid., 129.
[28] Chester Bowles, *Promises to Keep: My Years in Public Life, 1941–1969* (New York: Harper and Row, 1971), 407, 408, 409.
[29] Chester Bowles, "Memorandum from the Ambassador at Large (Bowles) to the Secretary of State", July 12, 1962, Washington, in *FRUS, 1961–1963*, vol. 2, document 241, pp. 516–19.

his support for Diem, who refused to support such a plan.[30] Soon after the Laotian settlement was signed, however, Harriman told Rusk that Bowles' proposal was unworkable, because it "would require us to take commitments without any assurance of the other side doing the same, with no enforcement procedures that would be workable."[31] Ironically, Harriman's words echoed those of President Diem and others who were against the original Laotian neutrality deal.

The American liberal idea that the pen was mightier than the sword, regardless of the facts on the ground with respect to the political and military prowess of the adversary, was based on an underlying false assumption that all the parties in a conflict want to stop the fighting more than they want to win the war. Because of their recent experience in Malaya, the British did not start from this assumption. They had found it necessary to steel themselves to accept the harsh reality that Communist insurgents will keep fighting until they are destroyed both politically and militarily. There was no point in negotiating with them before they were ready to surrender, and the British kept the pressure on them until they were.[32] The ruling American Democrats did not rest easy with the unsentimental British approach to counterinsurgency. Indeed, many of the Kennedy administration's "best and brightest" acted as though the Communists in Southeast Asia wanted nothing more than civil rights and peaceful coexistence with the non-Communists.

To powerful Democrat diplomats Bowles, Galbraith, and Harriman, President Diem stood in the way of their resolution to the conflicts in

---

[30] Bowles, *Promises to Keep*, 416–17.

[31] Averell Harriman, "Memorandum from the Assistant Secretary of State For Far Eastern Affairs (Harriman) to the Secretary of State", July 30, 1962, Washington, in *FRUS, 1961–1963*, vol. 2, document 253, pp. 565–66.

[32] "The main impact of government measures [in Malaya] occurred ... from 1952 to 1954, and it was during this period that the communists' organisation and military strength were broken, so that by the end of 1954 their eventual military defeat became apparent. Their strength was declining rapidly; they were losing arms at a higher rate than the government, and their subversive political organisation was being uprooted. Politically, this enabled the British to set the date for independence in 1957 and to inaugurate countrywide elections for a Malayan government, which was established in 1955 with Tunku Abdul Rahman as Chief Minister....With a new Malayan government in the saddle, pledged in its election platform to offer an amnesty to end war, the Communist Party accordingly put out peace feelers. The military pressure was temporarily taken off, and arrangements were made for peace talks to be held at Baling near the Malayan-Thai frontier." Robert Grainger Thompson, *Defeating Communist Insurgency: Experiences from Malaya and Vietnam* (London: Chatto and Windus, 1966), 45.

Southeast Asia, with his defiant stance against their demands to reform his government and his disgust with the Laotian deal. Anyone who supported Diem, such as Nolting and Colby, were cast in an unfavourable light by the Harriman group, which had direct access to President Kennedy. Outside the Washington "in-crowd", Nolting found that he had little means to explain or to defend his and Diem's actions. Indeed, Nolting came to realise that President Kennedy was basing his perceptions of the situation in Vietnam more on reports from his friends and the news media than on the official reports sent to him by his embassy in Saigon.[33] Roger Hilsman illustrated an example of Kennedy being swayed by Harriman. When suspicions about the Communists' intentions with regard to Laos were voiced in a National Security Council meeting, but there was no serious opposition to the basic policy, the president swung his chair around toward Harriman, saying, "Well, we'll go along with the governor."[34]

Going along with Harriman on Laos, who was actually going along with President Kennedy, proved to be a disaster for South Vietnam. In very short order, Diem's suspicions about the Communists' intentions in Laos were proved right and Harriman's "fingertips feelings" were proved wrong. Within a year of the accords being signed, the American press was carrying story after story of Communist violations of the settlement; it simultaneously portrayed the conflict as one between "Reds" and "Rightists", as if both sides were equally bad.[35]

As the security situation in Laos deteriorated, the Ngo Dinhs threatened to cut off diplomatic relations with Laos so that the GVN would not be legally bound by the treaty that forbade them from pursuing Communist insurgents who, after attacking South Vietnam, fled for

[33] Cf. Nolting, *From Trust to Tragedy*, 42–43

[34] Quoted in Roger Hilsman, *To Move a Nation: The Politics of Foreign Policy in the Administration of John F. Kennedy* (Garden City, N.Y.: Doubleday, 1967), 153.

[35] A small sampling of these reports includes the following: Associated Press, "Rightists in Laos Repel Red Drive: Call Leftists' Losses Heavy at Town in South as Fight among Factions Spreads", *New York Times*, June 14, 1963, 1, 10; United Press International, "South Laos Fighting at 2 Towns Noted", *New York Times*, June 16, 1963, 18 ("Neutralists and right-wing troops were reported battling Pathet Lao forces at two towns in southern Laos"); Reuters, "Laotian Reds Pound 'Rightist' Garrison", *New York Times*, June 21, 1963, 15; James Feron, "Britain Assails Soviet Account of How Laos Peace Broke Down", *New York Times*, June 22, 1963, 6; Hedrick Smith, "U.S. Says Hanoi Renews Laos Aid: Charges North Vietnamese Give Arms to Pro-Reds in Breach of Geneva Pact", *New York Times*, October 30, 1963, 1, 10.

refuge in Laos. Ambassador Nolting tried his best to persuade Diem and his brother not to break off diplomatic relations with Laos, as can be seen in his correspondence to Nhu at the time.[36] Harriman instructed Nolting to get tougher with Diem and his brother. In a telegram dated October 18, 1962, Harriman wrote: "I must tell you frankly that it will be diplomatic defeat if Diem severs relations with Laos. Diem cannot expect us to accept his refusal, in affronting disregard of request from the President, to stay in the fight to preserve Laos, Laos being on his own doorstep."[37]

At this time—on October 21, 1962, to be exact—a meeting was held at Gia Long Palace in Saigon between Vietnamese and American leaders. In attendance were Ngo Dinh Nhu, Frederick Nolting, and Admiral Harry D. Felt, representing the commander in chief of the U.S. Pacific Command (CINCPAC). The purpose of this meeting was to discuss South Vietnam's position on Laotian neutrality. This was a seminal meeting. Nhu illustrated very clearly how Southeast Asians viewed the problem and, particularly, why the South Vietnamese and the GVN were concerned. He pointed out many complexities about Laos that seemed to have eluded Harriman and his powerful supporters.

For example, Nhu had been in the process of negotiating the defection of two entire North Vietnamese regiments that had been stationed in Laos and did not want to return to Hanoi as stipulated under the Laotian neutrality agreement.[38] Nhu claimed that Laotian neutrality was working against his program for securing substantial defections from

---

[36] The following is from a letter Nolting sent to Nhu on October 13, 1962:

"Dear Mr. Counselor: I have already taken much time of your Government's officials, including the President, on the subject of relations with the Laotian Government, and I hope you will pardon my sending this note on the subject to express once again my Government's strong hope that the Government of Viet-Nam will find a way to continue diplomatic relations with the Laotian Government.... President Kennedy feels that the United States has the right to ask for the continued cooperation of the Government of Viet-Nam in this matter. He also recognizes and appreciates the fact that your Government has gone along thus far even despite grave misgivings. He feels that it would be a great mistake to break diplomatic relations at this point, regardless of what the Laotian Government may do in recognizing the Hanoi regime." Frederick Nolting, "Letter from the Ambassador in Vietnam (Nolting) to the Vietnamese President's Political Counselor (Nhu)", October 13, 1962, Saigon, in *FRUS, 1961–1963*, vol. 2, document 301, pp. 696–97.

[37] Averell Harriman, "Telegram from the Department of State to the Embassy in Vietnam", October 18, 1962, Washington, in *FRUS, 1961–1963*, vol. 2, document 304, p. 707.

[38] "Memorandum for the Record", October 21, 1962, Saigon, in *FRUS, 1961–1963*, vol. 2, document 305, pp. 708–9. This memorandum was prepared from the interpreter's notes.

the Viet Cong sequestered in Laos. Potential defectors now had questions about American intentions in the region: Would American policy change again? Would the Americans abandon those who switched sides the way they were abandoning tribesmen (such as the Hmong) in other parts of Laos to the Pathet Lao and the North Vietnamese?[39] Nhu mentioned another new South Vietnamese concern: rather than fearing the Americans would stay too long, they now worried that Laotian neutrality had opened a door through which the Americans would leave Vietnam.[40]

What is particularly important and readily discernible in Nhu's concerns, is that deep fears and suspicions had been aroused within the Vietnamese by the developments in Laos. These fears were based not only on the current situation, but on the Americans' allowing their allies in Eastern Europe to fall into the hands of the Soviets at the end of the Second World War. During the meeting, in fact, Nhu made this the centrepiece of his argument, and it struck home because Averell Harriman had presided over what the Vietnamese believed were failed Soviet agreements.[41]

To sum up, Laotian neutrality was causing far more problems in Southeast Asia than it was solving. At the end of the day, the Americans could always go home, but the non-Communist Vietnamese could not, since they were fighting for their very homes.[42] Regardless of these

---

[39] Ibid., 711.

[40] From the memorandum recounting the meeting: "Admiral Felt said that he had never heard the faintest whisper of such an idea [i.e., the Americans using the neutrality accords as a reason to leave Vietnam]. Mr. Nhu then said that he, personally, was convinced the United States had no idea of abandoning Vietnam, but that others could not understand the reason for what had taken place in Laos. Those who had the desire to confront the Communists thought that Laos offered the perfect terrain for their struggle." Ibid., 714.

[41] From the memorandum recounting the meeting: "He [Nhu] then referred to Mr. Harriman's written account of the Yalta Agreements pointing out that these agreements rested on the signature and the word of Stalin. He quoted Harriman's question in which he asked Stalin why he had not lived up to the agreements—and Stalin's answer that the conditions which had made the agreements necessary no longer prevailed. Mr. Nhu then said that the events in Laos were the direct consequence of the Vienna discussions between Khrushchev and Kennedy.... Mr. Nhu replied that the actions of the countries of the Free World were such that the initiative was always left with the Communists. The 'agreements' in Laos were entirely dependent upon the will of Khrushchev." Ibid., 711–12.

[42] This point was driven home when South Vietnam collapsed under the Communists' assault. After the Communist victory in 1975, those who were not killed outright by the victors were subject to decades in concentration and reeducation camps.

concerns, Harriman was determined to bend the Vietnamese to his will, to prevent them from backing out of the neutrality agreement, even if that meant removing his opposition, meaning Diem and his brother. Nolting tried to soften Harriman's approach, writing in a telegram that the Americans must respect the sovereignty of South Vietnam to determine its own foreign policy and must not threaten to cut off aid.[43]

Harriman was incensed by Nolting's telegram, and he shot back the following brisk cable:

> Your 443 indicates that you and I are not on the same wavelength. The President's position is already doubly engaged, not only by his personal letter to Diem, but also by Laos settlement which must be made to achieve US objectives as far as possible. In making settlement we have made it plain to all concerned that we consider it not ending all conflict, but transferring conflict from military to political area. In this conflict we have a right to expect full support and assistance from GVN as ally as well as signatory. From your messages I gained the impression that you do not consider Diem's attitude towards Laos of prime importance.... You are instructed to make another approach along lines of Deptel 459 or in whatever manner in your judgment you consider most appropriate. We have never suggested application sanctions, and you are not to give any implication that US has any idea of applying them. When you talk to Diem you should talk as an ally to another expecting support due us and may inform him you are speaking under instructions.[44]

Although Harriman told Nolting to speak to Diem as one ally to another, his message was clear. He must make the GVN do what Washington wants as commanded by Harriman. The men in the Kennedy administration failed to appreciate that they were effectively trying to make Diem their puppet, which in turn would undermine the most valuable commodity he had: political legitimacy. They were opening the floodgates for Communist propaganda against Diem, which never failed to drive home the point that he was "My-Diem" ("America's Diem").

Over the course of the next year, according to Nolting, Harriman's "hatred of the Diem regime became greater and greater". It had originated with President Diem's reluctance to sign the Laotian agreement,

---

[43] Frederick Nolting, "Telegram from the Embassy in Vietnam to the Department of State", October 20, 1962, Saigon, in *FRUS, 1961–1963*, vol. 2, document 306, pp. 716–17.

[44] Averell Harriman, "Telegram from the Department of State to the Embassy in Vietnam", October 22, 1962, Washington, in *FRUS, 1961–1963*, vol. 2, document 307, pp. 717–18.

he explained, even though the Thais had objected to it just as strongly as the Vietnamese. "But this started a personal distrust that certainly made it much more difficult to get any reasonable exchange of views in the National Security Council meetings that followed in the fall of 1963. It was very, very difficult."[45] Thus, Ambassador Nolting became deeply concerned about the future of American–South Vietnamese relations. The rapprochement with Diem he had taken pains to build was crumbling. In fact, the foundation had already been laid for the Kennedy administration's betrayal of the South Vietnamese president.

[45] Frederick Nolting, "Kennedy, NATO, and Southeast Asia", in *Diplomacy, Administration, and Policy: The Ideas and Careers of Frederick E. Nolting, Jr., Frederick C. Mosher, and Paul T. David*, ed. Kenneth W. Thompson (Lanham, Md.: University Press of America; Charlottesville, Va.: Miller Center, University of Virginia, 1995), 24–25.

8

Nolting's Rearguard Action

As the Harriman faction worked to bring about a 180-degree turn in U.S. policy toward President Diem, it was helped along by journalists whose negative reporting soured public opinion about America's involvement in South Vietnam. Ambassador Nolting, meanwhile, stuck to his mission to maintain a working relationship between Washington and Saigon by assuring President Diem of America's support.

The Harriman group consisted, at one time or another, of Chester Bowles,[1] Michael Forrestal,[2] John Kenneth Galbraith,[3] Roger Hilsman,[4] Paul Kattenburg,[5] Joseph Mendenhall,[6] William Sullivan,[7] and James

---

[1] According to Arthur Schlesinger Jr.: "Chester Bowles, as Under Secretary, had the second place of responsibility in the State Department.... It was Bowles himself, with his sure instinct for appointments, who first proposed putting Harriman in charge of Far Eastern affairs." *A Thousand Days: John F. Kennedy in the White House* (Boston: Houghton Mifflin, 1965), 437, 443–44.

[2] Forrestal was a Harriman protégé who went to work for President Kennedy, transferring from DOS to the White House as the National Security Council's specialist on Far Eastern affairs. Rudy Abramson, *Spanning the Century: The Life of W. Averell Harriman, 1891–1986* (New York: William Morrow, 1992), 571, 581, 589.

[3] According to Arthur Schlesinger, Galbraith shared Harriman's dislike of Diem and supported Harriman in his battles to turn policy away from supporting him. See Schlesinger, *Thousand Days*, 547.

[4] Hilsman had been the DOS director of intelligence and research and then became the assistant secretary for Far Eastern affairs. For his anti-Diem opinions, see George W. Ball, *The Past Has Another Pattern: Memoirs* (New York: W.W. Norton, 1982), 288, 371–72.

[5] According to Ambassador Nolting, Kattenburg, who later became head of the Vietnam Task Force, held a very low opinion of Ngo Dinh Diem. Frederick Nolting, *From Trust to Tragedy: The Political Memoirs of Frederick Nolting, Kennedy's Ambassador to Diem's Vietnam* (New York: Praeger, 1988), 128.

[6] Mendenhall had been the Saigon embassy's counsellor for political affairs. Before his return to Washington he told Ambassador Nolting that he intended to write a thesis on alternatives to President Diem. See ibid., 24–25.

[7] Sullivan was a Harriman protégé who helped with the Laotian negotiations and who, with Harriman's help, became ambassador to Laos. Charles A. Stevenson, *The End of Nowhere: American Policy toward Laos since 1954* (Boston: Beacon Press, 1972), 157.

Thomson.[8] The common bonds that tied these men together were their loyalty to Averell Harriman, their relatively powerful positions within DOS and the Kennedy administration (thanks to Harriman), and their dislike of Ngo Dinh Diem and Ngo Dinh Nhu. In the judgement of these men, the insurgency in South Vietnam was a civil war caused principally by Ngo Dinh Diem's ineptitude and corruption.[9] Thus, they logically concluded that the solution to the conflict was the removal of President Diem. While some of these men may have disliked Diem because some of his actions to thwart the Communists violated their democratic ideals, Harriman's dislike of the man was "personal and unforgiving", and he had the power to translate that passion into policy.[10] He led the fight for a coup against Diem, said Robert Kennedy. "It became an emotional matter ... and in fact, his advice was wrong. In fact, he started us down a road which was quite dangerous."[11]

As previously stated, the so-called civil war in South Vietnam was, in fact, a Communist insurgency organised and supported by Communist powers outside the country. Even the Americans who lined up against Diem understood it as a critical battle in the overall Cold War. The Viet Cong predated Diem's government; its infrastructure had been in place and growing since the French Indochina wars. The depth of the infrastructure's organisation and the discipline with which operations were carried out betrayed the not-so hidden hand of Ho Chi Minh. While the Harriman group sought a replacement of Diem who could succeed against the Viet Cong, in part by making democratic reforms and therefore winning over some of his political enemies, including those in America, Robert Thompson stated that the president of South Vietnam—regardless of who he was and what reforms he implemented—would still be faced with an unrelenting Communist insurgency.

Roger Hilsman, a veteran of guerrilla warfare in Burma during World War II, praised Thompson's work and agreed with many of his ideas, as we have seen, but he nevertheless assigned much blame for the insurgency to President Diem, and he aggressively advanced the argument for

---

[8] Abramson, *Spanning the Century*, 611.

[9] Ibid., 611–12.

[10] Ellen J. Hammer, *A Death in November: America in Vietnam, 1963* (New York: E.P. Dutton, 1987), 31.

[11] Ibid, 33, quoting Robert F. Kennedy, interview by John Bartlow Martin, April 30, 1964, John F. Kennedy Oral History Collection, John F. Kennedy Presidential Library, Boston.

his removal. Even before top military brass, Hilsman was pugnacious. "He was known to correct high-ranking military briefers in the presence of the President, the secretary of state, and the secretary of defense, using their maps and charts to launch soaring military and geopolitical expositions that left his superiors with jaws set and gripping the arms of their chairs." Vice President Lyndon Johnson "took a simmering dislike to him because of the way he excoriated Diem and asserted himself in matters Johnson considered in the province of the military."[12]

By late 1962 the various men advising President Kennedy about Vietnam constituted a house divided, with the Harriman group on one side and Secretary Rusk, Vice President Johnson, and the Pentagon on the other. Thus, Harriman's biographer noted: "Averell was the godfather of the anti-Diem band; Rusk was the faithful ally of the Pentagon school that spoke in the same breath of defeating the communists and supporting the government in Saigon."[13] President Kennedy encouraged both sides, "accepting the McNamara-Pentagon advice to up the ante while encouraging Harriman and the Diem critics to keep up the pressure for reforms".[14]

The division within DOS, between Rusk and Harriman, led to mixed signals being sent to the White House as the two men vied for the president's ear.[15] President Kennedy had perceived that there were problems at DOS, but even after instituting its reorganisation he was still perplexed.[16] Arthur Schlesinger Jr. noted, "To the end, the Department remained a puzzle to the President. No one ran it; Rusk, Ball and Harriman constituted a loose triumvirate on the seventh floor and, passing things back and forth among themselves, managed to keep a few steps ahead of crisis."[17]

According to Secretary of Defense Robert McNamara, the Pentagon was pleased with the military progress being made in Vietnam and had no intentions of getting behind a coup in South Vietnam. General Paul D. Harkins, who headed up the U.S. military mission in Vietnam,

---

[12] Abramson, *Spanning the Century*, 612.

[13] Ibid., 614–15.

[14] Ibid., 615.

[15] Smith Simpson, *Anatomy of the State Department* (Boston: Beacon Press, 1968), 141.

[16] Simpson suggested that Kennedy's reorganisation caused considerable grief in the department and that, owing to the president's interference, over two hundred experienced diplomats retired from the U.S. Foreign Service. See ibid., 140–42.

[17] Schlesinger, *Thousand Days*, 446–47.

maintained that Diem was on the "right track" and so was U.S. policy in supporting him and his government. Until the Buddhist crisis in the summer of 1963, there was little to no support for the Harriman group at DOD.[18]

The foreign policy of the U.S. government toward Vietnam from 1961 to 1962 was summed up by an American reporter as "sink or swim with Diem". But with the strengthening position of the Harriman group, this policy was about to become, in the words of Thompson, "sinking without him". By heeding more and more the advice of his anti-Diem advisors, Thompson wrote, Kennedy made a great error in 1963, when he informed the South Vietnamese generals that, if they overthrew President Diem, they would continue to receive full American support. "It was one thing to threaten the withdrawal of aid from Diem but quite another to offer it instead to others. In any circumstances and by any standards it was monstrous interference in the internal political affairs of another state.... By it the United States was committed to an open-ended assistance policy towards Diem's successors and assumed full responsibility for the outcome of the war."[19]

By late 1962 it was apparent to Ambassador Nolting that "sinking without Diem" was precisely the direction the Harriman group was leading the Kennedy administration. What particularly confounded him, and the reason the Pentagon resisted the Harriman group, was that measureable progress against the Viet Cong was being made.[20] "When we first arrived with our families," wrote Nolting, "we could hardly go out of Saigon without an escort, and then you took a chance on getting ambushed. By 1962 we could drive to many provinces without escort and without much danger.... This was just one indication of the gradual pacification brought about by the Diem government with our help and advice."[21]

---

[18] Robert S. McNamara, *In Retrospect: The Tragedy and Lessons of Vietnam*, with Brian VanDeMark (New York: Times Books, 1995), 46–49.

[19] Robert Grainger Thompson, *No Exit from Vietnam*, updated ed. (New York: David McKay, 1970), 120.

[20] Even Arthur Schlesinger Jr., who was no friend of Diem or the GVN, was forced to acknowledge the success of 1962 in terms of defeating Communist insurgency and Diem's reclamation of authority. See Schlesinger, *Thousand Days*, 982.

[21] Frederick Nolting, "Kennedy, NATO, and Southeast Asia", in *Diplomacy, Administration, and Policy: The Ideas and Careers of Frederick E. Nolting, Jr., Frederick C. Mosher, and Paul T. David*, ed. Kenneth W. Thompson (Lanham, Md.: University Press of America; Charlottesville, Va.: Miller Center, University of Virginia, 1995), 22.

The proof of the substantial gains made by the GVN was clear to the experts in the spring of 1963. As Robert Thompson reported, "Now, in March 1963, I can say, and in this I am supported by all members of the mission, that the Government is beginning to win the shooting war against the Viet Cong."[22] Two months later, Secretary McNamara reported that the overall situation in Vietnam was improving: "In the military sector of the counter-insurgency, we are winning."[23]

The French, who were mostly critical of American efforts in Southeast Asia, praised the counterinsurgency of the early 1960s, stating that South Vietnam was being returned to a stabilised security environment within which their big businesses, such as the Michelin Rubber Company, were able to conduct business again.[24] Even the enemies of the GVN acknowledged the progress it had made. According to Australian radical Wilfred Burchett, 1962 was a year of defeat and setbacks for the Viet Cong. After making considerable gains in terms of territory and population, the Viet Cong were pushed back by the ARVN with the help of American military aid: "The use of helicopters and amphibious tanks to increase rapidity of movement and to avoid the devastating ambushes that the Diemist troops invariably fell into when they moved by road or river, caught the guerrillas off balance." Burchett added that "the drive to set up 'strategic hamlets' was also a problem" for the Viet Cong.[25]

The Harriman group was not content with these military successes, however, because the Diem government was still far from the Western-style democracy demanded by the idealists in the Kennedy administration, the press, and the American public. Nolting would later say that the group's insistence on government reform was the greatest blunder of the Kennedy administration. "The error was in its refusal to understand that

[22] Quoted in Schlesinger, *Thousand Days*, 982.

[23] Congress, House, Committee on Armed Services, "Introduction", in *Evolution of the War: Counterinsurgency; The Overthrow of Ngo Dinh Diem, May–November, 1963*, section IV.B.5 of bk. 3 of *United States–Vietnam Relations, 1945–1967: Study Prepared by the Department of Defense* (Washington, D.C.: United States Government Printing Office, 1971), 2.

[24] According to Nolting, French diplomat Maurice Couve de Murville told him on two occasions that the American effort in 1961 and 1962 was succeeding from the point of view of the French interests still in South Vietnam. "The Michelin Rubber Company, the major banks, and the major shipping companies were all saying, 'Keep it up; the country is beginning to get pacified; it is beginning to work.'" Nolting, "Kennedy, NATO, and Southeast Asia", 23.

[25] Wilfred G. Burchett, *Vietnam: Inside Story of the Guerrilla War* (New York: International Publishers, 1965), 189.

the elected constitutional government of Vietnam was the best available. If we were to help South Vietnam survive at all, the only available vehicle that could sustain and carry forward the country was the government that had been in power eight years (after two elections)."[26]

The role of the American press in focusing the Kennedy administration on Diem's government cannot be overstated. Historian George Herring recorded the successes of the CIP in South Vietnam between 1961 and 1962. He also noted, however, that the young news reporters of the American press corps in Saigon placed an entirely different story before the American public. In their version, they did to President Diem what American reporter Theodore White had done to President Chiang Kai-shek of Taiwan.[27] White, who won a Pulitzer Prize in 1962, first earned a name for himself by exposing the weaknesses and the abuses of the pro-American, anti-Communist General Chiang.[28] The comparison of the media's treatment of President Diem with White's treatment of General Chiang was also made by Clare Boothe Luce, who observed that both storylines included the obligatory dragon lady: in Taiwan Madame Chiang Kai-shek, in South Vietnam Madame Ngo Dinh Nhu.[29] In an ad in the *New York Times*, just before Diem's murder, the former ambassador and congresswoman asked the following rhetorical question about South Vietnam: "Is the history of the Liberal Press in Chunking and Havana going to repeat itself?" She answered: "The evidence is that it is."[30]

In 1962 and 1963, American journalists David Halberstam of the *New York Times* and Neil Sheehan of United Press International wrote that the war in South Vietnam was being lost mostly because of Diem's corrupt and self-serving government, which, amongst other things, made the

---

[26] Nolting, "Kennedy, NATO, and Southeast Asia", 22.

[27] George C. Herring, *America's Longest War: The United States and Vietnam, 1950–1975* (New York: John Wiley, 1975), 91–92.

[28] Theodore White and Annalee Jacoby penned the well-known *Thunder out of China* (New York: William Sloane Associates, 1946). Once White's credentials were established amongst liberal intellectuals, he was able to secure a Pulitzer Prize for his book *The Making of the President, 1960* (New York: Atheneum, 1961).

[29] Clare Boothe Luce, "The Lady Is for Burning: The Seven Deadly Sins of Madame Nhu", *National Review*, November 5, 1963, 395–99.

[30] Clare Boothe Luce, "The Lady is For Burning: The Seven Deadly Sins of Madame Wu", in a full-page advertisement taken out by the *National Review* in the *New York Times*, Wednesday, October 30, 1963, p. 40.

Strategic Hamlet Program a "sham" and caused avoidable military losses involving American casualties.[31] Despite his praise for their writing and research, which he described respectively as "brilliant" and "exhaustive", William Colby thought the conclusions reached by Sheehan and Halberstam were just plain wrong. Criticising a government was one thing, he wrote, but to recommend undoing a functioning government in a time of war pretty much guaranteed that whatever would follow would be worse. Intellectual capability has its place, but it is simply no substitute for wisdom, the latter being a virtue that Colby thought the reporters lacked.[32]

The press was causing difficulties for Nolting, and the ambassador, in his memoirs, addressed this directly. He noted that at the beginning of his mission in Saigon his relationship with the press had been amicable, and he wrote that he was at a loss as to what later made the reporters hostile.[33] He did not seem to realise that because the reporters in Saigon had already concluded that Diem was the wrong leader for South Vietnam,[34] no amount of goodwill he tried to create with them would protect him, or anyone who supported Diem against their better judgement, from their assaults.[35] He admitted that he had severely underestimated the antipathy of these men toward Ngo Dinh Diem and himself.[36]

During this period, Nolting stumbled upon a little-known fact: at least one American reporter in South Vietnam regarded the country as a career "backwater" and was looking for a sensational story to provide him with a star exit. On one occasion, when President Diem was dragging a whole entourage around on one of his quick-paced, long-distance marches to inspect all manner of crops and fish ponds while talking with the local farmers, *New York Times* reporter Homer Bigart made

[31] For Neil Sheehan's views on Diem's military leadership, see his *A Bright Shining Lie: John Paul Vann and America in Vietnam* (New York: Vintage Books, 1988).

[32] William E. Colby, *Lost Victory: A Firsthand Account of America's Sixteen-Year Involvement in Vietnam*, with James McCargar (Chicago: Contemporary Books, 1989), 236–37.

[33] Nolting, *From Trust to Tragedy*, 87.

[34] For David Halberstam's views on Diem's government, see his *The Making of a Quagmire* (New York: Random House, 1965), 68.

[35] Nolting, *From Trust to Tragedy*, 87.

[36] Halberstam on Nolting: "Nolting came to remind me of some white community leaders I had known in Mississippi and Tennessee, men who—at a time when their communities were about to blow up in racial disorder—reassured me that all was well, that the Negroes were satisfied with the status quo, that the problem was entirely the work of outside agitators and that writing about it would only make the situation worse. These men had no contact with the Negro community except for what their maids or hired people told them, and they went on believing what they wanted to believe." *Making of a Quagmire*, 73–74.

his discomfort more than clear to Nolting. As Nolting recalled, the day was hot and humid, and everyone had trouble keeping up with Diem, who seemed to come alive on these occasions when he could, as in his happier times as a village and then a provincial chief, be directly involved in the projects improving the lives of his people. Bigart, however, "was furious with the whole set-up".[37] He seemed not to realise that Diem's passion for solving the practical problems confronting the farmers was not feigned for the benefit of reporters or other onlookers. His interest in and talent for infrastructure development emerged during the rule of Emperor Bao Dai and the French, and Ambassador Nolting had witnessed both firsthand on many occasions.[38]

After this incident, when Bigart's visa expired, the GVN refused to renew it because of his negative reporting. Nolting went straightaway to President Diem—even before receiving instructions to do so from Washington—and argued that expelling a representative from one of America's leading newspapers could only harm their mutual efforts.[39] Diem poured out his frustration about the media's constant attacks against him and his government.[40] Yet in order to show good faith to

[37] Nolting explained that the tour occurred after the opening of a vocational school in the provinces at which President Diem and he were present. "After a brief ceremony, Diem, as was his custom, tramped around the countryside, looking at the rice paddies, the dikes, and the fish ponds, and talking with the people there.... [Bigart] did not like anything about it, and he made it clear that he most definitely did not want to be there." *From Trust to Tragedy*, 87–88.

[38] In a letter to war correspondent Marguerite Higgins, Ambassador Nolting noted: "Diem was an indefatigable traveller. He was out of Saigon in the provinces two–three days out of every week. He ran us ragged trying to keep up with him. In addition to Army headquarters and outposts, he visited the remotest villages and districts.... As you know, Diem had been a Province Chief under the French (a darned good one) and he was intensely interested in local rural problems—health conditions, schools, water supply, roads, canals, seeds, fertilizer, crop diversification, land ownership, land rents, housing, etc. He was especially interested in, and proud of, the agricultural improvement stations which his government had established, teaching many things, from fruit and nut-tree raising to fish-ponds, manioc-grinding, and even mushroom-raising in rice-straw stacks.... I accompanied Diem on many, many trips." Frederick Nolting to Marguerite Higgins, July 2, 1965, 1, Nolting Papers, box 12, Selected Correspondence—Higgins, Marguerite.

[39] *From Trust to Tragedy*, 88.

[40] American reporters faulted Diem for taking exception to their articles. Halberstam: "Nolting's job was difficult, but it was made even more difficult by the almost psychotic preoccupation of Diem and his family with the Western press—the one element operating in Vietnam, other than the Vietcong, which they could not control.... Diem devoted time and energy to reading what the American reporters were writing about him, far beyond what could be considered the understandable sensitivities of a leader whose country is engaged in a difficult war." *Making of a Quagmire*, 74–75.

the American ambassador, Diem telephoned the minister of the interior and asked him to renew Bigart's visa. The very next day Bigart called Nolting and accused him of ruining his newsworthy expulsion from Vietnam.[41]

David Halberstam soon replaced Bigart, and Nolting's initial impression of him was positive to the extent that the twenty-seven-year-old reporter seemed to be an improvement over the unhappy Bigart. Within a few weeks, however, "Halberstam became the leader of the 'get Diem' press group in Saigon." Nolting continued, "His articles implied that if we stuck with Diem, we would sink as if we were tied to a stone. Halberstam's considerable writing talent enhanced his influence. Beginning like drops of acid, his reports steadily conditioned the climate of American opinion. I suspect that Halberstam may have been catering to the Times' editorial line. He was, I think, influenced by his bosses and they by his reports, creating a crescendo of anti-Diem propaganda."[42] Later, in August 1963, Nolting's suspicions that Halberstam was catering to New York Times editorial bias were reinforced. He received reports from a trusted colleague that Halberstam had been at the Caravelle Bar (a popular place for American reporters to congregate) "proudly displaying a telegram from his newspaper in New York, which said, in substance: 'Good going. Keep it up. State Department is beginning to see it our way.' "[43]

Mike Mansfield, the Senate majority leader and an influential member of the Senate Foreign Relations Committee, touched upon the subject of American press coverage in a report about his December 1962 visit to South Vietnam. In a meeting with Ngo Dinh Nhu, Mansfield noted that relations between the American and the Vietnamese governments were excellent but for the negative news reports. The concern of the Kennedy administration, Mansfield said, was that the difficulties the South Vietnamese government was having with Western reporters, particularly Americans, was reflecting negatively on the Diem government back

---

[41] From Nolting's memoirs: "I expected a word of appreciation, possibly even a change of attitude. Instead, he expressed considerable annoyance. He informed me that he had wanted to get away from his Vietnam assignment for some time and that this expulsion would have made his exit sensational. My intervention had only prolonged his stay and spoiled his story." Nolting, From Trust to Tragedy, 88.

[42] Ibid.

[43] Ibid.

home. Nhu, in his reply to the senator, fully acknowledged this problem and placed the blame on the shoulders of the American reporters. Nhu claimed that their youth, immaturity in outlook, and passion were to blame, and that Vietnam needed older, more experienced reporters who could comprehend the difficulties the country was facing.[44]

Arthur Schlesinger Jr. also noted the deep antagonism that set in between the American reporters in South Vietnam and the U.S. diplomatic and military missions in the country. He quoted Halberstam, who wrote that the U.S. embassy had "turned into the adjunct of a dictatorship" and that the Strategic Hamlet Program was "a fake and a failure". The reporter took the moral high ground for himself and his colleagues: "We are representatives of a free society and we weren't going to surrender our principles to the narrow notions of a closed society."[45]

In a hasty reaction to the attacks that Halberstam and other newsmen were making about American involvement in Vietnam, Kennedy despatched Roger Hilsman and Michael Forrestal in late 1962 to make a report on the situation.[46] Although critical of Ngo Dinh Diem, Hilsman acknowledged that the Communists had indeed suffered serious setbacks in 1962. "The war in South Vietnam is clearly going better than it was a year ago.... The Viet Cong, in sum, are being hurt—they have somewhat less freedom than they had a year ago, they apparently suffer acutely from lack of medicines, and in some very isolated areas they seem to be having trouble getting food."[47] Hilsman did not praise Diem or the GVN. Rather he condensed his report to the following: "Our overall judgment, in sum, is that we are probably winning but certainly more slowly than we had hoped. At the rate it is now going the war will last longer than we would like, cost more in terms of both lives and

[44] See "Memorandum of a Conversation, Gia Long Palace, Saigon, December 1, 1962, 11:30 A.M. [subject: Senator Mike Mansfield's visit to Vietnam]", in *FRUS, 1961–1963*, vol. 2, document 323, pp. 752–53.

[45] Quoted in Schlesinger, *Thousand Days*, 984 and 983.

[46] Kennedy had just received Senator Mansfield's report (from Mansfield's December 1962 visit to Vietnam; see footnote 44 above), which was pessimistic, and had tried to have Halberstam recalled by the *New York Times*.

[47] Roger Hilsman and Michael V. Forrestal, "Memorandum from the Director of the Bureau of Intelligence and Research (Hilsman) and Michael V. Forrestal of the National Security Council Staff to the President: A Report on South Vietnam", January 25, 1963, Washington, in United States Department of State, *FRUS, 1961–1963*, ed. John P. Glennon, vol. 3, *Vietnam, January–August 1963* (Washington, D.C.: United States Government Printing Office, 1991), document 19, pp. 49–50.

money than we anticipated, and prolong the period in which a sudden and dramatic event would upset the gain already made."[48]

The White House requested the Hilsman-Forrestal report not only because of the press but also owing to the surprisingly negative tone of Senator Mike Mansfield's report on Vietnam—particularly as it related to the SHP—which reached Washington in December 1962. Mansfield was considered the Senate authority on Indochina and Vietnam.[49] He was well connected in the Democratic Party and enjoyed many years of friendship with Lyndon B. Johnson.[50] Along with Francis Cardinal Spellman and then senator John F. Kennedy, Mansfield had thrown his considerable political weight behind Diem in the mid-1950s.[51] In late 1954 the senator went on a fact-finding mission to Saigon and issued a report upon his return to Washington that gave powerful support to an official American commitment to Diem. He asserted that if Diem were to be removed from power—for example, by the French—then all U.S. aid should be suspended since Diem was the only nationalistic leader who was dedicated to a truly free Vietnam.[52]

Shortly after receiving the first Mansfield report, President Eisenhower heard negative reports about Diem from General Joseph Lawton Collins. Senator Mansfield immediately came to Diem's defence, arguing that General Collins was "playing with political dynamite". Mansfield told Eisenhower that "the remarkable aspect of Diem was [that], unlike most of the Vietnamese, he really was honest, incorruptible and a devoutly dedicated nationalist as well."[53] To back up his firm stand in

[48] Ibid., 52.

[49] Hammer, *Death in November*, 70.

[50] John S. Bowman, ed., *The Vietnam War: An Almanac* (New York: Random House, 1985), 491.

[51] Robert Scheer, "The Genesis of United States Support for Ngo Dinh Diem", in *Vietnam: History, Documents, and Opinions on a Major World Crisis*, ed. Marvin E. Gettlemen (Greenwich, Conn.: Fawcett Publications, 1965), 251–52.

[52] "He [Mansfield] said the issue 'is not Diem as an individual but rather the program for which he stands'. That program 'represents genuine nationalism,... is prepared to deal effectively with corruption and ... demonstrates a concern in advancing the welfare of the Vietnamese people'. The Senator felt it 'improbable' that any other leadership 'dedicated to these principles' could be found and recommended the Government 'consider an immediate suspension of all aid to Vietnam and the French Union Forces there, except that of a humanitarian nature, preliminary to a complete reappraisal of our present policies in Free Vietnam' if Diem fell." *The Pentagon Papers: The Defense Department History of United States Decisionmaking on Vietnam*, ed. Mike Gravel (Boston: Beacon Press, 1971), 1:222.

[53] Ibid.

support of Diem, Mansfield asserted that he spoke for all the Democratic leaders and that their position was unequivocal: they would not agree to the support of any government in Vietnam other than that of Diem.[54]

Given Senator Mansfield's earlier absolute support for Diem, his December 1962 report stunned Diem supporters within the Kennedy administration. In it he warned against expecting too much too soon from the SHP. He observed that while Diem remained "a dedicated, sincere, hardworking, incorruptible and patriotic leader", he was older and faced problems that were far more complex than those he had faced a decade ago. Mansfield continued:

> The energizing role which he played in the past appears to be passing to other members of his family, particularly Ngo Dinh Nhu. The latter is a person of great energy and intellect who is fascinated by the operations of political power and has consummate eagerness and ability in organizing and manipulating it. But it is Ngo Dinh Diem, not Ngo Dinh Nhu, who has such popular mandate to exercise power as there is in South Vietnam. In a situation of this kind there is a great danger of the corruption of unbridled power.[55]

President Kennedy was alarmed by this assessment and hence called for a second opinion, by sending Hilsman and Forrestal to Vietnam in December 1962.[56]

At this time, Secretary of State Dean Rusk argued that the information he had received "cited improvements in supply and intelligence operations and in the Vietnam command structure as evidence, in fact, the Vietnamese were winning the war".[57] Therefore, another fact-finding mission was not necessary. But between the time Hilsman and Forrestal visited South Vietnam and submitted their report, a sensationalised story about a military blunder made headlines.

Lieutenant Colonel John Paul Vann provided American reporters in Vietnam with information about the failed Battle of Ap Bac, an

[54] Ronald H. Spector, *The United States Army in Vietnam: Advice and Support; The Early Years* (Washington, D.C.: Center of Military History, United States Army, 1983), 248.

[55] Mike Mansfield, "Report by the Senate Majority Leader (Mansfield): Southeast Asia—Vietnam", December 18, 1962, Washington, in *FRUS, 1961–1963*, vol. 2, document 330, pp. 780–82.

[56] Herring, *America's Longest War*, 93.

[57] Thomas J. Schoenbaum, *Waging Peace and War: Dean Rusk in the Truman, Kennedy, and Johnson Years* (New York: Simon and Schuster, 1988), 395.

American-Vietnamese military operation in which he took part. Here is William Colby's description of Vann's involvement with both the battle on January 2, 1963, and the news reports that followed:

> The [ARVN] division he advised bottled up a Communist unit there but with a combination of laxity and disinclination to close had allowed the enemy to escape through a gap conveniently left in the lines around them. The Vietnamese force had lost eighty dead and over a hundred wounded and the Americans five helicopters, with three from their crews dead and eight wounded.... With his usual forcefulness, Vann had exploded to the press that highlighted the affair as a further indication that the Diem regime and its Army were unworthy of American support. Vann became so incensed at the official American reaction to the affair, in his mind condoning the ineffectiveness of the Vietnamese unit and its commander and trying to muzzle his protests, that he resigned from the Army.[58]

Colonel Vann's outrage at the bungling of the ARVN at the cost American lives gave reporters a sensational story. From the perspective of the Pentagon, the action revealed nothing more than the fact that the ARVN was a fledgling, or "green", fighting force at this level of engagement; in short, there really was no surprise in what happened. Indeed, some very experienced U.S. senior commanders were more than willing to give the ARVN the benefit of the doubt: they noted that, while the army seemed somewhat hesitant and lacked co-ordination in the face of enemy fire, the soldiers nevertheless did not break down and flee. Vann, however, saw the behaviour of the ARVN differently, and in addition to informing the press, he filed an official complaint of the operation that ended up in the hands of the Joint Chiefs of Staff. In it "Vann attributed the failure to the poor state of training of the South Vietnamese units, a system of command that never placed a Vietnamese officer above the rank of captain on the battlefield, a reluctance to incur casualties, an inability to take advantage of air superiority, and a lack of discipline."[59]

Newsmen like Sheehan and Halberstam included Vann's criticisms in their reports.[60] In due course their articles created a furore back home

---

[58] Colby, *Lost Victory*, 236.

[59] Summary telegram 677 from U.S. Army, Pacific, to Joint Chiefs of Staff, January 4, 1963; Kennedy Library, National Security Files, Vietnam Country Series, 1/63. "Editorial Note", in "Reassessment, January 1–March 14, 1963: Hilsman-Forrestal Report, Wheeler Mission, Mansfield Report, Comprehensive Plan, Thompson Report", pt. 1 of *FRUS, 1961–1963*, vol. 3, document 1, p. 1.

[60] For Sheehan's account of the Battle of Ap Bac, see his *Bright Shining Lie* (203–65).

in the United States. The *New York Times* used the battle to launch a full-scale attack on Diem and his government, claiming that Ap Bac had been a major military defeat and that Americans were not getting the full story of what was going on in Vietnam.[61]

It is worth quoting some excerpts from the news reports of the battle. In the article "Vietnamese Reds Win Major Clash", which appeared in the New York Times on January 4, 1963, Halberstam wrote: "Communist guerrillas, refusing to play by their own hide-and-seek rules in the face of Government troops, stood their ground and inflicted a major defeat on a larger force of Vietnamese regulars yesterday and today."[62] In another story two days later, Halberstam wrote that the battle "has bewildered high United States officials in Saigon.... United States advisers in the field, however, have long felt that conditions here made a defeat like this virtually inevitable.... American officers throughout the Mekong Delta feel that what happened at Ap Bac goes far deeper than one battle."[63] On January 10, 1963, Halberstam blamed the problems with the ARVN on Diem's leadership:

> The advisers feel that there is still too much political interference in the Vietnamese Army and that promotion too often depends on political loyalty rather than military ability....
>
> These Americans recalled that in a recent shuffle of the high command two officers widely respected by the Americans were removed from field

[61] From the editors of *FRUS, 1961–1963*: "The battle of Ap Bac was reported in the press in the United States as a 'major defeat' in which 'communist guerrillas shot up a fleet of United States helicopters carrying Vietnamese troops into battle'" (*The Washington Post*, January 3, 1963; *The New York Times*, January 4, 1963). On January 7, *The Washington Post* printed a front-page assessment of the battle by Neil Sheehan in which he wrote that 'angry United States military advisers charged today that Vietnamese infantrymen refused direct orders to advance during Wednesday's battle at Ap Bac and that an American Army captain was killed while out front pleading with them to attack.' An assessment done in the Department of State on January 15 of press reaction across the country to the battle of Ap Bac noted that 'since Ap Bac the complaint has been increasingly heard that the American public is not "getting the facts" on the situation in Viet-Nam, even at this time when American casualties are mounting.'" "Editorial Note", in "Reassessment, January 1–March 14, 1963", pt. 1 of *FRUS, 1961–1963*, vol. 3, document 1, p. 2. The editorial note quotes "'Alert' on Viet-Nam: Current American Concern and Misunderstanding", National Archives and Records Administration, RG 59, Files of the Office of Public Opinion Studies, U.S. Policy on S. Vietnam, April–Dec. 1963.

[62] David Halberstam, "Vietnamese Reds Win Major Clash: Inflict 100 Casualties in Fighting Larger Force", *New York Times*, January 4, 1963, 2.

[63] David Halberstam, "Vietnam Defeat Shocks U.S. Aides: Saigon's Rejection of Advice Blamed for Setback", *New York Times*, January 7, 1963, 2.

commands and that officers promoted and given field commands were men who had shown loyalty to President Ngo Dinh Diem at moments when his regime was threatened with internal revolt....

These sources also feel that one of the basic problems now hindering military improvement is a fear among many Vietnamese commanders of incurring casualties. Some commanders are said to feel that they will not be promoted and may lose command if they suffer too many casualties....

Americans who deal with President Diem, however, say that he knows there will be casualties and is willing to allow for this. If this is true, the field commanders say, the word has not reached the Vietnamese in the field.[64]

The editorial "What's Wrong in Vietnam?", which appeared in the *New York Times* on January 15, 1963, plainly targeted Diem and his government as being the cause of the Ap Bac defeat:

> It is worthwhile being reminded that losses in one battle, or even a dozen battles, do not portend loss of the war in South Vietnam. The fact remains, however, that serious defects of political policy and leadership in South Vietnam do seriously hamper the spirit and effectiveness of the South Vietnamese military forces. A defensive reaction to adverse reports about last week's battle should not obscure a deficiency that is well-documented and is often cited by Americans on the spot in Vietnam.
>
> Plainly, the South Vietnamese armed forces are not so good and spirited as they might be because a suspicious, dictatorial government in Saigon must preoccupy itself with preserving itself in power, not just from Communists but from many patriotic Vietnamese who oppose the Communists. Loyalty to President Diem is the criterion for preferment among Vietnamese officers, rather than ability.[65]

The Joint Chiefs of Staff countered the press assaults against the GVN with a direct report to the president stating that news accounts of the battle were misleading: "It appears that the initial press reports have distorted both the importance of the action and the damage suffered by the US/GVN forces. Although unexpectedly stiff resistance was apparently encountered contact has been maintained and the operation is being continued."[66] General Paul Harkins, commander of the Military Assistance Command in Vietnam, tried to avoid placing too much blame on

---

[64] David Halberstam, "Harkins Praises Vietnam Troops: Defends Soldiers' Courage against U.S. Criticism", *New York Times*, January 11, 1963, 3.

[65] "What's Wrong in Vietnam?", special ed., *New York Times*, January 15, 1963, 6.

[66] "Editorial Note", in "Reassessment, January 1–March 14, 1963", 2.

the relatively green ARVN. As an experienced soldier who had been under General George Patton in World War II, Harkins noted in a report to President Kennedy that the errors of the South Vietnamese forces were largely errors of courage rather than cowardice: "It took a lot of guts on the part of those pilots and crews to go back into the area to try to rescue their pals."[67]

Ambassador Nolting later recalled that Vann's description of a cowardly army under the control of a despotic and corrupt leader further diminished the reputation of the South Vietnamese in the eyes of the American public: "Colonel Vann, who later gave his life in Vietnam, caused great damage by his press interview. His outburst stemmed, no doubt, from genuine frustration, but it was unfair to the South Vietnamese Army and government and did great harm in terms of American public opinion."[68] Nolting countered the charges that Diem had been telling his army to avoid casualties. Nolting explained that the leader did tell his military not to allow innocent civilians to be killed just so that one or two fleeing or fighting guerrillas could be brought down on the spot. The ability to win over the fence-sitters in South Vietnam was harmed whenever innocent civilians were killed. Many American military advisors recognised then (and still recognise now) an almost golden rule of effective counterinsurgency: do not create more guerrillas by killing innocents.[69]

In his memoirs, Hilsman claimed that Diem had a "go slow" policy that even Harkins and Nolting did not know about: "It could be argued that he sensed that defeating the guerrillas would be a long, slow process and that it would be better to husband the strength of the government forces rather than dissipate it in too much American 'gung ho' offensive-mindedness.... But he never raised this question with either

[67] Quoted in FRUS, 1961–1963, 2–3.

[68] Nolting, From Trust to Tragedy, 96.

[69] "No one, not President Diem, not Paul Harkins after his many talks with Diem, not Nguyen Dinh Thuan, the effective Defense Minister, ever said or intimated to me that the South Vietnamese government was ordering the Army to hold its punches. I never saw or heard of any orders to avoid combat. I do recall many discussions with Diem and other officials who thought the fewer the casualties among the Army, the villagers, the fence sitters, and even the Viet Cong, the sooner pacification of the countryside could take place. Both the Vietnamese armed units and their American advisors were instructed to be careful about whom they attacked, since we wanted to bring dissenters over to our side, not kill them." Ibid., 96–97.

General Harkins or Ambassador Nolting, who did not learn of Diem's 'go slow' instructions until much, much later." Hilsman added that the motive he ascribed to Diem for his "go slow" policy gave credibility to the accusation being made by "a few of the military advisers" and "most of the American press, particularly David Halberstam of the *New York Times* and Neil Sheehan of the United Press International".[70] But his memoirs seem to be inconsistent with the Hilsman-Forrestal report of January 1963, which stated that the American press corps was playing loose with the facts: "Although our report, for example, is not rosily optimistic, it certainly contains the factual basis for a much more hopeful view than the pessimistic (and factually inaccurate) picture conveyed in the press."[71]

One way the press conveyed an inaccurate picture, according to Ambassador Nolting, was by focusing on the failures of the ARVN and ignoring its successes. "There were far more successful military actions than there were debacles like Ap Bac. These successful battles did not make dramatic headlines because we expected our side to win.... The media tended to feature the setbacks, creating a false impression of the ARVN's capabilities and of American training and advice."[72]

In December 1962, as Hilsman gathered information on Vietnam for his report, he began to criticise Ambassador Nolting's loyalty to Diem. In a series of memoranda for the record, he questioned Nolting's optimism about the leader's abilities with respect to the SHP.[73] While Hilsman, with many caveats, accepted much of what Nolting had to tell him during his visit to Vietnam, he balked at Nolting's defence of Diem's leadership with, for example, the SHP. His "net reaction was that the case [for Diem] was not entirely persuasive".[74] He grudgingly admitted that Diem's understanding of what was going on throughout South

[70] Roger Hilsman, *To Move a Nation: The Politics of Foreign Policy in the Administration of John F. Kennedy* (Garden City, N.Y.: Doubleday, 1967), 446.

[71] Hilsman and Forrestal, "Memorandum from Director of Bureau of Intelligence and Research and Michael V", 59.

[72] Nolting, *From Trust to Tragedy*, 97.

[73] Roger Hilsman, "Memorandum for the Record by the Director of the Bureau of Intelligence and Research (Hilsman)", January 1963, Saigon, in *FRUS, 1961–1963*, vol. 3, document 3, pp. 5–11.

[74] Roger Hilsman, "Memorandum for the Record by the Director of the Bureau of Intelligence and Research (Hilsman); Subject: Country Team Meeting on Wednesday, January 2, 1963", January 2, 1963, in *FRUS, 1961–1963*, vol. 3, pp. 12–13.

Vietnam was staggering in its scope and detail. Yet he did not believe that Ngo Dinh Diem was the best man, or the only man, available to lead the country. The others who aspired to take his place paled in comparison, as the coup in Vietnam later proved. Knowing this, Nolting continued his attempts to persuade Hilsman, and anyone who would listen in Washington, that U.S. and Vietnamese interests were both served by staying the course with Ngo Dinh Diem.

According to Nolting, "Hilsman seemed quite optimistic during his visit." The ambassador found Forrestal less so: "Echoing Harriman, [Forrestal] urged more democratic institutions and methods, pressing Diem to broaden the base of his government and become more 'popular.' "[75] Nolting observed that Forrestal spent a lot of the time with the American press while he was in Saigon, presumably gathering information "untainted by the Embassy".

Nolting thought the overall tone of the Hilsman-Forrestal report was positive, and he wrote in his memoirs that it did not call for any dramatic changes in U.S. foreign policy in Vietnam. He did note, however, that the report called for more to be done, and to be done more quickly.[76] For those looking for reasons to remove Diem, they could find them in the report. Between the Mansfield report, the Hilsman-Forrestal report, and the ongoing negative reporting in the press, an anti-Diem momentum was building in Washington that could not be stopped by Ambassador Nolting or even Secretary Rusk. All of this carefully groomed pessimism acquired a weight of its own, and it became the foundation upon which Harriman was able to build the case and to marshal the forces for Diem's removal.

Meanwhile, Ambassador Nolting fought against the inevitable. In 1963, Nolting's last year in South Vietnam, his rearguard action begun in 1962 became an all-out fight to defend the honour of the American people, for as he understood it, they had given their word, through their president John F. Kennedy, that there would be no interference with the government of South Vietnam. Nolting argued right up to and after the murders of Diem and Nhu that it would be better for the United States to walk away from Vietnam than to breach its promise made to an ally.

[75] Nolting, *From Trust to Tragedy*, 96.
[76] Ibid.

9

The Decline of the Nolting Influence

The year 1963 was one of decision with regard to the future of American-Vietnamese relations. William Colby recalled the pressures that were building in Saigon and the split that developed within the Kennedy administration over South Vietnam: "On the American side, the differences grew between those who saw the problem as chiefly one requiring a strong effort in the countryside, military and paramilitary, and those who believed the effort was doomed unless Diem changed his authoritarian regime to attract popular support and include oppositionists in a national effort."[1] In the end the latter group won and eclipsed the efforts of Ambassador Nolting to stick with the original U.S. policy in support of the Diem regime.

The historical record places the responsibility for the fate of South Vietnam upon the shoulders of specific individuals, powerful men within the Kennedy administration who directly and intentionally abrogated America's pledges to President Diem's government. Their decisions resulted in the destruction of the South Vietnamese government and created a moral imperative for the United States to fill the political vacuum they produced with military might. Ambassador Nolting, as the senior State Department man on the ground in South Vietnam at that time, stood against these men. During the course of his protest, however, he was replaced as ambassador in the summer of 1963. Michael Forrestal of the National Security Council had advised President Kennedy that a successor was needed for Nolting, whose tour was up in

[1] William E. Colby, *Lost Victory: A Firsthand Account of America's Sixteen-Year Involvement in Vietnam*, with James McCargar (Chicago: Contemporary Books, 1989), 114.

April of that year. Forrestal had bluntly stated: "More vigor is needed in getting Diem to do what we want."[2]

There was considerable irony at work, because the beginning of 1963 seemed to be the harbinger for the same kind of success that the year 1962 had proved to be in the American-Vietnamese fight against the Viet Cong. This success was summarised in the "Current Intelligence Memorandum Prepared in the Office of Current Intelligence, Central Intelligence Agency". Much of this document has been redacted, or sanitised, and its full content remains unknown. Nevertheless, given its documentation of the accomplishments of the GVN with American help, it supported a continued relationship between Washington and President Diem. With regard to the progress of the counterinsurgency, for example, the document indicated the favourable seizure rate of Communist weaponry and the positive impact of the strategic hamlets.[3]

Specifically, the CIA report noted that the GVN was probably holding its own against the insurgents and even reducing the threat of the guerrillas in some areas. Cautiously, the CIA analysts explained it was too early to declare that the back of the Communist organisation had been broken. They did report, however, that the South Vietnamese were successfully curbing the insurgency through extensive American assistance. U.S. tactical advice had resulted in the ARVN being more efficient, mobile, and aggressive against the insurgents. The Diem government was gaining ground; the future disaster being predicted by reporters such as Halberstam and Sheehan was unlikely.[4] The United States was not sinking with Diem; it was at least treading water, and the Communists were doing no better. In some ways, thanks to the strategic hamlets, they were doing a good deal worse.[5]

[2] Michael V. Forrestal, "Memorandum from Michael V. Forrestal of the National Security Council Staff to the President; [subject:] South Vietnam", January 28, 1963, Washington, in *FRUS, 1961–1963*, vol. 3, document 21, pp. 63–64.

[3] "Current Intelligence Memorandum Prepared in the Office of Current Intelligence, Central Intelligence Agency", January 11, 1963, Washington, in *FRUS, 1961–1963*, vol. 3, document 11, pp. 19–21. The source text is labelled "sanitized copy", and the original classification has been obliterated. Ellipses throughout the document are in the source text.

[4] Sheehan intimated that a disaster was in store for the GVN and the ARVN based upon the poor performance at Ap Bac and the subsequent attempts at a cover-up. See Neil Sheehan, *A Bright Shining Lie: John Paul Vann and America in Vietnam* (New York: Vintage Books, 1988), 271–78.

[5] "Current Intelligence Memorandum", 22.

The CIA opinion was by no means the only official report done on the situation in South Vietnam in early 1963. The Joint Chiefs of Staff submitted a lengthy assessment based on General Earle G. Wheeler's observations in the country. In the Wheeler assessment, Ambassador Nolting was doing an impressive job at making the U.S. effort work. Wheeler and his team also noted that General Paul Harkins had established cordial, direct, and trustworthy relations with Diem's government.[6] They praised the substantial value of the strategic hamlets in the counterinsurgency effort against the Communists.

In specific terms, the Wheeler report labelled the military measures being taken in South Vietnam as vital. These measures would pave the way for security and stability, without which political and economic growth could not occur. The main problem that plagued rural South Vietnam was the lack of law and order; reestablishing government control would allow the GVN's measures for political and economic growth to take hold. Attached to this fundamental problem was the historical reality that the central government had never before done anything to improve the lives of the peasants. Nor had the peasants ever linked themselves, their activities, or their futures with the central government. As a result, they had no comprehension of national political issues, of what really was at stake if the Communists took over the whole country. The Wheeler report team did note, however, that the slow dawning of change was taking place.[7]

The Wheeler report identified the SHP as the greatest single political-military instrument the GVN had for making themselves relevant to rural South Vietnamese. The defence of the strategic hamlets allowed the GVN the opportunity to inaugurate political, economic, and social reforms at the hamlet level. As a result, elections had been held in over one thousand hamlets. The American team noted that these were fair and democratic elections. As such, they allowed councils and hamlet chiefs to represent the people in the efforts to defend and to improve the villages. While noting that the democratisation process was slow, the team recognised that democracy could not be forced on the people from

[6]Earle G. Wheeler, "Report by an Investigative Team Headed by the Chief of Staff, United States Army (Wheeler), to the Joint Chiefs of Staff", January 1963, Washington, in *FRUS, 1961–1963*, vol. 3, document 26, pp. 81–87.
[7]Ibid., 81–82.

legislative action in Saigon, due to pressure from abroad, but could grow through the political participation afforded by the strategic hamlets.

The Wheeler report concluded that the Americans were not in a position to direct the GVN. It recommended that the Kennedy administration do precisely what Nolting and Harkins had been urging all along: influence the GVN through good relations and friendly advice. The relationship between Washington and Saigon would only continue to improve if the excellent partnership put into place by Nolting and Harkins were maintained.

Wheeler's team recognised that opposite their positive view was the American media's negative one. The constant cynical and pessimistic reporting was causing serious problems for Secretary of State Dean Rusk and his attempts to stay the course with official U.S. foreign policy toward South Vietnam.[8] Rusk even sent a brief telegram to Nolting requesting his evaluation of what the U.S. newsmen were doing and what he thought could be done.[9] As noted by the Wheeler report, American journalists were also creating problems for Diem's family, the GVN, and the military effort.[10] Specifically they were making a serious public relations predicament for the war effort in Vietnam.

As a result of the negative reporting, the Wheeler report noted, the GVN had come to regard the foreign press as completely untrustworthy. Reporters had a predilection for publishing unreliable information derived from private, biased sources. News stories tended to portray the GVN and its undertakings in the worst possible light by focusing on mistakes and failures; rarely did they record anything being done well. To illustrate this point, the Wheeler report pointed to the scandal caused by the stories about the Battle of Ap Bac, which were discussed in the previous chapter.[11]

---

[8] Thomas J. Schoenbaum, *Waging Peace and War: Dean Rusk in the Truman, Kennedy, and Johnson Years* (New York: Simon and Schuster, 1988), 395.

[9] Dean Rusk, "Telegram from the Department of State to the Embassy in Vietnam", January 24, 1963, Washington, in *FRUS, 1961–1963*, vol. 3, document 17, pp. 34–35.

[10] In the conclusions of the Wheeler team's report to the Joint Chiefs of Staff, the following was noted: "The schism between the United States press and the Government of Vietnam is more than a simple lack of communications. To span the gap requires great effort and, on our side, much patience. An objective, on-the-spot appraisal of the war by mature, responsible newsmen is gravely needed as a counter to the sometimes frustrated reporting of the resident correspondents." Wheeler, "Report by Investigative Team", 93.

[11] Ibid.

Wheeler's team summed up the effect of American newswriting: great harm had been done to the combined U.S.-GVN effort to defeat the insurgency. There was no gainsaying the fact that both Congress and the American public had been influenced by the newsmen to think that the war effort in South Vietnam was badly off track. The ARVN and the GVN were seen as lacking drive, determination, courage, training, and competence. In turn, within South Vietnam, there was a serious backlash to declining American opinion. It was apparent to the Wheeler team that the Vietnamese bitterly resented the derogatory portrait of them being painted by the media.

The growing public antagonism toward South Vietnam could only hinder the continuation of current U.S. foreign policy toward the country. Even Harriman, who certainly wanted a change in policy, was worried about the influence U.S. newspapers were exerting on Washington, and he noted as much in a letter to Nolting at the end of January 1963. Harriman asked for Nolting's help in improving the news reports coming from South Vietnam, because of "the need for support and understanding at home for the expensive, continuing and sometimes dangerous programs which we are carrying out in Viet-Nam". Harriman mentioned that the administration was requesting more balanced reporting from the media. While waiting for that, Harriman wrote, Nolting must do something to stop the criticisms of the South Vietnamese made to the press by U.S. military personnel: "Nothing could be more destructive of the cooperation we must have with the Vietnamese or more helpful to the Communist propagandists."[12] Ambassador Nolting responded immediately to Harriman. He suggested that he be recalled to Washington for several weeks of consultations, during which he could devote much of the time to public relations work concerned with U.S. policy toward the government of South Vietnam.[13]

On February 5, 1963, Nolting sent a lengthy cable to the State Department that acknowledged the U.S. press problem in South Vietnam, which he said "is not unparalleled in other new countries".[14] He

---

[12] W. Averell Harriman, "Letter from the Assistant Secretary of State for Far Eastern Affairs (Harriman) to the Ambassador in Vietnam (Nolting)", January 30, 1963, Washington, in *FRUS, 1961–1963*, vol. 3, document 24, pp. 67–69.

[13] *FRUS, 1961–1963*, vol. 3, document 24, p. 69n5.

[14] Frederick E. Nolting, "Telegram from the Embassy in Vietnam to the Department of State", February 5, 1963, Saigon, in *FRUS, 1961–1963*, vol. 3, document 30, pp. 98–100.

explained that older, more experienced correspondents in South Vietnam "are able to take the larger view of what's at stake here and logic of US policy under circumstances". Younger reporters, however, often finding news sources amongst equally young American advisors, "tend to be shocked, angry, indignant because they think US is being 'suckered', though most of them accept basic US policy intellectually when considered in calmer moments." Nolting suggested that these young reporters and advisors additionally failed to understand the "petty, often rather pathetic, maneuvers to save face" often employed in Asian cultures. "And they forget that the face of the government has vital bearing on support of its people in conduct of war." He continued that these particular reporters and this particular regime disliked each other to a "degree that verges on neurotic".[15]

William Colby observed that the failure of American reporters to move beyond a short-term tactical view of events caused much of the bad blood between them and the Diem government. He recalled that when things were quieter in Vietnam, between 1956 and 1960, the American press generally ignored Diem's programs and his attempts to modernise South Vietnam socially, politically, and economically. When the Communists began the insurgency in earnest, the regional reporters from Tokyo and Hong Kong began to make more visits to South Vietnam, and the resident press corps began to expand.[16] Once in South Vietnam, the reporters, like many of the American civilian officials, naturally gravitated toward contacts with Saigon officials and members of the quarrelsome political elite who were fluent in French or English. The reporters, according to Colby, made their rounds in Saigon, where intrigue was constant and fascinating, and they only occasionally varied their gossip-column approach with trips to the countryside where the real story of South Vietnam was unfolding.

---

[15] Nolting elaborated, "Besides their public dispatches, newsmen have reported at length by mail and private cable to editors back home on indignities of working Vietnam. Chances are when Ap Bac story broke, GVN had hardly a friend in any editorial room in United States. What happened looks from here like savagely emotional delayed reaction to ousters of [reporters] Sully and Robinson, Mme. Nhu's charge that whole American press is 'communist' and every other harassment over past six months. Ap Bac was reported as major GVN failure at cost of American lives, and it appears from here that American editorial writers, commentators, columnists licked chops with delight and reached for simplest adjectives they could muster." Ibid., 100.

[16] Colby, *Lost Victory*, 112–14.

These trips, however, were often problematic, because interviews were hampered not only by laborious and time-consuming translations of questions and answers but also by an immense cultural gap. With deadlines for filing stories ever present, reporters understandably preferred the convenient Saigon gossip-circle interview over the far-flung, difficult, and often dangerous interview with a peasant in a remote hamlet. Because it was impossible to interview the Communists—their clandestine nature made such attempts futile—the reporters could focus only on the GVN and their American support structure. Additionally, the reporters were professionally trained to seek out the flaws in the banal statements made by officials, and in this regard both American and South Vietnamese officials were treated the same, with disdain and distrust.[17]

In summarizing his analysis of this issue, William Colby acknowledged that Saigon had been seen by journalists as a secondary story source for years before the Communist insurgency. After the insurrection began, Saigon attracted young and inexperienced reporters hopeful of launching their careers with a sensational story that could make the front page. For this and the other reasons cited above, distortions of the situation in South Vietnam were bound to occur.

The aftermath of Ap Bac was having an ugly influence on American-Vietnamese relations. The American press was poised to seize on anything that could be held as proof of failed American policy and Vietnamese government corruption. Well into February 1963, Ambassador Nolting was still doing damage control. He sent a cable to DOS stating that Ngo Dinh Nhu had assured the American embassy that the GVN was truly going to pull all of its punches in any future dealings with the young reporters from the United States. This was Nhu's way of suggesting that the GVN might even attempt to effect some sort of rapprochement with the editors back in New York and Washington.[18]

Regardless of Nolting's efforts to improve U.S.-Vietnamese relations, a policy shift was underway in Washington. A classified memo to Assistant Secretary of State Averell Harriman from Michael Forrestal of the National Security Council staff outlined some initial moves for making this change. The embassy was to create some distance between

---

[17] Ibid.
[18] Nolting, "Telegram from Embassy in Vietnam to Department of State", February 5, 1963, p. 101.

U.S. diplomatic personnel and President Diem by making themselves available to members of Diem's non-Communist opposition. Forrestal explained that there were two major reasons for doing this: "First, it would be part of a carefully designed program to establish a somewhat more independent U.S. position in SVN. Second, it should eventually increase our alternatives in the event of an accident which results in a shift in the government."[19] Forrestal wrote that although he agreed with Nolting that such activity could reawaken Diem's suspicions about U.S. intentions, "the risks in remaining too closely tied to Diem's government will increase rather than decrease as time goes on."

Nolting saw the writing on the wall and immediately objected strongly to it in a letter to Secretary Harriman. First he objected to the implication that he and his staff had isolated themselves in "cocoons" and had not already reached out to opposition leaders to hear their concerns and to pass them along to the GVN when appropriate. "There is, of course," he wrote, "a great difference between being accessible to oppositionists and giving them encouragement. Many of them tend towards radical solutions and we give them no encouragement. If we are not crystal clear on this, we would stimulate revolution."[20] Second Nolting objected to the idea that Americans should be building up "an alternative to the present government". He reiterated his belief that there was no workable alternative to Diem, that the civilian opposition was not capable of running a government. William Colby, his successor John Richardson, and Robert Thompson all agreed with Nolting's estimation of the civilian opposition in Saigon, that they were not fit to lead a coup or a headless country. Colby and the others therefore surmised that the real political threat to Diem lay within the army. Any attempt to remove Diem from power, Nolting continued, would "ruin the carefully built base of our advisory and supporting role here, which must rest on persuasion and on confidence in our integrity". In conclusion, he stated that he could not be "the agent in a change of US policy away from forthright support of the legitimate government".[21]

---

[19] Michael V. Forrestal, "Memorandum from Michael V. Forrestal of the National Security Council Staff to the Assistant Secretary of State for Far Eastern Affairs (Harriman)", February 8, 1963, Washington, in *FRUS, 1961–1963*, vol. 3, document 33, pp. 105–6.

[20] Frederick Nolting, "Letter from the Ambassador in Vietnam (Nolting) to the Assistant Secretary of State for Far Eastern Affairs (Harriman)", February 27, 1963, Saigon, in *FRUS, 1961–1963*, vol. 3, document 45, pp. 126–28.

[21] Ibid.

In a later interview, Nolting repeated some of the same points he made in his letter to Harriman. He said the shift in policy away from supporting Diem happened gradually: "It just happened, little by little, with people with a new slant coming in, sending me a telegram to do something which was quite contrary to what the original basic instructions had been, including, for example, instructions to cultivate the opposition to Diem.... This was a very serious change of instructions, and I questioned it very strongly."[22] Ambassador Nolting questioned the change in policy not only because of his practical and moral considerations but also because of his expectation that 1963 was going to witness even more progress in the fight against the insurgents. The Hilsman-Forrestal and Wheeler visits reinforced his feelings that the United States was "on the right track".[23] Furthermore, results on the ground in South Vietnam also seemed to demonstrate the counterinsurgency was working: "The pacified area in the country continued to expand, government services to the people continued to increase and improve, and the Strategic Hamlets program appeared to be consolidating these gains. The infiltration rate from North Vietnam was estimated at less than 500 a month."[24] Nolting was therefore confident that Washington would stay the course in South Vietnam.

Then the Mansfield report was made public in March 1963 and shattered Nolting's confidence. Senator Mike Mansfield, as previously noted, was a respected and powerful Democratic politician; thus, his report to President Kennedy carried substantial weight. Senator Mansfield called for a thorough reassessment of U.S. security interests in Southeast Asia. Such a study, he stated, might lead to the conclusion that America should be doing less rather than more in the region.[25] Nolting was astounded at the report's negative analysis of South Vietnam and GVN, which hurt Diem deeply because he had always considered Mansfield a personal friend.[26] The report, which the Harriman group used

[22] Frederick Nolting, interview by Dennis O'Brien, May 7, 1970, Washington, D.C., interview 3, transcript, 93–94, John F. Kennedy Oral History Collection, John F. Kennedy Presidential Library, Boston.

[23] Frederick Nolting, *From Trust to Tragedy: The Political Memoirs of Frederick Nolting, Kennedy's Ambassador to Diem's Vietnam* (New York: Praeger, 1988), 97–98.

[24] Ibid.

[25] Mike Mansfield, "Report by the Senate Majority Leader (Mansfield): Southeast Asia—Vietnam", December 18, 1962, Washington, in *FRUS, 1961–1963*, vol. 2, document 330, pp. 780–82.

[26] Nolting, *From Trust to Tragedy*, 98.

as proof of the Diem regime's incompetence, served as a warning to Nolting that the Kennedy administration, while still claiming to follow the original policy toward South Vietnam, was embarking on another course. It marked the beginning of the end of Nolting's influence.

Nolting disagreed with Mansfield's allegations that Diem was isolated from the people and absolutely dependent on the advice of his family. His observations were being used by those calling for immediate democratic reforms, which Nolting knew would be destructive of Washington-Saigon relations. Efforts to broaden the GVN to include its opposition, Nolting perceived, would have an effect in South Vietnam exactly the opposite of that which was intended. Encouraging the non-Communist dissidents would likely drive Diem to come down even harder on threats to his government, thereby narrowing his base instead of broadening it. Equally disastrous would be the response of the Viet Cong, who would view the report as evidence that support for Diem was weakening in the United States. "In retrospect," observed Nolting, "I consider the Mansfield report the first nail in Diem's coffin. Diem was right to fear its effect on President Kennedy and other policymakers in Washington."[27]

The Mansfield report stood in opposition to what Nolting had been telling Washington about the successes of the counterinsurgency. It also contradicted the Wheeler report to the Joint Chiefs of Staff, which declared that the ARVN, with American help, was slowly winning against the Viet Cong. Ominously, though, the Wheeler report warned against too much interference with the way the Vietnamese were conducting the war—including introducing large amounts of U.S. forces and demanding the United States be given control of the war.[28]

Given the fallout of the Mansfield report and the continued negative reporting in the press, Nolting tried to avert another public relations disaster for Diem. He wrote Harriman to defer indefinitely the public release of a U.S. General Accounting Office (GAO) report on South Vietnam (for the period 1958 to mid-1962), which he had read in draft form and which was severely critical of the GVN. He explained that "signs of reluctance and disillusionment on part of certain segments of US opinion, have without doubt encouraged coup plotting, have made the govt here tighten up rather than liberalize, and have encouraged the enemy. I do not think in these circumstances we can afford

---

[27] Ibid.
[28] Wheeler, "Report by Investigative Team", 91.

a public chastisement of the GVN (and/or our own policy) by a US agency."[29] He stated that the report would not give the Americans any kind of leverage over the GVN but only weaken it. "Any sign of weakening could well result in another attempt to overthrow the government," he wrote. "The predictable result of such an attempt—whether successful or not—would be, in my judgment, a bonanza for Hanoi."[30]

On March 28, 1963, Ambassador Nolting telegraphed the State Department regarding an intense meeting he had with Defence Minister Nguyen Dinh Thuan about the GVN's reluctance to collaborate with Washington on a counterinsurgency fund containing U.S. aid dollars. Thuan claimed that Ngo Dinh Nhu was backing away from a previous agreement to the fund in principle because of "doubts and misgivings engendered by the Mansfield report, by editorial and press pressures against the GVN in America, [and] by what appeared to Nhu to be indications of US uncertainty in continued support of GVN".[31] Ambassador Nolting reported that he did his best to overcome GVN fears of American duplicity: he emphasised that the agreement could restore the mutual confidence of both governments, and he promised to find ways to answer the GVN's objections. Nolting ended his despatch to the State Department by warning Secretary Rusk that these reactions of the South Vietnamese had been brewing for some time and that Washington needed to do something to reassure Diem and Nhu.

Rusk replied immediately to Nolting, telling the ambassador to assure Diem and Nhu of continuing U.S. support: "You are also authorized tell Nhu and Diem that you instructed assure them US policy remains full support of Diem's government in its efforts defend VN against VC attack and bring better life to VN people. Mansfield report does not mean change in US policy of support for GVN against Communist threat. This connection you may wish quote President Kennedy's March 6 press conference remarks on Mansfield report."[32] He then quoted what President Kennedy had said when asked whether

---

[29] Frederick Nolting, "Telegram from the Embassy in Vietnam to the Department of State", March 18, 1963, Saigon, in *FRUS, 1961–1963*, vol. 3, document 62, pp. 161–62.

[30] Ibid.

[31] Frederick Nolting, "Telegram from the Embassy in Vietnam to the Department of State", March 28, 1963, Saigon, in *FRUS, 1961–1963*, vol. 3, document 68, pp. 183–84.

[32] Dean Rusk, "Telegram from the Department of State to the Embassy in Vietnam", March 29, 1963, Washington, in *FRUS, 1961–1963*, vol. 3, document 69, p. 185.

he would implement the recommendation of the Mansfield report to cut back American support of Southeast Asia: "I don't see how we are going to be able, unless we are going to pull out of Southeast Asia and turn it over to the Communists, how we are going to be able to reduce very much our economic programs and military programs in South Viet-Nam in Cambodia, in Thailand."[33] Rusk's message also contained a warning: "If GVN unwilling trust us to extent of continuing successful and vital CI programs under proven machinery, difficulties of working together for common goals will be greatly increased." Despite the thinly veiled threat, the day after receiving Rusk's telegram, Nolting cabled back and expressed his appreciation for the authority to reassure Diem and Nhu.[34]

On April 1, 1963, in the early afternoon at the State Department, a peculiar conversation took place between Assistant Secretary of State Averell Harriman and Sir Robert Thompson, the head of the British Advisory Mission to Vietnam. Two other supporters of Harriman were also in attendance: Michael Forrestal of the National Security Council and William H. Sullivan, who served as Harriman's deputy during the Laotian negotiations and later became President Johnson's ambassador to Laos. These men were accompanied by Chalmers B. Wood, director of the Vietnam Working Group, who sent a report on the discussion to Nolting in Saigon. While Thompson sketched a favourable but not perfect picture of South Vietnam, wrote Wood, Harriman asked provocative questions and made sceptical comments, which betrayed the storm of doubt Harriman was unleashing in Washington against the Diem government. For example, when Thompson emphasised the necessity of building confidence, Harriman asked whether that were possible. Harriman said better leaders were needed at the local level, while Thompson countered that their calibre had already improved. On the issue of press relations, Harriman said the Kennedy administration had done everything it could to improve them; the rest was up to Diem.[35]

---

[33] John F. Kennedy, *Public Papers of the Presidents of the United States: John F. Kennedy*, vol. 3, *1963* (Washington, D.C.: United States Government Printing Office, 1964), 243–44, quoted in Rusk, "Telegram from Department of State to Embassy in Vietnam", March 29, 1963, 185.

[34] Frederick Nolting, "Telegram from the Embassy in Vietnam to the Department of State", March 30, 1963, Saigon, in *FRUS, 1961–1963*, vol. 3, document 70, p. 186.

[35] Chalmers B. Wood, "Memorandum of a Conversation, Department of State, Washington, April 1, 1963, Noon", in *FRUS, 1961–1963*, vol. 3, document 73, pp. 193–94.

Oddly enough it was Thompson, an Englishman, who was defending the core and the continuity of American policy toward South Vietnam even as it appeared that some U.S. officials had lost faith in it. He championed the CIP, the SHP, and the role of the GVN in both. His visit to Washington included meetings at the highest levels. In a meeting with President Kennedy, at which Wood and British Ambassador to the United States David Ormsby Gore were present, Thompson emphasised that Diem did indeed have support in rural Vietnam. He also said that if Diem were removed from power, the repercussions would be devastating.[36]

Thompson underlined what Nolting, Colby, and Harkins had already reported to Washington about the successes of the counterinsurgency against the Viet Cong. He said that war was moving in the right direction. "He cited particularly the increased number of defectors (from an average of 15–20 a week in early 1962 to 148 for the week ending March 25, 1963)."[37] He stressed that the special attention given the losses at Ap Bac was misguided and that the Americans had to be ready for occasional battlefield reverses. He cautioned against expecting major victories, adding that patience and time were key elements to the successful conclusion of the campaign.

Given the progress that had been made so far, as evidenced by the fact that "an observer in a plane could distinguish, on the one hand, GVN-controlled territories where roads and bridges were repaired and strategic hamlets built, and, on the other hand, VC territory where the bridges were generally down and the roads cut", Thompson said that by the end of the year, if the United States stayed the course, it would be able to announce a reduction in its forces in South Vietnam by about one thousand men. This, he said, would have three good effects: "It would show that the South Vietnamese were winning; it would take the steam out of the Communists' best propaganda line, i.e., that this was an American war and the Vietnamese were an American satellite; and it would reaffirm the honesty of American intentions."[38] He advised President Kennedy to downplay or ignore the heavy criticism of Diem and American policy in the press.

[36] Chalmers B. Wood, "Memorandum of a Conversation, White House, Washington, April 4, 1963, 10 A.M.", in *FRUS, 1961–1963*, vol. 3, document 77, p. 198.
[37] Ibid., 199.
[38] Ibid., 199–200.

Kennedy was cautious and sceptical. He asked Thompson: Why had the Viet Minh been able to defeat the French? Thompson's reply was immediate and straightforward: the French never had a hope of getting the Vietnamese on their side. Thompson stressed that the SHP was what was making the difference in Vietnam. The strategic hamlets were giving the Vietnamese a degree of security that the French had never been able to provide.

Thompson made a specific point of praising the quality of the American military personnel and their behaviour in South Vietnam. He also noted that the morale of the Vietnamese civilian and military authorities had improved. Communist terror was on the decline but would increase again when it became obvious to the Viet Cong that their position was desperate. He warned Kennedy that helicopters, while useful for surprising the insurgents and for preventing them from concentrating, were not capable of winning large-scale victories. In counterguerrilla warfare, he said, such victories are attained only by using one's "brains and feet".[39] The British were not without considerable expertise in this area, since they had been the first to use rotary-winged aircraft in a counter-insurgent environment (in Malaya).

In one of his final points on counterinsurgency tactics and programs, Thompson told Kennedy that the surrender policy put into place by Ngo Dinh Nhu for the GVN's erstwhile guerrilla enemies was a good one. He told the president that the United States should give the policy public support when it was announced. This would bolster Diem's political legitimacy by demonstrating the subordination of U.S. policy to that of South Vietnam. Too much U.S. involvement, he added, undermined Diem's credentials as a legitimate Vietnamese nationalist and provided the Communists with proof of their claim that Diem was an American puppet.

Later in the afternoon of the same day, April 4, Thompson met with the Special Group for Counterinsurgency, which included Harriman, Attorney General Robert Kennedy, Roswell Gilpatric, CIA Director John McCone, Michael Forrestal, and General Maxwell Taylor, amongst others. Thompson repeated much that he had told President Kennedy. He stressed the importance of American patience, the fact that the U.S. news media were out of control, and that the reporting

<hr>

[39] Ibid., 199.

in American papers concerned with the overall effort in Vietnam could be improved.[40] In the presence of counterinsurgency warfare experts, Thompson handed Harriman a rebuttal to his claim that the fault for negative reporting lay with Diem. The most important point made by Thompson was about what would happen if Diem were removed from office. He bluntly told the Americans that the entire government would collapse without Diem and that the counterinsurgency effort would be left in serious disarray.[41]

Wood sent Nolting a report also about this meeting with the counterinsurgency group. Particularly noteworthy was Wood's mention of Thompson emphasising that America would lose the fight against the Viet Cong if it lost Diem, that inflammatory press reporting should not cause Washington to panic, and that Harriman actually paid attention to what Thompson was saying. About the last point, Wood said that Harriman "kept his hearing aid in with the volume up. This is, I believe, a record for undivided gubernatorial attention."[42] Wood added in his letter to Nolting that Thompson had met with Defense Secretary Robert S. McNamara, Roger Hilsman, and Warren Unna of the *Washington Post* and that these meetings had gone well. Thompson had repeatedly raised the question about what the American press was trying to accomplish in South Vietnam.[43]

The apparent success of the Thompson visit to Washington notwithstanding, the direction the press was driving official opinion in America continued to be a major concern for Ambassador Nolting. The press corps did not irritate him, he said, but caused him "great alarm and pain" because "they were quite unjust, quite unjust, in the overall picture they gave of what the Vietnamese government was trying to do and what it was, in fact, doing for the benefit of its own people."[44] Also unjust,

[40] James W. Dingeman [executive secretary of the Special Group for Counterinsurgency], "Minutes of a Meeting of the Special Group for Counterinsurgency, Washington, April 4, 1963, 2 P.M.", in *FRUS, 1961–1963*, vol. 3, document 78, pp. 201–3.

[41] Ibid., 202.

[42] Chalmers P. Wood, "Letter from Director of Vietnam Working Group (Wood) to Ambassador in Vietnam (Nolting)", April 4, 1963, Washington, in *FRUS 1961–1963*, vol. 3, doc. 79, pp. 203–6.

[43] Ibid., 205.

[44] Frederick Nolting, interview by Dennis O'Brien, May 6, 1970, New York, interview 2, transcript, 70–71, John F. Kennedy Oral History Collection, John F. Kennedy Presidential Library, Boston.

according to Nolting, was the 1962 Mansfield report, which American reporters continued to cite as a source of information. Ironically, the report was based, in part, on those very same reporters. When it came to the description of Diem as isolated, cut off from his countrymen, Nolting said Mansfield "had gotten most of his information, I think, on this point from the American press corps in Saigon. And I think it was a mistake. I think it was an injustice."[45]

Returning to the matter of the American-Vietnamese counterinsurgency fund, Nolting's earlier talks with Thuan had failed to produce an agreement. Thus, Nolting sought a meeting with Diem to convince him of the necessity of coming to terms with the Americans on this key issue. During the course of this meeting, Nolting had to tell Diem that his protracted reluctance could result only in a further deterioration of U.S.-GVN relations and a change in U.S. policy. Diem continued to express his concerns that if he gave this kind of control to the Americans, he would be surrendering his legitimacy in the eyes of his people.[46] One other key factor that had caused Diem to stand so firmly on this issue was the fact that lower-level American officials were interfering with the direction in which Saigon wished to go and were reporting negatively back to Washington. In the aforementioned discussion with Diem, Nolting denied this interference, but he admitted many years later that he had found out that Diem had been correct in the allegation.[47]

In an April 7, 1963, telegram to Washington, Nolting informed DOS that he had consulted with General Harkins and Joseph L. Brent, director of the Operations Mission in Vietnam. The three men had agreed that before the United States took any actions to show Diem that they were serious about reducing aid if he did not comply with the joint counterinsurgency fund, they should ask him for a written rejection or acceptance of the proposal. Their concern was that forcing Diem's hand risked further deterioration of the Washington-Saigon relationship and

[45] Ibid., 77.

[46] Frederick Nolting, "Telegram from the Embassy in Vietnam to the Department of State", April 5, 1963, Saigon, in FRUS, 1961–1963, vol. 3, document 81, pp. 208, 212–13.

[47] Nolting described the impact of these negative reports: "I didn't realize at the time how much of this there was, and I still don't know how much there was. But I did discover later on that a lot of Washington thinking had been changed by this type of sort of informal and unofficial communication." Nolting, interview by O'Brien, interview 2, p. 97.

"might light coup fuse". He again reiterated that nothing good would be gained by such an outcome.[48] By April 17, 1963, Nolting was able to report back to Washington that Diem had softened his stance considerably and that the way was open for an agreement.[49] Nolting also mentioned in this report that he had spoken to Diem about Madame Nhu's penchant for making inflammatory remarks to the U.S. press and that this undermined their joint position. Diem defended Madame Nhu but also admitted that she tended to overstate her points.

By this breakthrough, in addition to many others, it would seem that Ambassador Nolting had fought hard to preserve a steady course in U.S. policy toward South Vietnam. He had consistently stated very firmly his opposition to the removal of President Diem. He had also made it plain to Diem that the Vietnamese president had to meet the Americans at least halfway on many issues, including the counterinsurgency fund. In Nolting's efforts to preserve continuity in direction for the U.S. mission in South Vietnam, the ambassador had received powerful support from Robert Thompson, who had argued the Nolting position very effectively in Washington.

Despite all of the above, the evidence indicates that the covert and overt powers of Harriman and those who agreed with him had already subtly and effectively undermined the old policy of support for Diem. The Mansfield report, according to Nolting, acted in Washington as evidence in favour of the direction Harriman wanted the Kennedy administration to go. It also had an impact in Saigon, where it weakened the GVN's trust in America's intentions. Ambassador Nolting ran headlong into this distrust in his initial attempts to seek GVN compliance with agreement over the joint counterinsurgency fund. This fund, proposed by Washington, was a test of Diem's cooperation by the Kennedy administration.

Despite the Harriman group's suggestions that the United States should distance itself from Diem in order to find a government to replace him, there is no documentary evidence that proves anyone in the group ever found a viable alternative to the Vietnamese president. Like the U.S. newsmen, they knew what they did not like and what they did

[48] Frederick Nolting, "Telegram from the Embassy in Vietnam to the Department of State", April 7, 1963, Saigon, in *FRUS, 1961–1963*, vol. 3, document 82, p. 214.

[49] Frederick Nolting, "Telegram from the Embassy in Vietnam to the Department of State", April 17, 1963, Saigon, in *FRUS, 1961–1963*, vol. 3, document 91, p. 227.

not want, but they had failed to produce another leader in South Vietnam who had the same prestige amongst ordinary Vietnamese as Diem.
Simply put, there was no political legitimacy beyond the Diem administration, and this is precisely what Nolting, Colby, and Thompson had
told Washington. Yes, Diem, his family, and his regime were far from
perfect, but he was a rare man in South Vietnam at that time: a genuine,
traditional, nationalistic Vietnamese leader with political legitimacy. His
enemies knew that a major crisis was needed to pull him down from
that pillar.

The Buddhist Crisis of 1963

The Buddhist crisis of 1963 was seized upon by President Diem's enemies as the final proof he must be replaced. The crisis began in the city
of Hue, where Diem's elder brother was the Catholic archbishop. In
May, during celebrations of the birth of the Buddha, Buddhists were
told to stop flying religious flags. Although there was a law against public displays of religious flags, some Buddhists believed the prohibition
had been unfairly enforced in their case by the government, which they
were told had been made into an intolerant Catholic regime by Diem
and his family. Hard feelings led to a violent protest against the government, which was suppressed by government troops, and nine unarmed
civilians died. News reports blamed the riot police for the deaths, while
the GVN blamed the protestors for the violence and the Viet Cong
for the deaths. More protests followed, including those by Buddhist
monks setting themselves ablaze, leading to more government suppression and civilian deaths. More news reports of the protests, along with
poignant photos of monks immolating themselves, spread throughout
the world, as did demands for Diem's removal. U.S. support for the
beleaguered South Vietnamese president then appeared to the Kennedy
administration as politically untenable.

Before the roots and the effects of the Buddhist crisis are explored,
this author must first maintain that President Diem was no religious
bigot or enemy of Buddhism. He had almost single-handedly brought
South Vietnamese Buddhism back from near extinction. Diem was
an equal-opportunity supporter of those who would provide a pro-
Vietnamese, non-Communist religious influence in the country in the
wake of French rule—whether they followed Buddha, Confucius, or
Christ. His government gave aid for the rebuilding of religious structures
and communities destroyed by colonialism and war.

The essential data indicating the Buddhist renaissance under the Ngo Dinh Diem regime are recorded by Father Piero Gheddo, an Italian Catholic missionary who researched the situation of the Catholic Church in Vietnam and other countries in Southeast Asia. He found that Diem's allocation of government funds to rebuild Buddhist infrastructure— including pagodas and schools—played a substantial role in the revival of the religion. Under his patronage, "the upper schools for bonzes in South Vietnam increased from 4 to 10; of the 4,766 pagodas in the country, 1,275 were built after 1954 and 1,295 were renovated or rebuilt after that year. The Diem government at the same time gave nine million piastres for the building of Buddhist pagodas (about $1,600,000), and President Diem himself gave a major contribution for the reconstruction of the famous Xa Loi pagoda."[1]

Father Gheddo also discovered that in South Vietnam during the Diem years, under the direction of the General Association of Buddhists of Vietnam, "three communities were organized, including 3,000 bonzes and 300 nuns, and another three communities of lay followers, even in the most deserted villages; these three communities grouped together about one million Buddhist laymen, to whom were joined the non-affiliated laymen."[2] Additionally, the GVN encouraged Buddhist programs, periodicals, conferences, lectures, and libraries.

Even before the Buddhist crisis, Diem's critics had accused him of creating an intolerant regime led only by his Catholic family members and cronies. As we have seen, this characterization had already found its way into American newspapers. Those making this accusation either did not know or simply failed to mention "his not wanting the name of God in the 1956 Constitution, as the Catholics requested, but only the name 'Most High,' as the representatives of Buddhism and the Buddhist sects asked."[3] Diem did hire and promote many Catholics, and one reason for this was mentioned earlier: the Catholic schools prepared more people for government and military leadership positions than other schools at that time. Many of his advisors and most of his generals and cabinet members, however, were Buddhists or other non-

---

[1] Piero Gheddo, *The Cross and the Bo-Tree: Catholics and Buddhists in Vietnam*, trans. Charles Underhill Quinn (New York: Sheed and Ward, 1970), 176. See also Mai Tho Truyen, *Le Bouddhisme au Vietnam* (Saigon: Xa Loi Pagoda, 1962).

[2] Gheddo, *Cross and Bo-Tree*, 177.

[3] Ibid., 133.

Catholics.[4] General Nguyen Khanh, who participated in the 1963 military coup that removed Diem from power, scoffed at the idea of Diem persecuting or discriminating against Buddhists. In an interview with the author, he said he, a Buddhist, enjoyed the president's trust and friendship.[5] Diem "entrusted the most important positions only to the most trusted persons," explained Father Gheddo, "but this was not on the basis of the individuals' religious persuasion but on the basis of their anti-Communism. The Diem regime could in no way be called 'Catholic.' "[6]

Diem was keenly aware of the claim that his Catholicism coloured the way he led the country and worked hard to create a balanced government that was truly representative of the Vietnamese people. It is ironic that the spark that set off the Buddhist crisis was his enforcement of a law prohibiting the public display of religious flags. According to Ambassador Frederick Nolting, Diem agreed to enforce the law precisely because Vatican flags had been inappropriately given prominence at a recent Catholic celebration in Hue.[7]

From where came the idea that Diem was anti-Buddhist? According to Ambassador Nolting, if Diem had a prejudice it was against the Saigon bourgeoisie; everyone who knew him had observed that he preferred the company of farmers to that of those he described as "spoiled middle class, always complaining, not worth anything".[8] The

---

[4] Here are the precise figures for Diem's government with regard to religious affiliation: "Diem chose a Buddhist to be his Vice-President during his two terms in office. In his cabinet during the last year of his administration, the Vice-President, Nguyen Ngoc Tho, was a devoted Buddhist. His Foreign Minister, Vu Van Mau, was another outstanding Buddhist. Among the 18 members of Diem's cabinet in 1963, five were Catholics, eight were Buddhists, and five were Confucians. The military governor of Saigon-Cholon, General Ton That Dinh, and the Commander-in-Chief, General Le Van Ty, were also Buddhists. Among the top 19 generals, there were only three Catholics. The others were Buddhists, Confucians, and Taoists. Although many of the best schools were Catholic, there were only 12 Catholics among the 38 provincial governors. The rest were Buddhists, Confucians, and Taoists." Stephen Pan and Daniel Lyons, *Vietnam Crisis* (New York: East Asian Research Institute, 1966), 115.

[5] Nguyen Khanh, interview by author, June 16, 1994, United States Air Force Special Operations School, Hurlburt Field, Fla., transcript, 61, Vietnam Center and Archive at Texas Tech University, Lubbock, Tex., and the United States Air Force Special Operations School, Hurlburt Field, Fla.

[6] Gheddo, *Cross and Bo-Tree*, 133–77.

[7] Frederick Nolting, *From Trust to Tragedy: The Political Memoirs of Frederick Nolting, Kennedy's Ambassador to Diem's Vietnam* (New York: Praeger, 1988), 106.

[8] Quoted in Ellen J. Hammer, *A Death in November: America in Vietnam, 1963* (New York: E. P. Dutton, 1987), 77.

disdain was mutual, and this group helped to characterise Diem as an intolerant man.

As noted previously, some of Diem's detractors had drafted a manifesto of complaint during a meeting at the Caravelle Hotel in Saigon in 1960. The Caravellists were intellectuals, professionals, and politicians who desired a more open and democratic government with a place for themselves within it. Although the group was not Communist, it cannot be overlooked that the Caravellists served a propaganda purpose for the Viet Cong, albeit unwittingly. Their complaints were eagerly received by the American reporters who frequented the Caravelle Bar and whose stories helped to turn U.S. policy makers against the Diem regime, which in the end helped the Viet Cong to take over the country. Another way the Caravellists helped the Viet Cong was the route they took to spread their cause against Diem. In seeking to build a larger political base, they ironically sought support from a group Diem had restored to a prominent place in Vietnamese society: the Buddhists. The Caravellists formed an underground political opposition within the urban pagodas, and Buddhism gave them an air of legitimacy they lacked on their own.[9]

The Buddhists they collaborated with were a small, radicalised coterie who had fallen under the sway of Thich Tri Quang, a bonze whose political activities had begun in the 1940s during the wars against French rule. While there is no hard evidence that he was a Communist Party member, it has been documented in North Vietnam that he worked alongside Vietnamese Communists in their campaigns against Western colonialism.[10] According to Marguerite Higgins, one of the few reporters to interview him at length, he was a disciple of Thich Tri Do, the leader of the Buddhist organization in Hanoi approved by the Communist regime there.[11] To Higgins, Thich Tri Quang was quite unlike the peaceful, meditative Buddhist monks of her acquaintance. "Deep, burning eyes stared out from a gigantic forehead. He had an air of massive intelligence, total self-possession, and brooding suspicion."[12]

[9] Gheddo, Cross and Bo-Tree, 178–79.

[10] Ho Son Dai and Tran Phan Chan, Lich Su Saigon-Cho Lon-Gia Dinh Khan Chien, 1945–1975 (Ho Chi Minh City: Ho Chi Minh City Publishing House, 1994) 364. In interviews with the author, William Colby, Lindsay Nolting, and General Nguyen Khanh all said that although they lacked proof they believed that Thich Tri Quang was a Communist agent.

[11] Marguerite Higgins, Our Vietnam Nightmare (New York: Harper and Row, 1965), 28–29.

[12] Ibid., 25.

Throughout the Buddhist crisis, Higgins watched him stir up protest-ers. "The results were frightening. By the time Thich Tri Quang was through with the mobs, they would cheerfully go drown themselves in the Saigon River, if that were what he wanted. He was, and is, a true demagogue. Hate emanates from the man. Mobs thrive on hate."[13]

An alliance of the Caravellists, Thich Tri Quang, and other radical bonzes could not have come at better time for the Viet Cong. During the period leading up to the Buddhist crisis, the Communists in South Vietnam were struggling, according to Viet Cong expert Douglas Pike.

> Diem was proving more durable than expected.... For the NLF it was a period that began with high hopes and ended with disillusionment. Most significantly, for rural Vietnamese it was a time of disenchantment in the NLF, its cause, and its increasing use of repression and terror.... Internal reports of the period stressed over and over the assessment that the Revolution was not moving with the necessary speed, that it had encountered far more resistance and hostility than anticipated, that the Diem government's counter-insurgency efforts, even if unpopular, might fatally injure the Revolution.... They feared that the GVN might with short-run measures destroy the NLF structure and crush the insurgency. This attitude became strongest in April 1963, which conversely was the high-water mark of the Diem government.[14]

After the Buddhist crisis, everything went downhill for the GVN.

Because the core of the struggle for South Vietnam concerned polit-ical legitimacy, the Communists needed a group who, through protest and subversion, could cause doubt about the righteousness of Diem's leadership in the minds of ordinary Vietnamese. Of equal or perhaps even greater importance to the Communists was the need to divorce American support from Diem in order to undo his effective counterin-surgency campaign.[15] Diem's record as a legitimate nationalist concerned

---

[13] Ibid., 30.

[14] Douglas Pike, *Viet Cong: The Organization and Techniques of the National Liberation Front of South Vietnam* (Cambridge, Mass.: MIT Press, 1966), 157–58.

[15] Mieczyslaw Maneli spent five years in Vietnam (1954–1955 and 1962–1964) as head of Poland's delegation to the International Control Commission and was in constant contact with Hanoi during this time. He admitted that in the spring and summer of 1963 the North was willing to go along with any plan that would divorce the Americans from Diem. See Mieczyslaw Maneli, *War of the Vanquished*, trans. Maria de Görgey (New York: Harper and Row, 1971), 134–35.

for the welfare of the average peasant in South Vietnam was near unassailable, so another route of subversion needed to be found. The Communists concluded that the Vietnamese president's weakest point was American reluctance to continue supporting an undemocratic leader. They were astute enough to realise that the tail wagging the dog of U.S. foreign policy was American public opinion, which is largely shaped by the media. In May 1963 the Communists had found the necessary tool to pry U.S. support away from Diem: radical Buddhists whose dramatic protests could commandeer the attention of newsmen in Saigon.

The question of whether the Viet Cong were actively helping the radical bonzes cannot be answered with certainty with the current evidence. In his research of Viet Cong propaganda in spring 1963, for example, Pike found no mention of the Buddhist protests:

> Attacks on Americans mounted in intensity and hysteria. Radio Liberation acted as though the Buddhists did not exist. Nor, as had been anticipated, did the NLF agit-prop teams flood the countryside with anti–Diem leaflets in the name of Buddhism. The leadership appeared unwilling or unable to capitalize on the most significant struggle movement in Vietnamese history.... Had the NLF leadership wished to do so, it could have used its impressive struggle machine to launch in the name of Buddha a nation-wide struggle movement that conceivably could have ended with its long-pursued General Uprising. The NLF's reluctance to involve itself deeply in the Buddhist struggle was somewhat puzzling.[16]

Pike could have added, however, that the Viet Cong's lack of public identification with the Buddhist uprising was outright suspicious. He discovered that two leading bonzes in the Buddhist protests, Thich Thien Hao and Thich Thom Me The Nhem, were members of the National Liberation Front and met with Communist leaders in China and North Vietnam.[17]

An educated guess might be that the Buddhist protests were carried out with the full support of Communist leaders from Hanoi to Moscow who told the Viet Cong leaders in South Vietnam to maintain a hands-off position for obvious reasons. This kind of political sophistication was well within the capabilities of Ho Chi Minh and his backers in China and Russia. Stephen C. Y. Pan of the East Asian Research

---

[16] Pike, *Viet Cong*, 353.
[17] Ibid., 431.

Institute in New York City met and interviewed Ho Chi Minh, Ngo Dinh Diem, and other Southeast Asian leaders. This expert on Vietnamese politics concluded that the Buddhist crisis was indeed a Communist front: "The communists knew how to cope with Diem's appeals. Highly skilled at spreading false propaganda, they created incidents, and launched demonstrations. Masters of cold war strategy, they decided that the Achilles heel in Vietnam was the Buddhist associations. They realised the acute sensitivity of Americans, in particular, to the charge of religious persecution."[18]

What unfolded in the spring and summer of 1963 was no spontaneous uprising of persecuted Buddhists who could no longer stand the "burden of oppression"—because there simply was no oppression. "Among the other freedoms granted by the Diem regime there was that of religion, of non-political assembly, freedom to demonstrate, a certain freedom of the press and finally the open admission into the country of many foreign journalists of every political stripe who were able to report abroad the opinions of the opponents of the regime, and the regime's mistakes."[19] The Buddhist protests therefore would seem to have been masterfully planned acts of political manipulation carefully directed at American public opinion in order to destroy U.S. policy in South Vietnam. Ambassador Nolting said a few years later in an interview, "The charge that this was a spontaneous uprising of Buddhists because of religious persecution was, in my opinion, false."[20] While the Buddhist crisis might not have been spontaneous in the sense that it lacked behind-the-scenes planning and organisation, to Nolting and other U.S. officials it did appear to come out of nowhere.

In early 1963, Ambassador Nolting asked Secretary of State Rusk to replace him in Saigon.[21] The assistant secretary of state Harriman replied to Nolting that, owing to the progress that was being made in South Vietnam, Nolting should remain indefinitely according to the discretion of DOS. He advised Nolting to plan for a holiday sometime in the spring or summer. Reports from the DOS and the DOD verify that

[18] Pan and Lyons, *Vietnam Crisis*, 110–11.

[19] Gheddo, *Cross and Bo-Tree*, 133.

[20] Frederick Nolting, interview by Joseph E. O'Connor, May 14, 1966, Paris, interview 1, transcript, 19, John F. Kennedy Oral History Collection, John F. Kennedy Presidential Library, Boston.

[21] Nolting, *From Trust to Tragedy*, 95.

from the American point of view the American-Vietnamese counterinsurgency effort was making considerable headway in spring 1963. Secretary of Defense McNamara told White House officials: "The over-all situation in Vietnam is improving. In the military sector of the counterinsurgency, we are winning. Evidences of improvement are clearly visible, as the combined impact of the programs which involve a long lead time begin to have effect on the Viet Cong."[22] American intelligence reports made similar claims.[23] Everything appeared to be moving along quite satisfactorily in South Vietnam, albeit, according to Hilsman and Forrestal, a bit slower than Washington would wish.[24] No American official seems to have realised that Buddhists were about to explode onto the political stage of South Vietnam.

No American reporter seems to have realised this either. Researcher Ellen Hammer was in South Vietnam just before the breaking of the Buddhist crisis. When she visited Hue in April and asked a local doctor for the latest news, "he did not speak of war but of peace. 'Something important,' he said. 'The Buddhist Youth are organising.'"[25] Hammer was intrigued by this bit of news, she said, but the American press was not: "What the upsurge in Buddhism might portend did not interest American reporters that spring. They were in Vietnam to cover a war, and their articles reported complaints of American officers that the Vietnamese did not want to fight or fought badly."[26]

The upsurge in Buddhist political activity reached a critical mass with the protest against the flag law in early May, just before Ambassador

[22] Quoted in *Evolution of the War: Counterinsurgency; The Overthrow of Ngo Dinh Diem, May–November, 1963*, section IV.B.5 of bk. 3 of *United States–Vietnam Relations, 1945–1967: Study Prepared by the Department of Defense*, by Congress, House, Committee on Armed Services (Washington, D.C.: United States Government Printing Office, 1971), 2.

[23] The details of these reports and their estimations can be found in "National Intelligence Estimate: NIE 53–63; Prospects in South Vietnam", April 17, 1963, Washington, in *FRUS, 1961–1963*, vol. 3, document 94, pp. 232–35. A CIA report stated: "The strategic hamlet program has so well proven itself in those areas where it has been well executed that there is every reason for optimism and confidence." Rufus Phillips, "Memorandum from the Assistant Director for Rural Affairs, United States Operations Mission in Vietnam (Phillips), to the Director of the Mission (Brent); Subject: An Evaluation of Progress in the Strategic Hamlet–Provincial Rehabilitation Program", May 1, 1963, Saigon, in *FRUS, 1961–1963*, vol. 3, document 102, p. 258.

[24] Nolting, *From Trust to Tragedy*, 95.

[25] Hammer, *Death in November*, 83.

[26] Ibid., 84.

Nolting was to go on holiday with his family. Here is his account of what happened:

> President Diem directed that the Vietnamese flag be given precedence over religious banners flown in public displays. He issued the order in response to the prominence given the Vatican flag at a recent Catholic celebration in Hué. Two days later, a large crowd assembled in Hue to celebrate the birth of Gautama Buddha. Buddhist flags were displayed ahead of the national flag. As the crowd attempted to take possession of the radio station, Vietnamese troops were called in by the province chief to enforce the recent decree and to protect the radio station. The demonstration became violent. Several shots (or explosions) occurred. Eight people died.[27]

The first official telegram about the protest sent by John J. Helble, the American consul in Hue, to the State Department was not as informative as it should have been, given the circumstances.[28] It did not give any context or background, and it was noncommittal as to what exactly had killed the demonstrators. It seemed to indicate that gunfire had been the cause of the fatalities, but the American embassy in Saigon added to this the possibility that explosions had killed the demonstrators.[29]

There were serious and substantial discrepancies in reports on the incident, and these spilled over into the news media. Some reports indicated that GVN gunfire had been responsible for the carnage, while others claimed that grenades or even bombs had been thrown or planted. The discrepancies attracted the notice of war correspondent Marguerite Higgins, who after investigating the incident concluded that some of the news reports about the protest were false: "For example, on June 30, 1963, a dispatch from Saigon to *The New York Times* said, 'The Buddhists said that they would not join a commission to investigate the alleged Buddhist grievances unless the government accepted responsibility for the incident on May 8, 1963, that set off the crisis. Troops fired then on Buddhists demonstrating against a ban on displaying their religious flag. Nine Buddhists were killed.' But these three sentences do not reflect the true situation."[30] Higgins went on to lament that false

---

[27] Nolting, *From Trust to Tragedy*, 106.

[28] Cf. John J. Helble, "Telegram from the Consulate at Hue to the Department of State", May 9, 1963, Hue, in *FRUS, 1961–1963*, vol. 3, document 112, p. 277.

[29] Telegram 1005 from American embassy, May 9, 1963, Saigon, ibid., 277n2.

[30] Higgins, *Our Vietnam Nightmare*, 89–90.

information made it all the way to the White House, where it effected a change in U.S. foreign policy: "And yet the account given in *The New York Times'* news dispatch represents what many Americans, even some in official positions, still believe to be the truth about Hue. I find this appalling, because crucial national policy was, it now appears, based on 'facts' of highly doubtful authenticity."[31]

Given the differing reports about the Buddhist crisis and the tremendous impact they had on U.S. foreign policy, historian Ellen Hammer and reporter Marguerite Higgins researched the incident in order to set the record straight. First they discovered, as has been already documented, no evidence that Diem was practicing or endorsing the persecution of Buddhists. Nor did they find any evidence that his enforcement of the flag law in May 1963 was an attack on Buddhists. According to Higgins, Diem's choice to enforce the decree about displaying the Vietnamese flag before any others, including religious banners, was actually aimed at his own brother, Archbishop Ngo Dinh Thuc, who had permitted ceremonies celebrating the silver anniversary of his ordination to the priesthood to be too lavish. At that event Vatican flags were many and national Vietnamese ones few, and President Diem rightly believed this was provocative and insensitive to non-Catholics. Hence Higgins' claim that the description of the law in the *New York Times* was false: "[As for the] assertion that there was a ban on Buddhist flags, no such thing existed. This dispatch implied also that there was some ruling applying solely to Buddhists. Again, this is not true.... The regulation applied to all religions.... There is no doubt, however, that the Vietnamese government's decision to revive these flag regulations on May 6, 1963, made possible the Hue tragedy."[32]

Hammer uncovered another twist in the story of how that decision was made.[33] Archbishop Ngo Dinh Thuc was upset by the prominence of Buddhist flags being displayed to celebrate the birth of Buddha, which he personally observed as he drove through Hue on May 7, 1963. Thuc ordered Ho Dac Khuong, the man who represented the Saigon government in Hue, to have the flags removed according to the decree. Khuong immediately protested, arguing that it was too late and that such a move would deeply offend the Buddhist community. Khuong even appealed

[31] Ibid.
[32] Ibid., 91.
[33] Hammer, *Death in November*, 110, 112–13.

to Saigon, but to no avail. Minister of the Interior Bui Van Luong, who
was in Hue at the time, visited the pagodas to reassure the bonzes that
their flags could be flown and that the order to have them taken down
had been rescinded; he later told United Nations representatives about
his efforts to reassure the Buddhists. Unfortunately, these GVN efforts
were too late: the police had already taken down some flags. This gave
Thich Tri Quang the excuse he needed to begin a campaign that would
bring down Diem and his government.

According to Higgins and Hammer, Thich Tri Quang, in Higgins'
words "a kind of Machiavelli with incense" played a leading role in the
way the protests developed.[34] First some of the Buddhist flags Thich had
displayed were inscribed with antigovernment slogans. The government
tolerated religious assemblies but not antigovernment ones; the political
slogans might have been one of the reasons the flags upset the archbishop and some GVN officials. After the GVN ordered the removal
of the flags, the minister of the interior, trying to avoid a provocation,
told Tri Quang privately that they did not have to come down. Yet Tri
Quang turned around and ordered his monks to take down the flags, as
if to provoke their outrage. Tri Quang also told his monks to inform the
citizens of Hue that the banners were coming down because of Diem's
order to ban Buddhist flags. Next he told people in the crowd, "Go
to the radio station—something very interesting will happen there."[35]
When Tri Quang and his followers reached the radio station, the Buddhist leader demanded that the station director broadcast a speech calling
for Diem's overthrow instead of the government-approved taped message commemorating Buddha's birthday.[36] Tri Quang and the crowd
grew raucous when the station director said he could not broadcast an
unauthorised political speech. Fearing that a riot would break out, the
director telephoned the deputy province chief who was in charge of
public security, Major Dang Sy.

Major Dang Sy reached the radio station two hours later. He and his
men arrived in rubber-tired armoured cars, not tanks as some reports
alleged. They were equipped with stun grenades and tear gas canisters.
While they were still in their armoured cars, more than fifty yards away

[34] Higgins, *Our Vietnam Nightmare*, 30.
[35] Ibid., 92–93.
[36] Hammer, *Death in November*, 113.

from the station, two massive explosions ripped through the crowd, scattering the shocked people. Dang Sy feared that a Viet Cong attack was underway and ordered his men to deploy their stun grenades and gas canisters. When the smoke cleared and the crowd had fled, he found seven dead adults and one dying child lying on the ground. The bodies of the dead had been mutilated, some even decapitated, by the force of the two explosions. A Buddhist doctor who examined the bodies of the victims said that their injuries had to have been caused by something exceeding the capacity of GVN anti-riot gear. Some therefore concluded that the blasts had been caused by homemade bombs, perhaps plastic and fertiliser bombs planted beforehand. Such bombs would indicate the handiwork of the Viet Cong.[37]

Back to Higgins' point about the discrepancies between what her research uncovered what the American media reported on Vietnam, here is an alternate and widely accepted version of the incident from a popular history of Vietnam written by American journalist Stanley Karnow:

> Several thousand [Buddhists] gathered peacefully in front of the city's radio station to listen to loudspeakers broadcast a speech by Tri Quang, a Buddhist leader. The station director cancelled the address, claiming that it had not been censored. He also telephoned Major Xi, who dispatched five armoured cars to the scene. The commander ordered the crowd to disperse, then told his men to fire. The people stampeded. A woman and eight children died, either shot or trampled in the melee.[38]

According to journalist John Mecklin, the American press in South Vietnam during the Buddhist crisis had been guilty of inaccurate or even biased reporting.

> In a scathing article (September 20, 1963) that led to the protest resignation of Charles Mohr, its chief correspondent for Southeast Asia, *Time* asserted: "The press corps on the scene is helping to compound the very confusion that it should be untangling for its readers at home.... They pool their convictions, information, misinformation and grievances.... They have covered a complex situation from only one angle, as if their own conclusions offered all the necessary illumination."[39]

[37] Ibid.,114–15.

[38] Stanley Karnow, *Vietnam: A History* (New York: Viking, 1983), 279.

[39] John Mecklin, *Mission in Torment: An Intimate Account of the U.S. Role in Vietnam* (Garden City, N.Y.: Doubleday, 1965), 120.

Mecklin noted that columnist Joseph Alsop, like Clare Boothe Luce, compared the work of some Saigon newsmen with the campaign against Chiang Kai-Shek by some of the correspondents in China in 1944.[40]

President Diem perceived that disaster lay in the Buddhist revolt, especially since it threatened to undo all that he had accomplished to build bridges between Buddhists and Catholics and to convince Buddhists that the program of his government was better for the country than the one the Communists would bring if they seized power. Bonze Nhat Hanh, remarked, "Under the Diem government there came to light an awareness of a distinction existing between the Communists and the national resistance, and this was Diem's most valid contribution to the country."[41] In order for that distinction to remain in view after the protest in Hue, Diem met with Buddhist leaders, offering generous indemnification for the families who had suffered losses in the protest.[42] In addition, he formed a special commission directed by a Buddhist, Vice President Nguyen Ngoc Tho, to reach amicable agreements between the GVN and the Buddhist communities.[43] Diem, confident that government forces had not caused the deaths in Hue, refused to accept blame for the killings prior to an internationally supervised investigation, which had been requested by Thich Tri Quang. A critical fact that should have drawn more attention to the monk's motives in requesting such an investigation was that, once Diem had agreed to it, Tri Quang rejected the idea.[44]

During the first meeting with the Buddhist leaders, Diem explained to them that errors had been made by GVN officials with respect to the flags. He reminded them that they were guaranteed freedom of worship under the constitution of the Republic of South Vietnam, and he also reminded them that there were troublemakers at the Hue radio station who had nothing to do with Buddhism; indeed, Catholics were amongst the injured.[45] Diem went to great lengths to assuage Buddhist fears and to meet their demands. He issued a joint communiqué with Thich Tinh

---

[40] Ibid, 120.
[41] Gheddo, Cross and Bo-Tree, 109.
[42] Higgins, Our Vietnam Nightmare, 101.
[43] Pan and Lyons, Vietnam Crisis, 112–13.
[44] Higgins, Our Vietnam Nightmare, 101.
[45] Hammer, Death in November, 117.

Kiet, head of the General Association of Buddhists, which addressed all of the Buddhist demands except the one from Thich Tri Quang wherein Diem was to admit guilt before any inquiry.[46] The reasons for Diem's position were relayed to Washington in a telegram from Ambassador Nolting on May 22, 1963.[47] The American journalists, almost to a man, ignored Diem's substantial efforts, which included presidential clemency for all bonzes who had broken the law in the riot,[48] because they believed his government was responsible for causing the protests and the deaths that resulted from it.

American journalists, though, were not alone in blaming the GVN for the Hue killings and in believing the protests arose from GVN mistreatment of Buddhists. Here is how Consul Helble described the situation in Hue following the initial protest:

> Population must be judged as tense. Duration and intensity of crisis unusual in view generally passive nature Vietnamese in terms public demonstrations. People seem to have taken seriously Bonze speech morning 8th 'now is time to fight.' While word fight perhaps overemphatic, desire of people seems to be to have some sort of showdown following years of frustration for Buddhists. Student banner morning 9th 'please kill us'. Man on street expressing great desire for world to know of killings on 8th. While GVN line is VC responsible, no credibility this among population.[49]

[46] The contents of the Buddhists' demands closely match the points President Diem addressed. See "Manifesto of Vietnamese Buddhist Clergy and Faithful", May 10, 1963, Hue, in *FRUS, 1961–1963*, vol. 3, document 118, pp. 287–88.

[47] "From Diem's extensive remarks to me, it was quite clear that he is convinced that (a) Hue incident was provoked by Buddhist leaders, (b) deaths were caused by grenade or grenades thrown by VC or other dissidents and not by GVN, and (c) certain Buddhist leaders are seeking to use Hue affair as means of enhancing their own positions within Buddhist movement." Frederick Nolting, "Telegram from the Embassy in Vietnam to the Department of State", May 22, 1963, Saigon, in *FRUS, 1961–1963*, vol. 3, document 131, p. 314.

[48] According to Gheddo, the agreement included "a new and carefully worked out regulation on the public display of religious banners (art. 1); the government's promise to pass at the beginning of 1964 a new law on religious assemblies and associations (art. 2); the setting up of an enquiry commission on the injustices denounced by the Buddhists and the act of presidential clemency for all who in the Buddhist demonstrations had broken the law (art. 3); the renewal of the guarantees for more ample religious freedom in all its aspects (art. 4) and, finally, the punishment of the members of the police who were proven guilty in the clash with Buddhists and the agreement to give aid to the families of the victims (art. 5)." Gheddo, *Cross and Bo-Tree*, 181.

[49] John J. Helble, "Telegram from the Consulate at Hue to the Department of State", May 10, 1963, Hue, 2 A.M., in *FRUS, 1961–1963*, vol. 3, document 116, p. 285.

Helble added that Thich Tri Quang was propelling the Buddhist campaign forward by trying to organise a massive funeral rally for the victims of the Hue incident to be attended by international Buddhist leaders.[50] Some hours later Helble wrote DOS that Tri Quang was trying to incite a nationwide Gandhi-styled protest against the GVN. He noted that another prominent Buddhist leader, whose name still remains classified, tried to prevent further violence by telling Quang-incited crowds that, in fact, Diem's government was a good one.[51]

At the time of the Buddhist protests, Ambassador Nolting was still trying to resolve the disagreements between Saigon and Washington over joint control of U.S. counterinsurgency funding, as mentioned in the previous chapter. Correspondence from Nolting shows that differences between the two governments were being overcome and that, counterinsurgency funding would rest on a better foundation than before.[52] Nolting stated in his memoirs that resolving the differences seemed routine enough at the time. Yet information that subsequently came his way revealed that it did not appear routine to the Kennedy administration. The National Security Council (NSC) was scheduled to discuss whether counterinsurgency funding should continue if Saigon did not agree to share control over it with Washington. The discussion never took place, Nolting wrote, and Diem eventually agreed to joint control, but the "dispute deepened Washington's perception that Diem was a difficult person to deal with and enhanced its impression that Nhu was even more stubborn than his brother.... [T]he argument left a bad taste in officialdom's mouth."[53]

The issue of Ngo Dinh Nhu's stubbornness related to his views about the American military presence in South Vietnam. In an interview with Warren Unna, a reporter for the *Washington Post*, Nhu had raised

[50] Ibid., 284–85.

[51] John J. Helble, "Telegram from the Consulate at Hue to Department of State", May 10, 1963, Hue, 3 P.M., in *FRUS, 1961–1963*, vol. 3, document 117, p. 285.

[52] Frederick Nolting, "Letter from the Ambassador in Vietnam (Nolting) to Secretary of State at the Presidency and Assistant Secretary of State for National Defense Thuan", May 10, 1963, Saigon, in *FRUS, 1961–1963*, vol. 3, document 119, pp. 289–90. In addition to Nolting's correspondence with Thuan, on May 17, 1963, President Diem and Nolting issued a joint communiqué that announced that the U.S. and South Vietnamese governments had reached an agreement on counterinsurgency funding. "Editorial Note", in *FRUS, 1961–1963*, vol. 3, document 127, pp. 307–9.

[53] Nolting, *From Trust to Tragedy*, 103–4.

pointed questions about the number of American troops in South Vietnam and the need for its reduction. Specifically, Ngo Dinh Nhu pointed out that their high profile was playing right into the hands of Communist propaganda. Secretary of State Dean Rusk sent a telegram to Ambassador Nolting complaining about the interview.[54] Four days later, Roger Hilsman sent a brisk telegram to Nolting in which he claimed that Nhu was making support for the GVN very difficult in Washington. Essentially, Hilsman wanted Nolting to persuade Diem to reign in his brother.[55] Nolting replied there was not much more that he could do in this regard. He added that much of the unfortunate impact of the interview was due to way it was handled by the *Washington Post*.[56]

There was little for Nolting to do because, as Ellen Hammer pointed out, Nhu and Diem had genuine concerns over what would happen to Vietnamese sovereignty if American armed forces started to deploy in increasing numbers in their country without the oversight of the Vietnamese government. Before the outbreak of the Buddhist crisis, Diem's main concern was about American intentions for South Vietnam, hence the disagreements over a jointly controlled counterinsurgency fund. "The real problem troubling the Vietnamese President was not money but men—the American advisers who seemed to be everywhere, too numerous, too deeply involved in Vietnamese affairs."[57] As a nationalist, Diem was alarmed at the growing number of the American men in South Vietnam, who were increasingly bypassing his administration, leaving him wondering if South Vietnam had gotten rid of French colonialism only to see it replaced with an American version.[58]

President Diem might have dodged the joint funding bullet and the Nhu bullet, but it can be argued that those in Washington who wanted

[54] Dean Rusk, "Telegram from the Department of State to the Embassy in Vietnam", May 13, 1963, Washington, in *FRUS, 1961–1963*, vol. 3, document 122, pp. 294–96. (Drafted by Heavner and cleared by Hilsman.)

[55] "I hope you able to find additional opportunities continue impress on Diem and Nhu fact that we having rough going defending our Viet-Nam program at best and this incident likely leave lasting bad impression in spite of communiqué. You may say we hope future statements will be more helpful to joint effort defeat VC." Roger Hilsman, "Telegram from the Department of State to the Embassy in Vietnam", May 17, 1963, Washington, in *FRUS, 1961–1963*, vol. 3, document 128, pp. 308–9.

[56] Nolting to Department of State, telegram, May 20, 1963, Saigon, ibid., 309n3.

[57] Hammer, *Death in November*, 120–21.

[58] Ibid.

him out of the way found exactly what they were looking for in the Buddhist crisis, which lasted for months both in South Vietnam and on the front pages of the *New York Times* and other newspapers.

As can be seen from his *Times'* articles, David Halberstam couched the issue as a conflict between an oppressive minority government and an oppressed majority population. Given that the regime was an ally of America, its apparent violations of religious rights and freedoms was both troubling and embarrassing for the Kennedy administration. Here are typical excerpts:

> The conflict between the South Vietnamese Government and Buddhist Priests is sorely troubling American officials here....
>
> For a variety of reasons Americans wish to dissociate themselves from the Saigon Government's role in the religious crisis....
>
> It is reported that Washington has already told its officials here to express extreme concern over the developments and the Government's handling of them, and to press for a solution to the religious strife....
>
> Americans are deeply embarrassed by the events, and frustrated in the face of persistent questioning by individual Vietnamese, who ask: "Why does your Government allow this to go on? Why don't you Americans say or do something?"...
>
> American political officials here are worried about the effect of the crisis on the war effort in a country where an estimated 70 per cent of the population considers itself Buddhist. Since President Diem and most of his close associates are Roman Catholic, it is almost impossible to maintain the Government's stand that it is only interested in keeping order, and that the struggle has no religious overtones.[59]

Halberstam's claims about the religious profile of South Vietnam and its government, which shaped American public opinion and ultimately American foreign policy, deserve scrutiny. As we have seen, the GVN was religiously diverse. Also, however many Buddhists there were in the country, the question should have been asked whether the leaders of

---

[59] David Halberstam, "Americans Vexed by Inability to Act in Vietnam Dispute", *New York Times*, June 10, 1963, 1, 6. For more articles in this vein, see David Halberstam, "U.S. Avoids Part in Saigon Dispute: Tells Its Troops Not to Help Stop Buddhist Protests", *New York Times*, June 11, 1963, 6; Max Frankel, "U.S. Warns South Vietnam on Demands of Buddhists: Diem Is Told He Faces Censure If He Fails to Satisfy Religious Grievances, Many of Which Are Called Just", *New York Times*, June 14, 1963, 1, 10; David Halberstam, "Saigon Buddhists Clash with Police", *New York Times*, June 16, 1963, 1, 18; David Halberstam, "Discontent Rises in Vietnam Crisis: Regime Losing Ground over Treatment of Buddhists", *New York Times*, June 22, 1963, 6.

the protests were, in fact, speaking on behalf of all or even most of them. Later, after more protests and some of the monks immolated themselves, one Buddhist monk told war correspondent Higgins, "No true Buddhist would commit suicide. It is written in the verses of Buddha that suicide is wrong. Buddha says that a man's responsibility is to mend his own life, not to meddle in politics. So those men who are, according to your newspaper article, marching in the streets [of Hue and Saigon] are not Buddhists. They betray Buddhism." Higgins replied, "These people are believed by the Americans to represent Buddhism." Then the monk said, "White men have brought many things to Vietnam. But white men have not brought much understanding to Vietnam."[60]

While the Kennedy administration was growing restless from the political fallout of the Buddhist crisis, other positive reports about the counterinsurgency surfaced. One in particular was given by Colonel Francis Philip "Ted" Serong, head of the Australian Training Mission to South Vietnam, at a high-level meeting of the Special Group for Counterinsurgency on May 23, 1963, attended by Averell Harriman, Robert Kennedy, John McCone, and Generals Victor Krulak and Maxwell Taylor, amongst others. Colonel Serong told the group that the war against the Viet Cong was being won.[61] Several indicators displayed the favourable trends, he said, not least of which was the substantial increase in spontaneous intelligence given to the GVN. Colonel Serong attributed this to the strategic hamlets, since they afforded the people greater security from the threats of the Communists. He put the success within the context of frustration that was being leaked by American advisors to the press. While acknowledging that things in South Vietnam were far from perfect, he stated that the real success story was being overlooked in Washington. Additionally, in his laconic soldier's style he noted that the American press, for some strange reason, was ignoring the story too.[62]

[60] Higgins, *Our Vietnam Nightmare*, 41.

[61] James W. Dingeman [executive secretary of the Special Group for Counterinsurgency], "Minutes of a Meeting of the Special Group for Counterinsurgency, Washington, May 23, 1963, 2 P.M.", in *FRUS, 1961–1963*, vol. 3, document 132, pp. 315–16.

[62] According to the minutes of the meeting: "He [Serong] pointed out that there are problems with the press in Viet-Nam, but they are reporting what they see or are being told. He believes this situation can be improved by working more closely with them in the field. Our U.S. military advisors are reflecting in their comments to the press their frustrations to get the Vietnamese to accept their advice. The big success story in Viet-Nam is the strategic hamlet program and this story has not yet been fully told. He stated that out of a total population of about 16 million some 8 million have been moved into the strategic hamlets, resulting in one of the biggest population moves in history." Ibid., 315.

A significant point made by Colonel Serong was that Ambassador Nolting had effectively and positively influenced relations between Washington and Saigon in such a manner as to allow the CIP to succeed. Nevertheless, the wheels had already been put into motion to replace Ambassador Nolting with a different sort of man. In a memorandum to President Kennedy two weeks before Serong's report, Michael Forrestal of the National Security Council staff stated, with regard to the embassy in Saigon: "What we need is fresh leadership in the field."[63] As we have seen, the Harriman group had already begun a search for a replacement government in South Vietnam,[64] and Nolting, in his loyalty to Diem, was not cooperating.

Indeed, Nolting had cautioned his own countrymen that their hubris and zeal would undo the patient work he had accomplished. He strongly hinted at this when he told Secretary of Defense McNamara that "it was difficult, if not impossible, to put a Ford engine into a Vietnamese ox-cart."[65] According to Nolting, McNamara agreed with his analogy but claimed that the United States had the capability to do just that and to make it work in short order.

---

[63] Michael V. Forrestal, "Memorandum from Michael V. Forrestal of the National Security Council Staff to the President", May 10, 1963, Washington, in *FRUS, 1961–1963*, vol. 3, document 120, p. 291.

[64] One of the best documents supporting the argument that Harriman was already looking for another, more compliant leader for South Vietnam is a telegram he sent to Nolting February 18, 1963—that is, before the Buddhist crisis—asking him to seek alternative leaders and to lend support to Diem's opponents: "However you, and your very competent Labor Attaché, might wish to consider using CIA to supply some discreet support to Mr. Buu's labor union in order to counteract repressive measures taken against it by GVN." W. Averell Harriman to Frederick E. Nolting, February 18, 1963, 1, Nolting Papers, box 12, Selected Correspondence—Harriman, W. Averell. The State Department claims that it could not find this document, which was mentioned by Nolting in a return telegram to Harriman; see Frederick E. Nolting, "Letter from the Ambassador in Vietnam (Nolting) to the Assistant Secretary of State for Far Eastern Affairs (Harriman)", February 27, 1963, Saigon, in *FRUS, 1961–1963*, vol. 3, document 45, p. 126n2.

[65] Michael Charlton, "The New Frontiersmen Hold the Line", program 4 of *Many Reasons Why: The American Involvement in Vietnam*, British Broadcasting Corporation, 1977, manuscript copy, 4, Nolting Papers, box 13, Professional Papers.

Washington Isolates Diem

The violence at the Buddhist protest in Hue deeply troubled Ambassador Nolting, but he believed the affair would be handled properly by all parties involved and, when the country seemed relatively calm, he left for his planned holiday on May 23, 1963. This proved to be a fateful decision: once Nolting was out of the country, Diem's foes amongst the radical Buddhists—and in the State Department—redoubled their efforts to bring down the president of South Vietnam. According to journalist John Mecklin,

> There was a personal drama behind the scenes of the American reaction to the Buddhist upheaval. It arose out of the coincidence that Ambassador Nolting had left Saigon on a well-earned home leave with his family just before the crisis developed.... It was a last-straw touch to Nolting's anguished tour of duty that in his absence the U.S. switched back to a "tough" policy with Diem and it failed miserably. It will remain one of the unanswerable "ifs" of history that Nolting's low-key way, at the moment of ultimate challenge, might have been more effective.[1]

As can be seen from his memoir, Nolting agreed: "I could not have made a worse mistake. I left my post on the eve of the storm—a storm that eventually destroyed nine years of constructive American help and support for South Vietnam's independence."[2]

During Nolting's absence from Saigon, his deputy, William Trueheart, was in charge of the embassy. Nolting left him strict instructions to contact him immediately if any sort of crisis or serious problem

---

[1] John Mecklin, *Mission in Torment: An Intimate Account of the U.S. Role in Vietnam* (Garden City, N.Y.: Doubleday, 1965), 168.

[2] Frederick Nolting, *From Trust to Tragedy: The Political Memoirs of Frederick Nolting, Kennedy's Ambassador to Diem's Vietnam* (New York: Praeger, 1988), 108–9.

[3] Ibid., 108.

developed.[3] Unfortunately for all concerned, the Buddhist crisis escalated while Nolting was out of the country, and Trueheart failed to contact the ambassador. This was a serious breach of trust, and it had long-term ramifications for U.S. policy. Later, in August 1963, when Nolting was back at the State Department in Washington, he filed a report on Trueheart with the personnel division. In it he stated that Trueheart,

> through no fault of his own, was faced by a dangerously developing crisis shortly after my departure. It was of such magnitude as to threaten to destroy the base on which United States policy in Viet-Nam was founded and to cause great changes in the relationships between the United States Mission and the Vietnamese Government.... Mr. Trueheart failed to let me know of these developments. This was contrary to our understanding and, in my view, not in keeping with the responsibilities and loyalties of a Deputy Chief of Mission to a Chief of Mission, irrespective of previous understandings.[4]

In May 1966, Nolting claimed in an interview that Trueheart had failed to communicate with him because he had been won over by the Harriman group.[5] The historical question is, what happened in Nolting's absence that undermined the constructive and mutually respectful relationship he had built between the American and Vietnamese governments? The answer is the Buddhist crisis. This simple answer, however, reflects only the surface of the problem, because the relationship between Saigon and Washington might have withstood the crisis but for the way Trueheart treated Ngo Dinh Diem. And his treatment of the South Vietnamese president was prescribed by Averell Harriman and Roger Hilsman.

Nolting summarised in his memoirs what happened in Vietnam during his leave. He noted that the Buddhists continued their agitation regardless of Diem's efforts to placate them;[6] and a respected elderly Buddhist monk, Thich Quang Duc, ceremoniously burned himself to

---

[4] Frederick E. Nolting, "Final Report on Mr. William C. Trueheart, Deputy Chief of Mission", August 17, 1963, 1–2, Nolting Papers, box 13, Selected Correspondence—Trueheart, William.

[5] Frederick Nolting, interview by Joseph E. O'Connor, May 14, 1966, Paris, interview 1, transcript, 21, John F. Kennedy Oral History Collection, John F. Kennedy Presidential Library, Boston.

[6] These attempts by Diem to placate the bonzes were duly noted in the cable traffic between the embassy in Saigon and DOS in Washington. In a telegram June 15, 1963, Trueheart explained that the South Vietnamese government was having difficulty keeping the bonzes

death on June 11, 1963.[7] The leaders of the radical Xa Loi and Tu Dam pagodas had arranged this self-immolation, which took place outside the Cambodian embassy.[8] Hence, amongst other things, the suicide was an appeal to Cambodia, whose leader, Prince Norodom Sihanouk, was no friend of Diem.

The anti-Diem Buddhists received encouragement and support from Cambodia. Adherents of the Hinayana form of Buddhism that prevailed in Cambodia were in the South Vietnamese Buddhist movement. Consequently, the Ngo Dinhs suspected that Prince Sihanouk was using the movement to impose on Vietnam the neutrality of his own country, where he attempted to steer a middle course between the Communists and the West. The Ngo Dinhs feared neutrality would eventually lead to Communist control, as it had in Laos. They had therefore sponsored plots against Sihanouk, both with the Americans and on their own.[9]

Prince Sihanouk had made public statements against the Ngo Dinhs. He asserted, for example, that Hanoi was bound to be victorious over them. At the Seventh World Buddhist Congress, held in Phnom Penh in November 1961, the Buddhist delegation from South Vietnam had been introduced to delegations from North Vietnam and China. Both of these delegations were firmly under Communist Party control.[10] While it cannot be proved with certainty, the claim that the Cambodians facilitated connections between the Viet Cong and the South Vietnamese Buddhist radicals appears to have some substance. According to Douglas Pike, Thich Thom Me The Nhem, "an ethnic Cambodian and a Buddhist monk, acted as leader of the Cambodian minority in Vietnam as well as the chief NLF liaison figure with the Vietnamese Buddhist organizations."[11] There existed an ideological common ground

---

at the table because the latter had many reasons for not negotiating with the government, including the sympathy of the press. See William Trueheart, "Telegram from the Embassy in Vietnam to the Department of State", June 15, 1963, Saigon, in *FRUS, 1961–1963*, vol. 3, document 176, p. 395. A note on another copy of this telegram indicates that President Kennedy read it.

[7] Associated Press, "Monk Suicide by Fire in Anti-Diem Protest", *New York Times*, June 11, 1963, 4.

[8] Marguerite Higgins, *Our Vietnam Nightmare* (New York: Harper and Row, 1965), 18.

[9] See Ellen J. Hammer, *A Death in November: America in Vietnam, 1963* (New York: E.P. Dutton, 1987), 140–41.

[10] Ibid., 141.

[11] Douglas Pike, *Viet Cong: The Organization and Techniques of the National Liberation Front of South Vietnam* (Cambridge: Mass.: MIT Press, 1966), 431.

between Communism and certain strains of Buddhism, as established in the research of Father Piero Gheddo of the Pontifical Institute for Foreign Missions of Milan.[12]

The salient point is that, behind the public image of the Buddhist monk in flames, there was much intrigue and manipulation. This is an important consideration because of the devastating impact this crafted image had on the GVN's ability to appear legitimate in the eyes of the American people. Ambassador Nolting recalled in his memoirs how a Vietnamese acquaintance explained the background of the suicide. Diem's own personal physician, who also happened to treat Thich Quang Duc on a regular basis at the Xa Loi Pagoda, warned Diem that Thich Quang Duc would burn himself to death.[13] This doctor, whose name Nolting would not divulge for security reasons, told Diem that several new monks were trying to persuade Quang Duc to kill himself. Several years earlier, Quang Duc had made a suicide pact with a Buddhist monk in Hanoi who had carried out his part of the bargain and burned himself to death in protest against the persecution of Buddhists in North Vietnam.[14] When leaders of the Buddhist uprising in South Vietnam learned that Quang Duc wanted to redeem his pledge, they encouraged him to do so. The monk's desire for suicide had little to do with Diem's government until they made it so.[15]

---

[12] Father Piero Gheddo's investigations uncovered an article entitled "World Coexistence of Buddhism and Communism" in a radical Japanese Buddhist publication from Tokyo, *Young East*, no. 56 (1965): 18–24. This article made plain that there was "a desire to show that the oppression in Asia comes from Christianity and white people, while salvation comes from Buddhism united with Communism since both complement one another and have the same aspirations and the same goals." Father Gheddo went on to explain that this article's main argument was that "between Buddhism and Communism there is more that unites than divides." Fr. Piero Gheddo, *The Cross and the Bo-Tree: Catholics and Buddhists in Vietnam*, trans. Charles Underhill Quinn (New York: Sheed and Ward, 1970), 206.

[13] Nolting, *From Trust to Tragedy*, 115.

[14] The American newspapers did not concern themselves with the outright persecution of Buddhists by the Communist Party in North Vietnam. According to Father Gheddo: "That there were discriminations [in South Vietnam] in favor of the Catholics (not qua Catholics but as certain foes of Communism) is undeniable, but that Diem 'declared a religious war against four-fifths of the population, who were Buddhists' passed for the truth only with a certain kind of Western press which never raised the least protest about the absolute authentic persecutions suffered by Buddhism in North Vietnam....

"It is enough to say that the two largest Buddhist organizations of North Vietnam (North Vietnam Buddhist Association and the North Vietnam Sangha) have, and had even in Diem's time, settled in Saigon, after having fled from the North (*World Buddhism*, January, 1963, p. 20)." Gheddo, *Cross and Bo-Tree*, 184, 204.

[15] Nolting, *From Trust to Tragedy*, 115–16.

Before Quang Duc's death, monks at Xa Loi pagoda told American reporters that "an important event was going to take place" and directed them where to go. As a result, Associated Press journalist Malcolm Browne was able to photograph his award-winning "Buddha in the Fire", which was published in newspapers throughout the world. Thus, "the world, and particularly the United States, was filled with shock and horror."[16] Indeed, Senator Frank Church, a member of the Senate Foreign Relations Committee, said, "Such grisly scenes have not been witnessed since the Christian martyrs marched hand in hand into the Roman arenas."[17]

According to Nolting, this shocking image and the articles that accompanied it constituted the final blow to American public opinion of President Diem.[18] And this is exactly the outcome the Buddhist radicals had intended. As Higgins discovered in interviews with Thich Tri Quang, the leader of the Buddhist insurrection, the monks were using self-immolation not because of harsh treatment by the GVN but because it had shock value in the Western world and would separate Diem's regime from its supporters in America. Then the bonzes, or so they thought, would be able to install a government of their own.[19] According to Ellen Hammer, "The activist bonzes found they had a weapon of choice that had captured the horrified imagination of people in many places throughout the world. They would use that weapon time and again in their struggle with the Diem government."[20]

While this author has made links between the radical bonzes and the Communists, it must be said that apart from the possibility of some actual Communist agents amongst them, the bonzes were not Communists per se. William Colby compared the bonzes to the radicalised Muslims who led the 1979 Iranian Revolution against the shah. The political ideology of the bonzes, he explained, included "a total rejection of the changes going on, modernization, [and] an idealistic return to some religious base."[21] Colby discerned a distinction between the impact of the

[16] Stephen Pan and Daniel Lyons, *Vietnam Crisis* (New York: East Asian Research Institute, 1966), 113–14.

[17] Quoted in Hammer, *Death in November*, 145–46.

[18] Nolting, *From Trust to Tragedy*, 112.

[19] Higgins, *Our Vietnam Nightmare*, 33–35.

[20] Hammer, *Death in November*, 145–46.

[21] William Colby, interview by Ted Gittinger, June 2, 1981, Washington, D.C., interview 1, transcript, 20, Lyndon Baines Johnson Presidential Library Oral History Collection, University of Texas at Austin.

burning bonzes on the American public—and hence on President Kennedy's policy—and that on the political legitimacy President Diem still enjoyed in Vietnam. By adroitly manipulating the media, the bonzes, were able to convince the world that they had more political power than they really possessed and that Diem had less political legitimacy than he still had. "They [the bonzes] were not a major problem," Colby said, "and he [Diem] had not lost the authority of his state. Sure, there were unhappy people, but he hadn't lost authority and he had been through tough challenges like that before."[22]

The emotion stirred up by the media's reporting of the Buddhist crisis nevertheless caused Washington to lose sight of its strategic assets and goals in South Vietnam. Nolting discerned this loss of focus in Trueheart's actions during the ambassador's absence. Looking later at the cable traffic between Washington and Saigon from this period, he saw that "the whole machinery of co-operation between the American mission and the South Vietnamese government nearly collapsed."[23] He noted that the embassy had taken a "get tough" approach with Diem, and Higgins supported his claim with her observation that under Trueheart American diplomacy was reduced to crude table hammering and threats.[24] As a result, the South Vietnamese president was isolated, and deliberately so. Nolting wrote, "It is still incomprehensible to me that my deputy in Saigon and my colleagues in the State Department allowed this crisis in US-GVN relations to develop without letting me know what was happening. They had our daily schedule. I had their assurances. Upon timely notification, I could have returned within twenty-four hours, and I believe that I could have helped to prevent the tragedies that followed."[25] Nolting concluded that the Kennedy administration did not want him back in Saigon. "In Washington I met with Hilsman and Harriman and once with President Kennedy.... Harriman was testy and uncommunicative. He appeared not to want me to return to Saigon. I suspect that I had not been notified during my vacation because the anti-Diem forces in Washington had not wanted me to return to Vietnam. Seeing in this crisis a chance for a fresh start, they may have wanted it to come

[22] Ibid.
[23] Nolting, *From Trust to Tragedy*, 112.
[24] Higgins, *Our Vietnam Nightmare*, 100.
[25] Nolting, *From Trust to Tragedy*, 113.

to a head, to make a change in government in Saigon inevitable."[26] Judging from Harriman's negative reaction to Nolting's request to get back to South Vietnam and from the remarks made by Roger Hilsman about Nolting's bias in favour of Diem, which he called "localitis",[27] it would seem that the Harriman group did not want Nolting to improve Washington's relationship with President Diem.[28]

Another perspective on the Buddhist crisis, by an eyewitness, lends credence to the conclusion that there was more behind the Buddhist protests then alleged religious intolerance by the GVN. John Mecklin, a U.S. Information Agency officer attached to Ambassador Nolting's mission in Saigon, explained how the Buddhist crisis expanded exponentially just after Nolting had gone on leave. On June 1, 1963, the day after Diem had met with Buddhist leaders and promised to consider their demands, some four thousand Buddhists demonstrated in Hue. William Trueheart reported this protest to Washington, informing the Kennedy administration that the bonze leading the protest, Thich Tri Quang, was telling his followers that the "situation in his view [was] beyond compromise and [that], in direct confrontation with GVN, Buddhists should seek help from any source, including VC."[29] DOS responded to this intelligence with the following advice: "Agree that unrest has political as well as religious motivation, but believe it would be unwise for GVN to make any further moves to place blame on Communists. Naming them would make them an officially recognized party to the dispute and downgrade genuine grievances Buddhists themselves have. Would seem best ignore Communists and deal as reasonably as possible with Buddhists."[30]

[26] Ibid.

[27] "Kennedy would send people out there, you know, like myself or Mike Forrestal and others, and they would come back and say Nolting has become wedded to Diem. Localitis, we used to call it, you know.... Then you see Nolting goes on leave and Bill Trueheart his deputy, his protégé, after a month of Nolting's leave, begins to be anti-Diem. So it is almost unanimous." Michael Charlton, "The New Frontiersmen Hold the Line", program 4 of *Many Reasons Why: The American Involvement in Vietnam*, British Broadcasting Corporation, 1977, manuscript copy, 11–12, Nolting Papers, box 13, Professional Papers.

[28] Nolting, *From Trust to Tragedy*, 113.

[29] William Trueheart, "Telegram from the Embassy in Vietnam to the Department of State", Saigon, June 1, 1963, in *FRUS, 1961–1963*, vol. 3, document 142, p. 341.

[30] Chalmers B. Wood, "Telegram from the Department of State to the Embassy in Vietnam", June 1, 1963, Washington, in *FRUS, 1961–1963*, vol. 3, document 143, p. 342. (Cleared by Rice and Hilsman. Signed "Rusk".)

According to Mecklin, on June 2, 1963, there was violent rioting in Hue that GVN troops tried to suppress with tear gas grenades, which owing to their age burned about sixty people.[31] The American consul in Hue reported to the American embassy in Saigon that the soldiers must have used blister gas against the demonstrators.[32] Trueheart, acting as chargé d'affaires in Nolting's absence, immediately stormed Secretary Thuan's office, threatening the GVN with public condemnation in Washington. Thuan allowed Trueheart to rant and then forcefully explained to him that the Vietnamese forces did not possess blister gas but had used very old tear gas grenades leftover from the French. The acid, which activates the smoke, had broken through and burned the protesters. Nevertheless, an American reporter spread the story that the suppression of the peaceful bonzes in Hue had been brutally accomplished by means of blister gas.[33] Mecklin, a former war correspondent himself, questioned the professional ethics of the reporter who wrote about blister gas before it was confirmed. An investigation later proved that the burns had been caused by old tear gas, but the political damage had already been done by the false report.[34]

Though highly critical of the GVN, Mecklin took seriously their concern that the Buddhist revolt had Communist connections. The police chief for central Vietnam, for example, told an American observer he had no doubt the three leading bonzes in Hue were Viet Cong.[35] Mecklin observed that their anti-government campaign was "executed with such sophisticated skill as to suggest that they had been trained on Madison Avenue".[36] He asked questions that American newsman were failing

[31] Mecklin, *Mission in Torment*, 155.

[32] William Trueheart, "Telegram from the Embassy in Vietnam to the Department of State", June 4, 1963, Saigon, in *FRUS, 1961–1963*, vol. 3, document 146, p. 346.

[33] Hammer, *Death in November*, 136.

[34] "The professional ethics of the Saigon newsmen occasionally were at least debatable.... On one occasion we had received a preliminary report indicating that Vietnamese police had used some kind of 'blister gas' against a Buddhist demonstration in Hue. Since this could provoke serious repercussions, I persuaded the chargé d'affaires, William Trueheart, to call in the newsmen, tell them all we knew, and then appeal for omission of references to 'blister gas' until the report could be investigated. The newsmen agreed, but one of them immediately filed a dispatch that was widely published in the U.S. accusing the government of using 'blister gas.' As we had hoped, investigation revealed that the burns had been caused by deteriorated tear gas grenades, but by then the damage had been done." Mecklin, *Mission in Torment*, 127.

[35] Trueheart, "Telegram from Embassy to Department of State", June 4, 1963, 346n2.

[36] Mecklin, *Mission in Torment*, 157.

to ask: Who benefited from and who had organised this unprecedented foray into politics by Buddhist monks? Additionally, Mecklin wanted to know how it had come about that Diem's enemies, who had previously dragged up every conceivable charge against him, had discovered so late in the day (May 8, 1963) that the man was also anti-Buddhist: "The experts [on Buddhism] were no less surprised than the rest of us when the Buddhists went into politics so spectacularly.... For years Diem's innumerable enemies had dredged up every possible charge against him, but it was only after the May 8 incident at Hue that they discovered that he was also guilty of oppressing the Buddhists."[37]

Mecklin maintained that it was never proved that the Communists planned the Buddhist crisis. He noted, however, that "for years it had been a standard Communist technique throughout the world secretly to infiltrate legitimate organisations, like American labor unions, to work into key positions of leadership, and to push openly for Communist objectives only when conditions offered the maximum chance of success. The Buddhist rebellion exactly fitted this pattern, and the Buddhists in Vietnam had long been vulnerable to exactly this kind of penetration."[38] He also noted that the Buddhists could not have succeeded in attaining their political goals without the help of the American media. "Expressed more bluntly, American news coverage of the upheaval contributed directly to the destruction of a national U.S. policy of direct importance to the security of the United States, in an area where we had deployed nearly twenty thousand Americans, where we were spending some $500 million a year, at the only point in the world where we engaged in support of a shooting war against a Communist enemy."[39]

Marguerite Higgins, who had covered the Korean War alongside Pulitzer Prize winner Keyes Beech, was no stranger to Southeast Asia, and particularly South Vietnam. Her extensive travels around the country during the summer of 1963 demonstrated the power of the news media to distort the situation. For example, in her trips to the countryside, the phrase she heard the most often from American advisers was that "we are inching ahead." Therefore, she wrote, she "was amazed upon returning to Saigon to find the town buzzing with news of recent

[37] Ibid., 158–59.
[38] Ibid.
[39] Ibid.

newspaper dispatches proclaiming that the Buddhist crisis was 'spreading to the countryside,' that it was 'deep and smouldering' in the army, that the war in the delta had 'deteriorated,' and that the situation was 'ominous.' "[40] She was stunned not only by these false conclusions but by the lack of reporting on the gains being made against the insurgents during this critical period. She contrasted the attention given to the defeat at Ap Bac in January with that given to the victory scored by the South Vietnamese at Quang Ngai four months later. The former made headlines for weeks, while the latter made no headlines at all. Yet, "the Twenty-fifth Vietnamese Division at Quang Ngai not only stood its ground but also fought four days and nights running. When the battle was over two hundred and twenty-six Viet Cong dead were picked off the field with their weapons (including Chinese and Czech machine guns)."[41] The focus on the negative, she said, "was a recurring phenomenon, and it embittered the United States mission."

The Ap Bac coverage in the *New York Times* had led the American public to conclude that something was seriously wrong with the government of South Vietnam, and its coverage of the Buddhist crisis very handily lent support to this conclusion. David Halberstam's reporting introduced the notion that the Diem government was staggering and most likely entering a terminal phase. His *New York Times* article "Discontent Rises in Vietnam Crises: Regime Losing Ground over Treatment of Buddhists" put forward a number of allegations and rumours as facts. The article started off by stating that Diem's government was "engaged in an all-out struggle for political survival".[42] Halberstam also wrote that the unrest in Saigon represented all of South Vietnam and that the GVN's mishandling of the Buddhist crisis had irreparably damaged the war effort. He added, "Some well-informed observers believe there will be an attempt to oust the Government."

Halberstam wrote a follow-up article that appeared on the front page of the *New York Times* on July 3. Entitled "Some U.S. Officials in Saigon Dubious about Diem Regime", it raised the issue of American officials wanting to see Diem's government replaced: "Some United States officials in South Vietnam who two months ago were praising President

[40] Higgins, quoted in ibid.,122–23.

[41] Higgins, quoted in ibid.,127–28.

[42] David Halberstam, "Discontent Rises in Vietnam Crises: Regime Losing Ground over Treatment of Buddhists", *New York Times*, June 22, 1963, 6.

Ngo Dinh Diem have changed their minds about him and his chances of winning the war against the Communists. They would like to see a new government in Saigon."[43] The article reiterated the claim that during the initial protest in Hue nine Buddhists were killed by government troops firing at them. In another article in the same issue of the *New York Times*, Secretary of State Dean Rusk declared the conflict in Vietnam a "dirty, untidy, disagreeable" war.[44] Another official in Washington blurted out in anger, "What do you want us to do? We're in a box. We don't like that Government but it's the only one around. We can't fight a war and a revolution at the same time, so lay off."[45]

The *New York Times* did not lay off, and as it kept the pressure on the Kennedy administration, William Trueheart, at the behest of the Harriman group in Washington,[46] engaged in "direct, relentless, table-hammering pressure on Diem such as the United States had seldom before attempted with a sovereign friendly government".[47] Lindsay Nolting said that her husband believed Trueheart had jumped ship and joined what he thought was the winning side in the State Department. Trueheart had been a close confidant, supporter, and friend of the ambassador, she explained, and therefore was trusted by the Ngo Dinh brothers. Yet, soon after he took over as chargé d'affaires at the American embassy in Saigon, he betrayed his boss and friend, and even the position he had previously held vis-à-vis Diem, in order to curry favour with the Harriman group.[48] Frederick Nolting said in an interview that he and Trueheart had completely agreed on policy until the ambassador left for his holiday. When he returned, he discovered that "Trueheart had shifted with the winds blowing from Washington—he had joined the Harriman-Hilsman group. He had adjusted his views."[49]

While Nolting was on holiday, the only high-level contact President Diem had with Washington, William Trueheart, offered neither

[43] *New York Times*, July 3, 1963, 1.

[44] Max Frankel, "Vietnam's 'Untidy' War: Washington Is Unhappy with Saigon, but Thinks That Support Is Necessary", *New York Times*, July 3, 1963, 8.

[45] Ibid.

[46] Trueheart's orders can be seen in DOS telegrams 1171 (June 3, 1963), doc. 147; 1173 (June 3, 1963), doc. 148; 1194 (June 8, 1963), doc. 158; 1196 (June 8, 1963), doc. 159; and 1207 (June 11, 1963), doc 167 in *FRUS, 1961–1963*, vol. 3, pp. 147–167.

[47] John Mecklin, quoted in Higgins, *Our Vietnam Nightmare*, 100.

[48] Lindsay Nolting, interview by Geoffrey D. T. Shaw, January 29, 1998.

[49] Nolting, interview by O'Connor, interview 1, p. 21.

understanding nor even normal diplomatic give-and-take; rather, he made threats. In his telegram of June 12, 1963, to Hilsman and Harriman, Trueheart boasted of following their instructions, which were "of course very strong medicine and will be very hard for Diem to take.... I believe we can be satisfied that we have done everything reasonably possible to get President Diem to save himself."[50] In particular, Trueheart threatened a formal dissociation, per Harriman's order, if Diem did not follow DOS directives to restore the confidence of the protesting bonzes.[51] Trueheart's hard-line approach accomplished two things: first, the honing of Diem's wariness and doubts about his alliance with the Americans; and second, the hardening of Diem's stance on the Buddhists.

As can be seen in DOS correspondence, President Kennedy was not immediately aware that his State Department had threatened Diem with formal dissociation. When Kennedy did find out on June 14, he was furious, because it had been done without his permission. He told DOS that no further threats were to be made without his personal approval.[52] Regardless of Kennedy's disapprobation, Averell Harriman and Roger Hilsman instructed Trueheart in a top secret telegram to "consider steps gradually [to] increase covert and overt contacts with non-supporters of GVN. In present situation this should only be done if you feel our (overt or covert) contacts with those who might play major roles in event of coup are now inadequate."[53] Trueheart replied, "We have all the lines out that we know how to put out and have had for some days."[54]

When Nolting returned to Vietnam for four weeks in July 1963, he saw that the Harriman group had destroyed nearly all the confidence Diem had placed in the American government. "The Embassy in Saigon

---

[50] William Trueheart, "Telegram from the Embassy in Vietnam to the Department of State", June 12, 1963, Saigon, in *FRUS, 1961–1963*, vol. 3, document 169, pp. 386–87.

[51] Chalmers B. Wood and Roger Hilsman, "Telegram from the Department of State to the Embassy in Vietnam", June 11, 1963, Washington, in *FRUS, 1961–1963*, vol. 3, document 167, p. 381. (Drafted by Wood and Hilsman and cleared in draft by Harriman. Signed "Rusk".)

[52] Trueheart, "Telegram from Embassy to Department of State", June 12, 1963, 386n5, 387n5.

[53] Chalmers B. Wood, "Telegram from the Department of State to the Embassy in Vietnam", June 14, 1963, Washington, in *FRUS, 1961–1963*, vol. 3, document 175, p. 394. (Cleared by Hilsman and Harriman. Signed "Rusk".)

[54] Trueheart, "Telegram from Embassy to Department of State", June 16, 1963, 398–99.

when I was away had broken the bridge of confidence by which we had worked with the Diem government. I tried to restore it during my remaining four weeks, after I got back to Saigon, but I was a 'lame duck.' I had more influence then with Diem than with Washington."[55] According to Nolting, three things destroyed U.S. support of President Diem that summer. First, President Kennedy's sensitivity to the claims in the American news media that he was supporting a Roman Catholic dictatorship permeated with nepotism.[56] Second, the Harriman group's profound dislike of the Vietnamese president and his family, which was fed by the news media.[57] Third, the Buddhist crisis, which became the Kennedy administration's justification to encourage a coup.

A meeting about the forthcoming coup took place with President Kennedy at the White House on July 4, 1963. In attendance were Undersecretary of State George W. Ball, Harriman, Special Assistant for National Security Affairs McGeorge Bundy, Hilsman, and Forrestal. In a memo about the meeting, Hilsman summarised the opinion of the Harriman group: "Our estimate was that no matter what Diem did there will be coup attempts over the next four months."[58] To convince the president that the coup would not interfere with the war effort, Hilsman and Forrestal reversed earlier warnings about the Buddhist crisis hindering the progress of the counterinsurgency. Hilsman said, "The war between the Vietnamese forces and the Viet Cong has been pursued throughout the Buddhist crisis without noticeable let-up."[59] Forrestal buttressed Hilsman with General Krulak's contention that, regardless of the rancour in Saigon, "the military units in the field continue to confront the Communists."[60] In other words, said both men, there would be no great loss to America's security interests in the region if Diem were removed from power. Said Hilsman in his memo, "Everyone agreed that the chances of chaos in the wake of a coup are considerably less than they were a year ago."[61] Hilsman directly refuted what Nolting and

[55] Nolting, interview by O'Connor, interview 1, pp. 22–23.

[56] Ibid., interview 3, pp. 102–3.

[57] Ibid.,103.

[58] Roger Hilsman, "Memorandum of a Conversation, White House, Washington, July 4, 1963, 11–11:50 A.M.; Subject: Situation in South Viet-Nam", in FRUS, 1961–1963, vol. 3, document 205, pp. 451–52.

[59] Ibid., 452.

[60] Ibid., 453.

[61] Ibid., 452.

Colby had been telling Washington, saying that Nolting had overstated the matter when he said a civil war could result from a coup.[62]

At this point in the discussion, President Kennedy asked about returning Nolting to Washington and moving Henry Cabot Lodge to Saigon.[63] He delegated the authority of deciding the timing of Nolting's return to Hilsman. The Harriman group wanted Hilsman to act upon this decision as soon as possible. Indeed, in a memorandum Forrestal sent Bundy, he stressed that they might need to recall Nolting before Lodge's arrival in South Vietnam. Forrestal praised Trueheart over the pro-Diem Nolting because Trueheart, unlike Nolting, had been obedient to the instructions of the Harriman group.[64] Hilsman did not need any encouragement to recall Nolting as soon as possible.[65] Not only had Nolting been a thorn in the side of those wanting to remove Diem, sometime between the end of July and August 1, Nolting told the press, to the embarrassment of DOS, that Diem was not persecuting Buddhists.[66]

Ambassador Nolting first heard about his replacement by Henry Cabot Lodge on the ship's radio aboard an ocean liner to New York City, when he and his family were returning from their holiday.[67] After his arrival in the United States at the end of June 1963, Nolting finally

[62] Ibid., 453.

[63] According to Hilsman's memorandum of the conversation: "The President volunteered that Ambassador Nolting had done an outstanding job, that it was almost miraculous the way he had succeeded in turning the war around from the disastrously low point in relations between Diem and ourselves that existed when Ambassador Nolting took over ... and the President said that he hoped a way could be found to commend Ambassador Nolting publicly so as to make clear the fine job he had done and that he hoped an appropriate position could be found for him in Washington." Ibid.

[64] Michael V. Forrestal, "Memorandum from Michael V. Forrestal of the National Security Council Staff to the President's Special Assistant for National Security Affairs (Bundy)", July 9, 1963, Washington, in *FRUS, 1961–1963*, vol. 3, document 215, pp. 481–82.

[65] The following is from a memorandum of a telephone conversation that took place between Harriman and Hilsman: "WAH [Harriman] told RH [Hilsman] that he was disturbed about the reports of Nolting's statement on the Buddhists, WAH said he ought to be recalled at once. RH said he couldn't agree more." "Memorandum of a Telephone Conversation between the Under Secretary of State for Political Affairs (Harriman) and the Assistant Secretary of State for Far Eastern Affairs (Hilsman), Washington, August 1, 1963, 9:55 A.M.", transcribed by Eleanor G. McGann of Harriman's staff, in *FRUS, 1961–1963*, vol. 3, document 243, p. 550.

[66] Frederick Nolting, telegram, August 1, 1963, Saigon, no. 161, quoted in ibid., 550n2.

[67] Nolting, *From Trust to Tragedy*, 111.

received a personal message about the new assignment from Trueheart. The memo also stated that a major crisis involving the Buddhists had developed in Vietnam during his absence.

On July 5, 1963, the day after the coup discussion at the White House, Nolting attended a meeting at DOS with Undersecretary of State Ball and two other officials, Chalmers B. Wood and George S. Springsteen. Ball, who was not known to have any sympathy for the Diem government, asked Nolting what he thought would happen in South Vietnam if there were a coup.[68] Nolting answered that a coup would be a disaster and could very well unleash feuds between various factions with the result that the United States might have to withdraw, leaving the country open to the Communists. When DOS officials asked whether Diem could be pressured into tolerating the Buddhist protestors, Nolting said Diem would stop suppressing them if they stopped trying to overthrow his government. He further explained that, should Diem's government collapse—which he believed it would if the United States pressed any further—the Communists would stand to gain the prize. At the end of this meeting, Nolting warned Ball about his replacement, Henry Cabot Lodge, that "the more Lodge was built up to be a strong man who was going to tell Diem where to get off, the harder it would be for Lodge to do his job in Viet-Nam."[69]

Two days later, in spite of the direction Washington was headed with respect to South Vietnam, Trueheart defended the GVN against accusations that it was suppressing the media being made by correspondents Malcolm Browne, David Halberstam, Peter Kalischer, Neil Sheehan, and Peter Arnett. Buddhist protestors had tipped off the reporters about a demonstration. After the reporters arrived, a scrum had ensued between protestors and plainclothes police who were there monitoring the situation. According to the reporters the police knocked Peter Arnett to the ground and smashed a camera.[70] Nevertheless, Trueheart reported to Washington that the situation was far less serious than the reporters were claiming.

[68] Chalmers B. Wood, "Memorandum of a Conversation, Department of State, Washington, July 5, 1963; Subject: Current Situation in Viet-Nam", in FRUS, 1961–1963, vol. 3, document 208, p. 466.

[69] Ibid., 467.

[70] William Trueheart, "Telegram from the Embassy in Vietnam to the Department of State", July 7, 1963, Saigon, in FRUS, 1961–1963, vol. 3, document 210, p. 470.

Browne, Halberstam, Kalischer, and Sheehan sent a telegram of protest concerning the incident to President Kennedy on July 7. They said they had been covering a peaceful Buddhist religious ceremony when they were attacked by plainclothes policemen. Regular uniformed police would not come to their aid, they added. They concluded that the GVN had begun a campaign of open intimidation and violence against American newsmen; therefore, they wanted the president to make a strong protest to Diem, "since the United States Embassy here does not deem this incident serious enough to make a formal protest".[71] At least to Nolting, President Kennedy seemed unmoved by the incident. In his meeting with Kennedy on July 8, he wrote, the president's "manner was more calm and cordial than what I had encountered in the State Department. It was he who agreed that I should return as promptly as possible to Saigon, telling me to do my best to help restore confidence and trust until Lodge arrived."[72]

Trueheart cabled Washington again on July 10 and informed DOS that the reporters in question had lost all objectivity and were openly calling for Diem to be overthrown.[73] The same day DOS made a clear statement on July 10, 1963: "There has been no change in our policy toward Viet-Nam, or our support for the program against the Communist Viet Cong in that country."[74] Nolting, however, once back in Saigon, found that the previous policy had been overturned. He reported that the "patient" (i.e., U.S.-GVN relations) was on the "critical list" and that Diem's confidence in U.S. intentions had been badly shaken. Most disturbing of all, Nolting found Diem in what he called a "martyr's

[71] Malcolm Browne et al., "Telegram from Malcolm Browne of the Associate Press, David Halberstam of *The New York Times*, Peter Kalischer of CBS News, and Neil Sheehan of United States Press International to the President", July 7, 1963, Saigon, in *FRUS, 1961–1963*, vol. 3, document 211, p. 472.

[72] *From Trust to Tragedy*, 113.

[73] "Department should be aware that in recent weeks resident correspondents have become so embittered towards GVN that they are saying quite openly to anyone who will listen that they would like to see regime overthrown. GVN no doubt has this well-documented. GVN also unquestionably considers that correspondents have been actively encouraging Buddhists. Diem is therefore most unlikely to accept view that correspondents merely carrying on normal functions of keeping US public informed." William Trueheart, embassy in Vietnam to Department of State, telegram, July 10, 1963, Saigon, no. 65, quoted in *FRUS, 1961–1963*, vol. 3, document 211, p. 472, unnumbered footnote.

[74] Quoted in Nolting, "Telegram from Embassy to Department of State", July 11, 1963, 486n1.

mood", with heightened suspicions and resentments, some of them well founded, about American pressures and Buddhist intentions.[75] He informed Washington of what he thought was the best course of action:

> While making our views and especially US domestic considerations amply clear, we should not try to blueprint his course for him. Specifically, we should not reiterate our threat of disassociation, nor feel stuck with it if other means of easing the situation (even the passage of time) work in favor of a political modus vivendi here. Rather, I think, we should continue, as has been done, to tell him the facts of life about public opinion at home and let him work out his own accommodation.... But I think we must accept the fact that we will probably continue to have a generally bad press for some time, until political calm returns and we can demonstrate the success of the overall strategy and plan. With luck—I emphasize this—[and?] an appearance of calm determination on the part of Americans to see this crisis surmounted, I believe there is a reasonably good chance of re-establishing the basis for continued progress here.[76]

After a Buddhist demonstration July 16 outside the American embassy in Saigon, Nolting cabled Washington and confirmed what many had already suspected: "Buddhist agitation is now predominantly controlled by activists and radical elements aimed at the overthrow of GVN."[77] Nolting also warned Washington that even if the Buddhists were not connected to coup plots against Diem by military officers, they were nonetheless well aware of them and their potential. In his response, Secretary Rusk stated that they must be prepared for further Buddhist demonstrations. He recommended that Nolting continue trying to persuade Diem to accommodate Buddhists.[78] Nolting wrote back that he was disappointed by Rusk's recommendation: "It gives us nothing to work with, on either side of equation. A wait-and-see attitude on our part at this juncture will lead only, in my judgment, to further undermining of stability here and to further jeopardizing US vital interests. It

---

[75] Frederick Nolting, "Telegram from the Embassy in Vietnam to the Department of State", July 15, 1963, Saigon, in *FRUS, 1961–1963*, vol. 3, document 219, p. 487.

[76] Ibid., 487–88.

[77] Frederick Nolting, "Telegram from the Embassy in Vietnam to the Department of State", July 17, 1963, Saigon, in *FRUS, 1961–1963*, vol. 3, document 223, pp. 493–94.

[78] Theodore J.C. Heavner, "Telegram from the Department of State to the Embassy in Vietnam", July 19, 1963, Washington, in *FRUS, 1961–1963*, vol. 3, document 230, pp. 517–18. (Cleared by Kattenberg, Rice, and Rusk. Signed "Rusk".)

will encourage more agitation and demand on part of Buddhists; it will discourage further conciliatory action on part of government; it will increase prospects of a coup."[79]

Toward the end of Nolting's tenure as ambassador to South Vietnam, another public relations problem with the GVN was added to the Buddhist crisis: Madame Nhu, the wife of President Diem's brother Ngo Dinh Nhu. The de facto first lady of South Vietnam, Madame Nhu had a special talent for saying exactly the wrong thing at the most inconvenient moment. For example, when Thich Quang Duc had burned himself to death, Madame Nhu used the word "barbecue" to describe the shocking event.[80] This indeed stung American sensibilities, but no one seemed to question where she had picked up such an un-Vietnamese description; in fact, her daughter had told her that that was what the American journalists were privately calling the suicide.[81] That didn't stop the American newsmen from seizing upon everything the very politically incorrect Madame Nhu had to say and using this material against Diem in the court of American public opinion.

Both Ellen Hammer and Marguerite Higgins interviewed Madame Nhu on various occasions and found her to be a strident Vietnamese nationalist and, in a Vietnamese fashion, an equally strident feminist.[82] She had a strong will, an unbridled tongue, and—unfortunately for relations between Saigon and Washington—a very poor grasp of English, her first and preferred language being French. All of these factors combined to create, with the help of some very eager American journalists, an unflattering image of a notorious dragon lady.[83] Harriman had a

[79] Frederick Nolting, "Telegram from the Embassy in Vietnam to the Department of State", July 20, 1963, Saigon, in *FRUS, 1961–1963*, vol. 3, document 232, p. 521.

[80] Marguerite Higgins wrote: "I asked her why she had used the word 'barbecue' to describe the Buddhist suicides.... 'If I had it all to do over again, I would say the same thing,' she said defiantly. 'I used those terms because they have shock value. It is necessary to somehow shock the world out of this trance in which it looks at Vietnam with false vision about religious persecution that does not exist." Higgins, *Our Vietnam Nightmare*, 62–63.

[81] Hammer, *Death in November*, 145.

[82] Higgins, *Our Vietnam Nightmare*, 64.

[83] From Nolting's memoirs: "She had little formal education in the Western sense, but she had extraordinary vitality and energy. Being young, photogenic, and only too willing to talk, she was a natural target for the press. Her command of English seemed much greater than it was (she never used English in private conversation if there was a choice), and while her indiscreet public pronouncements influenced history, I think she did not understand the implications of some of her own outrageous remarks." Nolting, *From Trust to Tragedy*, 99.

much more venal and blunt name for Madame Nhu: he referred to her as "that bitch", and he made sure that everyone in the State Department knew exactly what he thought of her.[84]

On August 8, 1963, George Ball cabled Nolting and instructed him to seek an interview with President Diem to secure Madame Nhu's silence since Halberstam had just run another story in the *New York Times* with another one of her unflattering outbursts.[85] Nolting cabled Washington back on August 10, "Fact is Madame Nhu is out of control of everybody—her father, mother, husband and brother-in-law."[86] Nolting relayed that Diem promised he would find a way to place Madame Nhu on holiday status, although his attempts up to that point had been less than successful. Regardless of the Madame Nhu annoyance, Nolting stressed that it was most important that the United States let Diem maintain authority in his own way and that urging Diem "to have Nhu make [a] public statement of support for Diem's policy" was not a good idea, "as this brings into question who is running the GVN and related problems. Please reconsider."[87]

For all the criticism of Madame Nhu, justified or not, she did make some prescient remarks. For example, she had predicted that if the United Nations sent in a team to determine whether the government of Ngo Dinh Diem had persecuted Buddhists, they would find it had not. The United Nations did send in a team and found no justification for

[84] Nolting recalled: "At a conference of American regional ambassadors at Baguio called by Averell Harriman, while some fifteen of us were seated at a long table, the chairman, Harriman, was handed a telegram from Saigon. It contained a description of another 'anti-American' speech made by Madame Nhu. Harriman read it and passed it down the table with a note to me: 'Nolting—what are you going to do about this b—ch?' I passed it back with a note: 'What would you propose, Sir?'" Ibid., 101–2.

[85] Specifically, Ball told Nolting: "You are accordingly to seek new interview with Diem and tell him again that while we recognize Mme Nhu is private citizen rather than GVN official it clear we cannot ignore such destructive and insulting statements by person so clearly identified with him. Diem cannot overlook effect this has of undercutting his authority and creating image abroad that he being led around by apron strings.... We have in mind action similar to that taken in early years Diem regime when she sent to Hong Kong convent." George Ball, "Telegram from the Department of State to the Embassy in Vietnam", August 8, 1963, Washington, in *FRUS, 1961–1963*, vol. 3, document 248, pp. 557–58. (Drafted by Heavner and Kattenburg, cleared by Harriman and Forrestal, and approved by Hilsman.)

[86] Frederick Nolting, "Telegram from the Embassy in Vietnam to the Department of State", August 10, 1963, Saigon, in *FRUS, 1961–1963*, vol. 3, document 250, p. 560.

[87] Ibid., 561–62.

accusing the GVN of religious persecution.[88] By the time the United Nations committee's investigations were complete, however, Diem had already been murdered and his government destroyed; thus, the report was never published. William F. Buckley Jr. obtained a copy and published its findings in his magazine *National Review*. The U.N. committee's findings were a damning indictment of the story newsmen such as Halberstam told the American public, as well as of the story that the Harriman faction foisted onto the Kennedy administration. The Costa Rican member of the U.N. fact-finding mission said: "The charges made in the General Assembly against the Diem Government were not sustained.... There was no religious discrimination or persecution, no encroachment of freedom of religion.... There is no other way to see it. The clash between a part—not all—of the Buddhist community and the Diem regime was on political grounds.... It [is] a political question, not a religious question."[89]

Because of the ongoing bad press, the Kennedy administration sent Robert J. Manning, the assistant secretary of state for public affairs, along with his special assistant, Marshall Wright, to meet with Ngo Dinh Nhu to see what could be done about it.[90] The meeting took place on July 17, 1963, and was also attended by Troung Buu Khanh (of the Vietnamese press) and John Mecklin, who at that time was serving as the public affairs officer of the U.S. embassy in Saigon. The American visitors were astonished by the political acumen and sheer intelligence of Nhu, who had been portrayed so negatively by American newspapers. The document that resulted from the meeting shows that Nhu had a firm and ready grasp of all the pertinent facts. Conversely, the Americans were caught rather short, and what was supposed to have been a dressing down of Nhu turned into almost an apology by Manning, who blurted out a reassurance of American support for the GVN. He said the

---

[88] Higgins, *Our Vietnam Nightmare*, 62–63.

[89] United Nations, "The Violation of Human Rights in South Vietnam", document A/5630, December 7, 1963, quoted by William F. Buckley, in Nolting Papers, box 23, Professional Papers—Newsclippings, 1 of 2.

[90] According to the editors of *FRUS, 1961–1963*: "Manning was sent to Vietnam by President Kennedy to investigate and report on the type of problems relating to American journalists which had led to the telegram sent to the President by a group of journalists on July 7, Document 211 [of *FRUS, 1961–1963*; see footnote 71 above]." "Memorandum of a Conversation, Saigon, July 17, 1963", in *FRUS, 1961–1963*, vol. 3, document 226, pp. 496–97n1.

journalists were not the tail that wagged the dog of American foreign policy, as Nhu proposed. He agreed that reporters such as Halberstam and Sheehan had abandoned professional ethics and were running on emotions, and he said he would urge editors in the United States to send reporters who would practice more self-discipline. Manning did point out, however, that 1964 was an election year, "and as the campaign heats up, it will become more and more necessary that the President have the necessary tools to insure a continuance of American public support for the effort in Vietnam."[91] This high-level meeting, which began with an inquisitor's imperious manner on Manning's part and ended with positive agreement, amounted to nothing. Manning's efforts evidently had no effect on the biased reporting. Likewise, the Harriman group did not veer from its steady course to have Diem removed from power.

Two days after Manning's assurances to Nhu, Chester Bowles, who had replaced John Kenneth Galbraith as ambassador to India,[92] sent a top secret letter in favour of a coup to McGeorge Bundy, the president's special assistant for national security affairs. In it the judgement of the Harriman group was laid bare: "We cannot achieve our objectives in Southeast Asia as long as Diem and his family run Vietnam." Bowles played the China card in this letter to assist Harriman and Hilsman in provoking the Kennedy cabinet to act against Diem: "In Diem and his family we have a set-up comparable to that presented by the Generalissimo in China in the 1940's. We failed in China largely because we failed to find an effective means of dealing with an inept ruling power that had lost touch with the people. We will fail in Southeast Asia, and

[91] Marshall Wright, "Memorandum of a Conversation, Saigon, July 17, 1963", in *FRUS, 1961–1963*, vol. 3, document 226, pp. 502–7.

[92] According to John Kenneth Galbraith, Bowles had been removed as undersecretary of state and made ambassador to India "ostensibly because of his unduly loquacious style, in fact because he was not in harmony with the brisk, sanguinary anti-Communist faith of Dean Rusk. Bowles had persuaded himself that beneath the evil of Communist design and supporting it were social discontents and political abuses that drove men and women to extreme solutions. That there were forthright military remedies he thought overly simple. And admittedly he was inclined to enlarge at length on these views as well as to be guided by them. The stern foreign-policy men of the time had responded with amused contempt but also with a firm determination to bring an end to such nonsense. In consequence, Bowles had been idling for many months in a face-saving White House post, that of presidential adviser on economic development. Now, to his great relief, he became my replacement. He had, of course, previously served as Ambassador to India (and Nepal) under Harry Truman." John Kenneth Galbraith, *A Life in Our Times: Memoirs* (Boston: Houghton Mifflin, 1981), 444.

perhaps even more decisively, if we repeat this mistake in Vietnam." To be accused of losing Vietnam as China had been lost held serious political ramifications in Washington, especially for a president seeking reelection in 1964. Bowles concluded by saying, "Almost any articulate, courageous, anti-Communist Vietnamese with a good reputation who puts himself at the head of a coup to overthrow Diem ... would find himself a national hero in a matter of weeks."[93]

According to William Colby, the Buddhist crisis not only weakened America's support for Diem, it also weakened the support of his generals. The protesting bonzes caused Diem's government to switch its focus from fighting the Viet Cong through war-winning strategic hamlets to fighting the radical Buddhists.[94] Taking on this new enemy led to a fight with the Americans. The diversion from the strategic imperative of protecting the rural villages and the conflicts with the Kennedy administration benefited the Communists. According to Colby, the Viet Cong had been so concerned about the success of the Strategic Hamlet Program that they had "instructed their people that they were to destroy this program at all costs, because it really did threaten them".[95] Colby maintained that during the Buddhist revolt, the Communists directed their fire at what threatened their lifeblood: the strategic hamlets. He said the people in the Kennedy administration who wanted Diem removed unwittingly paved the way for these attacks. "The program [strategic hamlets] was let lag at exactly the time when the communists had identified it as a major threat.... So they began to attack it in about June or July, and you can see the terrorist incidents grow at that time against it."[96] Meanwhile, because of the differences between Saigon and Washington over the protesting Buddhists, America threatened to withdraw its support of the counterinsurgency, which encouraged the eventual revolt by the ARVN generals. This threat, according to Colby, was the greatest mistake the Americans could have made.[97]

[93] Chester Bowles, "Letter from the Ambassador in India (Bowles) to the President's Special Assistant for National Security Affairs (Bundy)", July 19, 1963, New Delhi, in *FRUS, 1961–1963*, vol. 3, document 231, p. 519.

[94] Colby, interview by Gittinger, interview 1, p. 22.

[95] Ibid.

[96] Ibid.

[97] Those generals who sought power argued that Diem "was risking American support of Vietnam against the Communists.... He was going to lose the war because the Americans were going to back away.... [T]he fact was that they wouldn't have had a revolt if the United States had not encouraged it. There is no doubt about that whatsoever." Ibid., 21–22.

Colby knew his business well; what he was describing, in effect, was that the Buddhist crisis served as a holding attack while the real assault of the Communists went in at the strategic hamlet level. Normally, one has to provide one's own holding attack to focus enemy attention away from where the real attack will take place. The Communists, however, were fortunate in receiving timely assistance from the American press coverage of the Buddhist crisis: this diversionary holding attack was provided by the U.S. newsmen and, to a certain degree, the Harriman group in the State Department.

In support of what Nolting had argued all along, Colby said Diem could have sustained his government through the Buddhist crisis, the rioting in Saigon, and the unrest in the army if the Americans had maintained a steady course and adhered to their original policy of support. "But when the Americans indicated a change, then bing, it was gone, it went."[98] Colby understood, however, the tremendous pressure brought to bear on Washington by the press coverage of the Buddhist protests.

One of Ambassador Nolting's last cables to Washington in his capacity as U.S. ambassador to South Vietnam was sent on August 12, 1963. This telegram covered in depth Nolting's meetings with President Diem about Madame Nhu's attacks on the American media.[99] Nolting reported that Diem was not that annoyed with Madame Nhu for the content of her statements, but he was upset about the insensitive way she said them, which provoked more animosity from the press. During the course of these conversations, Nolting wrote, Diem "reverted again and again to the bad faith of the bonzes, to their sabotage of the war effort, etc. He also mentioned the pressure he was under from 'good people' in the provinces and elsewhere not to knuckle under to the false monks. He complained that nobody in the outside world recognized the falsity of the religious issue or the fact that it was being used for subversive action."[100]

Once again it was apparent to Nolting that Diem was everything the traditional Vietnamese demanded of a Confucian leader. His position vis-à-vis the Buddhists was not anchored to mere stubborn pride. Instead, his stance was founded on a deep-seated understanding. Even if

[98] Ibid.
[99] Frederick Nolting, "Telegram from the Embassy in Vietnam to the Department of State", August 12, 1963, Saigon, in *FRUS, 1961–1963*, vol. 3, document 251, p. 563.
[100] Ibid.

the capriciousness of chance was in favour of the radical bonzes, he still had to stand by what was true, correct, and proper.

The State Department, however, did not see Diem in this light. In one of the very last cables sent to Nolting, DOS said Diem's position vis-à-vis who had caused the deaths in Hue in May was unacceptable to Washington. Regardless of the forensic facts, which cleared Diem's officials, Washington insisted that Diem cave in to the bonzes' demands on this key issue.[101] The cynical observer of this episode in Washington-Saigon relations might presume that DOS knew Diem would not abide by such outrageous demands and that his impenitent stance would ensure the inevitability of a coup supported by the Kennedy administration. There can be little doubt that President Diem was being set up for removal when Washington pulled away its firmest pillar of support, Ambassador Frederick Nolting.

---

[101] From the State Department's cable to Nolting: "We note that [Vice President] Tho appears indicate GVN intends prosecute Buddhists for May 8 affair, which is in direct conflict with Buddhist insistence GVN officials responsible for May 8 deaths. Such action is not only refusal of Buddhist request that these officials be identified and punished but is sure to provide further and legitimate grounds for Buddhist charges of persecution." Theodore J. C. Heavner, "Telegram from the Department of State to the Embassy in Vietnam", August 13, 1963, Washington, in *FRUS, 1961–1963*, vol. 3, document 252, p. 564. (Cleared by Kattenburg and approved by Hilsman. Signed "Rusk".)

12

Nolting's Farewell

On August 14, 1963, Ambassador Nolting said his official farewell to President Diem. Because of State Department pressure, this last meeting was tense as it focused on the Buddhist question and Madame Nhu's intemperate public statements. Diem promised he would make a public statement through Marguerite Higgins and the *New York Herald Tribune* that would offer some conciliation to Americans affronted by Madame Nhu. On this point, Diem kept his word.[1] At the end of the meeting, Nolting recounted, Diem said that their frank exchange would not mar their friendship and that he considered Nolting's tenure in Saigon one of the best memories of his life.[2]

The next day, Nolting and his family left for the United States with many concerns still unresolved, especially with regard to U.S. policy toward South Vietnam and Ngo Dinh Diem's government. Recognising that American-Vietnamese relations were extremely tenuous, Nolting had requested to stay long enough to restore the old pattern of trust, but DOS had denied this request. The Harriman group wanted Nolting out even if there were no ambassador in Vietnam until Henry Cabot Lodge could take up the post.[3] Diem, Nolting recalled, was as

[1] According to the editors of *FRUS, 1961–1963*: "Diem's statement was made to newspaper correspondent Marguerite Higgins. As quoted in *The Herald Tribune*, August 15, Diem stated 'the policy of utmost reconciliation [with the Buddhists] is irreversible' and 'that neither any individual nor the government could change it at all.' In a veiled reference to Madame Nhu, Diem was quoted as saying, 'It is only because some have contributed, either consciously or unconsciously, to raising doubts about this government policy that the solution of the Buddhist affair has been retarded.'" Frederick Nolting, "Telegram from the Embassy in Vietnam to the Department of State", August 14, 1963, Saigon, in *FRUS, 1961–1963*, vol. 3, document 253, p. 566n1.

[2] Ibid.

[3] Frederick Nolting, *From Trust to Tragedy: The Political Memoirs of Frederick Nolting, Kennedy's Ambassador to Diem's Vietnam* (New York: Praeger, 1988), 118–19.

concerned about U.S. policy as he was. Prior to Nolting's departure he asked the ambassador if his return to the United States signalled a change.[4] "Does your departure mean that the American government has changed its policy from what you and I agreed two and one half years ago?" Diem asked. Nolting replied: "No, Mr. President, it does not."[5] Diem then asked Nolting to check with Washington just to be sure, and Nolting complied straightaway. Subsequently, Nolting received the reply from the U.S. president's office: "No change in policy and you can tell him that straight out."[6] When Nolting translated the telegram, Diem remarked, "Mr. Ambassador, I believe you, but I'm afraid your information is incorrect."[7] Diem knew, via his own intelligence sources, what Harriman was engineering, and he suspected that Washington was attempting to play both him and their own ambassador for fools.

All during the spring and summer of 1963, a distrustful American attitude toward Diem had been building. The way he was handling the Buddhist crisis and the response to it in the American media was one reason for this. Another reason was Diem's recalcitrance toward increasing American force levels and American control in South Vietnam. Diem had signed the agreement over the joint counterinsurgency funding program after much delay, ostensibly because he did not want to give up control of the money to the United States. However, the real reason the Vietnamese leader had hesitated was best stated by Nolting in a cable he had sent to Washington in early April 1963 during the negotiations over the joint fund: "In assessing Diem's rejection of our proposal for counter-insurgency fund, most significant point is that grounds advanced for rejection approach repudiation of concept of expanded and deepened US advisory effort, civil and military."[8]

Ellen Hammer also asserted that the real problem for Diem was not his giving the Americans control of the counterinsurgency funding. Rather,

[4] Ibid., 119.

[5] Frederick Nolting, Foreign Service Journal, July 1968, 20.

[6] Frederick E. Nolting, "Kennedy, NATO, and Southeast Asia", in Diplomacy, Administration, and Policy: The Ideas and Careers of Frederick E. Nolting, Jr., Frederick C. Mosher, and Paul T. David, ed. Kenneth W. Thompson (Lanham, Md.: University Press of America; Charlottesville, Va.: Miller Center, University of Virginia, 1995), 26.

[7] Ibid.

[8] Frederick Nolting, "Telegram from the Embassy in Vietnam to the Department of State", April 7, 1963, Saigon, in FRUS, 1961–1963, vol. 3, document 82, p. 213.

it was the numbers of Americans who would start entering the country and the kind of control the funding agreement would give them. One of Diem's chief complaints was that unaccounted-for and unaccountable U.S. advisors were already too involved in local Vietnamese political affairs. In the provinces there were at least two thousand American advisors—men who were essentially running the rural economic development plan and deliberately bypassing the Saigon government. With the joint funding agreement, more American military advisors would be deployed to Vietnam, and the rural areas would be under more direct administration by foreigners. The situation, which would amount to a new colonialism, was not only intolerable to any self-respecting national government but also helpful to the Viet Cong, who would have further proof that Diem had sold out to the Americans. Diem brought these issues to the U.S. embassy and asked that most of the two thousand advisors be withdrawn.[9]

Diem was so worried about the problem of American colonialism that he turned to the French for advice. He complained directly to the French ambassador, Roger Lalouette, about the influx of American military personnel. Diem told him that the new American advisors had not been invited and that they did not even have passports.[10] Lalouette tried to calm the frustrated Diem and suggested that a "gentle" request that some of the Americans leave would be Diem's best approach.[11] Lalouette, however, had mistaken the American mood, and Diem's "gentle" request that some of the provincial advisors be removed set off alarm bells in Washington.[12] Years later, in June 1970, Roger Lalouette told Ellen Hammer that he had traced the American decision to abandon Diem to this attempt to have American provincial advisors recalled in April 1963.[13]

The severity of the problem Diem was facing was mentioned in the South Vietnamese newspaper *Hoa Binh* in 1970. Vietnamese national Tran Kim Tuyen wrote, "Everyone close to Ngo Dinh Diem knew that for him the question of Vietnamese sovereignty was primordial; no

---

[9] Ellen J. Hammer, *A Death in November: America in Vietnam, 1963* (New York: E.P. Dutton, 1987), 120–21.

[10] Marianna P. Sullivan, *France's Vietnam Policy* (Westport, Conn.: Greenwich Press, 1978), 67.

[11] Ibid.

[12] Hammer, *Death in November*, 121.

[13] Ibid.

question of foreign aid could supersede that."[14] According to Hammer, Diem rejected all American proposals for a large base to be built at Cam Ranh Bay, and he maintained his defiant position on this issue into August 1963; in fact, the famous base received official approval to be built only after Diem was killed.[15]

William Colby also understood that Diem's pushback on the Americans was motivated by his concern for South Vietnam's national sovereignty. In 1961, when the situation in Laos had so deteriorated that Diem was calling for a greater American commitment to stemming the advance of Communism in Southeast Asia,[16] Diem was loath to accept American combat forces in his country without an agreement about the definition of their role. He was even willing to accept a division of nationalist Chinese troops from Taiwan if the Americans were unwilling to limit their role to training and advising. The Taiwanese offer went no further because the Americans assured Diem they would respect his boundaries.[17]

Another reason Americans were hardening toward Diem in the summer of 1963 was his apparent attempt at making peace with the Communists in the spring. Ngo Dinh Nhu had held talks with various Viet Cong leaders, but these had been concerned with negotiating large-scale defections of Viet Cong units.[18] Lindsay Nolting observed that this process of *chieu hoi*, or "open arms", did not originate with Nhu. The concept had been advanced by Sir Robert Thompson as an effective technique for breaking the solidarity of the Communist insurgent organisation.[19] Nolting informed Washington, through normal State Department channels, about Nhu's contacts with the Communist insurgents, which were no secret.[20] DOS replied that Nolting should not interfere with Nhu as long as the Saigon embassy was convinced he wasn't "selling out". Nolting was indeed "convinced that Nhu never had any idea of selling out to the Viet Cong. On the contrary, he was trying to get

[14] Tran Kim Tuyen, *Hoa Binh*, August 8, 1970, quoted in ibid.

[15] Hammer, *Death in November*, 121–22.

[16] William E. Colby, *Lost Victory: A Firsthand Account of America's Sixteen-Year Involvement in Vietnam*, with James McCargar (Chicago: Contemporary Books, 1989), 96.

[17] Ibid.

[18] Nolting, *From Trust to Tragedy*, 117–18.

[19] Lindsay Nolting, interview by Geoffrey D. T. Shaw, January 29, 1998.

[20] Frederick Nolting, interview by Dennis O'Brien, May 7, 1970, Washington, D.C., interview 3, transcript, 15, John F. Kennedy Oral History Collection, John F. Kennedy Presidential Library, Boston.

them, or units of the Viet Cong, to sell out, in effect, to the government."[21] Later, in his memoirs, Nolting admitted that there had been some unfavourable reaction to Nhu's meetings with Communist leaders, especially amongst the enemies he had made in the State Department, who mistrusted Nhu as much as they disliked him.[22]

American suspicion of a "sell out" was exacerbated by another development. A larger North-South dialogue was being planned before the Buddhist crisis erupted, according to Mieczyslaw Maneli, who spent five years in Vietnam (1954–1955 and 1962–1964) as head of the Polish delegation to the International Control Commission. During the spring of 1963, he wrote, Ramchundur Goburdhun, chairman of the ICC, French Ambassador Lalouette, and Italian Ambassador Giovanni d'Orlandi mentioned to him repeatedly that they were trying to arrange a meeting with him and Nhu on neutral ground.[23] This meeting could not be arranged before the Buddhist crisis, Maneli explained, and the protests delayed it. "Nevertheless, a dialogue between us began."[24]

In short, a Washington-Saigon separation was already underway before the Buddhist crisis, and the pressure directed at the GVN by American political leaders and newsmen during the crisis, discussed in the previous chapter, widened the distance between the two countries and encouraged South Vietnam to consider talks with North Vietnam. Nolting believed that Diem and Nhu considered these talks because without American support, which diplomat Trueheart had threatened to withdraw during Nolting's summer holiday, they would have no options for survival left.[25] Diem and Nhu were not delusional, as it was clear to Maneli, Goburdhun, Lalouette, and Orlandi that the Americans wished to be rid of them. Through their intervention, Maneli and Nhu finally met at a diplomatic reception attended by the new American ambassador to South Vietnam, Henry Cabot Lodge. Ellen Hammer was amongst the guests and quickly discerned that something was afoot that excluded the Americans.[26]

[21] Ibid.

[22] Nolting, *From Trust to Tragedy*, 118.

[23] Mieczyslaw Maneli, *War of the Vanquished*, trans. Maria de Görgey (New York: Harper and Row, 1971), 118.

[24] Ibid.

[25] Lindsay Nolting, interview by Shaw, January 29, 1998.

[26] Hammer, *Death in November*, 220–21.

Maneli explained the different views and objectives of the ambassadors who had helped to arrange the meeting.[27] Chairman Ramchundur, from India, represented his government's attitude toward Diem as a model Asian ruler whom they backed completely—a view representative of other nonaligned Asian governments. Ambassador d'Orlandi "was the most reticent of the three in this affair. Italy had no particular interests in Vietnam, outside of the general Western hope of maintaining a reasonable balance of power in Southeast Asia and of making decisions in a more thoughtful and restrained way than was the habit of the impetuous and inexperienced Americans." French Ambassador Lalouette, on the other hand, "had even more reason for arranging and watching over [Maneli's] future relations with Nhu.... His stakes in the game were incomparably higher and more portentous." Lalouette's long-term plan was "to open a dialogue between Saigon and Hanoi, and then a token cultural and economic exchange between the two regions. In this way, the ground would be laid for political talks. Tension, suspicion, and enmity between the two governments would be reduced and peace would be assured." A lasting peace and a political dialogue were the indispensable conditions for a long-term political solution in Vietnam, according to Lalouette, which would include the unification of North and South, free nationwide elections, and international controls. To achieve these ends, Lalouette proposed that Maneli conduct the necessary talks with Hanoi while he maintained contact on the subject with Saigon.

Maneli realised that the Americans were intent on divorcing themselves from Diem and his family in May 1963, when he sent a report to the Polish government, which would have been passed along to the Soviets, about the French plan to redeem the regime "from the reckless Americans". In this report, Maneli wrote that the French could not afford to support South Vietnam the way the Americans had been doing. "Thus, they advise this mistress to change her style of living to a less extravagant one: to make peace with the North and the National Liberation Front. The next step will be neutralization: not under the direction of India, but rather Charles de Gaulle. In this way Vietnam, in addition to neutral Cambodia and Laos, will again become a pearl in the 'grandeur de France.'" Maneli called the French scheme "one of the boldest plans in twentieth-century politics".[28]

[27] Maneli, *War of the Vanquished*, 118–21.
[28] From Manelli, "Report of May 5, 1963", quoted in ibid., 125–26.

Mieczyslaw Maneli was an interesting and complex man. He had been a partisan fighter in Poland against the Nazis during the Second World War and was eventually captured by the Germans and sent to Auschwitz, whence he escaped with other Polish officers. His patriotism won him a place in the Polish Communist Party after the war, and he worked in various prestigious jobs, eventually earning a law degree in 1954. He received an appointment as associate professor at Warsaw University, and it was from this job that the Polish Central Committee appointed him to the ICC in 1954. Regardless of his close party ties, he was attacked by the Stalinists as a "revisionist" sympathetic to "bourgeois liberalism" because he had spoken out against the intolerance and violence visited on the Polish people in the mid-1950s. He refused to condemn the Israelis after their victory in the Six-Day War, even though he had been pressured to do so, and eventually he was purged from Warsaw University because he was deemed antisocialist. During his tenure as Poland's ICC ambassador, he was sympathetic to the Communist cause in Vietnam and fully supported Ho Chi Minh's regime while harbouring open concerns about what the Chinese wanted in Vietnam. In short, Maneli was his own man, and he was a dedicated—if a somewhat unconventional—Communist.[29]

When Maneli argued for the Diem-Ho rapprochement with the Chinese ambassador to Hanoi, he revealed where he stood regardless of his keen socialist aversion to the Ngo Dinh brothers and their government. He said, "Diem and Nhu, fearing a coup inspired by the Americans, were switching their police and military forces for a defense against the Americans instead of the National Liberation Front." Then he asked, "Should not the socialist forces, in this new political situation, seek new methods and solutions?"[30]

When Maneli first broached the subject of talks with the North Vietnamese during one of his routine visits to Hanoi, their response was immediate and exhaustive. Pham Van Dong, the premier, and Ho Chi Minh were ready to begin negotiations at any time, and they had a list of goods they believed could be exchanged for South Vietnamese products to cement a direct economic foundation between the two Vietnams.[31] In their conversations with both Maneli and Lalouette, the

[29] Material on Maneli's background can be found in Maneli, *War of the Vanquished*, 1–18.
[30] Ibid., 129.
[31] Ibid., 121.

North Vietnamese dropped all pretence of viewing Diem as a monster and a puppet of the Americans. "In Hanoi, despite all the open, official hostility toward Diem-Nhu, there still existed an atmosphere that could be described as favourable to negotiations and contact with that government. Pham Van Dong even said that Nhu certainly was capable of thinking logically, since he was a graduate of the lycée in Chartres."[32]

Ellen Hammer's interviews with Lalouette and Goburdhun confirmed what Maneli claimed. She discovered that Ho told Goburdhun to convey his sympathy to Diem, "a patriot", with regard to the terrible position in which the Americans had placed him. Ho had foreseen that Diem, with his independent character, would have a hard time with the Americans, "who liked to control everything".[33] The irony is profound. When all the propaganda was stripped away, the North Vietnamese enemy accepted Ngo Dinh Diem as a Vietnamese patriot and leader. It was his American ally who could find little good in him or his government by this time. The Americans did have, however, a good reason to fear a rapprochement between North and South. When Maneli asked North Vietnamese leaders Pham Van Dong and Xuan Thuy what he should say if Ngo Dinh Nhu invited him for a talk, they said, "Everything you know about our stand on economic and cultural exchange and co-operation, about peace and unification. One thing is sure: the Americans have to leave. On this political basis, we can negotiate about everything."[34]

In this conversation, the North Vietnamese leaders tacitly acknowledged that they were responsible for the hostilities in the South, which they expressed a desire to end.[35] Further proof of Hanoi's control over the Viet Cong was made manifest when the foundations were being laid for talks between Hanoi and Saigon.[36] During this period, when Diem

---

[32] Ibid., 122.

[33] Hammer, *Death in November*, 222.

[34] Maneli, *War of the Vanquished*, 127–28.

[35] Maneli recalled: "I asked Pham Van Dong, in the presence of Ho Chi Minh, whether they see the possibility of some kind of federation with Diem-Nhu or something in the nature of a coalition government. Pham answered: 'Everything is negotiable on the basis of the independence and sovereignty of Vietnam.... We can come to an agreement with any Vietnamese.... We have a sincere desire to end hostilities, to establish peace and unification on a completely realistic basis. We are realists.'" Ibid.

[36] Maneli intimates that secret talks had already begun by July 1963: "Saigon is buzzing with rumors about secret contacts between Diem-Nhu and Ho Chi Minh. In Hanoi no one confirms this, but no one has given me—when I have asked—a clear, negative answer.... On

and his government were most vulnerable to attack—owing in no small part to American vacillation over the Buddhist crisis—the Viet Cong backed off and an unofficial cease-fire was accepted amongst opposing commanders.[37] Ellen Hammer explained that, while the talks were not about any detailed agreements—it was far too early in the day for that—they incorporated a recognition of similar actions that both sides could take, such as parallel limitations on military activities. In her discussions with Lalouette, he informed her that it was self-evident that cease-fires being put into place by Viet Cong commanders were to facilitate the talks with the North and to make it plain to Diem that they did not want to take advantage of him while he was having such difficulties with his erstwhile American supporters. In support of this Lalouette understanding, fighting in certain areas had ceased altogether, with local cease-fire arrangements made by each side's respective commanders.[38]

Charles de Gaulle recognised the opportunity for France to regain its foothold in Vietnam through a North-South dialogue. In August 1963, when the Americans were feverishly trying to find South Vietnamese generals to throw Diem out of office, the French president publicly called for peace and unity talks between Hanoi and Saigon.[39] De Gaulle's offer—a vague promise of French cooperation though it was—appealed to the older ties that still bound the Vietnamese to the French and the Vietnamese desire for a reunited country.[40] Ho Chi Minh followed-up De Gaulle's offer with a call for a cease-fire.

Ngo Dinh Nhu was cautious about these overtures, because he did not want to lose American support.[41] As Lalouette told Maneli, he

---

the basis of information I received strictly privately in the North, it is possible to conclude that some kind of Ngo-Ho talks have already begun: through direct emissaries of the North, with the help of the French—at least technical help at this stage." Ibid., 127.

[37] There was one notable exception to this unofficial cease-fire: the Communist propaganda venom directed at the strategic hamlets. Likewise, violence directed toward the strategic hamlets continued unabated until the program was abandoned.

[38] Hammer, *Death in November*, 224–25.

[39] Ibid., 225.

[40] Maneli explained: "There was no doubt that the French government, and de Gaulle personally, decided to seize the chance, to take control of the Diem government, make it dependent on the help of the French government, and somehow oust the Americans. In this way at last the barbarians from across the ocean would learn what French culture, intelligence, and experience meant.... De Gaulle and Lalouette were right. In 1963–64 it might have been possible to end the war and achieve neutralization in a sovereign Vietnamese state independent of Moscow and Peking." *War of the Vanquished*, 151–52.

[41] Hammer, *Death in November*, 228–29.

did "not want to burn his bridges behind him". But Lalouette thought Nhu was deluding himself that he could maintain his alliance with the Americans. He added, "If he does not rid himself of these illusions he will be lost. It is a tragic mistake."[42] According to Hammer, Lalouette could see that Lodge was deliberately undoing the goodwill Nolting had built between the Kennedy and Diem governments. He urged Lodge not to make a coup, to leave Diem in power, but by that time the French ambassador believed that Lodge had been sent to Vietnam with instructions to remove Diem as soon as he could. It was hopeless, Lalouette told Hammer later, because the Americans "had made up their minds to negotiate from a position of force."[43]

Here is another irony to emerge from the breakdown in relations between the Kennedy and Diem governments. At the inception of Ngo Dinh Diem's fledgling Republic of Vietnam, it was the Americans who defended him against the French; in late summer 1963, it was the French who were trying to save Diem from American impatience and wrath. Lalouette told Maneli that the French believed Diem and Nhu were the only ones who could bring about peace with the North because the Communists still respected their nationalist credentials. He believed in their continued political legitimacy even after they declared martial law in late August and ordered raids on the pagodas of the radical bonzes. He warned Lodge that a coup would cause irreparable harm to the country because any government the Americans put in place would lack the support of most Vietnamese and be even more dependent on the United States. The war would then continue to the detriment of everyone.[44]

The *New York Times* attacked the French ambassador for convincing other diplomats to pressure Lodge to soften the American stance toward Diem. According to Hammer, there were also newspaper reports that France was backing Nhu as the man to "lead a great national movement toward reunification".[45] The French position was officially denied in Paris, and assurances were given to the Americans that France had

---

[42] Maneli, *War of the Vanquished*, 151.

[43] Hammer, *Death in November*, 229.

[44] Maneli recounted Lalouette's words: "It is difficult to defend the Diem-Nhu regime since the raid on the pagodas. They are discredited, but nevertheless I feel that only Diem can conclude peace with the North and come to an agreement with the Front.... Any other government will be even more dependent on the Americans, will be obedient to them in all things, and so there will be no chance for peace.'" *War of the Vanquished*, 141–42.

[45] Hammer, *Death in November*, 229.

no intention of supporting Ngo Dinh Nhu. Lalouette told Ambassador Lodge on September 10 that he had been summoned to Paris for consultations for a week, but he never returned.[46] Even with the recall of Lalouette, the rumours in Saigon and amongst American newsmen about a North–South rapprochement continued.[47]

Seymour M. Hersh, in his book *The Dark Side of Camelot*, claimed that the North–South dialogue was the main reason the Kennedy administration removed Diem. Hersh interviewed a good friend of Kennedy, Charles Bartlett,[48] about this issue. Bartlett quoted Kennedy as saying: "Charlie, I can't let Vietnam go to the Communists and then go and ask these people [the voters of America] to re-elect me. Somehow we've got to hold that territory through the 1964 election. We've already given up Laos to the communists and if I give up Vietnam I won't really be able to go to the people. But we've got no future there. [The South Vietnamese] hate us. They want us out of there. At one point they'll kick our asses out of there."[49]

In this chat with Bartlett, Kennedy exposed many things about his administration. Not least of these was his recognition that his and Harriman's Laotian neutrality deal had handed the country over to the Communists. Diem and Nhu, regardless of State Department protests and assurances, had been right all along about Laos, and their fears about how Kennedy would treat them were equally well justified. Ambassador Nolting traced Kennedy's troubles with the Diem government to the abandonment of Laos by the United States. Nevertheless, Hersh's work ignores this earlier betrayal and focuses on the Ngo Dinh talks with the Communists as the main reason for the November coup.

The Hersh thesis, in its most fundamental form, is that President Kennedy believed he could not win the 1964 elections if South Vietnam had become "neutral" as a result of Nhu and Diem's dialogue with the North. This was because Kennedy's adversaries, the Republicans, would quite rightly point out that neutrality was nothing but political

[46] Ibid., 229–30.

[47] Ibid., 230.

[48] Charles Bartlett was such a close friend that when Kennedy became more secluded in the White House due to his duties as president, he still made time to go to dinner at Bartletts'. See Arthur M. Schlesinger Jr., *A Thousand Days: John F. Kennedy in the White House* (Boston: Houghton Mifflin, 1965), 94, 667.

[49] Quoted in Seymour M. Hersh, *The Dark Side of Camelot* (Boston: Little, Brown, 1997), 418.

doublespeak for having surrendered to the Communists. Kennedy's Laos neutrality accords would have been hauled out and presented by the Republicans as a case in point as to what neutrality really meant when the Democrats used such terminology.[50] Hence domestic political considerations were permitted to befuddle sound foreign policy. Hersh touched upon an old theme here, but it is a theme that continues to be relevant, even in the post-Vietnam era.

Hersh's argument has some credibility,[51] but it represents only the proverbial tip of a very deep-set iceberg. The Kennedy administration's double-mindedness in its policy toward Diem's GVN had its beginning in the bitter animosity that arose between Diem and Harriman over the Laos neutrality accords. As this work has shown, Averell Harriman was an extremely powerful man, and he had powerful and respected colleagues ranging from the eloquent Galbraith, who had the president's ear, to the persistent Roger Hilsman. His strong dislike of Diem probably numbered the South Vietnamese president's days well before the Buddhist crisis and the talks with the North Vietnamese. Nolting maintained that, while Kennedy truly liked President Diem and did not want to see him ousted, the American president's loyalty to the man was nevertheless weak. Regardless of his good intentions toward Diem, he could not stand up to the pressures exerted by Harriman and his cohorts in the State Department as well as those from the American press and the upcoming election.

---

[50] Hersch wrote: "If Diem made a deal, the deal was that the US would leave and South Vietnam would become a neutral country. Vietnam would still be divided. For Kennedy, this was anathema, because they [his political opponents in the 1964 elections] would say, 'He lost Vietnam because he let it go neutral.' So that meant you had to get rid of Diem." Ibid., 422–23.

[51] There is little doubt that the possibility of a deal done with the North by Diem and Nhu was worrying Washington. For example, Ambassador Lodge had sought the advice of Robert Thompson with regard to Nhu's capabilities for pulling off a deal with the North. Lodge reported the following to Washington through a classified cable: "Brother Nhu was always thinking of negotiating with North Vietnam and [Thompson] believed he was clever enough to bring it off now that, in his opinion, South Vietnam was somewhat stronger than it was two years ago. Thompson believed the only trump card Nhu had was the withdrawal of the US. For this, he said, North Vietnam would pay almost any price. What, he asked, would we do if the Govt of Vietnam invited us to leave?" Henry Cabot Lodge to secretary of state, telegram, September 12, 1963, Saigon, no. 496, p. 1, Nolting Papers, box 26, Professional Papers, 1963–1982, 1 of 3.

13

Washington Moves for a Coup

In the end, American policy toward President Diem "came down to a disgraceful one," wrote Frederick Nolting, "encouraging a coup while pretending we had nothing to do with it."[1] President Diem and his brother Nhu were aware that the Americans were contemplating a coup, and they knew that one of their reasons for such a move was the deepening Buddhist crisis. Nevertheless, they decided to take firm measures against the radical bonzes during the interim between U.S. ambassadors Nolting and Lodge, and this proved to be the catalyst that set the coup in motion.

The Buddhist uprising was threatening the very survival of the Diem government. Thus, the choice before Diem and Nhu was simple and the same one they had faced when the militant sects vied for power in the early days of the Republic of South Vietnam: either suppress the challenge or give up authority. They knew that if they chose to suppress the radical bonzes, they could expect no help from the Americans, for the Kennedy administration had done nothing but demand they placate a group intent on overthrowing the government. Nevertheless, on August 20, 1963, President Diem declared martial law and moved militarily against the Xa Loi and Tu Dam pagodas.

The news that martial law had been declared in South Vietnam and that the pagodas had been seized and cleared was met with shock and confusion in Washington, and the Kennedy administration scrambled to condemn publically the actions of their ally.[2] Nolting recalled that the

---

[1] Frederick Nolting, *From Trust to Tragedy: The Political Memoirs of Frederick Nolting, Kennedy's Ambassador to Diem's Vietnam* (New York: Praeger, 1988), 132.

[2] DOS noted in an internal document, "We expect to issue a statement on August 21 stating that the repressive measures against the Buddhists undertaken by the GVN represent a direct violation of its assurances that it was pursuing a policy of reconciliation with the

news shocked him as well and that he could not understand why Diem had acted so rapidly and against his own policy of conciliation. He sent Diem a telegram with a personal note to this effect. He later regretted the telegram when he learned Diem's reason for raiding the pagodas—"continued packing of arms in the Xa Loi and other pagodas, continued riots clamoring for the government's overthrow, and a total unwillingness on the part of Thich Tri Quang and his militants to compromise on anything".[3]

William Colby believed that the pagoda raids gave the GVN a position of strength vis-à-vis the Buddhists, from which they could finally negotiate a settlement regarding legitimate grievances, such as their losses at Hue.[4] Then the GVN would be able to put the counterinsurgency—particularly the Strategic Hamlet Program—back on course.[5] He also believed, however, that the massive show of force gave too much

---

Buddhists and consequently the actions of the GVN cannot be condoned by the United States." "Department of State Daily Staff Summary", August 21, 1963, Washington, in *FRUS, 1961–1963*, vol. 3, document 263, pp. 598–99.

In a telephone conversation on September 10, Senator Frank Church took Hilsman to task over why the United States still had not made an international public statement condemning Diem for religious persecution. Hilsman's memorandum of the conversation stated, "Mr. Hilsman said that Nolting and Maggie Higgins have insisted that there is no religious persecution. But, however, he [Hilsman] said that he could assist Senator Church with the language." Roger Hilsman, "Memorandum of a Telephone Conversation between the Assistant Secretary of State for Far Eastern Affairs (Hilsman) and Senator Frank Church, Washington, September 10, 1963, 11:55 A.M.", vol. 4, document 84, p. 168.

[3] Nolting, *From Trust to Tragedy*, 121. Nolting's recollection in his memoirs is consistent with earlier interviews he gave for the Lyndon Baines Johnson Presidential Library Oral History Collection, as noted by the editors of *FRUS, 1961–1963*: "In an oral history interview, Nolting remembers that he was 'shocked' at the raids and that he sent Diem a personal message from Honolulu in which he told Diem: 'This is the first time that you have ever gone back on your word to me.'" Johnson Library, Oral History Program, Frederick E. Nolting Jr., November 11, 1982, quoted in Bromley Smith, "Memorandum of a Conference with the President, White House, Washington, August 27, 1963, 4 P.M.; Subject: Vietnam", in *FRUS, 1961–1963*, vol. 3, document 303, p. 661n6.

[4] "From Colby:—endeavor to induce the GVN quickly to take a series of favorable actions respecting the Buddhists to exhibit that the repressive measures were necessary to establish the tranquillity in which the religious problem could be solved." Victor H. Krulak, "Memorandum for the Record by the Joint Chiefs of Staff's Special Assistant for Counterinsurgency and Special Activities (Krulak)", August 21, 1963, Washington, in *FRUS, 1961–1963*, vol. 3, document 265, pp. 601–2.

[5] Colby said that SHP stalled "when the attention of the palace drifted off after May of 1963 to the problems with the Buddhists and with the Americans." William Colby, interview by Ted Gittinger, March 1, 1982, interview 2, transcript, 6, Lyndon Baines Johnson Presidential Library Oral History Collection.

credence to the arguments of Diem's enemies in Washington, particularly within the State Department.[6] The raids also caused immediate problems for the CIA, because the organisation was thought to have been involved in them and therefore too close to Diem and Nhu.[7] The CIA's overall assessment nevertheless remained that America should continue its support of the Diem government. Colby underscored this position, which supported Nolting's arguments entirely, in an interview with the BBC several years after the fact. He said, "Our position was that Diem is about as good a leadership as you're going to get in Vietnam in this damn time. That America's main interest in Vietnam is not the small details of how it runs its internal government structure, but whether it's meeting the communist challenge."[8]

Using as a pretext the crackdown on the pagodas and the fictitious report that Nhu was consolidating power to take over the government, Hilsman sent a fateful telegram to involve the Kennedy administration in the direct planning of a coup. Hilsman's transmission, in some ways a reaction to earlier queries Lodge had sent from Saigon, was despatched to the U.S. embassy on the weekend of August 24, 1963, when President Kennedy was out of town.[9] It outlined the following steps:

[6] William Colby and Peter Forbath, *Honorable Men: My Life in the CIA* (New York: Simon and Schuster, 1978), 208–9.

[7] Colby explained this in his memoirs: "Because of the CIA's secrecy and its long-time close relations with Nhu and Diem, the immediate question was raised in many minds whether the Agency might be pursuing its own policy at cross purposes with the official United States position, and even have had something to do with the raids. For, as it developed, the troops who had carried out the raids had been led by the Vietnamese Special Forces which were supported by CIA.... In fact, however, they had been assembled for the pagoda raids totally without the CIA's knowledge, and it fell to me to convince Americans and Vietnamese alike that this was so." Ibid., 209.

[8] Colby continued, "Now, there were other people in Washington who claimed that it was hopeless with Mr. Diem, that the dislike for his authoritarian rule, the political opposition was so strong, that the communists could not help but win in the long term with that kind of government.... The key question was never answered. Which one are we interested in? Are we interested in a perfect constitutional democracy in a small under-developed country in Asia, recently freed from a hundred years of colonial rule? Or are we interested in some kind of a structure that will prevent further expansion of communist control?" Interview in Michael Charlton, "The New Frontiersmen Hold the Line", program 4 of *Many Reasons Why: The American Involvement in Vietnam*, British Broadcasting Corporation, 1977, transcript copy, 8–9, Nolting Papers, box 27, Professional Papers.

[9] Henry Cabot Lodge had taken over the post of U.S. ambassador to South Vietnam and had first set foot in Saigon on the night of August 22, 1963. See Anne E. Blair, *Lodge in Vietnam: A Patriot Abroad* (New Haven, Conn.: Yale University Press, 1995), 24.

(1) First, we must press on appropriate levels of GVN following line:

(a) USG [U.S. government] cannot accept actions against Buddhists taken by Nhu and his collaborators under cover of martial law. (b) Prompt dramatic actions redress situation must be taken, including repeal of decree 10, release of arrested monks, nuns, etc.

(2) We must at same time also tell key military leaders that US would find it impossible to continue support GVN militarily and economically unless above steps are taken immediately which we recognize requires removal of the Nhus from the scene. We wish give Diem reasonable opportunity to remove Nhus, but if he remains obdurate, then we are prepared to accept the obvious implication that we can no longer support Diem. You may also tell appropriate military commanders we will give them direct support in any interim period of breakdown central government mechanism....

Concurrently with above, Ambassador and country team should urgently examine all possible alternative leadership and make detailed plans as to how we might bring about Diem's replacement if this should become necessary....

... We will back you to the hilt on actions you take to achieve our objectives.[10]

Nolting saw this telegram just a short while after it had been sent as he stood in Hilsman's office at the State Department, and he perceived that the impact of the cable would be far-reaching, certainly beyond the combined imaginations of the group of men who were behind its content. "The telegram of August 24 turned out to be a decisive factor in leading our country into the longest and most unnecessary war in American history."[11] According to the editors of the State Department's *Foreign Relations of the United States, 1961–1963*, "The drafting and clearance of this message has occasioned subsequent controversy which is reflected in the memoirs and recollections of some of the principal personalities involved at the time." For an example, they quote General Maxwell Taylor's description of the cable as "ill-conceived, confusing, and would never have been approved had Hilsman and his colleagues not taken advantage of the absence from Washington of most of the high-level

---

[10] Roger Hilsman, "Telegram from the Department of State to the Embassy in Vietnam", August 24, 1963, Washington, in *FRUS, 1961–1963*, vol. 3, document 281, pp. 628–29. (Drafted by Hilsman and cleared by Hilsman, Forrestal, and Ball. Approved by Harriman for transmission and classification. Signed "Ball".)

[11] Nolting, *From Trust to Tragedy*, 124.

officials of the administration." The general also wrote that "the cable was an 'end run' by an anti-Diem faction in Washington including Hilsman, Harriman, and Forrestal."[12]

Nolting's assessment made plain the actual mechanics of how the telegram sneaked out of town with the tacit approval of all the key players: "They had cleared this text over the telephone with representatives of State (George Ball was acting Secretary because Rusk was away), Defense, CIA, and the White House staff. The President was consulted. Each person, including President Kennedy, who was vacationing on Cape Cod, had approved the telegram under the impression that other top officials had agreed with it. There was no formal meeting to discuss or co-ordinate the message."[13]

Robert McNamara, Kennedy's secretary of defense, remembered the details of how this cable was approved and sent forward. His description supports Nolting's assertion that everyone was presented with the cable having been told it had already been approved by everyone else.[14] McNamara also recalled that Maxwell Taylor, whom he considered far and away Kennedy's most capable geopolitical thinker and security advisor, was appalled by what Hilsman had done. Roswell Gilpatric, who initially had fallen prey to the efforts of Hilsman and Harriman to get

---

[12] Hilsman, "Telegram from Department of State to Embassy in Vietnam", August 24, 1963, 628n1.

[13] Nolting, *From Trust to Tragedy*, 124.

[14] Robert S. McNamara, *In Retrospect: The Tragedy and Lessons of Vietnam*, with Brian Van-DeMark (New York: Random House, 1995), 54. McNamara's description certainly supports Nolting's contention that the Harriman group had masterminded this effort: "After Hilsman completed the cable, on August 24, Averell Harriman, who had just become under-secretary of state for political affairs, approved it. Michael Forrestal, son of the first secretary of defense and a member of the NSC [National Security Council] staff, immediately sent the cable to President Kennedy in Hyannis Port, stating, 'Clearances are being obtained from [Under-secretary of State George] Ball and Defense.... Suggest you let me know if you wish ... to hold up action.' ... The cable's sponsors were determined to transmit it to Saigon that very day. They found George Ball on the golf course and asked him to call the President on Cape Cod. He did, and President Kennedy said he would agree to the cable's transmission if his senior advisers concurred. George [Ball] immediately telephoned Dean Rusk in New York and told him the president agreed. Dean [Rusk] endorsed it, though he was unenthusiastic. Averell, meanwhile, sought clearance from the CIA. Since John McCone was absent, he talked to Richard Helms, the deputy director for plans. Helms was reluctant, but, like Rusk, went along because the president had already done so.... Forrestal, meanwhile, called Ros [Roswell] Gilpatric at home and told him the same story: the president and the secretary of state had seen the cable and concurred." Ibid., 53.

instant approval of the telegram, had immediate doubts and, even while the cable was in the process of being sent, made sure that General Taylor got a copy immediately. Regardless of misgivings, the cable was sent, and McNamara recalled: "Lodge understood the August 24 cable as instructing him to initiate action to remove Diem as leader of South Vietnam."[15]

Years later—in 1977, in an interview with the BBC—Ambassador Lodge claimed that he was stunned by the content of the August 24 telegram:

> I was thunderstruck.... So I get on down to Saigon on Friday and then Sunday comes this telegram telling me to do whatever I could to overthrow Diem, and to, in effect, press the button.... I thought about asking for clarification of instructions and then I thought no, that I wouldn't do that.... I can read English, I could understand perfectly well what the telegram said, I thought it was very ill-advised; but I only had had twenty-four hours in the country and my opinion wasn't worth very much to me or anybody else. So I said I'm going to try to carry it out.[16]

Lodge went on to tell the BBC that he believed that the instigators of the telegram (i.e., the Harriman group in Washington) had gotten carried away. "In the State Department you had men who had devoted a large part of their lives to this thing, they were on it day and night and they'd get worked up and I think it's all done in the spirit of sincerity. That doesn't make it any less reprehensible."[17] The BBC interviewer then asked Lodge: "Do you think that a group in the State Department opposed to Diem seized their opportunity that weekend in a quite deliberate way?"[18] Lodge answered this question in the affirmative: "Well, that's the obvious explanation, that there was a group that had been working on this question for a long time and they were emotionally involved."[19] One of the Harriman group's chief accusations against Nolting was that he was emotionally involved with Diem, yet they could not perceive their own emotional involvement in a contrary direction.

Nolting recalled that McNamara was so upset by what he had read in the Hilsman telegram that the secretary called him and asked him

---

[15] Ibid., 54–55.
[16] Interview by Charlton in "New Frontiersmen", 27–29.
[17] Ibid., 29.
[18] Ibid., 30.
[19] Ibid.

to attend a meeting he was trying to set up with the president to have the telegram's instructions voided.[20] Nolting assured McNamara that he would attend if he were invited, whereupon he received an immediate invitation from President Kennedy's military aide, General Chester V. "Ted" Clifton. The meeting turned out to be, in Nolting's words, "a kind of National Security Council special group meeting, chaired by President Kennedy, who appeared to be harassed and worried".[21] The meeting illustrated yet again that a deep division existed in Kennedy's administration over policy toward President Diem.

Prior to this meeting, another had taken place at the White House on August 26, 1963, wherein all of the major forces in the Harriman group were involved. These included Ball, Forrestal, Harriman, and Hilsman. According to Nolting's memoirs, Kennedy was plainly annoyed at the way U.S. policy was being driven by certain individuals and was fed up with what the press had been doing. He said, "Halberstam of *The New York Times* is actually running a political campaign; and he is wholly unobjective, reminiscent of Mr. Matthews in the Castro days." He added that the reporter should not be unduly influencing the actions of his administration.[22] But did the president realise that the reporter's influence on policy had been given to him, at least in part, by State Department officials?

On August 14, for example, Assistant Secretary of State Roger Hilsman, in a broadcast on Voice of America, declared that the Buddhist crisis was "beginning to affect the war effort". Marguerite Higgins took Hilsman's statement to Ambassador Nolting, who was to leave Saigon the following day. Nolting told her that all his reports showed that the Buddhist crisis was not having any impact at all. He said, "I don't know what Hilsman based his statement on. But he isn't basing it on anything that went out of this embassy, the military mission, or the CIA."[23] When Higgins returned to New York, she telephoned Hilsman and asked him if the basis for his claim was the *New York Times*. "Partly that," said Hilsman, "the *Times* and other press dispatches out of Saigon." Higgins later wrote,

[20] Nolting, *From Trust to Tragedy*, 124–25.
[21] Ibid.
[22] Ibid., 638.
[23] Marguerite Higgins, *Our Vietnam Nightmare* (New York: Harper and Row, 1965), 124–25.

And thus is history recast. All those Vietnamese-speaking Americans circling the countryside for the purpose of testing Vietnamese opinion; all those American officers gauging the morale of the troops; all those C.I.A. agents tapping their sources (hopefully) everywhere; all those dispatches from Ambassador Nolting—an army of data—collectors in reasonable agreement had been downgraded in favor of press dispatches stating opposite conclusions. It was the first time that I began to comprehend, in depth and in some sorrow, what was meant by the power of the press.[24]

Perhaps she should also have been taken aback at the power of the powerful to use the press.

Back to the August 26 meeting at the White House, President Kennedy tried to find out if it were possible for the United States to live with Diem and Nhu. According to Nolting, Hilsman responded it would be horrible to contemplate because of "Nhu's grave emotional instability".[25] Hilsman pressed to have the regime overthrown, which seemed to annoy the president. Harriman supported Hilsman during this conference by stating that they had sent the August 24 telegram because they believed they had Vietnamese support to move against Diem as a result of the pagoda raids.

According to Robert McNamara's memory of this meeting, Hilsman tried to stop Kennedy from listening to Nolting. "The President told him he wanted another meeting the next day and asked that former Ambassador Nolting be present. Hilsman did not like that. He complained that Nolting's views were colored and that he had become emotionally involved in the situation. The president replied acidly, 'Maybe logically.' "[26] McNamara's recollections of this meeting match notes in State Department papers.[27]

As we saw, Nolting did attend the next meeting. During the next couple of weeks, he attended several meetings on Vietnam. In his

[24] Ibid., 125.

[25] For Nolting's description of this meeting, see *From Trust to Tragedy*, 638–41.

[26] McNamara, *In Retrospect*, 58.

[27] The official record observed: "Mr. Hilsman commented that Nolting's views are colored, in that he is emotionally involved in the situation. Upon hearing this, the President observed, 'Maybe properly.' " V. H. Krulak, "Memorandum for the Record of a Meeting at the White House, Washington, August 26, 1963, Noon", in *FRUS, 1961–1963*, vol. 3, document 265, p. 641.

memoirs, he described how he expressed his position in support of President Diem.

> The basic issue was whether the U.S. government should connive to overthrow the Diem government. I argued that it should not. A coup would create a political vacuum, encourage the Communists, and wipe out the nine years of relatively successful support we had given South Vietnam—without the use of American combat forces. Furthermore, in supporting a coup, the United States would be doing exactly what President Kennedy had promised President Diem we would not do, namely, interfering in South Vietnam's internal affairs. Our moral commitment, the integrity of the United States, was at stake. Finally, I argued that the generals would be ineffective leaders. They would not gain the support of the South Vietnamese people and would naturally turn to the United States for more and more military help, including, probably, U.S. combat forces. I was appalled that our government would encourage a coup of dissident generals to overthrow their elected government. It was wrong in principle and would, even if successfully executed, have disastrous long-range consequences for the United States as well as for Vietnam.[28]

Regardless of Nolting's efforts, and regardless of Kennedy's willingness to listen to his former ambassador, there is no evidence that the White House made any attempt to stop the coup. In fact, from what can be discerned in a top secret telegram Kennedy sent to Lodge on August 29, 1963, Kennedy approved the go-ahead for an overthrow of the Diem's civilian government by his generals:

> Top Secret, Eyes Only,
>   Emergency Personal For The Ambassador From The President—No Department or Other Distribution Whatever
>   I have approved all the messages you are receiving from others today, and I emphasize that everything in these messages has my full support.
>   We will do all that we can to help you conclude this operation successfully. Nevertheless, there is one point on my own constitutional responsibilities as President and Commander in Chief which I wish to state to you in this entirely private message, which is not being circulated here beyond the Secretary of State.
>   Until the very moment of the go signal for the operation by the Generals, I must reserve a contingent right to change course and reverse

---

[28] Nolting, *From Trust to Tragedy*, 125.

previous instructions. While fully aware of your assessment of the consequences of such a reversal, I know from experience that failure is more
destructive than an appearance of indecision. I would, of course, accept
full responsibility for any such change as I must bear also the full responsibility for this operation and its consequences. It is for this reason that I
count on you for a continuing assessment of the prospects of success and
most particularly desire your candid warning if current course begins to
sour. When we go, we must go to win, but it will be better to change
our minds than fail. And if our national interest should require a change
of mind, we must not be afraid of it.[29]

In sending such a telegram, Kennedy had ignored not just Colby,
Nolting, Taylor, and McNamara but also the opinions of several foreign governments. The French opinion can be seen in a cable Lodge
sent George Ball on August 30, 1963. In it Lodge explained that French
Ambassador Roger Lalouette urged the United States not to back a
coup. Lalouette defended Diem and Nhu as the best available leaders in
South Vietnam and said the war against the Viet Cong could be won
with them at the helm. He explained that the Buddhist protests had
been overdramatised by the press and that it was American opinion that
needed calming down.[30]

Similar to Lalouette's message was one by the Philippine government. A CIA report dated September 7, 1963, included statements by
Philippine Foreign Secretary Salvador Lopez, who said his government
backed President Diem and was willing to act as an agent of reconciliation between him and the United States. The Communist threat was
the most important issue in South Vietnam, he said. While Diem needed
U.S. support for the counterinsurgency, Lopez warned that without him
Washington could not succeed. He mentioned that the Buddhist uprising was a South Vietnamese internal matter and that according to Philippine intelligence the revolt was Communist inspired.[31]

[29] Kennedy had also instructed Lodge, if the latter chose to reply, to address his answer
"For President Only, Pass White House directly, no other distribution whatever." John F.
Kennedy to Henry Cabot Lodge, telegram, August 29, 1963, Washington, Nolting Papers,
box 26, Professional Papers, 2 of 3.

[30] Henry Cabot Lodge to George Ball, telegram, August 30, 1963, Saigon, 1–2, Nolting
Papers, box 26, Professional Papers, 1 of 3.

[31] CIA, "Philippine Foreign Secretary Lopez' Belief that the Philippines Must Support
the United States' Backing of Ngo Dinh Diem as an Anti-Communist Bulwark", telegram
information report TDCS 3/558,907, reference 17430, September 7, 1963, 1, Nolting Papers,
box 26, Professional Papers, 1963–1982, 1 of 3.

The Australian government's position was remarkably similar to this. A telegram sent from the American embassy in Canberra to the secretary of state in Washington spelled out the position of the Australian government that there was no alternative to Diem and that the regime was by no means beyond constructive influence. The radical Buddhists had shot their bolt for the time being, and the crisis had calmed down somewhat. The Australians were hopeful that the calm would allow the fight to be refocused on the Communists.[32]

The British ambassador to South Vietnam, Gordon Etherington-Smith, felt likewise, as noted by Lodge in his cable to Washington on September 11, 1963: "On the general situation, Etherington-Smith thinks that the Diem Govt. has overcome the Buddhist problem and is strongly in the saddle and that apparently nothing much can be gained by trying to bring about a change.... In other words, attempts to get another govt. will probably fail and therefore should not be undertaken."[33]

In her research on South Vietnam, Anne Blair asked a fundamental question: How did Kennedy become so divorced from what was really going on in South Vietnam so as to get behind a coup? Her answer coincided, for the most part, with those offered by Nolting and Colby. She identified the power of the Halberstam-Sheehan group of reporters to draw attention to and to amplify the Buddhist crisis at Kennedy's political expense. She highlighted the fact that Halberstam, Sheehan, and other reporters had made clear their support for a coup.[34] In Blair's assessment, Kennedy was so driven by domestic concerns related to bad publicity over Diem and South Vietnam that he made himself prey to a flawed and inexpert group headed by the powerful Averell Harriman.

---

[32] Jack Wilson Lydman to secretary of state, telegram, September 10, 1963, American embassy in Canberra, 1, Nolting Papers, box 26, Professional Papers, 1963–1982, 1 of 3.

[33] Henry Cabot Lodge to secretary of state, telegram, September 11, 1963, Saigon, no. 484, p. 1, Nolting Papers, box 26, Professional Papers, 1963–1982, 1 of 3.

[34] "By their own admission, they had taken up the story of a developing dispute between Diem and various Buddhist groups as a vehicle for writing about the political situation in South Vietnam with the quite conscious motive of promoting a coup against Diem. The Halberstam-Sheehan group made the 'Buddhist crisis' story their own; their copy was the basis for almost all the reports that appeared in major American daily newspapers and weekly magazines such as Time and Newsweek. The group's promotion of the story put Vietnam on front pages for several weeks, prompting many editorials and readers' letters abhorring U.S. support of Diem. This development threatened to open up public debate on the conduct of the war that Kennedy wished to avoid." Blair, Lodge in Vietnam, 13.

In turn, these domestic concerns prevented him from seeing or hearing what the most experienced Southeast Asian experts were saying: Stay the course with Diem.[35]

On August 29, 1963, Ambassador Lodge followed up on President Kennedy's cable with a momentous one of his own, wherein he declared: "We are launched on a course from which there is no respectable turning back: The overthrow of the Diem Government."[36] On this same date, the White House drafted another top secret, eyes only cable, approved by the president, Secretary of State Rusk, and Hilsman. It informed Lodge: "The USG will support a coup which has a good chance of succeeding but plans no direct involvement of U.S. Armed Forces."[37] This telegram was fleshing out what had been hinted in Kennedy's earlier message to Lodge. There is no record that would indicate that Nolting was aware of this last DOS cable, especially since at a White House meeting the same day, Nolting continued his fight against the coup. He argued that Diem was firmly in control of the government, working his usual eighteen-hour days, and that it was still not clear whether the generals wanted to get rid of both him and Nhu. He added that if the Nhus had to go, the United States could certainly live with a new government headed by Diem.[38]

At a State Department meeting the following day, Nolting tried to defend Nhu against the increasingly vicious attacks on his character. This

[35] According to Blair, "During the summer of 1963, Kennedy seems to have conceptualized Vietnam as a political and public relations issue rather than a war. He consulted only with a select few from State, especially Harriman and Hilsman. Representatives of the Defense Department, the Joint Chiefs of Staff, and the CIA were not included in these discussions. As a result, William Bundy recorded, these principals did not know the thinking of Harriman, Hilsman, Kennedy, and Lodge on the political situation in Saigon.... If Kennedy's bypassing key representatives of the National Security Council on Vietnam policy seems grave enough, there was yet another twist. In effect, the Department of State team had also cut themselves off from those officials most in a position to advise them on how to deal with Diem and his family. Two of these men were John Richardson of the CIA, whose special job it was to liaise with Ngo Dinh Nhu, and William Colby, then chief of the Far Eastern Division of the CIA in Washington and formerly head of the agency in Saigon." Ibid., 16–17.

[36] Henry Cabot Lodge, "Telegram from the Embassy in Vietnam to the Department of State", August 29, 1963, Saigon, in FRUS, 1961–1963, vol. 4, document 12, p. 21.

[37] Dean Rusk to Henry Cabot Lodge and Paul Harkins, telegram, August 29, 1963, Washington, no. 272, Nolting Papers, box 26, Professional Papers, 1963–1982, 1 of 3.

[38] Bromley Smith, "Memorandum of a Conference with the President, White House, Washington, August 29, 1963, Noon", in FRUS, 1961–1963, vol. 4, document 15, vol. 4, pp. 27, 31.

malice against Nhu made it unthinkable in Washington for him to serve in any future government supported by the United States. The question was raised whether Nhu was going to sell out to North Vietnam, and Nolting answered that while Nhu was "shifty", he was committed to an anti-Communist course.[39]

When the discussion turned to the coup, Secretary of Defense McNamara supported Nolting's position against it. He expressed his contempt for the generals plotting against their president and claimed they had no plan for a replacement government, "contrary to their assurances".[40] A day later, in another high-level DOS meeting, McNamara again argued against encouraging a coup. He said the United States should instead be helping Diem fight the Viet Cong. He stated: "We need to reopen communications with Diem to get his ideas about what comes next."[41] Later, when Paul Kattenburg, a DOS researcher, tried to condemn Diem as a petty tyrant who was alienating the people of South Vietnam, Nolting corrected him by pointing out that the political discontent as confined to the cities, which represented only 15 per cent of South Vietnam's population.[42] At this point in the meeting, Secretary Rusk swung his support behind Nolting. Taking exception to Kattenburg's statement, he said that during the first six months of the year the GVN had made steady progress in winning over people in the countryside and that an attempt should be made to recover this position.[43]

At this juncture, Vice President Johnson stated with considerable force that he never had any sympathy for the idea of changing the Vietnamese government by plotting with ARVN generals; he strongly recommended that the White House backtrack immediately, reestablish amicable relations with Diem, and then get on with the real fight, which

---

[39] Roger Hilsman, "Memorandum of a Conversation, Department of State, Washington, August 30, 1963, 2:30 P.M.", in *FRUS, 1961–1963*, vol. 4, document 26, p. 54.

[40] Ibid., 55.

[41] Roger Hilsman, "Memorandum of a Conversation, Department of State, Washington, August 31, 1963, 11 A.M.", in *FRUS, 1961–1963*, vol. 4, document 37, p. 73. General Krulak's memorandum of this meeting is printed in *U.S. Involvement in the War, Internal Documents: The Kennedy Administration, January 1961–November 1963, Book II*, section V.B.4 of bk. 12 of *United States–Vietnam Relations, 1945–1967: Study Prepared by the Department of Defense*, by Congress, House, Committee on Armed Services (Washington, D.C.: United States Government Printing Office, 1971), 540–44.

[42] Ibid., 74.

[43] Ibid.

was against the Communists.[44] During his stout defence of Diem, Johnson could not resist the opportunity to use his famous Texas humour: "Certainly there were bad situations in South Viet-Nam. However, there were bad situations in the U.S. It was difficult to live with Otto Passman, but we couldn't pull a coup on him."[45]

In another last-ditch effort to restore U.S. support for the Diem regime, Nolting told President Kennedy at a September 6 White House meeting not to use any more pressure tactics on Diem, because they would most likely trigger an "unfortunate reaction". The president then asked him if the American minimum requirement should be the removal of Nhu. Nolting replied that, for the sake of U.S. public opinion, Nhu would have to go. He quickly added that the removal of Nhu would be a loss for Vietnam, a loss that was difficult to justify even if there were a corresponding gain in public opinion of Kennedy.[46]

On September 10, at another White House meeting, Marine General Krulak and DOS advisor Joseph A. Mendenhall gave their two reports on their recent visits to Vietnam. Ambassador Nolting was in attendance. The two vastly different reports—Mendenhall's focusing on political intrigue in Saigon, and Krulak's focusing on the overall national picture and the counterinsurgency—prompted Kennedy to ask: "The two of you did visit the same country, didn't you?"[47] Mendenhall's report was strongly anti-Diem, while Krulak's report stated that progress in defeating the Viet Cong was tangible. General Krulak noted that, although there was still a lot of war left to fight, "the Viet Cong war will be won if the current U.S. military and sociological programs are pursued."[48] His message to the president was unmistakable: Stay the course.

Nolting liked what he heard from Krulak. He interrupted the meeting only after Rufus Phillips of the CIA put forward various scenarios through which Nhu and Colonel Le Quang Tung of the ARVN

[44] Ibid., 74n7.

[45] Ibid., 74. Otto Passman was a conservative-minded Democratic congressman from Louisiana.

[46] Bromley Smith, "Memorandum of a Conference with the President, White House, Washington, September 6, 1963, 10:30 A.M.", in FRUS, 1961–1963, vol. 4, document 66, p. 120.

[47] Roger Hilsman, "Memorandum of a Conversation, White House, Washington, September 10, 1963, 10:30 A.M.", in FRUS, 1961–1963, vol. 4, document 83, p. 162.

[48] Ibid.

Special Forces could be discredited and removed from power.[49] Nolting interjected with a query as to what the results would be from Phillips' intrigues if they were put into effect: "Military action against the Nhus? Military action against the government? ... Civil war?"[50] Phillips then tried another avenue to criticise the Diem government. He claimed that the strategic hamlets were "being chewed to pieces by the Viet Cong [in the Mekong Delta region]", that 60 per cent of them had been overrun.[51] Hilsman, who was taking notes, recalled that General Krulak strongly disagreed with Phillips. Krulak said that his "statement respecting military progress had its origins in a reservoir of many advisors who were doing nothing other than observe the prosecution of the war; that their view was shared and expressed officially by General Harkins." Krulak added that in a choice between Harkins and Phillips, he would go with the general.[52]

Owing to his continual defence of Diem, Nolting became a persona non grata within the Kennedy administration and was invited to fewer and fewer meetings. He was conspicuously absent at an important September 10 meeting at DOS, which was attended by Secretary McNamara, Attorney General Robert Kennedy, CIA Director John McCone, Undersecretary Harriman, General Taylor, General Krulak, Deputy Secretary Gilpatric, Assistant Secretary Hilsman, Colby, Phillips, and several others.[53] This meeting revealed the chasm that had grown between the Harriman faction and Diem's remaining supporters within the Kennedy administration. The divide became apparent when Robert Kennedy said they all agreed the war would go better without Diem and Secretary McNamara immediately disagreed: "He believed our present policy was not viable. He thought that we had been trying to overthrow Diem, but we had no alternative to Diem that we knew about. Therefore, we were making it impossible to continue to work with Diem on the one hand and, on the other, not

<hr />

[49] Although Phillips was ready to discredit and abandon Colonel Tung, William Colby—Phillips' predecessor—had had the utmost respect for the man. The CIA was very possibly as divided as DOS over Vietnam.

[50] Hilsman, "Memorandum of Conversation, September 10, 1963", 163–64.

[51] Ibid., 165.

[52] Quoted in ibid., 165n6.

[53] Bromley Smith, "Memorandum of a Conversation, Department of State, Washington, September 10, 1963, 5:45 P.M.", in FRUS, 1961–1963, vol. 4, document 85, p. 169.

developing an alternative solution. He felt that we should go back to what we were doing three weeks ago."[54] Harriman defended the change, claimed it was the president's policy, and stated it should therefore not be discussed any further. He said Diem, by persecuting the Buddhists, had made it impossible for the United States to back him. Diem had to be removed, he added, because he had "gravely offended the world community".[55]

The military men in the room did not buy Harriman's lofty logic. As can be seen in this message General Harkins sent the Joint Chiefs of Staff two days after the meeting with Harriman, they had come to believe that the Communist enemy, not President Diem, was to blame for the Buddhist uprising:

> I think we must all realize we are fighting a ruthless, crude, brutal enemy who is using every known trick in the Communist bag. In 1960 he saw he was losing the initial round so he openly flexed his biceps. Our tremendous effort of the past year and one half began to pay off early this year and he saw he was losing the military battle. In seeking a new approach he seized the religious one. Bonze Quang, the culprit we now are giving asylum to in our Embassy, has admitted in conversations since he entered his safe haven that he had been planning to go full out against the Diem regime prior to May 8th. He seized upon this episode as his opportunity. Though the government made concessions, Quang and his cohorts refused to accept them, always demanding more. He remained unable to unseat Diem. The 21st of August crackdown stopped the outward religious effort, and now the school children [protest organised against Diem]. This of course is another well-organized covertly led Communist trick.[56]

Ironically the military coup was being demanded by American diplomats and resisted by American generals. The former believed the removal of Diem was essential to winning the war; the latter believed the war was being won with Diem in place. On September 3 General Taylor hand carried a memorandum to President Kennedy stating that,

---

[54] Ibid., 169–70.

[55] Ibid., 170–71.

[56] Paul Harkins, "Telegram from the Commander, Military Assistance Command, Vietnam (Harkins) to the Joint Chiefs of Staff's Special Assistant for Counterinsurgency and Special Activities (Krulak)", September 12, 1963, Saigon, in *FRUS, 1961–1963*, vol. 4, document 96, p. 194.

regardless of Saigon's preoccupation with the unstable political situation, the whole month of August 1963 displayed favourable military trends in all areas of activity. In other words, the GVN was successfully prosecuting the counterinsurgency in spite of the Buddhist protests.[57] Nevertheless, Kennedy asked Secretary McNamara to determine the accuracy of reports in the *New York Times* stating the opposite. McNamara informed the president that Halberstam was understating the effectiveness of the ARVN and overstating the abilities of the Viet Cong. In addition, he said, Halberstam was failing to report on positive trends in ARVN operations.[58] The CIA prepared a memorandum for Director McCone to make available to the president, which was based on a review of all the articles written by Halberstam since June. The majority of these were "almost invariably pessimistic reports" about "the Buddhist crisis in South Vietnam and the injurious effects of the crisis on the struggle against the Viet Cong". The CIA found that Halberstam was "by and large accurate" in terms of his facts. His emphasis and conclusions, however, called "his objectivity into question".[59]

The CIA also prepared a report to address another concern of the Kennedy administration—that Diem and Nhu might conclude a neutrality deal with the North, which would essentially hand South Vietnam to the Communists. In late September 1963, the CIA reported that Diem and Nhu were feeling "boxed between two unacceptable alternatives: abject surrender to US demands or a loss of all political power". While they might be casting about for alternatives to American support, including some kind of agreement with Hanoi, they would not go along with a united Communist Vietnam.[60]

Irrespective of the positive reports—which essentially verified what Nolting had been telling the president—worries about Diem's ability

[57] See Maxwell D. Taylor, "Memorandum from the Chairman of the Joint Chiefs of Staff (Taylor) to the President" [September 3, 1963], Washington, in *FRUS, 1961–1963*, vol. 4, document 53, pp. 98–99.

[58] "Editorial Note", in "Period of Interlude, September 7–October 22, 1963: Assessment of the Progress of the War, U.S. Efforts to Reform the Diem Government, the McNamara-Taylor Mission to Vietnam and Report, U.S. Policy on Coup Plotting in Vietnam", pt. 2 of *FRUS, 1961–1963*, vol. 4, document 141, pp. 277–78.

[59] Quoted in ibid., 278.

[60] Ray S. Cline, "Memorandum Prepared for the Director of Central Intelligence (McCone); Subject: Possible Rapprochement between North and South Vietnam", September 26, 1963, Washington, in *FRUS, 1961–1963*, vol. 4, document 151, p. 297.

to lead the war effort continued to escalate in the Kennedy administration, and Nolting was effectively squeezed out of having any influence whatsoever on the final decisions with respect to the Diem government.[61] Also ignored was a late October congressional fact-finding visit to South Vietnam, which determined that the best course for U.S. policy was to stay with Diem. Congressman Clement Zablocki reported that in spite of Diem's faults—"his autocracy, his tolerance of venality and brutality"—his government was winning the war against the Communist insurgents. He stated that there was no reasonable alternative to Diem, and that therefore coup plots were harmful. He accused American reporters in the country of being "arrogant, emotional, un-objective and ill informed".[62]

Regardless of the meetings, the reports, and the fact-finding missions during late summer and early fall 1963, President Kennedy did nothing to halt the plot against Diem that he had set into motion. It is therefore remarkable that Averell Harriman later blamed its forward movement on Ambassador Lodge: "I don't think we could have [prevented Diem's overthrow]. Now it is true at the end there Lodge did not try to stop it. You would have to try to stop it. There was nothing we did that I know of that encouraged the coup."[63]

Making Lodge, a Republican, the fall guy for the coup was perhaps planned at the time of his appointment as ambassador to South Vietnam. According to Anne Blair, "Kennedy welcomed Rusk's nomination of Lodge. Lodge, he thought, would serve admirably as Republican asbestos against the heat of possible future criticism of his foreign policy.... As history was to show, the Lodge appointment did achieve the goal of deflecting criticism from Kennedy's involvement in Vietnam, although

[61] Frederick Nolting was excluded from all of the October 1963 White House conferences. Later, in 1964, Nolting informed the editor of the New York Times that he had had no voice in any matter of policy concerning Vietnam since August 27, 1963. See Frederick E. Nolting Jr., letter to the editor, New York Times, March 19, 1964, Nolting Papers, box 12, Editor, New York Times.

[62] Quoted in V. H. Krulak, "Memorandum for the Record by the Joint Chiefs of Staff's Special Assistant for Counterinsurgency and Special Activities (Krulak)", October 28, 1963, Washington, in FRUS, 1961–1963, vol. 4, document 222, p. 446.

[63] W. Averell Harriman, interview by Arthur M. Schlesinger Jr., January 17, 1965, Washington, D.C., interview 2, transcript 105–17, John F. Kennedy Oral History Collection, John F. Kennedy Presidential Library, Boston.

ultimately with great cost to America's reputation in the foreign relations field."[64]

The coup took place on November 1, 1963. With forces loyal to Diem deployed to the far-flung reaches of South Vietnam, rebel forces sealed off military bases in the capital and proceeded to assault the presidential palace, where the coup leaders discovered that Diem and Nhu had escaped during the night. The brothers had fled to the house of a friend in Cholon. Early on November 2 they attended Mass at the local Church of Saint Francis Xavier and spent some time afterwards in prayer, according to Father Clement Nguyen Van Thach, an eyewitness.[65] The brothers were outside the church, in the Grotto of the Virgin Mary, when General "Big" Duong Van Minh's soldiers arrived with a couple of American jeeps and an armoured personnel carrier. Sometime during that morning, General Minh, the leader of the coup, had been informed that the Ngo Dinh brothers were at the church. He made the plan to capture both brothers there and gave a direct order to his body guard to murder them. Once Diem and Nhu were secured in the hold of the personnel carrier, Minh's order was carried out promptly as the vehicle was driven away. The executioner, Major NguyenVan Nhung, cut out their gallbladders while they were still alive and then shot them.

Years later, visibly distraught at recalling the murder, General Nguyen Khanh said, "Nhu was alive when they put the knife in to take out some of the organs ... the gallbladder. And in the Orient when you are a big soldier, big man—this thing is very important.... They do it against Nhu when Nhu was alive.... And Diem had this happen to him, and later on they kill him by pistol and rifle. This is murder. A real murder.... It's very savage ... *très savage!*"[66] General Khanh, who had been involved in the coup, maintained that the Americans did not expect that Diem and Nhu would be killed, but he also said that the Americans had no idea with whom they were dealing when they accepted

[64] Blair, *Lodge in Vietnam*, 13.

[65] Thanh and Duc. *Why the Vietnam War? President Ngo Dinh Diem and the US: His Overthrow and Assassination* ([San Jose, Calif.:] Tuan-Yen and Quan-Viet Mai-Nam Publishers, 2001), 391.

[66] Nguyen Khanh, interview by Geoffrey D. T. Shaw, June 16, 1994, United States Air Force Special Operations School, Hurlburt Field, Fla., transcript, 46–48, Vietnam Center and Archive at Texas Tech University, Lubbock, Tex., and the United States Air Force Special Operations School, Hurlburt Field, Fla.

General Minh[67] as the leader of the coup. Khanh indicated that had the Americans known about the intrigues in which Minh was involved, they would have known murder was likely and would not have allied themselves with him.[68]

According to Minh, the Americans not only expected the murder but wanted it. The plotting generals wanted the Ngo Dinh brothers dead, and "the Americans had wanted the same thing too."[69] Minh attempted to justify the murder by saying, "They had to be killed. Diem could not be allowed to live because he was too much respected among simple, gullible people in the countryside, especially the Catholics and the refugees."[70] According to Tran Van Huong, who had signed the Caravelle Manifesto and became president of South Vietnam in 1975, "The top generals who decided to murder Diem and his brother were scared to death. The generals knew very well that having no talent, no moral virtues, no political support whatsoever, they could not prevent a spectacular comeback of the president and Mr. Nhu if they were alive."[71] Huong's testimony is especially significant because he had been jailed by Diem's government for participating in the Caravellists; he was no friend of the Ngo Dinh brothers.

---

[67] General "Big" Duong Van Minh harboured a grudge against the Ngo Dinh brothers for three reasons. After he was caught pilfering money in 1954, when he led ARVN troops against the criminal organisation Binh Xuyen, Ngo Dinh Nhu forced him to return the stolen money to the government. Nhu did not have Minh charged or dismissed from the government, since he seemed to have calculated that Minh's loss of face was punishment enough. After the defeat of the Binh Xuyen, Minh was charged with capturing Ba Cut, the leader of Hoa Hao sect. After two failed attempts, Nhu stepped in, criticised Minh for not being clever or brave enough in his efforts, and drew up a plan that succeeded. Finally, Minh was caught contacting the Viet Cong via his own Viet Cong brother, Duong Van Nhut. Nhu removed him from active duty and made him the army's comptroller. Source, Paul Nghia, editor of the newsletter of the Saigon Arts, Culture, and Education Institute (SACEI), e-mail to author, March 5, 2014.

[68] Khanh, interview by Shaw, 48–50.

[69] Hoang Ngoc Thanh and Than Thi Nhan Duc, *Why the Vietnam War?*, 419.

[70] Quoted in Howard Jones, *Death of a Generation: How the Assassinations of Diem and JFK Prolonged the Vietnam War* (New York: Oxford University Press, 2003), 435.

[71] Quoted in ibid, 435–36.

CONCLUSION

Rufus Phillips, the CIA operative who had met with Diem but a few days before the coup, was deeply saddened and distraught when he entered Gia Long Palace on the day after the overthrow: "I wanted to sit down and cry. And I was so upset when I heard that he'd been killed.... That was a stupid decision and, God, we paid, they paid, everybody paid."[1] Vice President Johnson had argued against the coup plotting; by all accounts, he genuinely liked Diem and thought him a good leader of his country. He was livid over the murder of Diem and did little to hide his contempt for those who had a hand in it. In 1966, when he was president, he confided in a telephone conversation with Senator Eugene McCarthy the truth of what the Kennedy administration had done to President Diem back in 1963: "[W]e killed him. We all got together and got a goddamn bunch of thugs and we went in and assassinated him. Now, we've really had no political stability since then."[2] William Colby stated nearly the same thing to this writer in 1996, when he confided that after Diem had been killed, South Vietnam never got back on track. On November 5, 1963, Madame Nhu stated at a press conference: "Whoever has the Americans as allies does not need any enemies.... I can predict to you all that the story in Vietnam is only at its beginning."[3] Her words proved to be prescient.

The coup almost immediately destroyed any harmony there had been amongst the Vietnamese generals who had launched it; in killing Diem, they had also killed their own chances at governing as any sort of cohesive body. General Tran Van Don took an instant loathing to his fellow

---

[1] Howard Jones, *Death of a Generation: How the Assassinations of Diem and JFK Prolonged the Vietnam War* (New York: Oxford University Press, 2003), 436.

[2] "Johnson Conversation with Eugene McCarthy", February 1, 1966, tape WH6602.01, conversation 9602, from Presidential Recordings of Lyndon B. Johnson, Miller Center, University of Virginia, http://millercenter.org/presidentialrecordings/lbj-wh6602.01-9601.

[3] Monique Brinson Demery, *Finding the Dragon Lady: The Mystery of Vietnam's Madame Nhu* (New York: PublicAffairs, 2013), 214.

conspirator General Minh for ordering the murders. He knew full well, however, the petty and vicious motivations of Minh, and he later admitted that he knew the man would most likely order the murders of Diem and Nhu. He told historian George McTurnan Kahin that if Diem and Nhu had been left alive, in about three months' time the Americans would have "fired" him (Don) and the other generals, and would have returned Diem and Nhu to power, probably with a sigh of relief.[4] And for good reason: soon after the coup Don and Minh had their daggers drawn at each other, and each had a following as considerable as the other.[5] Their rancour spilled over into all of the ruling junta's appointments and dealings, thus leaving it weak and vulnerable. The situation invited an overthrow, which occurred in 1964.

Also in 1964, Frederick Nolting resigned from the State Department in protest over the coup in South Vietnam. Here is an excerpt from his brief February 25 letter to President Johnson:

> I have today sent to the Secretary of State a request to be granted retirement from the Foreign Service, in order to accept an offer in private business. That my decision has been influenced by my strong disapproval of certain actions which were taken last fall in relation to Vietnam, with predictable adverse consequences, I do not deny. Nor do I deny that I have been uncomfortable in my association with the Department of State since returning from Vietnam six months ago.[6]

One of the last public comments Nolting made about the coup illustrates the long-term strategic costs of President Kennedy's pursuit of short-term tactical gains:

> Now the young president was caught in a dilemma; there was no question about it. There were several things he could have done, but the worst alternative was what he opted to do. Even worse than the practical consequences of the coup were the moral effects. I will not go into the sequence of events here because I believe it is now clear that after the revolution things went from bad to worse, regardless of the number of troops that we put in and regardless of the fact that the cost went

[4] Hoang Ngoc Thanh and Than Thi Nhan Duc, *Why the Vietnam War? President Ngo Dinh Diem and the US: His Overthrow and Assassination* ([San Jose, Calif.:] Tuan-Yen and Quan-Viet Mai-Nam Publishers, 2001), 418.

[5] Jones, *Death of a Generation*, 436.

[6] Frederick Nolting, *From Trust to Tragedy: The Political Memoirs of Frederick Nolting, Kennedy's Ambassador to Diem's Vietnam* (New York: Praeger, 1988), 134–35.

up dramatically: 57,000 American lives, eight years of dissension in our country, huge increases in public debt, and the inflation that afflicted us throughout the 1970s. The actions of the Kennedy administration set the stage for all this.[7]

General Harkins and the former ambassador, in correspondence between the two of them after the coup, tended to be harder on Hilsman, Harriman, and the American press than on the president for what went wrong in South Vietnam. For example, on March 27, 1964, in a letter Harkins wrote to Nolting in sorrow over the latter's resignation, the general claimed that the removal of Diem had set the counterinsurgency back about ten months, and he apportioned a good deal of the blame to the press: "As you know, the press took the sails out of Diem starting last June and July to make him practically ineffective."[8] Nolting replied to Harkins on April 7, 1964, and informed him that he and his wife, Lindsay, had gone over the tragedy of what had happened to Diem and Nhu so many times that it was driving them crazy. He wrote that he wished he had been allowed to stay longer in Saigon; however, in the final analysis, he had come to believe that the destruction of Diem's government was inevitable given the players inside DOS: "Among other things, these people were feeding to the press the very line that you and I were instructed to counteract—i.e., the 'can't win with Diem' line.... This is a most unsavory story, but some day the facts will be publicly known. They already are known around Washington, but not admitted, and the press doesn't like to eat crow."[9] In a letter handwritten to Nolting in 1971, Harkins enumerated the people and actions that alienated President Diem, resulted in his murder, and destroyed effective U.S. policy in Southeast Asia. Harkins listed Harriman, Hilsman, Senator Mansfield, and the American press corps, in descending order, as those he believed were most responsible.[10]

[7] Frederick E. Nolting, "Kennedy, NATO, and Southeast Asia", in *Diplomacy, Administration, and Policy: The Ideas and Careers of Frederick E. Nolting, Jr., Frederick C. Mosher, and Paul T. David*, ed. Kenneth W. Thompson (Lanham, Md.: University Press of America; Charlottesville, Va.: Miller Center, University of Virginia, 1995), 25.

[8] Paul D. Harkins to Frederick Nolting, March 27, 1964, 1–2, Nolting Papers, box 12, Selected Correspondence—Harkins, Paul D.

[9] Frederick Nolting to Paul D. Harkins, April 7, 1964, 1, Nolting Papers, box 12, Selected Correspondence—Harkins, Paul D.

[10] Paul D. Harkins to Frederick Nolting, July 22, 1971, 1–2, Nolting Papers, box 12, Selected Correspondence—Harkins, Paul D.

When Nolting started to go public with his views on the coup, he maintained that the ultimate responsibility for America's actions lay with President John F. Kennedy and Secretary of State Dean Rusk. Rusk claimed that he had asked Nolting to stay on in Saigon and that Nolting was the one who insisted on going home. Rusk's implications were clear: Nolting had deserted his post during a crucial and tough period. Rusk's position, however, cannot be sustained by the facts, and the weight of evidence is on Nolting's side. First, as previously noted, the cable traffic and memoranda from the State Department's files show that Harriman and Hilsman wanted Nolting out of Saigon as rapidly as possible, even if this meant that there would be no ambassador at the post. Hilsman had been given the authority by President Kennedy to determine the departure date of Nolting, and he acted upon this authority in short order. Second, at the time that Nolting placed a request to stay on as ambassador, his request was denied. Nevertheless, Nolting found himself engaged in a battle to defend his honour, which lasted for many years.

Nolting went to work for Morgan Guaranty Trust in Paris as its vice president. He worked at this post in from 1964 until 1969, when he became assistant to the chairman in New York City. In 1973 he became a consultant to the company and was able to maintain this position until 1976. All along and simultaneous with his business career, he reestablished his academic contacts.

From 1971 to 1973 Nolting served at the University of Virginia as diplomat-in-residence. He went on to hold teaching and administrative posts as the Olsson Professor of Business Administration in the Darden School of Business from 1973 to 1976. He became professor in the Woodrow Wilson Department of Government and Foreign Affairs and helped found the Miller Center of Public Affairs, of which he became the first director. He retired from his full-time academic commitments at the University of Virginia in 1982 and began the painstaking process of compiling documents for his critical analysis of the Kennedy administration's blunders in Vietnam. This work produced his political memoirs, *From Trust to Tragedy*. Frederick Nolting died on December 14, 1989, at the age of seventy-eight, only a year after *From Trust to Tragedy* was published.

As for Ngo Dinh Diem, General Nguyen Khanh told this writer that most of the Buddhists he knew who were in full support of the coup—and even of the subsequent killing of the man—changed their minds in the intervening decades and came to regard his murder as a mistake of unparalleled proportion for South Vietnam.[11] Catholic Vietnamese, as noted in the beginning of this work, venerate the memory of President Diem. They affirm what Josef Cardinal Frings, the archbishop of Cologne, stated in 1965: "The greater part of the world has not given just recognition of this noble man."[12]

[11] Nguyen Khanh, interview by Geoffrey D. T. Shaw, June 16, 1994, United States Air Force Special Operations School, Hurlburt Field, Fla., transcript, Vietnam Center and Archive at Texas Tech University, Lubbock, Tex., and the United States Air Force Special Operations School, Hurlburt Field, Fla.

[12] *Sunday Examiner* (Hong Kong), July 30, 1965, 12.

SELECTED BIBLIOGRAPHY

Primary Sources

1. United States Government Documents

Congress, House, Committee on Armed Services. *United States–Vietnam Relations, 1945–1967: Study Prepared by the Department of Defense.* Washington, D.C.: United States Government Printing Office, 1971.

Gibbons, William C. *The U.S. Government and the Vietnam War: Executive and Legislative Roles and Relationships.* Pts. 1–2. Washington, D.C.: Government Printing Office, 1984. Reprint, Princeton: Princeton University Press, 1986.

Jackson, Henry M., ed. *The Secretary of State and the Ambassador: Jackson Subcommittee Papers on the Conduct of American Foreign Policy.* New York: Frederick A. Praeger, 1966.

The John F. Kennedy National Security Files: Asia and the Pacific National Security Files, 1961–1963. Frederick, Md.: University Publications of America. 1988. Microfilm.

The John F. Kennedy National Security Files: Vietnam National Security Files, 1961–1963. Frederick, Md.: University Publications of America. 1987. Microfilm.

Specter, Ronald. *The United States Army in Vietnam: Advice and Support; The Early Years.* Washington, D.C.: Center of Military History, United States Army, 1983.

Thompson, Robert G. K. "Draft Paper by the Head of the British Advisory Mission in Vietnam (Thompson)". National Security Council, Policy Directive No. ... [ellipsis in original], Delta Plan. [February 7, 1962?], Saigon. In United States Department of State, *Foreign Relations, 1961–1963*, vol. 2, document 51, pp. 102–9.

United States Department of the Army. *United States Armed Forces in Vietnam, 1954–1975.* Frederick, Md.: University Publications of America, Indochina Studies, 1983. Microfilm.

United States Department of State. *Confidential U.S. State Department Special Files: Southeast Asia, 1944–1958.* Frederick, Md.: University Publications of America. 1989. Microfilm.

United States Department of State. *Foreign Relations of the United States, 1958–1960*. Edited by John P. Glennon. Vol. 1, *Vietnam*. Washington, D.C.: United States Government Printing Office, 1986.

United States Department of State. *Foreign Relations of the United States, 1961–1963*. Edited by John P. Glennon. Vol. 1, *Vietnam, 1961*. Washington, D.C.: United States Government Printing Office, 1988.

United States Department of State. *Foreign Relations of the United States, 1961–1963*. Edited by John P. Glennon. Vol. 2, *Vietnam, 1962*. Washington, D.C.: United States Government Printing Office, 1990.

United States Department of State. *Foreign Relations of the United States, 1961–1963*. Edited by John P. Glennon. Vol. 3, *Vietnam, January–August 1963*. Washington, D.C.: United States Government Printing Office, 1991.

United States Department of State. *Foreign Relations of the United States, 1961–1963*. Edited by John P. Glennon. Vol. 4, *Vietnam, August–December 1963*. Washington, D.C: United States Government Printing Office, 1991.

United States Department of State. *Foreign Relations of the United States, 1952–1954*. Edited by John P. Glennon. Vol. 13, pt. 2, *Indochina*. Washington, D.C: United States Government Printing Office, 1982.

United States Department of State. *Foreign Relations of the United States, 1958–1960*. Edited by John P. Glennon. Vol. 16, *East Asia–Pacific Region; Cambodia; Laos*. Washington, D.C.: United States Government Printing Office, 1992.

United States Senate Committee on Foreign Relations. *Top-Secret Hearings by the U.S. Senate Committee on Foreign Relations: First Installment, 1959–1966*. Frederick, Md.: University Publications of America, 1981. Microfilm.

United States Senate, Select Committee to Study Governmental Operations. *Alleged Assassination Plots Involving Foreign Leaders*. Washington, D.C.: United States Government Printing Office, 1975.

2. Autobiographical Material

Ball, George W. *The Past Has Another Pattern: Memoirs*. New York: W.W. Norton, 1982.

Bowles, Chester. *Promises to Keep: My Years in Public Life, 1941–1969*. New York: Harper and Row, 1971.

Colby, William, and Peter Forbath. *Honorable Men: My Life in the CIA*. New York: Simon and Schuster, 1978.

Collins, J. Lawton. *Lightning Joe: An Autobiography*. Baton Rouge: Louisiana State University Press, 1979.

Galbraith, John Kenneth. *Ambassador's Journal: A Personal Account of the Kennedy Years*. Boston: Houghton Mifflin, 1969.

_____. *A Life in Our Times: Memoirs*. Boston: Houghton Mifflin, 1981.

Johnson, Lyndon Baines. *The Vantage Point: Perspectives of the Presidency, 1963–1969*. New York: Popular Library, 1971.

Lansdale, Edward Geary. *In the Midst of Wars: An American's Mission to Southeast Asia*. New York: Harper and Row, 1972.

Nolting, Frederick. *From Trust to Tragedy: The Political Memoirs of Frederick Nolting, Kennedy's Ambassador to Diem's Vietnam*. New York: Praeger, 1988.

Nguyen Cao Ky, *Twenty Years and Twenty Days*. New York: Stein and Day, 1976.

Taylor, Maxwell D. *The Uncertain Trumpet*. New York: Harper and Brothers, 1960.

Tran Van Don. *Our Endless War: Inside Vietnam*. San Rafael, Calif.: Presidio Press, 1978.

3. Biographical Material

Abramson, Rudy. *Spanning the Century: The Life of W. Averell Harriman, 1891–1986*. New York: William Morrow, 1992.

Anderson, David L., ed. *Shadow on the White House: Presidents and the Vietnam War, 1945–1975*. Lawrence: University Press of Kansas, 1993.

Anderson, Joseph J. *Trapped by Success: The Eisenhower Administration and Vietnam, 1953–1961*. New York: Columbia University Press, 1991.

Blair, Anne E. *Lodge in Vietnam: A Patriot Abroad*. New Haven, Conn.: Yale University Press, 1995.

Bouscaren, Anthony Trawick. *The Last of the Mandarins: Diem of Vietnam*. Pittsburgh: Duquesne University Press, 1965.

Colvin, John. *Giap: Volcano under the Snow*. New York: Soho Press, 1996.

Currey, Cecil B. *Edward Lansdale: The Unquiet American*. Boston: Houghton Mifflin, 1989.

Douglas, William O. *North from Malaya*. New York: Doubleday, 1953.

Isaacson, Walter, and Evan Thomas. *The Wise Men: Six Friends and the World They Made; Acheson, Bohlen, Harriman, Kennan, Lovett, McCloy*. New York: Simon and Schuster, 1986.

Macdonald, Peter. *Giap: The Victor in Vietnam*. New York: W. W. Norton, 1993.

Nolting, Frederick E. "The Papers of Frederick (Fritz) Ernest Nolting Jr.: Personal Papers and Diaries". Accession 12804. Special Collections, Alderman Library, University of Virginia, Charlottesville.

Salinger, Pierre. *With Kennedy*. Garden City, N.Y.: Doubleday, 1966.

Schlesinger, Arthur M., Jr. *A Thousand Days: John F. Kennedy in the White House*. Boston: Houghton Mifflin, 1965.

_____. *Robert Kennedy and His Times.* Vol. 2. Boston: Houghton Mifflin, 1978.

Schoenbaum, Thomas J. *Waging Peace and War: Dean Rusk in the Truman, Kennedy, and Johnson Years.* New York: Simon and Schuster, 1988.

Smith, Sally Bedell. *Reflected Glory: The Life of Pamela Churchill Harriman.* New York: Simon and Schuster, 1997.

Stanfield, James Ronald. *John Kenneth Galbraith.* New York: St. Martin's Press, 1996.

4. Field Experience and Expertise

Andrews, William R. *The Village War: Vietnamese Communist Revolutionary Activities in Dinh Tuong Province, 1960–1964.* Columbia: University of Missouri Press, 1973.

Burchett, Wilfred. *The Furtive War: The United States in Vietnam and Laos.* New York: International Publishers, 1963.

_____. *Grasshoppers and Elephants: Why Viet Nam Fell.* New York: Urizen Books, 1977.

_____. *The Second Indochina War: Cambodia and Laos.* New York: International Publishers, 1970.

_____. *Vietnam: Inside Story of the Guerrilla War.* New York: International Publishers, 1965.

Colby, William E. *Lost Victory: A Firsthand Account of America's Sixteen-Year Involvement in Vietnam.* With James McCargar. Chicago: Contemporary Books, 1989.

Dallin, Alexander, and George W. Breslauer. *Political Terror in Communist Systems.* Stanford, Calif.: Stanford University Press, 1970.

Dai, Ho Son and Tran Phan Chan. *Lich Su Saigon-Cho Lon-Gia Dinh Khan Chien, 1945–1975.* Ho Chi Minh City: Ho Chi Minh City Publishing House, 1994.

Davison, W. P. *Some Observations on Viet Cong Operations in the Villages.* Santa Monica, Calif.: RAND Corporation, 1967.

Fall, Bernard B. *Last Reflections on a War: Bernard B. Fall's Last Comments on Vietnam.* Garden City, N.Y.: Doubleday, 1967.

Gheddo, Piero. *The Cross and the Bo-Tree: Catholics and Buddhists in Vietnam.* Translated by Charles Underhill Quinn. New York: Sheed and Ward, 1970.

Giap, Vo Nguyen. *Banner of People's War, the Party's Military Line.* New York: Frederick A. Praeger, 1970.

_____. *"Big Victory, Great Task": North Viet-Nam's Minister of Defense Assesses the Course of the War.* New York: Frederick A. Praeger, 1968.

_____. *People's War, People's Army: The Viet Cong Insurrection Manual for Under-developed Countries.* New York: Frederick A. Praeger, 1962.

_____. *Unforgettable Days.* Hanoi: Foreign Languages Publishing House, 1975.

Government of the Republic of Vietnam. *Violations of the Geneva Agreements by the Viet-Minh Communists: From July 1959 to June 1960.* Second White Book. Saigon: Republic of Vietnam Printing Office, 1960.

Gravel, Mike, ed. *The Pentagon Papers: The Defense Department History of United States Decisionmaking on Vietnam.* Vols. 1–3. Boston: Beacon Press, 1971.

Hammer, Ellen J. *A Death in November: America in Vietnam, 1963.* New York: E. P. Dutton, 1987.

_____. *The Struggle for Indochina.* Stanford, Calif.: Stanford University Press, 1954.

_____. *Vietnam: Yesterday and Today.* New York: Holt, Rinehart and Winston, 1966.

Harriman, W. Averell. *America and Russia in a Changing World: A Half Century of Personal Observation.* Garden City, N.Y.: Doubleday, 1971.

Hosmer, Stephen T. *Viet Cong Repression and Its Implications for the Future.* Report Prepared for the Advanced Research Projects Agency: R-475/1-ARPA. Santa Monica, Calif.: RAND Corporation, 1970.

Langer, Paul F., and Joseph J. Zasloff. *North Vietnam and the Pathet Lao: Partners in the Struggle for Laos.* Cambridge, Mass.: Harvard University Press, 1970.

Maneli, Mieczyslaw. *War of the Vanquished.* Translated by Maria de Görgey. New York: Harper and Row, 1971.

Mao Tse Tung. *Statement Opposing Aggression against Southern Viet Nam and Slaughter of Its People by the U.S.–Ngo Dinh Diem Clique.* Peking: Foreign Languages Press, 1963.

Nolting, Frederick E. "Kennedy, NATO, and Southeast Asia". In *Diplomacy, Administration, and Policy: The Ideas and Careers of Frederick E. Nolting, Jr., Frederick C. Mosher, and Paul T. David*, edited by Kenneth W. Thompson, 17–35. Lanham, Md.: University Press of America; Charlottesville, Va.: Miller Center, University of Virginia, 1995.

Pike, Douglas. *Brief History of the Government of Vietnam (GVN) during the Vietnam War.* Berkeley, Calif.: Indochina Studies, 1991.

_____. *History of Vietnamese Communism, 1925–1976.* Stanford, Calif.: Hoover Institution Press, 1978.

_____. *Viet Cong: The Organization and Techniques of the National Liberation Front of South Vietnam.* Cambridge, Mass.: MIT Press, 1966.

_____. *War, Peace, and the Viet Cong.* Cambridge, Mass.: MIT Press, 1969.

RAND Corporation and Military Assistance Command, Vietnam J-2. "Studies of the National Liberation Front of South Vietnam". DT-86, DT-99, DT-84, DT-88. Saigon, n.d.

Scheer, Robert. "The Genesis of United States Support for Ngo Dinh Diem". In *Vietnam: History, Documents, and Opinions on a Major World Crisis*, edited by Marvin E. Gettlemen, 147–252. Greenwich, Conn.: Fawcett Publications, 1965.

Thanh, Hoang Ngoc, and Than Thi Nhan Duc. *Why the Vietnam War? President Ngo Dinh Diem and the US: His Overthrow and Assassination.* [San Jose, Calif.:] Tuan-Yen and Quan-Viet Mai-Nam, 2001.

Thompson, Robert Grainger. *Defeating Communist Insurgency: Experiences from Malaya and Vietnam.* London: Chatto and Windus, 1966.

_____. *No Exit from Vietnam.* Updated ed. New York: David McKay, 1970.

_____. *Peace Is Not at Hand.* London: Chatto and Windus, 1974.

Thornton, Thomas Perry. "Terror as a Weapon of Political Agitation". In *Internal War: Problems and Approaches*, edited by Harry Eckstein. New York: Free Press, 1968.

Tran Van Dinh. "Why Every American Should Read Kim Van Kieu". In *We the Vietnamese: Voices from Vietnam*, edited by François Sully, 236–37. New York: Praeger, 1971.

5. Oral Histories

Carver, George A., Jr. "An Unheeded Firebell: The November 1960 Coup Attempt". In *Kennedy in Vietnam*, by William J. Rust and the editors of U.S. News Books. New York: Scribner, 1985.

Colby, William E. Interview by Michael Charlton in "The New Frontiersmen Hold the Line", program 4 of *Many Reasons Why: The American Involvement in Vietnam*. Transcript. British Broadcasting Corporation, 1977.

_____. Interview by Ted Gittinger, June 2, 1981, Washington, D.C. Interview 1. Transcript. Lyndon Baines Johnson Presidential Library Oral History Collection, University of Texas at Austin.

_____. Interview by Ted Gittinger, March 1, 1982, Washington, D.C. Interview 2. Transcript. Lyndon Baines Johnson Presidential Library Oral History Collection, University of Texas at Austin.

_____. Speech to the Miller Center at the University of Virginia, in *Diplomacy, Administration and Policy: The Ideas and Careers of Frederick E. Nolting, Jr., Frederick C. Mosher, and Paul T. David*, edited by Kenneth W. Thompson. Lanham, Md.: University Press of America, 1995.

Harriman, W. Averell. Interview by Michael V. Forrestal, April 13, 1964, Hobe Sound, Fla. Interview 1. Transcript. John F. Kennedy Oral History Collection, John F. Kennedy Presidential Library, Boston.

_____. Interview by Arthur M. Schlesinger Jr., January 17, 1965, Washington, D.C. Interview 2. Transcript. John F. Kennedy Oral History Collection, John F. Kennedy Presidential Library, Boston.

Hilsman, Roger. Interview by Dennis J. O'Brien, August 14, 1970, Hamburg Cove, Lyme, Conn. Transcript. John F. Kennedy Oral History Collection, John F. Kennedy Presidential Library, Boston.

Johnson, Lyndon B., "Johnson Conversation with Eugene McCarthy", February 1, 1966, tape WH6602.01, conversation 9601. Presidential Recordings of Lyndon B. Johnson. Charlottesville, Va: Miller Center, University of Virginia. http://millercenter.org/presidentialrecordings /lbj-wh6602.01-9601.

Kennedy, John F. "The President's News Conference of March 23, 1961". In *Public Papers of the Presidents of the United States: John F. Kennedy.* Vol. 1, *1961*, document 92, pp. 213–20. Washington, D.C.: United States Government Printing Office, 1962.

_____. "The President's News Conference of November 29, 1961". In *Public Papers of the Presidents of the United States: John F. Kennedy.* Vol. 1, *1961*, document 488. Washington, D.C.: United States Government Printing Office, 1962.

Kennedy, Robert F. Interview by John Bartlow Martin, April 30, 1964, n.p. Transcript. John F. Kennedy Oral History Collection, John F. Kennedy Presidential Library, Boston.

Khanh, Nguyen. Interview by Geoffrey D. T. Shaw, June 16, 1994, United States Air Force Special Operations School, Hurlburt Field, Fla. Transcript. Vietnam Center and Archive at Texas Tech University, Lubbock, Tex., and the United States Air Force Special Operations School, Hurlburt Field, Fla.

Miller, Anne. "And One for the People: The Life Story of President Ngo Dinh Diem". Unpublished manuscript, July 30, 1965. Microfilm, Indochina Studies Archive at the University of California at Berkeley.

Nolting, Frederick E. Interview by Joseph E. O'Connor, May 14, 1966, Paris. Interview 1. Transcript. John F. Kennedy Oral History Collection, John F. Kennedy Presidential Library, Boston.

_____. Interview by Dennis O'Brien, May 6, 1970, New York. Interview 2. Transcript. John F. Kennedy Oral History Collection, John F. Kennedy Presidential Library, Boston.

_____. Interview by Dennis O'Brien, May 7, 1970, Washington, D.C. Interview 3. Transcript. John F. Kennedy Oral History Collection, John F. Kennedy Presidential Library, Boston.

_____. "The Origin and Development of United States Commitment in Vietnam". Lecture, April 2, 1968. Transcript. John F. Kennedy Oral History Collection, John F. Kennedy Presidential Library, Boston.

Nolting, Lindsay. Interviews by Geoffrey D. T. Shaw, January 29, 1998; February 3, 1999; February 4, 1999.

Pham Kim Vinh. *The Politics of Selfishness: Vietnam the Past as Prologue*. San Diego: n.p., 1977. Vietnam Center and Archive, Texas Tech University, Lubbock, Tex.

Rusk, Dean. Interview by Paige E. Mulhollan, July 28, 1969, n.p. Interview 1. Transcript. Lyndon Baines Johnson Presidential Library Oral History Collection, University of Texas at Austin.

———. Interview by Paige E. Mulhollan, September 26, 1969, n.p. Interview 2. Transcript. Lyndon Baines Johnson Presidential Library Oral History Collection, University of Texas at Austin.

———. Interview by Paige E. Mulhollan, January 2, 1970, n.p. Interview 3. Transcript. Lyndon Baines Johnson Presidential Library Oral History Collection, University of Texas at Austin.

———. Interview by Paige E. Mulhollan, March 8, 1970, n.p. Interview 4. Transcript. Lyndon Baines Johnson Presidential Library Oral History Collection, University of Texas at Austin.

Streeb, Kent M. "A Fragmented Effort: Ngo Dinh Diem, the United States Military and State Department and the Strategic Hamlet Program of 1961–1963". Paper, George Mason University, December 10, 1994. Vietnam Center and Archive, Texas Tech University, Lubbock, Tex.

Weller, Jac. "Fire and Movement: Bargain-Basement Warfare in the Far East". Vietnam Center and Archive, Texas Tech University, Lubbock, Tex.

6. *Periodicals*

Associated Press. "Monk in Saigon Dies as U.N. Team Tours". *New York Times*. October 27, 1963, 1, 24.

———. "Monk Suicide by Fire in Anti-Diem Protest", *New York Times*, June 11, 1963, 6.

———. "Newsmen Beaten by Saigon Police: 6th Buddhist Burns Himself to Death—Crisis Grows". *New York Times*, October 6, 1963, 20.

———. "Priest Forecasts Red Gains in Asia: A Roman Catholic Missionary Predicted Last Week That Laos, Cambodia and Thailand Would Be Communist-Dominated within Ten to Twenty Years". *New York Times*, May 6, 1962, 27.

———. "Rebels Capture Laotian Center: Pro-Communist Forces Have Captured Nam Tha". *New York Times*, May 7, 1962, 1, 13.

_____. "Red Chinese Raid in Laos Affirmed: U.S. Aides Back Charges of Peiping Role in Drive That Captured Border Town". *New York Times*, May 6, 1962, 1, 28.

_____. "Reds Widen Gains: Push to Thai Border Seen as Peril to Capitals". *New York Times*, May 12, 1962, 1, 2.

_____. "Rightists in Laos Repel Red Drive: Call Leftists' Losses Heavy at Town in South as Fight among Factions Spreads". *New York Times*, June 14, 1963, 1, 10.

_____. "Troops and Tanks Quell Buddhist Riots in Saigon". *New York Times*, June 17, 1963, 1, 4.

Bigart, Homer. "Delays in Saigon Harass Newsmen: Anti-Press Campaign Seen—Flights Are Curbed". *New York Times*, May 7, 1962, 6.

_____. "McNamara Asks Vietnam Chief to Alter Tactics in Struggle: U.S. Is Showing Impatience over Lag on Mekong Delta Pacification Plan—American Pilot Wounded". *New York Times*, May 11, 1962, 7.

_____. "McNamara Backs Role in Vietnam: Says in Saigon U.S. Plans to Send No Combat Men". *New York Times*, May 10, 1962, 7.

_____. "McNamara Terms Saigon Aid Ample: Says It Is at Peak and Will Level Off—Diem's Fight against Reds Hailed". *New York Times*, May 12, 1962, 1, 2.

Billings-Yun, Melanie. "Ike and Vietnam". *History Today* 38 (November 1988): 13–19.

Browne, Malcolm W. "U.S. Intelligence Role Is Diverse in South Vietnam". *New York Times*, October 8, 1963, 21.

Feron, James. "Britain Assails Soviet Account of How Laos Peace Broke Down". *New York Times*, June 22, 1963, 6.

Frankel, Max. "U.S. Shifting Laos Policy, Writes Off Routed Army; Plans Asian Fleet Moves: Accord Is Sought, Kennedy Acts to Force Rightists to Join a 3-Faction Regime". *New York Times*, May 12, 1963, 1, 2.

_____. "U.S. Warns South Vietnam on Demands of Buddhists: Diem Is Told He Faces Censure If He Fails to Satisfy Religious Grievances, Many of Which Are Called Just". *New York Times*, June 14, 1963, 1, 10.

_____. "Vietnam's 'Untidy' War: Washington Is Unhappy with Saigon, But Thinks That Support Is Necessary". *New York Times*, July 3, 1963, 8.

_____. "Violence in Saigon Renews U.S. Debate on Vietnam Policy". *New York Times*, October 7, 1963, 1, 2.

Halberstam, David. "Americans Vexed by Inability to Act in Vietnam Dispute". *New York Times*, June 10, 1963, 1, 6.

_____. "Saigon Buddhists Clash with Police". *New York Times*, June 16, 1963, 1, 18.

———. "Diem Asks Peace in Religion Crisis: But Buddhists Still Protest—Dispute Seems Worse". *New York Times*, June 12, 1963, 3.

———. "Discontent Rises in Vietnam Crisis: Regime Losing Ground over Treatment of Buddhists". *New York Times*, June 22, 1963, 6.

———. "Harkins Praises Vietnam Troops: Defends Soldiers' Courage against U.S. Criticism". *New York Times*, January 11, 1963, 3.

———. "Lodge Deplores Mrs. Nhu's View of U.S. Officers: Calls Disparagement Cruel and Shocking—She Denies Slur Attributed to Her". *New York Times*, September 27, 1963, 1, 2.

———. "Motley U.S. Force Blocks Vietcong: Helps Trap 32 in Flight to Raise Costs of Defeat". *New York Times*, January 5, 1963, 2.

———. "Saigon Arrests 800 Teen-Agers Staging Protest". *New York Times*, September 8, 1963, 1, 3.

———. "Saigon Forces Seize 1,000 More in School Battle". *New York Times*, September 10, 1963, 1, 3.

———. "Some of U.S. Aid to Saigon Halted; Policy Reviewed; Washington Feels Vietnam May Be Easier to Guide if Funds Run Out $10 Million Reduction Ban on Commercial Exports Followed August Attacks on Buddhist Pagodas". *New York Times*, October 8, 1963, 1, 18.

———. "Some U.S. Officials in Saigon Dubious about Diem Regime". *New York Times*, July 3, 1963, 1, 8.

———. "Two U.S. Officials Arrive in Saigon: McNamara and Taylor Will Study War with Reds". *New York Times*, September 25, 1963, 3.

———. "U.N. Mission Sees Jailed Buddhists: It Questions 6 in Inquiry into Saigon's Policies". *New York Times*, October 30, 1963, 11.

———. "U.N. Team, in Vietnam, Pledges Impartiality in Buddhist Inquiry". *New York Times*, October 24, 1963, 8.

———. "U.N. Team Visits Pagoda in Saigon: Only 2 Monks at Protest Center—Kennedy Sends Cool Message to Diem". *New York Times*, October 26, 1963, 1, 8.

———. "U.S. Avoids Part in Saigon Dispute: Tells Its Troops Not to Help Stop Buddhist Protests". *New York Times*, June 11, 1963, 3.

———. "U.S. Starts Study in South Vietnam: McNamara Aide Says War on Reds Is Going Better". *New York Times*, September 26, 1963, 13.

———. "Vietcong Downs Five U.S. Copters, Hits Nine Others: Defeat Worst since Build-Up Began—Three Americans Killed in Vietnam". *New York Times*, January 3, 1963, 1 2.

———. "Vietnam Adopts New War Method: Communist Blunder Shows Effectiveness of Patrols". *New York Times*, January 9, 1963, 3.

———. "Vietnam Defeat Shocks U.S. Aides: Saigon's Rejection of Advice Blamed for Setback". *New York Times*, January 7, 1963, 2.

_____. "Vietnamese Reds Win Major Clash: Inflict 100 Casualties in Fighting Larger Force". *New York Times*, January 4, 1963, 2.

_____. "Vietnam Says U.S. Aided '60 Revolt: 19 Go on Trial for Uprising—Charges Considered Warning to Americans". *New York Times*, July 6, 1963, 1, 8.

Kenworthy, E. W. "President Scores Pro-Reds in Laos for Truce Breach". *New York Times*, May 10, 1962, 1, 5.

_____. "U.S. Asks Inquiry into Laos Attack as Truce Breach". *New York Times*, May 8, 1962, 1, 17.

King, Seth S. "U.N.'s Itinerary in Use in Saigon: Guidance by Regime Ends—Buddhist Is Suicide". *New York Times*, October 28, 1963, 12.

_____. "Vietnam Presses Hamlet Program: Shelters against Vietcong Vary in Effectiveness". *New York Times*, October 26, 1963, 8.

Luce, Clare Boothe. "The Lady Is for Burning: The Seven Deadly Sins of Madame Nhu". *National Review*, November 5, 1963, 395–99.

_____. "The Lady Is for Burning: The Seven Deadly Sins of Madame Nhu". *New York Times* (advertisement), October 30, 1963, 40.

New York Times. "Diem Tells Thant Asia Is Imperiled: Charges Foreigners Tried to Control Buddhists". Special ed., *New York Times*, September 25, 1963, 3.

_____. "Fact-Finder in Vietnam: Abdul Rahman Pazhwak". Special ed., *New York Times*, October 28, 1963, 12.

_____. "Laos, Long Ruled by Outsiders, Now Torn by Internal Conflict: Neutralists, Communists and Pro-Reds Have Struggled for Power since the End of French Rule in 1949". *New York Times*, May 12, 1962, 2.

_____. "Mrs. Nhu's Father Says Aid Cut Could Influence Saigon's Policy". Special ed., *New York Times*, October 9, 1963, 10.

_____. "Nhu Asserts Saigon's Struggle Forced Him into Political Role". Special ed., *New York Times*, September 25, 1963, 3.

_____. "Texts of Letters by Thant and Diem". Special ed., *New York Times*, September 25, 1963, 3.

_____. "U.N. Team Visits Camp in Vietnam: Interviews Students Seized in Buddhist Disorders". Special ed., *New York Times*, October 29, 1963, 7.

_____. "Vietcong Battered By Vietnam Troops". Special ed., *New York Times*, September 10, 1963, 1, 2.

_____. "Visa to Mrs. Nhu Is under Inquiry: Diplomatic Nature of Permit Questioned by Rep. Hayes". Special ed., *New York Times*, October 9, 1963, 10.

_____. "What's Wrong in Vietnam?" Special ed., *New York Times*, January 15, 1963, 6.

Osborne, John. "The Tough Miracle Man of Vietnam: Diem, America's Newly Arrived Visitor, Has Roused His Country and Routed the Reds". *Life*, May 13, 1957.

Reuters. "Laotian Reds Pound 'Rightists' Garrison". *New York Times*, June 21, 1963, 15.

Shaplen, Robert. "A Reporter in Vietnam: Diem". *New Yorker*, September 22, 1962.

Smith, Hedrick. "Lodge to Return from Saigon Soon for Policy Talks: Envoy to Brief Kennedy on the Political and Military Situation in Vietnam;—Air of Crisis Denied—Officials in U.S. Insist Visit Does Not Herald Major Changes in Planning". *New York Times*, October 24, 1963, 1, 8.

_____. "Rusk Condemns Attack in Saigon on U.S. Newsmen: Lodge Protests the Beating of 3 Who Watched another Suicide by a Buddhist; Mansfield Is Shocked; Senator Calls for Apology and Compensation for Victims of Assault". *New York Times*, October 6, 1963, 1, 21.

_____. "U.S. Says Hanoi Renews Laos Aid: Charges North Vietnamese Give Arms to Pro-Reds in Breach of Geneva Pact". *New York Times*, October 30, 1963, 1, 10.

Sunday Examiner (Hong Kong). "Cardinal Frings Raises Funds for Catholics in S. Vietnam: Calls Late President Diem a 'Noble Man'". Catholic News of the Week, July 30, 1965.

Teltsch, Kathleen. "Soviet, in U.N., Blocks Bid from Vietnam for Inquiry". *New York Times*, October 8, 1963, 1, 19.

Time. "South Viet-Nam: The Beleaguered Man". April 4, 1955.

Topping, Seymour. "Moscow Is Urged by U.S. and Britain to Curb Laos Reds". *New York Times*, May 9, 1962, 1, 2.

United Press. "Mrs. Nhu's Sister Calls Her 'Blind'". *New York Times*, October 26, 1963, 8.

_____. "New Red Advance in Laos Menaces Neutralist Base: Kong Le Says Pathet Lao Forces Are Only 5 Miles from His Headquarters". *New York Times*, June 10, 1963, 1, 7.

Wicker, Tom. "Kennedy Says Red Threat Bars Saigon Aid Cut Now". *New York Times*, September 10, 1963, 1, 3.

Secondary Sources

Ambrose, Stephen E. *Rise to Globalism: American Foreign Policy, 1938–1976*. Rev. ed. New York: Penguin Books, 1976.

Anderson, David L. "J. Lawton Collins, John Foster Dulles, and the Eisenhower Administration's 'Point of No Return' in Vietnam". *Diplomatic History*, no. 12 (Spring 1988): 127–47.

Anderson, Patrick. *The President's Men: White House Assistants of Franklin D. Roosevelt, Harry S. Truman, Dwight D. Eisenhower, John F. Kennedy and Lyndon B. Johnson.* Garden City, N.Y.: Anchor Books / Doubleday, 1969.

Arnold, James R. *The First Domino: Eisenhower, the Military, and America's Intervention in Vietnam.* New York: Morrow, 1991.

Asprey, Robert B. *War in the Shadows: The Guerrilla in History.* New York: William Morrow, 1994.

Ball, Moya Ann. *Vietnam-on-the-Potomac.* New York: Praeger, 1992.

Barber, Noel. *The War of the Running Dogs: Malaya, 1948–1960.* London: Arrow Books, 1989.

Bator, Victor M. *Vietnam: A Diplomatic Tragedy.* Dobbs Ferry, N.Y.: Oceana Publications, 1965.

Bell, J. Boyer. *The Myth of the Guerrilla: Revolutionary Theory and Malpractice.* New York: Alfred A. Knopf, 1971.

Bell, J. Boyer. *A Time of Terror: How Democratic Societies Respond to Revolutionary Violence.* New York: Basic Books, 1978.

Berman, Larry. *Planning a Tragedy: The Americanization of the War in Vietnam.* New York: W. W. Norton, 1982.

Berman, Paul. *Revolutionary Organization: Institution-Building within the People's Liberation Armed Forces.* Lexington, Mass.: Lexington Books / D. C. Heath, 1974.

Blaufarb, Douglas A. *The Counter-Insurgency Era: U.S. Doctrine and Performance, 1950 to the Present.* New York: Macmillan, 1977.

Bloodworth, Dennis. *An Eye for the Dragon: Southeast Asia Observed, 1954–1970.* New York: Farrar, Straus, and Giroux, 1970.

Blum, Robert. *Drawing the Line: The Origin of the American Containment Policy in East Asia.* New York: Norton, 1982.

Bodard, Lucien. *The Quicksand War: Prelude to Vietnam.* Translated and with an introduction by Patrick O'Brian. Boston: Little, Brown, 1967.

Boettiger, John R. *Vietnam and American Foreign Policy.* Boston: D. C. Heath, 1968.

Bouscaren, Anthony T., ed. *All Quiet on the Eastern Front: The Death of South Vietnam.* Old Greenwich, Conn.: Devin-Adair, 1977.

Brandon, Henry. *Anatomy of Error: The Inside Story of the Asian War on the Potomac, 1954–1969.* Boston: Gambit, 1969.

Briggs, Phillip J. *Making American Foreign Policy: President-Congress Relations from the Second World War to Vietnam.* Lanham, Md.: University Press of America, 1991.

Brocheux, Pierre. *The Mekong Delta: Ecology, Economy, and Revolution, 1860–1960.* Madison: Center for Southeast Asian Studies, University of Wisconsin, 1995.

Bromley, Dorothy D. *Washington and Vietnam: An Examination of the Moral and Political Issues*. Dobbs Ferry, N.Y.: Oceana Publications, 1966.

Brown, Weldon A. *Prelude to Disaster: The American Role in Vietnam, 1940–1963*. Port Washington, N.Y.: Kennikat Press, 1975.

Browne, Malcom W. *The New Face of War*. New York: Bobbs-Merrill, 1965.

Burke, John P., and Fred I. Greenstein. *How Presidents Test Reality: Decisions on Vietnam, 1954 and 1965*. New York: Russell Sage Foundation, 1989.

Buzzanco, Robert. "Prologue to Tragedy: U.S. Military Opposition to Intervention in Vietnam, 1950–1954". *Diplomatic History* 17 (Spring 1993): 201–22.

Cable, Larry E. *Conflict of Myths: The Development of American Counterinsurgency Doctrine and the Vietnam War*. New York: New York University Press, 1986.

Callison, Charles S. *Land-to-the-Tiller in the Mekong Delta: Economic, Social and Political Effects of Land Reform in Four Villages of South Vietnam*. Lanham, Md.: University Press of America, 1983.

Cao Van Vien and Dong Van Khuyen. *Reflections on the Vietnam War*. Indochina Monographs. Washington, D.C.: United States Army Center of Military History, 1980.

Catton, Philip E. *Diem's Final Failure: Prelude to America's War in Vietnam*. Lawrence: University Press of Kansas, 2002.

Charlton, Michael, and Anthony Moncrieff. *Many Reasons Why: The American Involvement in Vietnam*. New York: Hill and Wang, 1978.

Clutterbuck, Richard L. *Terrorism and Guerrilla Warfare*. New York: Routledge, 1990.

Cochran, David. "I. F. Stone and the New Left: Protesting U.S. Policy in Vietnam". *Historian* 53 (Spring 1991): 505–20.

Combs, Arthur. "The Path Not Taken: The British Alternative to U.S. Policy in Vietnam, 1954–1956". *Diplomatic History* 19 (Winter 1995): 33–57.

Condit, Kenneth W. *The History of the Joint Chiefs of Staff: The Joint Chiefs of Staff and National Policy*. Vols. 1–4. Wilmington: Michael Glazier, 1979.

Cooper, Chester L. *The Lost Crusade: America in Vietnam*. New York: Dodd, Mead, 1970.

Courtois, Stéphane, et al. *The Black Book of Communism: Crimes, Terror, Repression*. Translated by Mark Kramer and Jonathan Murphy. Cambridge, Mass.: Harvard University Press, 1999.

Critchfield, Richard. *The Long Charade: Political Subversion in the Vietnam War*. New York: Harcourt, Brace and World, 1968.

Dacy, Douglas C. *Foreign Aid, War, and Economic Development: South Vietnam, 1955–1975*. New York: Cambridge University Press, 1986.

Dallin, Alexander, and George W. Breslauer. *Political Terror in Communist Systems*. Stanford, Calif.: Stanford University Press, 1970.

Dalloz, Jacques. *The War in Indo-China, 1945–54*. Dublin: Gill and Macmillan, 1990.

Davidson, Phillip B. *Vietnam at War: The History, 1946–1975*. Novato, Calif.: Presidio Press, 1988.

DeConde, Alexander. *The American Secretary of State: An Interpretation*. New York: Praeger, 1962.

Deitchman, Seymour J. *Limited War and American Defense Policy*. Cambridge: MIT Press, 1964.

Demery, Monique Brinson. *Finding the Dragon Lady: The Mystery of Vietnam's Madame Nhu*. New York: Public-Affairs, 2013.

Destler, I. M., Leslie H. Gelb, and Anthony Lake. *Our Own Worst Enemy: The Unmaking of American Foreign Policy*. Rev. ed. New York: Touchstone Books / Simon and Schuster, 1984.

Dietz, Terry. *Republicans and Vietnam, 1961–1968*. Westport, Conn.: Greenwood, 1986.

Dommen, Arthur J. *Laos: Keystone of Indochina*. Boulder, Colo.: Westview Press, 1985.

Dowdy, Homer E. *The Bamboo Cross*. Harrisburg, Pa.: Christian Publications, 1964.

Drachman, Edward R. *United States Policy toward Vietnam, 1940–1945*. Farleigh Dickinson, 1970.

Duiker, William J. *The Communist Road to Power in Vietnam*. 2nd ed. Boulder, Colo.: Westview Press, 1996.

———. *Sacred War: Nationalism and Revolution in a Divided Vietnam*. New York: McGraw-Hill, 1995.

Duncanson, Dennis J. *Government and Revolution in Vietnam*. London: Oxford University Press / Royal Institute of International Affairs, 1968.

Emerson, Gloria A. *Winners and Losers: Battles, Retreats, Gains, Losses and Ruins from a Long War*. 2nd ed. New York: Random House, 1976.

Fair, Charles. *From the Jaws of Victory*. New York: W. W. Norton, 1972.

Fall, Bernard B. *Anatomy of a Crisis: The Laotian Crisis of 1960–1961*. New York: Doubleday, 1969.

———. *Last Reflections on a War: Bernard B. Fall's Last Comments on Viet-Nam*. Garden City, N.Y.: Doubleday, 1967.

———. *The Two Viet-Nams: A Political and Military Analysis*. New York: Praeger, 1963.

———. *Vietnam Witness, 1953–66*. London: Pall Mall Press, 1966.

Ferrell, Robert H. *American Diplomacy: A History*. 3rd ed. New York: W. W. Norton, 1975.

Field, Michael. *The Prevailing Wind: Witness in Indo-China*. London: Methuen, 1965.

Fifield, Russell H. *Americans in Southeast Asia: The Roots of Commitment*. New York: Thomas Crowell, 1973.

Fishel, Wesley, ed. *Vietnam: Anatomy of a Conflict*. Itasca, Ill.: F. E. Peacock, 1968.

Fitzgerald, Frances. *Fire in the Lake: The Vietnamese and the Americans in Vietnam*. New York: Vintage Books, 1989.

Gabriel, Richard A., and Paul L. Savage, *Crisis in Command: Mismanagement in the Army*. New York: Hill and Wang, 1978.

Galula, David. *Counter-Insurgency Warfare: Theory and Practice*. New York: Frederick A. Praeger, 1964.

Gates, John M. "People's War in Vietnam". *Journal of Military History* 54 (July 1990): 325–44.

Gelb, Leslie H. *The Irony of Vietnam: The System Worked*. Washington, D.C.: Brookings Institution, 1979.

Gettleman, Marvin E., ed. *Vietnam: History, Documents and Opinions on a Major World Crisis*. New York: Fawcett Publications, 1965.

Glick, Edward Bernard. *Peaceful Conflict: The Non-Military Use of the Military*. Harrisburg, Pa.: Stackpole Books, 1967.

Goldstein, Martin E. *American Policy toward Laos*. Cranbury, N.J.: Associated University Presses, 1973.

Goodman, Allan E. *An Institutional Profile of the South Vietnamese Officer Corps*. Santa Monica, Calif.: RAND Publications, 1970.

Goodman, Allan E. *Politics in War: The Bases of Political Community in South Vietnam*. Cambridge, Mass.: Harvard University Press, 1973.

Goodwin, Richard N. *Triumph or Tragedy: Reflections on Vietnam*. New York: Random House, 1966.

Gurtov, Melvin. *The First Vietnam Crisis: Chinese Communist Strategy and United States Involvement, 1953–1954*. New York: Columbia University Press, 1967.

Halberstam, David. *Ho*. London: Barrie and Jenkins, 1971.

_____. *The Making of a Quagmire: America and Vietnam during the Kennedy Era*. New York: Random House, 1965.

_____. *The Making of a Quagmire: America and Vietnam during the Kennedy Era*. Rev. ed. New York, Alfred A. Knopf, 1988.

Hamilton-Merritt, Jane. *Tragic Mountains: The Hmong, the Americans, and the Secret Wars for Laos, 1942–1992*. Bloomington: Indiana University Press, 1993.

Hammond, William M. "The Press in Vietnam as Agent of Defeat: A Critical Examination". *Reviews in American History* 17 (June 1989): 312–23.

Hannah, Norman B. *The Key to Failure: Laos and the Vietnam War*. New York: Madison Books, 1987.

Harrison, James. *The Endless War: Vietnam's Struggle for Independence.* New York: McGraw-Hill, 1983.

Hatcher, Patrick Lloyd. *The Suicide of an Elite: American Internationalists and Vietnam.* Stanford, Calif.: Stanford University Press, 1990.

Hayes, Samuel P., ed. *The Beginning of American Aid to Southeast Asia: The Griffin Mission of 1950.* Lexington, Mass.: Heath, 1971.

Henderson, William D. *Why the Viet Cong Fought: A Study of Motivation and Control in a Modern Army in Combat.* Westport, Conn.: Greenwood, 1979.

Herring, George C. *America's Longest War: The United States and Vietnam, 1950–1975,* New York: John Wiley, 1975.

_____. *America's Longest War: The United States and Vietnam, 1950–1975.* 2nd ed. New York: Alfred A. Knopf, 1986.

_____. *Vietnam: An American Ordeal.* St. Louis: Forum Press, 1976.

Herrington, Stuart A. *Silence Was a Weapon: The Vietnam War in the Villages; A Personal Perspective.* Novato, Calif.: Presidio Press, 1982.

Hersh, Seymour M. *The Dark Side of Camelot.* Boston: Little, Brown, 1997.

Hess, Gary R. "Historiography: The Unending Debate—Historians and the Vietnam War". *Diplomatic History* 18, no. 2 (Spring 1994): 239–64.

_____. *The United States' Emergence as a Southeast Asian Power, 1940–1950.* New York: Columbia University Press, 1987.

Hickey, Gerald C. *Village in Vietnam.* New Haven, Conn.: Yale University Press, 1964.

_____. Hickey, Gerald C. *The American Military Advisor and His Foreign Counterpart: The Case of Vietnam.* Santa Monica, Calf.: RAND Publications, 1965.

Higgins, Marguerite. *Our Vietnam Nightmare.* New York: Harper and Row, 1965.

Hilsman, Roger. *The Politics of Policy Making in Defense and Foreign Affairs.* New York: Harper and Row, 1971.

_____. *To Move a Nation: The Politics of Foreign Policy in the Administration of John F. Kennedy.* Garden City, N.Y.: Doubleday, 1967.

Hilsman, Roger, and Robert C. Good, eds. *Foreign Policy in the Sixties: The Issues and the Instruments.* Baltimore: John Hopkins Press, 1965.

Hunt, Richard A. *Pacification: The American Struggle for Vietnam's Hearts and Minds.* Boulder, Colo.: Westview Press, 1995.

Huntington, Samuel P. *Military Interventions, Political Involvement and the Unlessons of Vietnam.* Chicago: Adlai Stevenson Institute of International Affairs, 1968.

Iriye, Akira. *The Cold War in Asia.* Englewood Cliffs, N.J.: Prentice-Hall, 1974.

Jackson, Henry M., ed. *The Secretary of State and the Ambassador: Jackson Subcommittee Papers on the Conduct of American Foreign Policy.* New York: Frederick A. Praeger, 1966.

Jamieson, Neil L. *Understanding Vietnam.* Berkeley: University of California Press, 1993.

Jervis, Robert, and Jack Snyder, eds. *Dominoes and Bandwagons: Strategic Beliefs and Great Power Competition in the Eurasian Rimland.* New York: Oxford University Press, 1990.

Jones, Howard. *Death of a Generation: How the Assassinations of Diem and JFK Prolonged the Vietnam War.* New York: Oxford University Press, 2003.

Kahin, George McTurnan. *Intervention: How America Became Involved in Vietnam.* New York: Alfred Knopf, 1986.

Karnow, Stanley. *Vietnam: A History.* New York: Viking Press, 1983.

Kattenburg, Paul. *The Vietnam Trauma in American Foreign Policy, 1945–1975.* New Brunswick, N.J.: Transaction Books, 1980.

Keith, Charles. *Catholic Vietnam: A Church from Empire to Nation.* Berkeley: University of California Press, 2012.

Kemp, Anthony. *The SAS: Savage Wars of Peace, 1947 to the Present.* London: Penguin/Signet Books, 1995.

Kern, Montague, Patricia W. Levering, and Ralph B. Levering. *The Kennedy Crisis: The Press, the Presidency, and Foreign Policy.* Chapel Hill: University of North Carolina Press, 1983.

Kimball, Jeffrey P., ed. *To Reason Why: The Debate about the Causes of U.S. Involvement in the Vietnam War.* New York: McGraw-Hill, 1990.

Kinnard, Douglas. *The Certain Trumpet: Maxwell Taylor and the American Experience in Vietnam.* McLean, Va.: Brassey's, 1991.

Kitson, Frank. *Low Intensity Operations: Subversion, Insurgency, Peace-Keeping.* London: Faber and Faber, 1971.

Knightly, Philip. *The First Casualty: From Crimea to Vietnam; The War Correspondent as Hero, Propagandist, and Myth Maker.* New York: Harcourt Brace Jovanovich, 1975.

Kolko, Gabriel. *Anatomy of a War: Vietnam, the United States, and the Modern Historical Experience.* New York: Pantheon Books, 1985.

Komer, Robert W. *Bureaucracy at War: U.S. Performance in the Vietnam Conflict.* Boulder, Colo.: Westview Press, 1986.

Krepinevich, Andrew F., Jr. *The Army and Vietnam.* Baltimore: Johns Hopkins University Press, 1986.

Lake, Anthony, ed. *The Vietnam Legacy: The War, American Society, and the Future of American Foreign Policy.* New York: New York University Press, 1976.

Langer, Paul F., and Joseph J. Zasloff. *North Vietnam and the Pathet Lao: Partners in the Struggle for Laos.* Cambridge, Mass.: Harvard University Press, 1970.

Lanning, Michael Lee, and Dan Cragg. *Inside the VC and NVA: The Real Story of North Vietnam's Armed Forces.* New York: Fawcett, 1992.

Leacacos, John P. *Fires in the In-Basket: The ABC's of the State Department.* Cleveland: World Publishing, 1968.

Lewy, Guenther. *America in Vietnam.* New York: Oxford University Press, 1978.

Logevall, Fredrik. "De Gaulle, Neutralization, and American Involvement in Vietnam". *Pacific Historical Review* 61 (February 1992): 69–102.

Lomperis, Timothy J. *From People's War to People's Rule: Insurgency, Intervention, and the Lessons of Vietnam.* Chapel Hill: University of North Carolina Press, 1996.

_____. *The War Everyone Lost and Won: America's Intervention in Viet Nam's Twin Struggles.* Baton Rouge: Louisiana State University Press, 1984. Paperback, Washington, D.C.: Congressional Quarterly Press, 1987; rev. ed., 1992.

Luce, Don, and John Summer. *Viet Nam: The Unheard Voices.* Ithaca, N.Y.: Cornell University Press, 1969.

MacDonald, Douglas J. *Adventures in Chaos: American Intervention for Reform in the Third World.* Cambridge, Mass.: Harvard University Press, 1992.

Mai Tho Truyen. *Le Bouddhisme au Vietnam.* Saigon: Xa Loi Pagoda, 1962.

Mallin, Jay. *Terror in Vietnam.* Princeton, N.J.: Van Nostrand, 1966.

McCoy, James W. *Secrets of the Viet Cong.* New York: Hippocrene, 1992.

McNamara, Robert S. *The Essence of Security.* London: Hodder and Stoughton, 1968.

_____. *In Retrospect: The Tragedy and Lessons of Vietnam.* With Brian VanDe-Mark. New York: Times Books, 1995.

McNeill, Ian. *The Team: Australian Advisors in Vietnam, 1962–1972.* St. Lucia, Australia: University of Queensland Press, 1984.

_____. *To Long Tan: The Australian Army and the Vietnam War, 1950–1966.* St. Leonards, Australia: Allen and Unwin, 1993.

Mecklin, John. *Mission in Torment: An Intimate Account of the U.S. Role in Vietnam.* Garden City, N.Y.: Doubleday, 1965.

Metzner, Edward P. *More than a Soldier's War: Pacification in Vietnam.* College Station, Tex.: Texas A&M University Press, 1995.

Middleton, Drew. *Retreat from Victory: A Critical Appraisal of American Foreign and Military Policy from 1920 to the 1970s.* New York: Hawthorn Books, 1973.

Mohr, Charles. "Once Again—Did the Press Lose Vietnam?" *Columbia Journalism Review* 22 (November–December 1983): 51–80.

Moyar, Mark. *Triumph Forsaken: The Vietnam War, 1954–1965.* Cambridge, U.K.: Cambridge University Press, 2006.

Murti, B. S. N. *Vietnam Divided: The Unfinished Struggle.* New York: Asia Publishing House, 1964.

Nasution, Abdul Harris. *Fundamentals of Guerrilla Warfare*. New York: Praeger, 1965.

Newman, John M. *JFK and Vietnam: Deception, Intrigue, and the Struggle for Power*. New York: Warner Publications, 1992.

Nguyen Thi Tuyet Mai. *The Rubber Tree*. Edited by Monique Senderowicz. Jefferson, N.C.: McFarland, 1994.

Nighswonger, William A. *Rural Pacification in Vietnam*. Praeger Special Studies in International Politics and Public Affairs. New York: Frederick A. Praeger, 1966.

O'Ballance, Edgar. *The Wars in Vietnam, 1954–1980*. New York: Hippocrene Books, 1981.

O'Neill, Bard E. *Insurgency and Terrorism: Inside Modern Revolutionary Warfare*. New York: Brassey's, 1990.

Osanka, Franklin Mark, ed. *Modern Guerrilla Warfare: Fighting Communist Guerrilla Movements, 1941–1961*. New York: Free Press of Glencoe / Macmillan, 1962.

Osborne, Milton E. *Strategic Hamlets in South Viet-Nam: A Survey and Comparison*. Data Paper 55. Ithaca, N.Y.: Southeast Asia Program, Department of Asian Studies, Cornell University Press, 1965.

Palmer, Gregory. *The McNamara Strategy and the Vietnam War: Program Budgeting in the Pentagon, 1960–1968*. Westport, Conn.: Greenwood, 1978.

Pan, Stephen, and Daniel Lyons. *Vietnam Crisis*. New York: East Asian Research Institute, 1966.

Paret, Peter, and John W. Shy. *Guerrillas in the 1960's*. Rev. ed. New York: Frederick A. Praeger, 1962, 1966.

Paterson, Thomas G. *Meeting the Communist Threat: Truman to Reagan*. Oxford: Oxford University Press, 1988.

Pfeffer, Richard M., ed. *No More Vietnams? The War and the Future of American Foreign Policy*. New York: Harper and Row, 1968.

Pho, Hai B. *Vietnamese Public Management in Transition: South Vietnam Public Administration, 1955–1975*. Lanham, Md.: University Press of America, 1990.

Pike, Douglas. "South Vietnam: Autopsy of a Compound Crisis". In *Friendly Tyrants: An American Dilemma*, edited by Daniel Pipes and Adam Garfinkle. New York: St. Martin's Press, 1991.

Podhoretz, Norman. *Why We Were in Vietnam*. New York: Simon and Schuster, 1982.

Pomeroy, William J., ed. *Guerrilla Warfare and Marxism: A Collection of Writings from Karl Marx to the Present on Armed Struggles for Liberation and for Socialism*. New York: International Publishers, 1968.

Poole, Peter A. *The United States and Indochina: From FDR to Nixon.* Hinsdale, Ill.: Dryden Press, 1973.

Pustay, John S. *Counterinsurgency Warfare.* New York: Free Press, 1965.

Pye, Lucian W. *Guerrilla Communism in Malaya: Its Social and Political Meaning.* Westport, Conn.: Greenwood Press, 1981.

Race, Jeffrey. *War Comes to Long An.* Berkeley: University of California Press, 1972.

Ramsay, Jacob. *Mandarins and Martyrs: The Church and the Nguyen Dynasty in Early Nineteenth-Century Vietnam.* Stanford, Calif.: Stanford University Press, 2008.

Rice, Edward E. *Wars of the Third Kind: Conflict in Underdeveloped Countries.* Berkeley: University of California Press, 1988.

Rotter, Andrew J. *The Path to Vietnam.* Ithaca, N.Y.: Cornell University Press, 1989.

Rust, William J., and the editors of U.S. News Books. *Kennedy in Vietnam.* New York: Scribners, 1985.

Sanger, Richard H. *Insurgent Era: New Patterns of Political, Economic, and Social Revolution.* Washington, D. C.: Potomac Books, 1967.

Sansom, Robert L. *The Economics of Insurgency in the Mekong Delta.* Cambridge, Mass.: MIT Press, 1970.

Sapin, Burton M. *The Making of United States Foreign Policy.* New York: Praeger, 1966.

Sarkesian, Sam Charles. *America's Forgotten Wars: The Counter-Revolutionary Past and Lessons for the Future.* Westport, Conn.: Greenwood Press, 1984.

———. *The New Battlefield: The United States and Unconventional Conflicts.* Westport, Conn.: Greenwood Press, 1986.

———. *Unconventional Conflict in a New Security Era: Lessons from Malaya and Vietnam.* Westport, Conn.: Greenwood, 1993.

Schurmann, Franz, Peter Dale Scott, and Reginald Zelnik. *The Politics of Escalation in Vietnam.* Boston: Beacon Press, 1966.

Schlesinger, Arthur M., Jr. *The Bitter Heritage: Vietnam and American Democracy, 1941–1966.* Boston: Houghton Mifflin, 1967.

Scigliano, Robert. *South Vietnam: Nation under Stress.* Boston: Houghton Mifflin, 1964.

Scigliano, Robert, and Guy Fox. *Technical Assistance in Vietnam: The Michigan State University Experience.* New York: Praeger, 1965.

Shackleton, Ronald. *Village Defense: Initial Special Forces Operations in Vietnam.* Arvada, Colo.: Phoenix Press, 1975.

Shafer, D. Michael. *Deadly Paradigms: The Failure of U.S. Counterinsurgency Policy.* Princeton, N.J.: Princeton University Press, 1989.

Shaplen, Robert. *The Lost Revolution: The Story of Twenty Years of Neglected Opportunities in Vietnam and of America's Failure to Foster Democracy There*. New York: Harper and Row, 1965.

Sharp, U.S. Grant. *Strategy for Defeat: Vietnam in Retrospect*. San Rafael, Calif.: Presidio Press, 1978.

Sheehan, Neil. *A Bright Shining Lie: John Paul Vann and America in Vietnam*. New York: Vintage Books, 1988.

Simpson, Smith. *Anatomy of the State Department*. Boston: Beacon Press, 1968.

Smith, Ralph. *Viet-Nam and the West*. Ithaca, N.Y.: Cornell University Press, 1971.

Smith, R.B. *An International History of the Vietnam War*. Vol. 1, *Revolution versus Containment, 1955–1961*. London: St. Martin's Press, 1983.

Stanton, Shelby L. *Green Berets at War: US Army Special Forces in Southeast Asia, 1956–1975*. Novato, Calif.: Presidio Press, 1985; New York: Dell, 1991.

Stevenson, Charles A. *The End of Nowhere: American Policy toward Laos since 1954*. Boston: Beacon Press, 1972.

Sullivan, Marianna P. *France's Vietnam Policy*. Westport, Conn.: Greenwich Press, 1978.

Summers, Harry G., Jr. *On Strategy: A Critical Analysis of the Vietnam War*. Novato, Calif.: Presidio Press, 1982.

Tanham, George K. *War without Guns: American Civilians in Rural Vietnam*. With W. Robert Warne, Earl J. Young, and William A. Nighswonger. New York: Praeger, 1966.

Taylor, Maxwell D. *Responsibility and Response*. New York: Harper and Row, 1967.

———. *Swords and Plowshares*. New York: W.W. Norton, 1972.

Thayer, Carlyle A. *War by Other Means: National Liberation and Revolution in Viet-Nam, 1954–60*. Cambridge, Mass.: Unwin Hyman, 1989.

Thayer, Charles W. *Guerrilla*. New York: Harper and Row, 1963.

Thompson, Kenneth W., ed. *Diplomacy, Administration, and Policy: The Ideas and Careers of Frederick E. Nolting, Jr., Frederick C. Mosher, and Paul T. David*. Lanham, Md.: University Press of America; Charlottesville, Va.: Miller Center, University of Virginia, 1995.

Thompson, Leroy. *Ragged War: The Story of Unconventional and Counter-Revolutionary Warfare*. London: Arms and Armour Press, 1994.

Thompson, Robert Grainger, ed. *War in Peace: Conventional and Guerrilla Warfare since 1945*. New York: Harmony Books, 1982.

Thompson, W. Scott, and Donaldson D. Frizzell, eds. *The Lessons of Vietnam*. New York: Crane, Russak, 1977.

Trinquier, Roger. *Modern Warfare: A French View of Counterinsurgency*. New York: Praeger, 1964.

Trullinger, James. *Village at War*. New York: Longman, 1980.

Turley, William S. *The Second Indochina War: A Short Political and Military History, 1954–1975*. Boulder, Colo.: Westview Press, 1986.

Wade, Betsy, ed. *Forward Positions: The War Correspondence of Homer Bigart*. Fayetteville: Arkansas University Press, 1992.

Warner, Denis. *The Last Confucian: Vietnam, Southeast Asia, and the West*. Rev. ed. Sydney, Australia: Angus and Robertson, 1964.

_____. *Reporting Southeast Asia*. Australia: Angus and Robertson, 1966.

Warner, Geoffrey. "The United States and the Fall of Diem, Part I". *Australian Outlook* (December 1974).

_____. "The United States and the Fall of Diem, Part II". *Australian Outlook* (April 1975).

Weigley, Russell F. *The American Way of War: A History of United States Military Strategy and Policy*. New York: Macmillan, 1973.

Weil, Martin. *A Pretty Good Club: The Founding Fathers of the U.S. Foreign Service*. New York: W. W. Norton, 1978.

White, Theodore. *The Making of the President, 1960*. New York: Atheneum, 1961.

White, Theodore, and Annalee Jacoby. *Thunder out of China*. New York: William Sloane Associates, 1946.

Wyatt, Clarence R. "At the Cannon's Mouth: The American Press and the Vietnam War". *Journalism History* 13 (Autumn/Winter 1986): 104–13.

INDEX

Abdul Rahman, Tunku, 116, 152n32
Adams, John Quincy, 100
Affluent Society, The (Galbraith), 146
Agroville Program, 50, 120–22, 124
Alsop, Joseph, 206
American Military Assistance Advisory
  Group (MAAG). *See* MAAG
American press. *See* United States press
An Xa village, 95
Andrews, William R., 42–44, 47n21,
  48n24
Annamite Mountains, 97n44
Anspacher, John, 82–83
Ap Bac, Battle of, 169–72, 174, 177n4,
  179, 181n15, 182, 188, 222
Aristotle, 70n42
Army of the Republic of Vietnam
  (ARVN), 50n37, 54, 58–60, 66, 162,
  169–74, 177, 179–82, 234
  and the CIP, 107, 109–12, 118–19,
    123–24
  and the coup against Diem, 261–62,
    265, 268n67
  effectiveness of, 185, 265
  the press and, 174, 180
  and the SHP, 133–35, 138, 140–41
  US aid for, 75
  See also Ap Bac, Battle of
Arnett, Peter, 227
ARVN. *See* Army of the Republic of
  Vietnam
Australia, 12, 83, 162, 211, 259

Ba Cut (leader of Hoa Hao sect),
  268n67
Ball, George W., 158n4, 160, 225, 227,
  231, 252n10, 253, 255, 258

Bao Dai (Emperor of French
  Indochina), 10, 26n8, 32–33, 35,
  67, 165
Bartlett, Charles, 247
Bay of Pigs invasion of Cuba, 76, 98,
  107n2
Beech, Keyes, 221
Benedictine Order, 37
Bigart, Homer, 164–66
Binh Xuyen (private South Vietnamese
  Army/criminal organization), 45,
  115n24, 268n67
Black, Edwin F., 77n26
Black River campaign (1952), 96n41
Blair, Anne, 259–60, 266–67
Boun Oum, Prince, 88–89
Bowles, Chester "Chet", 94–95, 103,
  151–52, 158, 233–34
Brent, Joseph L., 191
Britain/the British, 150–51, 259
  See also Malaya; Thompson, Sir
    Robert G. K.
British Advisory Mission, 116, 123, 132,
  134, 135n28, 142, 187
Brown, Weldon A., 84
Browne, Malcolm, 43n9, 217, 227–28
Buckley, William F., Jr., 232
Buddhism/Buddhists, 17, 23, 26n6, 27,
  30, 60–61, 194
  and Communism, 216–17
  Diem's attitude toward, 13, 39,
    194–97
  North Vietnamese agents among, 13,
    197, 199–200, 215, 220
  North Vietnamese persecution of,
    216
  See also Buddhist crisis